MAKING SENSE OF
WHO
GOD IS

Works by Wayne Grudem

Bible Doctrine: Essential Teachings of the Christian Faith

Christian Beliefs: Twenty Basics Every Christian Should Know

Counterpoints: Are Miraculous Gifts for Today? (General Editor)

Politics According to the Bible

Systematic Theology

Systematic Theology Laminated Sheet

Making Sense of Series

Making Sense of the Bible

Making Sense of Who God Is

Making Sense of Man and Sin

Making Sense of Christ and the Spirit

Making Sense of Salvation

Making Sense of the Church

Making Sense of the Future

MAKING SENSE OF
WHO GOD IS

ONE OF SEVEN PARTS FROM GRUDEM'S
SYSTEMATIC THEOLOGY

WAYNE GRUDEM

ZONDERVAN®

ZONDERVAN.com/
AUTHORTRACKER
follow your favorite authors

ZONDERVAN

Making Sense of Who God Is
Copyright © 1994, 2011 by Wayne Grudem

Previously published in *Systematic Theology*

This title is also available as a Zondervan ebook. Visit www.zondervan.com/ebooks.

Requests for information should be addressed to:

Zondervan, *Grand Rapids, Michigan* 49530

This edition: ISBN 978-0-310-49312-9 (softcover)

The Library of Congress has cataloged the complete volume as:

Grudem, Wayne Arden.
    Systematic theology: an introduction to biblical doctrine / Wayne Grudem.
        p. cm.
    Includes index.
    ISBN 978-0-310-28670-7
    1. Theology, Doctrinal. I. Title.
BT75.2.G78 — 1994
230'.046—dc20   94-8300

Cover design: *Rob Monacelli*
Interior design: *Mark Sheeres*

Printed in the United States of America

11 12 13 14 15 16 /DCI/ 33 32 31 30 29 28 27 26 25 24 23 22 21 20 19 18 17 16 15 14 13 12 11 10 9 8 7 6 5 4 3 2 1

CONTENTS

PREFACE

I have not written this book for other teachers of theology (though I hope many of them will read it). I have written it for students—and not only for students, but also for every Christian who has a hunger to know the central doctrines of the Bible in greater depth.

I have tried to make it understandable even for Christians who have never studied theology before. I have avoided using technical terms without first explaining them. And most of the chapters can be read on their own, so that someone can begin at any chapter and grasp it without having read the earlier material.

Introductory studies do not have to be shallow or simplistic. I am convinced that most Christians are able to understand the doctrinal teachings of the Bible in considerable depth, provided that they are presented clearly and without the use of highly technical language. Therefore I have not hesitated to treat theological disputes in some detail where it seemed necessary.

Yet this book is still an *introduction* to systematic theology. Entire books have been written about the topics covered in each chapter of this book, and entire articles have been written about many of the verses quoted in this book. Therefore each chapter is capable of opening out into additional study in more breadth or more depth for those who are interested. The bibliographies at the end of each chapter give some help in that direction.

The following six distinctive features of this book grow out of my convictions about what systematic theology is and how it should be taught:

1. A Clear Biblical Basis for Doctrines. Because I believe that theology should be explicitly based on the teachings of Scripture, in each chapter I have attempted to show where the Bible gives support for the doctrines under consideration. In fact, because I believe that the words of Scripture themselves have power and authority greater than any human words, I have not just given Bible references; I have frequently quoted Bible passages at length so that readers can easily examine for themselves the scriptural evidence and in that way be like the noble Bereans, who were "examining the scriptures daily to see if these things were so" (Acts 17:11). This conviction about the unique nature of the Bible as God's words has also led to the inclusion of a Scripture memory passage at the end of each chapter.

2. Clarity in the Explanation of Doctrines. I do not believe that God intended the study of theology to result in confusion and frustration. A student who comes out of a course in theology filled only with doctrinal uncertainty and a thousand unanswered questions is hardly "able to give instruction in sound doctrine and also to confute those who contradict it" (Titus 1:9). Therefore I have tried to state the doctrinal positions of this book clearly and to show where in Scripture I find convincing evidence for those positions. I do not expect that everyone reading this book will agree with me at every point of doctrine; I do think that every reader will understand the positions I am arguing for and where Scripture can be found to support those positions.

This does not mean that I ignore other views. Where there are doctrinal differences within evangelical Christianity I have tried to represent other positions fairly, to explain why I disagree with them, and to give references to the best available defenses of the opposing positions. In fact, I have made it easy for students to find a conservative evangelical statement on each topic from within their own theological traditions, because each chapter contains an index to treatments of that chapter's subject in thirty-four other theology texts classified by denominational background.

3. Application to Life. I do not believe that God intended the study of theology to be dry and boring. Theology is the study of God and all his works! Theology is meant to be lived and prayed and sung! All of the great doctrinal writings of the Bible (such as Paul's epistle to the Romans) are full of praise to God and personal application to life. For this reason I have incorporated notes on application from time to time in the text, and have added "Questions for Personal Application" at the end of each chapter, as well as a hymn related to the topic of the chapter. True theology is "teaching which accords with godliness" (1 Tim. 6:3), and theology when studied rightly will lead to growth in our Christian lives, and to worship.

4. Focus on the Evangelical World. I do not think that a true system of theology can be constructed from within what we may call the "liberal" theological tradition—that is, by people who deny the absolute truthfulness of the Bible, or who do not think the words of the Bible to be God's very words. For this reason, the other writers I interact with in this book are mostly within what is today called the larger "conservative evangelical" tradition—from the great Reformers John Calvin and Martin Luther, down to the writings of evangelical scholars today. I write as an evangelical and for evangelicals. This does not mean that those in the liberal tradition have nothing valuable to say; it simply means that differences with them almost always boil down to differences over the nature of the Bible and its authority. The amount of doctrinal agreement that can be reached by people with widely divergent bases of authority is quite limited. I am thankful for my evangelical friends who write extensive critiques of liberal theology, but I do not think that everyone is called to do that, or that an extensive analysis of liberal views is the most helpful way to build a positive system of theology based on the total truthfulness of the whole Bible. In fact, somewhat like the boy in Hans Christian Andersen's tale who shouted, "The Emperor has no clothes!" I think someone needs to say that it is doubtful that liberal theologians have given us any significant insights into the doctrinal teachings of Scripture that are not already to be found in evangelical writers.

It is not always appreciated that the world of conservative evangelical scholarship is so rich and diverse that it affords ample opportunity for exploration of different viewpoints and insights into Scripture. I think that ultimately we will attain much more depth of understanding of Scripture when we are able to study it in the company of a great number of scholars who all begin with the conviction that the Bible is completely true and absolutely authoritative. The cross-references to thirty-four other evangelical systematic theologies that I have put at the end of each chapter reflect this conviction: though they are broken down into seven broad theological traditions (Anglican/Episcopalian, Arminian/Wesleyan/Methodist, Baptist, Dispensational, Lutheran, Reformed/Presbyterian, and Renewal/Charismatic/ Pentecostal), they all would hold to the inerrancy of the Bible and would belong to what would be called a conservative evangelical position today. (In addition to these thirty-four conservative evangelical works, I have also added to each chapter a section of cross-references to two representative Roman Catholic theologies, because Roman Catholicism continues to exercise such a significant influence worldwide.)

5. Hope for Progress in Doctrinal Unity in the Church. I believe that there is still much hope for the church to attain deeper and purer doctrinal understanding, and to overcome old barriers, even those that have persisted for centuries. Jesus is at work perfecting his church "that he might present the church to himself in splendor, without spot or wrinkle or any such thing, that she might be holy and without blemish" (Eph. 5:27), and he has given gifts to equip the church "until we all attain to the unity of the faith and of the knowledge of the Son of God" (Eph. 4:13). Though the past history of the church may discourage us, these Scriptures remain true, and we should not abandon hope of greater agreement. In fact, in this century we have already seen much greater understanding and some greater doctrinal agreement between Covenant and Dispensational theologians, and between charismatics and noncharismatics; moreover, I think the church's understanding of biblical inerrancy and of spiritual gifts has also increased significantly in the last few decades. I believe that the current debate over appropriate roles for men and women in marriage and the church will eventually result in much greater understanding of the teaching of Scripture as well, painful though the controversy may be at the present time. Therefore, in this book I have not hesitated to raise again some of the old differences (over baptism, the Lord's Supper, church government, the millennium and the tribulation, and predestination, for example) in the hope that, in some cases at least, a fresh look at Scripture may provoke a new examination of these doctrines and may perhaps prompt some movement not just toward greater understanding and tolerance of other viewpoints, but even toward greater doctrinal consensus in the church.

6. A Sense of the Urgent Need for Greater Doctrinal Understanding in the Whole Church. I am convinced that there is an urgent need in the church today for much greater understanding of Christian doctrine, or systematic theology. Not only pastors and teachers need to understand theology in greater depth—the whole church does as well. One day by God's grace we may have churches full of Christians who can discuss, apply, and live the doctrinal teachings of the Bible as readily as they can discuss the details of their own jobs or hobbies—or the fortunes of their favorite sports team or television program. It is not that Christians lack the ability to understand doctrine; it is just that they must have access to it in an understandable form. Once that happens, I think that many Christians will find that understanding (and living) the doctrines of Scripture is one of their greatest joys.

> *"O give thanks to the LORD, for he is good; for his steadfast love endures for ever!" (Ps. 118:29).*

> *"Not to us, O LORD, not to us, but to your name give glory" (Ps. 115:1).*

WAYNE GRUDEM
Phoenix Seminary
4222 E. Thomas Road/Suite 400
Phoenix, Arizona 85018
USA

ABBREVIATIONS

BAGD	*A Greek-English Lexicon of the New Testament and Other Early Christian Literature.* Ed. Walter Bauer. Rev. and trans. Wm. Arndt, F. W. Gingrich, and F. Danker. Chicago: University of Chicago Press, 1979.
BDB	*A Hebrew and English Lexicon of the Old Testament.* F. Brown, S. R. Driver, and C. Briggs. Oxford: Clarendon Press, 1907; reprinted, with corrections, 1968.
BETS	*Bulletin of the Evangelical Theological Society*
BibSac	*Bibliotheca Sacra*
cf.	compare
CRSQ	*Creation Research Society Quarterly*
CT	*Christianity Today*
CThRev	*Criswell Theological Review*
DPCM	*Dictionary of Pentecostal and Charismatic Movements.* Stanley M. Burgess and Gary B. McGee, eds. Grand Rapids: Zondervan, 1988.
EBC	*Expositor's Bible Commentary.* Frank E. Gaebelein, ed. Grand Rapids: Zondervan, 1976.
ed.	edited by, edition
EDT	*Evangelical Dictionary of Theology.* Walter Elwell, ed. Grand Rapids: Baker, 1984.
et al.	and others
IBD	*The Illustrated Bible Dictionary.* Ed. J. D. Douglas, et al. 3 vols. Leicester: Inter-Varsity Press, and Wheaton: Tyndale House, 1980.
ISBE	*International Standard Bible Encyclopedia.* Revised edition. G. W. Bromiley, ed. Grand Rapids: Eerdmans, 1982.
JAMA	*Journal of the American Medical Association*
JBL	*Journal of Biblical Literature*
JETS	*Journal of the Evangelical Theological Society*
JSOT	*Journal for the Study of the Old Testament*
KJV	King James Version (Authorized Version)
LSJ	*A Greek-English Lexicon,* ninth edition. Henry Liddell, Robert Scott, H. S. Jones, R. McKenzie. Oxford: Clarendon Press, 1940.
LXX	Septuagint
mg.	margin or marginal notes
n.	note
n.d.	no date of publication given
n.p.	no place of publication given

NASB	New American Standard Bible
NDT	*New Dictionary of Theology.* S. B. Ferguson, D. F. Wright, J. I. Packer, eds. Leicester and Downers Grove, Ill.: InterVarsity Press, 1988.
NIDCC	*New International Dictionary of the Christian Church.* Ed. J. D. Douglas et al. Grand Rapids: Zondervan, 1974.
NIDNTT	*The New International Dictionary of New Testament Theology.* 3 vols. Colin Brown, gen. ed. Grand Rapids: Zondervan, 1975–78.
NIGTC	New International Greek Testament Commentaries
NIV	New International Version
NKJV	New King James Version
NTS	*New Testament Studies*
ODCC	*Oxford Dictionary of the Christian Church.* Ed. F. L. Cross. London and New York: Oxford University Press, 1977.
rev.	revised
RSV	Revised Standard Version
TB	*Tyndale Bulletin*
TDNT	*Theological Dictionary of the New Testament.* 10 vols. G. Kittel and G. Friedrich, eds.; trans. G. W. Bromiley. Grand Rapids: Eerdmans, 1964–76.
TNTC	Tyndale New Testament Commentaries
TOTC	Tyndale Old Testament Commentaries
trans.	translated by
TrinJ	*Trinity Journal*
vol.	volume
WBC	Word Biblical Commentary
WTJ	*Westminster Theological Journal*

Chapter 1

INTRODUCTION TO SYSTEMATIC THEOLOGY

What is systematic theology?
Why should Christians study it?
How should we study it?

EXPLANATION AND SCRIPTURAL BASIS

A. Definition of Systematic Theology

What is systematic theology? Many different definitions have been given, but for the purposes of this book the following definition will be used: *Systematic theology is any study that answers the question, "What does the whole Bible teach us today?" about any given topic.*[1]

This definition indicates that systematic theology involves collecting and understanding all the relevant passages in the Bible on various topics and then summarizing their teachings clearly so that we know what to believe about each topic.

1. Relationship to Other Disciplines. The emphasis of this book will not therefore be on *historical theology* (a historical study of how Christians in different periods have understood various theological topics) or *philosophical theology* (studying theological topics largely without use of the Bible, but using the tools and methods of philosophical reasoning and what can be known about God from observing the universe) or *apologetics*

---

[1]This definition of systematic theology is taken from Professor John Frame, now of Westminster Seminary in Escondido, California, under whom I was privileged to study in 1971–73 (at Westminster Seminary, Philadelphia). Though it is impossible to acknowledge my indebtedness to him at every point, it is appropriate to express gratitude to him at this point, and to say that he has probably influenced my theological thinking more than anyone else, especially in the crucial areas of the nature of systematic theology and the doctrine of the Word of God. Many of his former students will recognize echoes of his teaching in the following pages, especially in those two areas.

(providing a defense of the truthfulness of the Christian faith for the purpose of convincing unbelievers). These three subjects, which are worthwhile subjects for Christians to pursue, are sometimes also included in a broader definition of the term *systematic theology*. In fact, some consideration of historical, philosophical, and apologetic matters will be found at points throughout this book. This is because historical study informs us of the insights gained and the mistakes made by others previously in understanding Scripture; philosophical study helps us understand right and wrong thought forms common in our culture and others; and apologetic study helps us bring the teachings of Scripture to bear on the objections raised by unbelievers. But these areas of study are not the focus of this volume, which rather interacts directly with the biblical text in order to understand what the Bible itself says to us about various theological subjects.

If someone prefers to use the term *systematic theology* in the broader sense just mentioned instead of the narrow sense which has been defined above, it will not make much difference.[2] Those who use the narrower definition will agree that these other areas of study definitely contribute in a positive way to our understanding of systematic theology, and those who use the broader definition will certainly agree that historical theology, philosophical theology, and apologetics can be distinguished from the process of collecting and synthesizing all the relevant Scripture passages for various topics. Moreover, even though historical and philosophical studies do contribute to our understanding of theological questions, only Scripture has the final authority to define what we are to believe,[3] and it is therefore appropriate to spend some time focusing on the process of analyzing the teaching of Scripture itself.

Systematic theology, as we have defined it, also differs from *Old Testament theology, New Testament theology,* and *biblical theology.* These three disciplines organize their topics historically and in the order the topics are presented in the Bible. Therefore, in Old Testament theology, one might ask, "What does Deuteronomy teach about prayer?" or "What do the Psalms teach about prayer?" or "What does Isaiah teach about prayer?" or even, "What does the whole Old Testament teach about prayer and how is that teaching developed over the history of the Old Testament?" In New Testament theology one might ask, "What does John's gospel teach about prayer?" or "What does Paul teach about prayer?" or even "What does the New Testament teach about prayer and what is the historical development of that teaching as it progresses through the New Testament?"

"Biblical theology" has a technical meaning in theological studies. It is the larger category that contains both Old Testament theology and New Testament theology as we have defined them above. Biblical theology gives special attention to the teachings of *individual authors and sections* of Scripture, and to the place of each teaching in the *historical development* of Scripture.[4] So one might ask, "What is the historical development

---

[2]Gordon Lewis and Bruce Demarest have coined a new phrase, "integrative theology," to refer to systematic theology in this broader sense: see their excellent work, *Integrative Theology* (Grand Rapids: Zondervan, 1996). For each doctrine, they analyze historical alternatives and relevant biblical passages, give a coherent summary of the doctrine, answer philosophical objections, and give practical application.

[3]Charles Hodge says, "The Scriptures contain all the Facts of Theology" (section heading in *Systematic Theology,* 1:15). He argues that ideas gained from intuition or observation or experience are valid in theology only if they are supported by the teaching of Scripture.

[4]The term "biblical theology" might seem to be a natural and appropriate one for the process I have called

of the teaching about prayer as it is seen throughout the history of the Old Testament and then of the New Testament?" Of course, this question comes very close to the question, "What does the whole Bible teach us today about prayer?" (which would be *systematic theology* by our definition). It then becomes evident that the boundary lines between these various disciplines often overlap at the edges, and parts of one study blend into the next. Yet there is still a difference, for biblical theology traces the historical development of a doctrine and the way in which one's place at some point in that historical development affects one's understanding and application of that particular doctrine. Biblical theology also focuses on the understanding of each doctrine that the biblical authors and their original hearers or readers possessed.

Systematic theology, on the other hand, makes use of the material of biblical theology and often builds on the results of biblical theology. At some points, especially where great detail and care is needed in the development of a doctrine, systematic theology will even use a biblical-theological method, analyzing the development of each doctrine through the historical development of Scripture. But the focus of systematic theology remains different: its focus is on the collection and then the summary of the teaching of all the biblical passages on a particular subject. Thus systematic theology asks, for example, "What does the whole Bible teach us today about prayer?" It attempts to summarize the teaching of Scripture in a brief, understandable, and very carefully formulated statement.

2. Application to Life. Furthermore, systematic theology focuses on summarizing each doctrine as it should be understood by present-day Christians. This will sometimes involve the use of terms and even concepts that were not themselves used by any individual biblical author, but that are the proper result of combining the teachings of two or more biblical authors on a particular subject. The terms *Trinity, incarnation,* and *deity of Christ,* for example, are not found in the Bible, but they usefully summarize biblical concepts.

Defining systematic theology to include "what the whole Bible *teaches us* today" implies that application to life is a necessary part of the proper pursuit of systematic theology. Thus a doctrine under consideration is seen in terms of its practical value for living the Christian life. Nowhere in Scripture do we find doctrine studied for its own sake or in isolation from life. The biblical writers consistently apply their teaching to life. Therefore, any Christian reading this book should find his or her Christian life enriched and deepened during this study; indeed, if personal spiritual growth does not occur, then the book has not been written properly by the author or the material has not been rightly studied by the reader.

3. Systematic Theology and Disorganized Theology. If we use this definition of systematic theology, it will be seen that most Christians actually do systematic theology (or at least make systematic-theological statements) many times a week. For example: "The Bible says that everyone who believes in Jesus Christ will be saved." "The Bible says

---

"systematic theology." However, its usage in theological studies to refer to tracing the historical development of doctrines throughout the Bible is too well established, so that starting now to use the term biblical theology to refer to what I have called systematic theology would only result in confusion.

that Jesus Christ is the only way to God." "The Bible says that Jesus is coming again." These are all summaries of what Scripture says and, as such, they are systematic-theological statements. In fact, every time a Christian says something about what the whole Bible says, he or she is in a sense doing "systematic theology"—according to our definition—by thinking about various topics and answering the question, "What does the whole Bible teach us today?"[5]

How then does this book differ from the "systematic theology" that most Christians do? First, it treats biblical topics in a *carefully organized way* to guarantee that all important topics will receive thorough consideration. This organization also provides one sort of check against inaccurate analysis of individual topics, for it means that all other doctrines that are treated can be compared with each topic for consistency in methodology and absence of contradictions in the relationships between the doctrines. This also helps to ensure balanced consideration of complementary doctrines: Christ's deity and humanity are studied together, for example, as are God's sovereignty and man's responsibility, so that wrong conclusions will not be drawn from an imbalanced emphasis on only one aspect of the full biblical presentation.

In fact, the adjective *systematic* in systematic theology should be understood to mean something like "carefully organized by topics," with the understanding that the topics studied will be seen to fit together in a consistent way, and will include all the major doctrinal topics of the Bible. Thus "systematic" should be thought of as the opposite of "randomly arranged" or "disorganized." In systematic theology topics are treated in an orderly or "systematic" way.

A second difference between this book and the way most Christians do systematic theology is that it treats topics in *much more detail* than most Christians do. For example, an ordinary Christian as a result of regular reading of the Bible may make the theological statement, "The Bible says that everyone who believes in Jesus Christ will be saved." That is a perfectly true summary of a major biblical teaching. However, it can take several pages to elaborate more precisely what it means to "believe in Jesus Christ," and it could take several chapters to explain what it means to "be saved" in all of the many implications of that term.

Third, a formal study of systematic theology will make it possible to formulate summaries of biblical teachings with *much more accuracy* than Christians would normally arrive at without such a study. In systematic theology, summaries of biblical teachings must be worded precisely to guard against misunderstandings and to exclude false teachings.

Fourth, a good theological analysis must find and treat fairly *all the relevant Bible passages* for each particular topic, not just some or a few of the relevant passages. This

---

[5]Robert L. Reymond, "The Justification of Theology with a Special Application to Contemporary Christology," in Nigel M. Cameron, ed., *The Challenge of Evangelical Theology: Essays in Approach and Method* (Edinburgh: Rutherford House, 1987), pp. 82–104, cites several examples from the New Testament of this kind of searching through all of Scripture to demonstrate doctrinal conclusions: Jesus in Luke 24:25–27 (and elsewhere); Apollos in Acts 18:28; the Jerusalem Council in Acts 15; and Paul in Acts 17:2–3; 20:27; and all of Romans. To this list could be added Heb. 1 (on Christ's divine Sonship), Heb. 11 (on the nature of true faith), and many other passages from the Epistles.

often means that it must depend on the results of careful exegesis (or interpretation) of Scripture generally agreed upon by evangelical interpreters or, where there are significant differences of interpretation, systematic theology will include detailed exegesis at certain points.

Because of the large number of topics covered in a study of systematic theology and because of the great detail with which these topics are analyzed, it is inevitable that someone studying a systematic theology text or taking a course in systematic theology for the first time will have many of his or her own personal beliefs challenged or modified, refined or enriched. It is of utmost importance therefore that each person beginning such a course firmly resolve in his or her own mind to abandon as false any idea which is found to be clearly contradicted by the teaching of Scripture. But it is also very important for each person to resolve not to believe any individual doctrine simply because this textbook or some other textbook or teacher says that it is true, unless this book or the instructor in a course can convince the student from the text of Scripture itself. It is Scripture alone, not "conservative evangelical tradition" or any other human authority, that must function as the normative authority for the definition of what we should believe.

4. What Are Doctrines? In this book, the word *doctrine* will be understood in the following way: *A doctrine is what the whole Bible teaches us today about some particular topic.* This definition is directly related to our earlier definition of systematic theology, since it shows that a "doctrine" is simply the result of the process of doing systematic theology with regard to one particular topic. Understood in this way, doctrines can be very broad or very narrow. We can speak of "the doctrine of God" as a major doctrinal category, including a summary of all that the Bible teaches us today about God. Such a doctrine would be exceptionally large. On the other hand, we may also speak more narrowly of the doctrine of God's eternity, or the doctrine of the Trinity, or the doctrine of God's justice.[6]

Within the major doctrinal category of this book, many more specific teachings have been selected as appropriate for inclusion. Generally these meet at least one of the following three criteria: (1) they are doctrines that are most emphasized in Scripture; (2) they are doctrines that have been most significant throughout the history of the church and have been important for all Christians at all times; (3) they are doctrines that have become important for Christians in the present situation in the history of the church (even though some of these doctrines may not have been of such great interest earlier in church history). Some examples of doctrines in the third category would be the doctrine of the inerrancy of Scripture, the doctrine of baptism in the Holy Spirit, the doctrine of Satan and demons with particular reference to spiritual warfare, the doctrine of spiritual gifts in the New Testament age, and the doctrine of the creation of man as male and female in relation to the understanding of roles appropriate to men and women today.

---

[6]The word *dogma* is an approximate synonym for *doctrine,* but I have not used it in this book. *Dogma* is a term more often used by Roman Catholic and Lutheran theologians, and the term frequently refers to doctrines that have official church endorsement. *Dogmatic theology* is another term for *systematic theology.*

Finally, what is the difference between systematic theology and *Christian ethics?* Although there is inevitably some overlap between the study of theology and the study of ethics, I have tried to maintain a distinction in emphasis. The emphasis of systematic theology is on what God wants us to *believe* and to *know,* while the emphasis in Christian ethics is on what God wants us to *do* and what *attitudes* he wants us to have. Such a distinction is reflected in the following definition: *Christian ethics is any study that answers the question, "What does God require us to do and what attitudes does he require us to have today?" with regard to any given situation.* Thus theology focuses on ideas while ethics focuses on situations in life. Theology tells us how we should think while ethics tells us how we should live. A textbook on ethics, for example, would discuss topics such as marriage and divorce, lying and telling the truth, stealing and ownership of property, abortion, birth control, homosexuality, the role of civil government, discipline of children, capital punishment, war, care for the poor, racial discrimination, and so forth. Of course there is some overlap: theology must be applied to life (therefore it is often ethical to some degree). And ethics must be based on proper ideas of God and his world (therefore it is theological to some degree).

This book will emphasize systematic theology, though it will not hesitate to apply theology to life where such application comes readily. Still, for a thorough treatment of Christian ethics, another textbook similar to this in scope would be necessary.

B. Initial Assumptions of This Book

We begin with two assumptions or presuppositions: (1) that the Bible is true and that it is, in fact, our only absolute standard of truth; (2) that the God who is spoken of in the Bible exists, and that he is who the Bible says he is: the Creator of heaven and earth and all things in them. These two presuppositions, of course, are always open to later adjustment or modification or deeper confirmation, but at this point, these two assumptions form the point at which we begin.

C. Why Should Christians Study Theology?

Why should Christians study systematic theology? That is, why should we engage in the process of collecting and summarizing the teachings of many individual Bible passages on particular topics? Why is it not sufficient simply to continue reading the Bible regularly every day of our lives?

1. The Basic Reason. Many answers have been given to this question, but too often they leave the impression that systematic theology somehow can "improve" on the Bible by doing a better job of organizing its teachings or explaining them more clearly than the Bible itself has done. Thus we may begin implicitly to deny the clarity of Scripture or the sufficiency of Scripture.

However, Jesus commanded his disciples and now commands us also to *teach* believers to observe all that he commanded:

> Go therefore and make disciples of all nations, baptizing them in the name of the Father and of the Son and of the Holy Spirit, *teaching them* to observe all

that I have commanded you; and lo, I am with you always, to the close of the age. (Matt. 28:19–20)

Now to teach all that Jesus commanded, in a narrow sense, is simply to teach the content of the oral teaching of Jesus as it is recorded in the gospel narratives. However, in a broader sense, "all that Jesus commanded" includes the interpretation and application of his life and teachings, because in the book of Acts it is implied that it contains a narrative of what Jesus *continued* to do and teach through the apostles after his resurrection (note that 1:1 speaks of "all that Jesus *began* to do and teach"). "All that Jesus commanded" can also include the Epistles, since they were written under the supervision of the Holy Spirit and were also considered to be a "command of the Lord" (1 Cor. 14:37; see also John 14:26; 16:13; 1 Thess. 4:15; 2 Peter 3:2; and Rev. 1:1–3). Thus in a larger sense, "all that Jesus commanded" includes all of the New Testament.

Furthermore, when we consider that the New Testament writings endorse the absolute confidence Jesus had in the authority and reliability of the Old Testament Scriptures as God's words, and when we realize that the New Testament epistles also endorse this view of the Old Testament as absolutely authoritative words of God, then it becomes evident that we cannot teach "all that Jesus commanded" without including all of the Old Testament (rightly understood in the various ways in which it applies to the new covenant age in the history of redemption) as well.

The task of fulfilling the Great Commission includes therefore not only evangelism but also *teaching*. And the task of teaching all that Jesus commanded us is, in a broad sense, the task of teaching what the whole Bible says to us today. To effectively teach ourselves and to teach others what the whole Bible says, it is necessary to *collect* and *summarize* all the Scripture passages on a particular subject.

For example, if someone asks me, "What does the Bible teach about Christ's return?" I could say, "Just keep reading your Bible and you'll find out." But if the questioner begins reading at Genesis 1:1 it will be a long time before he or she finds the answer to his question. By that time many other questions will have needed answers, and his list of unanswered questions will begin to grow very long indeed. What does the Bible teach about the work of the Holy Spirit? What does the Bible teach about prayer? What does the Bible teach about sin? There simply is not time in our lifetimes to read through the entire Bible looking for an answer for ourselves every time a doctrinal question arises. Therefore, for us to learn what the Bible says, it is very helpful to have the benefit of the work of others who have searched through Scripture and found answers to these various topics.

We can teach others most effectively if we can direct them to the most relevant passages and suggest an appropriate summary of the teachings of those passages. Then the person who questions us can inspect those passages quickly for himself or herself and learn much more rapidly what the teaching of the Bible is on a particular subject. Thus the necessity of systematic theology for teaching what the Bible says comes about primarily because we are finite in our memory and in the amount of time at our disposal.

The basic reason for studying systematic theology, then, is that it enables us to teach ourselves and others what the whole Bible says, thus fulfilling the second part of the Great Commission.

2. The Benefits to Our Lives. Although the basic reason for studying systematic theology is that it is a means of obedience to our Lord's command, there are some additional specific benefits that come from such study.

First, studying theology helps us *overcome our wrong ideas.* If there were no sin in our hearts, we could read the Bible from cover to cover and, although we would not immediately learn everything in the Bible, we would most likely learn only true things about God and his creation. Every time we read it we would learn more true things and we would not rebel or refuse to accept anything we found written there. But with sin in our hearts we retain some rebelliousness against God. At various points there are—for all of us—biblical teachings which for one reason or another we do not want to accept. The study of systematic theology is of help in overcoming those rebellious ideas.

For example, suppose there is someone who does not want to believe that Jesus is personally coming back to earth again. We could show this person one verse or perhaps two that speak of Jesus' return to earth, but the person might still find a way to evade the force of those verses or read a different meaning into them. But if we collect twenty-five or thirty verses that say that Jesus is coming back to earth personally and write them all out on paper, our friend who hesitated to believe in Christ's return is much more likely to be persuaded by the breadth and diversity of biblical evidence for this doctrine. Of course, we all have areas like that, areas where our understanding of the Bible's teaching is inadequate. In these areas, it is helpful for us to be confronted with the *total weight of the teaching of Scripture* on that subject, so that we will more readily be persuaded even against our initial wrongful inclinations.

Second, studying systematic theology helps us to be *able to make better decisions later on new questions of doctrine that may arise.* We cannot know what new doctrinal controversies will arise in the churches in which we will live and minister ten, twenty, or thirty years from now, if the Lord does not return before then. These new doctrinal controversies will sometimes include questions that no one has faced very carefully before. Christians will be asking, "What does the whole Bible say about this subject?" (The precise nature of biblical inerrancy and the appropriate understanding of biblical teaching on gifts of the Holy Spirit are two examples of questions that have arisen in our century with much more forcefulness than ever before in the history of the church.)

Whatever the new doctrinal controversies are in future years, those who have learned systematic theology well will be much better able to answer the new questions that arise. The reason for this is that everything that the Bible says is somehow related to everything else the Bible says (for it all fits together in a consistent way, at least within God's own understanding of reality, and in the nature of God and creation as they really are). Thus the new question will be related to much that has already been learned from Scripture. The more thoroughly that earlier material has been learned, the better able we will be to deal with those new questions.

This benefit extends even more broadly. We face problems of applying Scripture to life in many more contexts than formal doctrinal discussions. What does the Bible teach about husband-wife relationships? About raising children? About witnessing to a friend at work? What principles does Scripture give us for studying psychology, or economics, or the natural sciences? How does it guide us in spending money, or in saving, or in tithing? In every area of inquiry certain theological principles will come to bear, and those who have learned well the theological teachings of the Bible will be much better able to make decisions that are pleasing to God.

A helpful analogy at this point is that of a jigsaw puzzle. If the puzzle represents "what the whole Bible teaches us today about everything" then a course in systematic theology would be like filling in the border and some of the major items pictured in the puzzle. But we will never know everything that the Bible teaches about everything, so our jigsaw puzzle will have many gaps, many pieces that remain to be put in. Solving a new real-life problem is analogous to filling in another section of the jigsaw puzzle: the more pieces one has in place correctly to begin with, the easier it is to fit new pieces in, and the less apt one is to make mistakes. In this book the goal is to enable Christians to put into their "theological jigsaw puzzle" as many pieces with as much accuracy as possible, and to encourage Christians to go on putting in more and more correct pieces for the rest of their lives. The Christian doctrines studied here will act as guidelines to help in the filling in of all other areas, areas that pertain to all aspects of truth in all aspects of life.

Third, studying systematic theology will *help us grow as Christians.* The more we know about God, about his Word, about his relationships to the world and mankind, the better we will trust him, the more fully we will praise him, and the more readily we will obey him. Studying systematic theology rightly will make us more mature Christians. If it does not do this, we are not studying it in the way God intends.

In fact, the Bible often connects sound doctrine with maturity in Christian living: Paul speaks of "*the teaching which accords with godliness*" (1 Tim. 6:3) and says that his work as an apostle is "to further the faith of God's elect and their knowledge of *the truth which accords with godliness*" (Titus 1:1). By contrast, he indicates that all kinds of disobedience and immorality are "contrary to sound doctrine" (1 Tim. 1:10).

In connection with this idea it is appropriate to ask what the difference is between a "major doctrine" and a "minor doctrine." Christians often say they want to seek agreement in the church on major doctrines but also to allow for differences on minor doctrines. I have found the following guideline useful:

> A major doctrine is one that has a significant impact on our thinking about other doctrines, or that has a significant impact on how we live the Christian life. A minor doctrine is one that has very little impact on how we think about other doctrines, and very little impact on how we live the Christian life.

By this standard doctrines such as the authority of the Bible, the Trinity, the deity of Christ, justification by faith, and many others would rightly be considered major doctrines. People who disagree with the historic evangelical understanding of any of these doctrines will have wide areas of difference with evangelical Christians who affirm these doctrines. By contrast, it seems to me that differences over forms of church government or some details about the Lord's Supper or the timing of the great tribulation concern minor doctrines. Christians who differ over these things can agree on perhaps every other area of doctrine, can live Christian lives that differ in no important way, and can have genuine fellowship with one another.

Of course, we may find doctrines that fall somewhere between "major" and "minor" according to this standard. For example, Christians may differ over the degree of significance that should attach to the doctrine of baptism or the millennium or the extent of the atonement. That is only natural, because many doctrines have *some* influence on other doctrines or on life, but we may differ over whether we think it to be a "significant" influence. We could even recognize that there will be a range of significance here and just say that the more influence a doctrine has on other doctrines and on life, the more "major" it becomes. This amount of influence may even vary according to the historical circumstances and needs of the church at any given time. In such cases, Christians will need to ask God to give them mature wisdom and sound judgment as they try to determine to what extent a doctrine should be considered "major" in their particular circumstances.

D. A Note on Two Objections to the Study of Systematic Theology

1. "The Conclusions Are 'Too Neat' to be True." Some scholars look with suspicion at systematic theology when — or even because — its teachings fit together in a noncontradictory way. They object that the results are "too neat" and that systematic theologians must therefore be squeezing the Bible's teachings into an artificial mold, distorting the true meaning of Scripture to get an orderly set of beliefs.

To this objection two responses can be made: (1) We must first ask the people making the objection to tell us at what specific points Scripture has been misinterpreted, and then we must deal with the understanding of those passages. Perhaps mistakes have been made, and in that case there should be corrections.

Yet it is also possible that the objector will have no specific passages in mind, or no clearly erroneous interpretations to point to in the works of the most responsible evangelical theologians. Of course, incompetent exegesis can be found in the writings of the less competent scholars in *any* field of biblical studies, not just in systematic theology, but those "bad examples" constitute an objection not against the scholar's field but against the incompetent scholar himself.

It is very important that the objector be specific at this point because this objection is sometimes made by those who — perhaps unconsciously — have adopted from our culture a skeptical view of the possibility of finding universally true conclusions about anything, even about God from his Word. This kind of skepticism regarding theological truth is especially common in the modern university world where "systematic theology" — if it is studied at all — is studied only from the perspectives of philosophical theology and historical theology (including perhaps a historical study of the various ideas that were believed by the early Christians who wrote the New Testament, and by other Christians at that time and throughout church history). In this kind of intellectual climate the study of "systematic theology" as defined in this chapter would be considered impossible, because the Bible would be assumed to be merely the work of many human authors who wrote out of diverse cultures and experiences over the course of more than one thousand years: trying to find "what the whole Bible teaches" about any subject would be thought nearly as hopeless as trying to find "what all philosophers teach" about some question, for the answer in both cases would be thought to be not one view but many diverse and often conflicting views. This skeptical viewpoint must be rejected by evangelicals who see Scripture as the product of human *and* divine authorship, and therefore as a collection of writings that teach noncontradictory truths about God and about the universe he created.

(2) Second, it must be answered that in God's own mind, and in the nature of reality itself, *true* facts and ideas are all consistent with one another. Therefore if we have accurately understood the teachings of God in Scripture we should expect our conclusions to "fit together" and be mutually consistent. Internal consistency, then, is an argument for, not against, any individual results of systematic theology.

2. "The Choice of Topics Dictates the Conclusions." Another general objection to systematic theology concerns the choice and arrangement of topics, and even the fact that such topically arranged study of Scripture, using categories sometimes different from those found in Scripture itself, is done at all. Why are *these* theological topics treated rather than just the topics emphasized by the biblical authors, and why are the topics *arranged in this way* rather than in some other way? Perhaps—this objection would say—our traditions and our cultures have determined the topics we treat and the arrangement of topics, so that the results of this systematic-theological study of Scripture, though acceptable in our own theological tradition, will in fact be untrue to Scripture itself.

A variant of this objection is the statement that our starting point often determines our conclusions on controversial topics: if we decide to start with an emphasis on the divine authorship of Scripture, for example, we will end up believing in biblical inerrancy, but if we start with an emphasis on the human authorship of Scripture, we will end up believing there are some errors in the Bible. Similarly, if we start with an emphasis on God's sovereignty, we will end up as Calvinists, but if we start with an emphasis on man's ability to make free choices, we will end up as Arminians, and so forth. This objection makes it sound as if the most important theological questions could probably be decided by flipping a coin to decide where to start, since *different* and *equally valid* conclusions will inevitably be reached from the different starting points.

Those who make such an objection often suggest that the best way to avoid this problem is not to study or teach systematic theology at all, but to limit our topical studies to the field of biblical theology, treating only the topics and themes the biblical authors themselves emphasize and describing the historical development of these biblical themes through the Bible.

In response to this objection, much of the discussion in this chapter about the necessity to teach Scripture will be relevant. Our choice of topics need not be restricted to the main concerns of the biblical authors, for our goal is to find out what God requires of us in all areas of concern to us today.

For example, it was not the *main* concern of any New Testament author to explain such topics as "baptism in the Holy Spirit," or women's roles in the church, or the doctrine of the Trinity, but these are valid areas of concern for us today, and we must look at all the places in Scripture that have relevance for those topics (whether those specific terms are mentioned or not, and whether those themes are of primary concern to each passage we examine or not) if we are going to be able to understand and explain to others "what the whole Bible teaches" about them.

The only alternative—for we *will* think *something* about those subjects—is to form our opinions haphazardly from a general impression of what we feel to be a "biblical" position on each subject, or perhaps to buttress our positions with careful analysis of one or two relevant texts, yet with no guarantee that those texts present a balanced view of "the whole counsel of God" (Acts 20:27) on the subject being considered. In fact this approach—one all too common in evangelical circles today—could, I suppose, be called "unsystematic theology" or even "disorderly and random theology"! Such an alternative is too subjective and too subject to cultural pressures. It tends toward doctrinal fragmentation and widespread doctrinal uncertainty, leaving the church theologically immature, like "children, tossed to and fro and carried about with every wind of doctrine" (Eph. 4:14).

Concerning the objection about the choice and sequence of topics, there is nothing to prevent us from going to Scripture to look for answers to *any* doctrinal questions, considered in *any sequence.* The sequence of topics in this book is a very common one and has been adopted because it is orderly and lends itself well to learning and teaching. But the chapters could be read in any sequence one wanted and the conclusions should not be different, nor should the persuasiveness of the arguments—if they are rightly derived from Scripture—be significantly diminished. I have tried to write the chapters so that they can be read as independent units.

E. How Should Christians Study Systematic Theology?

How then should we study systematic theology? The Bible provides some guidelines for answering this question.

1. We Should Study Systematic Theology With Prayer. If studying systematic theology is simply a certain way of studying the Bible, then the passages in Scripture that talk about the way in which we should study God's Word give guidance to us in this task. Just as the psalmist prays in Psalm 119:18, "Open my eyes, that I may behold wondrous things out of your law," so we should pray and seek God's help in understanding his Word. Paul tells us in 1 Corinthians 2:14 that "the unspiritual man does not receive the gifts of the Spirit of God, for they are folly to him, and he is not able to understand them because they are spiritually discerned." Studying theology is therefore a spiritual activity in which we need the help of the Holy Spirit.

No matter how intelligent, if the student does not continue to pray for God to give him or her an understanding mind and a believing and humble heart, and the student does not maintain a personal walk with the Lord, then the teachings of Scripture will be misunderstood and disbelieved, doctrinal error will result, and the mind and heart of the student will not be changed for the better but for the worse. Students of systematic theology should resolve at the beginning to keep their lives free from any disobedience to God or any known sin that would disrupt their relationship with him. They should resolve to maintain with great regularity their own personal devotional lives. They should continually pray for wisdom and understanding of Scripture.

Since it is the Holy Spirit who gives us the ability rightly to understand Scripture, we need to realize that the proper thing to do, particularly when we are unable to understand some passage or some doctrine of Scripture, is to pray for God's help. Often what we need is not more data but more insight into the data we already have available. This insight is given only by the Holy Spirit (cf. 1 Cor. 2:14; Eph. 1:17–19).

2. We Should Study Systematic Theology With Humility. Peter tells us, "Clothe yourselves, all of you, with humility toward one another, for 'God opposes the proud, but gives grace to the humble'" (1 Peter 5:5). Those who study systematic theology will learn many things about the teachings of Scripture that are perhaps not known or not known well by other Christians in their churches or by relatives who are older in the Lord than they are. They may also find that they understand things about Scripture that some of their church officers do not understand, and that even their pastor has perhaps forgotten or never learned well.

In all of these situations it would be very easy to adopt an attitude of pride or superiority toward others who have not made such a study. But how ugly it would be if anyone were to use this knowledge of God's Word simply to win arguments or to put down a fellow Christian in conversation, or to make another believer feel insignificant in the Lord's work. James' counsel is good for us at this point: "Let every man be quick to hear, slow to speak, slow to anger, for the anger of man does not work the righteousness of God" (James 1:19–20). He tells us that one's understanding of Scripture is to be imparted in humility and love:

> Who is wise and understanding among you? By his good life let him show his works in the meekness of wisdom. . . . But the wisdom from above is first pure, then peaceable, gentle, open to reason, full of mercy and good fruits, without uncertainty or insincerity. And the harvest of righteousness is sown in peace by those who make peace. (James 3:13, 17–18)

Systematic theology rightly studied will not lead to the knowledge that "puffs up" (1 Cor. 8:1) but to humility and love for others.

3. We Should Study Systematic Theology With Reason. We find in the New Testament that Jesus and the New Testament authors will often quote a verse of Scripture and then draw logical conclusions from it. They *reason* from Scripture. It is therefore not wrong to use human understanding, human logic, and human reason to draw conclusions from the statements of Scripture. Nevertheless, when we reason and draw what we think to be correct logical deductions from Scripture, we sometimes make mistakes. The deductions we draw from the statements of Scripture are not equal to the statements of Scripture themselves in certainty or authority, for our ability to reason and draw conclusions is not the ultimate standard of truth—only Scripture is.

What then are the limits on our use of our reasoning abilities to draw deductions from the statements of Scripture? The fact that reasoning to conclusions that go beyond the mere statements of Scripture is appropriate and even necessary for studying Scripture, and the fact that Scripture itself is the ultimate standard of truth, combine to indicate to us that *we are free to use our reasoning abilities to draw deductions from any passage of Scripture so long as these deductions do not contradict the clear teaching of some other passage of Scripture.*[7]

This principle puts a safeguard on our use of what we think to be logical deductions from Scripture. Our supposedly logical deductions may be erroneous, but Scripture itself cannot be erroneous. Thus, for example, we may read Scripture and find that God the Father is called God (1 Cor. 1:3), that God the Son is called God (John 20:28; Titus 2:13), and that God the Holy Spirit is called God (Acts 5:3–4). We might deduce from this that there are three Gods. But then we find the Bible explicitly teaching us that God is one (Deut. 6:4; James 2:19). Thus we conclude that what we *thought* to be a valid logical deduction about three Gods was wrong and that Scripture teaches both (a) that there are three separate persons (the Father, the Son, and the Holy Spirit), each of whom is fully God, and (b) that there is one God.

We cannot understand exactly how these two statements can both be true, so together they constitute a *paradox* ("a seemingly contradictory statement that may nonetheless be true").[8] We can tolerate a paradox (such as "God is three persons and one God") because we have confidence that ultimately God knows fully the truth about himself and about the nature of reality, and that in his understanding the different elements of a paradox are fully reconciled, even though at this point God's thoughts are higher than our thoughts (Isa. 55:8–9). But a true contradiction (such as, "God is three persons and God is not three persons") would imply ultimate contradiction in God's own understanding of himself or of reality, and this cannot be.

---

[7]This guideline is also adopted from Professor John Frame at Westminster Seminary.

[8]The *American Heritage Dictionary of the English Language,* ed. William Morris (Boston: Houghton-Mifflin, 1980), p. 950 (first definition). Essentially the same meaning is adopted by the *Oxford English Dictionary* (1913 ed., 7:450), the *Concise Oxford Dictionary* (1981 ed., p. 742), the *Random House College Dictionary* (1979 ed., p. 964), and the *Chambers Twentieth Century Dictionary* (p. 780), though all note that *paradox* can also mean "contradiction" (though less commonly); compare the *Encyclopedia of Philosophy,* ed. Paul Edwards (New York: Macmillan and The Free Press, 1967), 5:45, and the entire article "Logical Paradoxes" by John van Heijenoort on pp. 45–51 of the same volume, which proposes solutions to many of the classical paradoxes in the history of philosophy. (If *paradox* meant "contradiction," such solutions would be impossible.)

When I use the word *paradox* in the primary sense defined by these dictionaries today I realize that I am differing somewhat with the article "Paradox" by K. S. Kantzer in the *EDT,* ed. Walter Elwell, pp. 826–27 (which takes *paradox* to mean essentially "contradiction"). However, I am using *paradox* in an ordinary English sense and one also familiar in philosophy. There seems to me to be available no better word than *paradox* to refer to an apparent but not real contradiction.

There is, however, some lack of uniformity in the use of the term *paradox* and a related term, *antinomy,* in con-temporary evangelical discussion. The word *antinomy* has sometimes been used to apply to what I here call *paradox,* that is, "seemingly contradictory statements that may nonetheless both be true" (see, for example, John Jefferson Davis, *Theology Primer* [Grand Rapids: Baker, 1981], p. 18). Such a sense for *antinomy* gained support in a widely read book, *Evangelism and the Sovereignty of God,* by J. I. Packer (London: Inter-Varsity Press, 1961). On pp. 18–22 Packer defines *antinomy* as "an appearance of contradiction" (but admits on p. 18 that his definition differs with the *Shorter Oxford Dictionary*). My problem with using *antinomy* in this sense is that the word is so unfamiliar in ordinary English that it just increases the stock of technical terms Christians have to learn in order to understand theologians, and moreover such a sense is unsupported by any of the dictionaries cited above, all of which define *antinomy* to mean "contradiction" (e.g., *Oxford English Dictionary,* 1:371). The problem is not serious, but it would help communication if evangelicals could agree on uniform senses for these terms.

A paradox is certainly acceptable in systematic theology, and paradoxes are in fact inevitable so long as we have finite understanding of any theological topic. However, it is important to recognize that Christian theology should never affirm a *contradiction* (a set of two statements, one of which denies the other). A contradiction would be, "God is three persons and God is not three persons" (where the term *persons* has the same sense in both halves of the sentence).

When the psalmist says, "The sum of your word is truth; and every one of your righteous ordinances endures for ever" (Ps. 119:160), he implies that God's words are not only true individually but also viewed together as a whole. Viewed collectively, their "sum" is also "truth." Ultimately, there is no internal contradiction either in Scripture or in God's own thoughts.

4. We Should Study Systematic Theology With Help From Others. We need to be thankful that God has put teachers in the church ("And God has appointed in the church first apostles, second prophets, third *teachers . . .*" [1 Cor. 12:28]. We should allow those with gifts of teaching to help us understand Scripture. This means that we should make use of systematic theologies and other books that have been written by some of the teachers that God has given to the church over the course of its history. It also means that our study of theology should include *talking with other Christians* about the things we study. Among those with whom we talk will often be some with gifts of teaching who can explain biblical teachings clearly and help us to understand more easily. In fact, some of the most effective learning in systematic theology courses in colleges and seminaries often occurs outside the classroom in informal conversations among students who are attempting to understand Bible doctrines for themselves.

5. We Should Study Systematic Theology by Collecting and Understanding All the Relevant Passages of Scripture on Any Topic. This point was mentioned in our definition of systematic theology at the beginning of the chapter, but the actual process needs to be described here. How does one go about making a doctrinal summary of what all the passages of Scripture teach on a certain topic? For topics covered in this book, many people will think that studying the chapters in this book and reading the Bible verses noted in the chapters is enough. But some people will want to do further study of Scripture on a particular topic or study some new topic not covered here. How could a student go about using the Bible to research its teachings on some new subject, perhaps one not discussed explicitly in any of his or her systematic theology textbooks?

The process would look like this: (1) Find all the relevant verses. The best help in this step is a good concordance, which enables one to look up key words and find the verses in which the subject is treated. For example, in studying what it means that man is created in the image and likeness of God, one needs to find all the verses in which "image" and "likeness" and "create" occur. (The words "man" and "God" occur too often to be useful for a concordance search.) In studying the doctrine of prayer, many words could be looked up (*pray, prayer, intercede, petition, supplication, confess, confession, praise, thanks, thanksgiving,* et al.)—and perhaps the list of verses would grow too long to be manageable, so that the student would have to skim the concordance entries without looking up the verses, or the search would probably have to be divided into sections or limited in some other way. Verses can also be found by thinking through the overall history of the Bible and then turning to sections where there would be information on the topic at hand—for example, a student studying prayer would want to read passages like the one about Hannah's prayer for a son (in 1 Sam. 1), Solomon's prayer at the dedication of the temple (in 1 Kings 8), Jesus' prayer in the Garden of Gethsemane (in Matt. 26 and parallels), and so forth. Then in addition to concordance work and reading other passages that one can find on the subject, checking the relevant sections in some systematic theology books will often bring to light other verses that had been missed, sometimes because none of the key words used for the concordance were in those verses.[9]

(2) The second step is to read, make notes on, and try to summarize the points made in the relevant verses. Sometimes a theme will be repeated often and the summary of the various verses will be relatively easy. At other times, there will be verses difficult to understand, and the student will need to take some time to study a verse in depth (just by reading the verse in context over and over, or by using specialized tools such as commentaries and dictionaries) until a satisfactory understanding is reached.

(3) Finally, the teachings of the various verses should be summarized into one or more points that the Bible affirms about that subject. The summary does not have to take the exact form of anyone else's conclusions on the subject, because we each may see things in Scripture that others have missed, or we may organize the subject differently or emphasize different things.

On the other hand, at this point it is also helpful to read related sections, if any can be found, in several systematic theology books. This provides a useful check against error and oversight, and often makes one aware of alternative perspectives and arguments that may cause us to modify or strengthen our position. If a student finds that others have argued for strongly differing conclusions, then these other views need to be stated fairly and then answered. Sometimes other theology books will alert us to historical or philosophical considerations that have been raised before in the history of the church, and these will provide additional insight or warnings against error.

The process outlined above is possible for any Christian who can read his or her Bible and can look up words in a concordance. Of course people will become faster and more accurate in this process with time and experience and Christian maturity, but it would be a tremendous help to the church if Christians generally would give much more time to searching out topics in Scripture for themselves and drawing conclusions in the way outlined above. The joy of discovery of biblical themes would be richly rewarding. Especially pastors and those who lead Bible studies would find added freshness in their understanding of Scripture and in their teaching.

6. We Should Study Systematic Theology With Rejoicing and Praise. The study of theology is not merely a theoretical exercise of the intellect. It is a study of the living God, and of the wonders of all his works in creation and redemption. We cannot study this subject dispassionately! We must love all that God is, all that he says and all that he does. "You shall love the LORD your God with all your heart" (Deut. 6:5). Our response to the study of the theology of Scripture should be that of the psalmist who said, "How precious to me are your thoughts, O God!" (Ps. 139:17). In the study of the teachings of

---

[9]I have read a number of student papers telling me that John's gospel says nothing about how Christians should pray, for example, because they looked at a concordance and found that the word *prayer* was not in John, and the word *pray* only occurs four times in reference to Jesus praying in John 14, 16, and 17. They overlooked the fact that John contains several important verses where the word *ask* rather than the word *pray* is used (John 14:13–14; 15:7, 16, et al.).

God's Word, it should not surprise us if we often find our hearts spontaneously breaking forth in expressions of praise and delight like those of the psalmist:

> The precepts of the LORD are right,
>   rejoicing the heart. (Ps. 19:8)

> In the way of your testimonies I delight
>   as much as in all riches. (Ps. 119:14)

> How sweet are your words to my taste,
>   sweeter than honey to my mouth! (Ps. 119:103)

> Your testimonies are my heritage for ever;
>   yea, they are the joy of my heart. (Ps. 119:111)

> I rejoice at your word
>   like one who finds great spoil. (Ps. 119:162)

Often in the study of theology the response of the Christian should be similar to that of Paul in reflecting on the long theological argument that he has just completed at the end of Romans 11:32. He breaks forth into joyful praise at the richness of the doctrine which God has enabled him to express:

> O the depth of the riches and wisdom and knowledge of God! How unsearchable are his judgments and how inscrutable his ways!

> "For who has known the mind of the Lord,
> or who has been his counselor?"
> "Or who has given a gift to him
> that he might be repaid?"

> For from him and through him and to him are all things. To him be glory for ever. Amen. (Rom. 11:33–36)

QUESTIONS FOR PERSONAL APPLICATION

These questions at the end of each chapter focus on application to life. Because I think doctrine is to be felt at the emotional level as well as understood at the intellectual level, in many chapters I have included some questions about how a reader *feels* regarding a point of doctrine. I think these questions will prove quite valuable for those who take the time to reflect on them.

1. In what ways (if any) has this chapter changed your understanding of what systematic theology is? What was your attitude toward the study of systematic theology before reading this chapter? What is your attitude now?

2. What is likely to happen to a church or denomination that gives up learning systematic theology for a generation or longer? Has that been true of your church?

3. Are there any doctrines listed in the Contents for which a fuller understanding would help to solve a personal difficulty in your life at the present time? What

are the spiritual and emotional dangers that you personally need to be aware of in studying systematic theology?

4. Pray for God to make this study of basic Christian doctrines a time of spiritual growth and deeper fellowship with him, and a time in which you understand and apply the teachings of Scripture rightly.

SPECIAL TERMS

apologetics
biblical theology
Christian ethics
contradiction
doctrine
dogmatic theology
historical theology
major doctrine

minor doctrine
New Testament theology
Old Testament theology
paradox
philosophical theology
presupposition
systematic theology

BIBLIOGRAPHY

Baker, D. L. "Biblical Theology." In *NDT*, p. 671.

Berkhof, Louis. *Introduction to Systematic Theology*. Grand Rapids: Eerdmans, 1982, pp. 15–75 (first published 1932).

Bray, Gerald L., ed. *Contours of Christian Theology*. Downers Grove, Ill.: InterVarsity Press, 1993.

_____. "Systematic Theology, History of." In *NDT*, pp. 671–72.

Cameron, Nigel M., ed. *The Challenge of Evangelical Theology: Essays in Approach and Method*. Edinburgh: Rutherford House, 1987.

Carson, D. A. "Unity and Diversity in the New Testament: The Possibility of Systematic Theology." In *Scripture and Truth*. Ed. by D. A. Carson and John Woodbridge. Grand Rapids: Zondervan, 1983, pp. 65–95.

Davis, John Jefferson. *Foundations of Evangelical Theology*. Grand Rapids: Baker, 1984.

_____. *The Necessity of Systematic Theology*. Grand Rapids: Baker, 1980.

_____. *Theology Primer: Resources for the Theological Student*. Grand Rapids: Baker, 1981.

Demarest, Bruce. "Systematic Theology." In *EDT*, pp. 1064–66.

Erickson, Millard. *Concise Dictionary of Christian Theology*. Grand Rapids: Baker, 1986.

Frame, John. *Van Til the Theologian*. Phillipsburg, N.J.: Pilgrim, 1976.

Geehan, E. R., ed. *Jerusalem and Athens*. Nutley, N.J.: Craig Press, 1971.

Grenz, Stanley J. *Revisioning Evangelical Theology: A Fresh Agenda for the 21st Century*. Downers Grove, Ill.: InterVarsity Press, 1993.

House, H. Wayne. *Charts of Christian Theology and Doctrine*. Grand Rapids: Zondervan, 1992.

Kuyper, Abraham. *Principles of Sacred Theology*. Trans. by J. H. DeVries. Grand Rapids: Eerdmans, 1968 (reprint; first published as *Encyclopedia of Sacred Theology* in 1898).

Machen, J. Gresham. *Christianity and Liberalism*. Grand Rapids: Eerdmans, 1923. (This 180-page book is, in my opinion, one of the most significant theological studies ever written. It gives a clear overview of major biblical doctrines and shows the vital differences with Protestant liberal theology at every point, differences that still confront us today. It is required reading in all my introductory theology classes.)

Morrow, T. W. "Systematic Theology." In *NDT*, p. 671.

Poythress, Vern. *Symphonic Theology: The Validity of Multiple Perspectives in Theology*. Grand Rapids: Zondervan, 1987.

Preus, Robert D. *The Theology of Post-Reformation Lutheranism: A Study of Theological Prolegomena*. 2 vols. St. Louis: Concordia, 1970.

Van Til, Cornelius. *In Defense of the Faith*, vol. 5: *An Introduction to Systematic Theology*. N.p.: Presbyterian and Reformed, 1976, pp. 1–61, 253–62.

_____. *The Defense of the Faith*. Philadelphia: Presbyterian and Reformed, 1955.

Vos, Geerhardus. "The Idea of Biblical Theology as a Science and as a Theological Discipline." In *Redemptive History and Biblical Interpretation*, pp. 3–24. Ed. by Richard Gaffin. Phillipsburg, N.J.: Presbyterian and Reformed, 1980 (article first published 1894).

Warfield, B. B. "The Indispensableness of Systematic Theology to the Preacher." In *Selected Shorter Writings of Benjamin B. Warfield*, 2:280–88. Ed. by John E. Meeter. Nutley, N.J.: Presbyterian and Reformed, 1973 (article first published 1897).

_____. "The Right of Systematic Theology." In *Selected Shorter Writings of Benjamin B. Warfield*, 2:21–279. Ed. by John E. Meeter. Nutley, N.J.: Presbyterian and Reformed, 1973 (article first published 1896).

Wells, David. *No Place for Truth, or, Whatever Happened to Evangelical Theology?* Grand Rapids: Eerdmans, 1993.

Woodbridge, John D., and Thomas E. McComiskey, eds. *Doing Theology in Today's World: Essays in Honor of Kenneth S. Kantzer*. Grand Rapids: Zondervan, 1991.

SCRIPTURE MEMORY PASSAGE

Students have repeatedly mentioned that one of the most valuable parts of any of their courses in college or seminary has been the Scripture passages they were required to memorize. "I have hidden your word in my heart that I might not sin against you" (Ps. 119:11 NIV). In each chapter, therefore, I have included an appropriate memory passage so that instructors may incorporate Scripture memory into the course requirements wherever possible. (Scripture memory passages at the end of each chapter are taken from the RSV. These same passages in the NIV and NASB may be found in appendix 2.)

Matthew 28:18–20: *And Jesus came and said to them, "All authority in heaven and on earth has been given to me. Go therefore and make disciples of all nations, baptizing them in the name of the Father and of the Son and of the Holy Spirit, teaching them to observe all that I have commanded you; and lo, I am with you always, to the close of the age."*

HYMN

Systematic theology at its best will result in praise. It is appropriate therefore at the end of each chapter to include a hymn related to the subject of that chapter. In a classroom setting, the hymn can be sung together at the beginning or end of class. Alternatively, an individual reader can sing it privately or simply meditate quietly on the words.

For almost every chapter the words of the hymns were found in *Trinity Hymnal* (Philadelphia: Great Commission Publications, 1990),[10] the hymnal of the Presbyterian Church in America and the Orthodox Presbyterian Church, but most of them are found in many other common hymnals. Unless otherwise noted, the words of these hymns are now in public domain and no longer subject to copyright restrictions: therefore they may be freely copied for overhead projector use or photocopied.

Why have I used so many old hymns? Although I personally like many of the more recent worship songs that have come into wide use, when I began to select hymns that would correspond to the great doctrines of the Christian faith, I realized that the great hymns of the church throughout history have a doctrinal richness and breadth that is still unequaled. For several of the chapters in this book, I know of no modern worship song that covers the same subject in an extended way—perhaps this can be a challenge to modern songwriters to study these chapters and then write songs reflecting the teaching of Scripture on the respective subjects.

For this chapter, however, I found no hymn ancient or modern that thanked God for the privilege of studying systematic theology from the pages of Scripture. Therefore I have selected a hymn of general praise, which is always appropriate.

"O for a Thousand Tongues to Sing"

This hymn by Charles Wesley (1707–88) begins by wishing for "a thousand tongues" to sing God's praise. Verse 2 is a prayer that God would "assist me" in singing his praise throughout the earth. The remaining verses give praise to Jesus (vv. 3–6) and to God the Father (v. 7).

O for a thousand tongues to sing
My great Redeemer's praise,
The glories of my God and King,
The triumphs of His grace.

My gracious Master and my God,
Assist me to proclaim,
To spread through all the earth abroad,
The honors of Thy name.

Jesus! the name that charms our fears,
That bids our sorrows cease;

---

[10]This hymn book is completely revised from a similar hymnal of the same title published by the Orthodox Presbyterian Church in WW 1961.

'Tis music in the sinner's ears,
'Tis life and health and peace.

He breaks the pow'r of reigning sin,
He sets the prisoner free;
His blood can make the foulest clean;
His blood availed for me.

He speaks and, list'ning to His voice,
New life the dead receive;
The mournful, broken hearts rejoice;
The humble poor believe.

Hear him, ye deaf; his praise, ye dumb,
Your loosened tongues employ,
Ye blind, behold your Savior come;
And leap, ye lame, for joy.

Glory to God and praise and love
Be ever, ever giv'n
By saints below and saints above—
The church in earth and heav'n.

AUTHOR: CHARLES WESLEY, 1739, ALT.

Chapter 2

THE EXISTENCE OF GOD

How do we know that God exists?

EXPLANATION AND SCRIPTURAL BASIS

How do we know that God exists? The answer can be given in two parts: First, all people have an inner sense of God. Second, we believe the evidence that is found in Scripture and in nature.

A. Humanity's Inner Sense of God

All persons everywhere have a deep, inner sense that God exists, that they are his creatures, and that he is their Creator. Paul says that even Gentile unbelievers "knew God" but did not honor him as God or give thanks to him (Rom. 1:21). He says that wicked unbelievers have "exchanged the truth about God for a lie" (Rom. 1:25), implying that they actively or willfully rejected some truth about God's existence and character that they knew. Paul says that "what can be known about God is plain to them," and adds that this is "because God has shown it to them" (Rom. 1:19).

Yet Scripture also recognizes that some people deny this inner sense of God and even deny that God exists. It is "the *fool*" who says in his heart, "There is no God" (Ps. 14:1; 53:1). It is the wicked person who first "curses and renounces the LORD" and then in pride repeatedly thinks "there is no God" (Ps. 10:3–4). These passages indicate both that sin leads people to think irrationally and to deny God's existence, and that it is someone who is thinking irrationally or who has been deceived who will say, "There is no God."

Paul also recognizes that sin will cause people to *deny* their knowledge of God: he speaks of those who "by their wickedness *suppress the truth*" (Rom. 1:18) and says that those who do this are "without excuse" for this denial of God (Rom. 1:20). A series of active verbs indicates that this is a willful suppression of the truth (Rom. 1:23, 25, 28, 32).[1]

---

[1]Some people deny that they have an inner sense of God. But their awareness of God will often make itself evident in a time of personal crisis, when deep-seated convictions of the heart show themselves in outward words and deeds. Several years ago I was a passenger in a car with several friends, including a young woman who in conversation was firmly denying

In the life of a Christian this inner awareness of God becomes stronger and more distinct. We begin to know God as our loving Father in heaven (Rom. 8:15), the Holy Spirit bears witness with our spirits that we are children of God (Rom. 8:16), and we come to know Jesus Christ living within our hearts (Eph. 3:17; Phil. 3:8, 10; Col. 1:27; John 14:23). The intensity of this awareness for a Christian is such that though we have not seen our Lord Jesus Christ, we indeed love him (1 Peter 1:8).

B. Believing the Evidence in Scripture and Nature

In addition to people's inner awareness of God that bears clear witness to the fact that God exists, clear evidence of his existence is to be seen in Scripture and in nature.

The evidence that God exists is of course found throughout the Bible. In fact, the Bible everywhere assumes that God exists. The first verse of Genesis does not present evidence for the existence of God but begins immediately to tell us what he has done: "In the beginning God created the heavens and the earth." If we are convinced that the Bible is true, then we know from the Bible not only that God exists but also very much about his nature and his acts.

The world also gives abundant evidence of God's existence. Paul says that God's eternal nature and deity have been "clearly perceived in the things that have been made" (Rom. 1:20). This broad reference to "the things that have been made" suggests that in some sense every created thing gives evidence of God's character. Nevertheless, it is man himself, created in the image of God, who most abundantly bears witness to the existence of God: whenever we meet another human being, we should (if our minds are thinking correctly) realize that such an incredibly intricate, skillful, communicative living creature could only have been created by an infinite, all-wise Creator.

In addition to the evidence seen in the existence of living human beings, there is further excellent evidence in nature. The "rains and fruitful seasons" as well as the "food and gladness" that all people experience and benefit from are also said by Barnabas and Paul to be witnesses to God (Acts 14:17). David tells us of the witness of the heavens: "*The heavens are telling the glory of God; and the firmament proclaims his handiwork. Day to day pours forth speech, and night to night declares knowledge*" (Ps. 19:1–2). To look upward into the sky by day or by night is to see sun, moon, and stars, sky and clouds, all continually declaring by their existence and beauty and greatness that a powerful and wise Creator has made them and sustains them in their order.

This wide variety of testimonies to God's existence from various parts of the created world suggests to us that in one sense *everything that exists* gives evidence of God's existence. For those who have eyes to see and evaluate the evidence correctly, every leaf on every tree, every blade of grass, every star in the sky, and every other part of creation all cry out continuously, "God made me! God made me! God made me!" If our hearts and minds were not so blinded by sin, it would be impossible for us to look closely at

that she had any inner awareness of God's existence. Shortly thereafter the car hit a patch of ice and spun around in a complete circle at high speed. Before the car came to rest in a large snow bank (with no serious damage) this same woman could be heard distinctly calling out, "Lord Jesus, please help us!" The rest of us looked at her in amazement when we realized that her agnosticism had been disproved by words from her own mouth.

a leaf from any tree and say, "No one created this: it just happened." The beauty of a snowflake, the majestic power of a thunderstorm, the skill of a honeybee, the refreshing taste of cold water, the incredible abilities of the human hand—all these and thousands of other aspects of creation simply could not have come into existence apart from the activity of an all-powerful and all-wise Creator.

Thus, for those who are correctly evaluating the evidence, *everything* in Scripture and *everything* in nature proves clearly that God exists and that he is the powerful and wise Creator that Scripture describes him to be. Therefore, when we believe that God exists, we are basing our belief *not* on some blind hope apart from any evidence, but on *an overwhelming amount of reliable evidence from God's words and God's works.* It is a characteristic of true faith that it is a confidence based on reliable evidence, and faith in the existence of God shares this characteristic.

Furthermore, these evidences can all be seen as valid proofs for the existence of God, even though some people reject them. This does not mean that the evidence is invalid in itself, only that those who reject the evidence are evaluating it wrongly.

C. Traditional "Proofs" for the Existence of God

The traditional "proofs" for the existence of God that have been constructed by Christian (and some non-Christian) philosophers at various points in history are in fact attempts to analyze the evidence, especially the evidence from nature, in extremely careful and logically precise ways, in order to persuade people that it is not rational to reject the idea of God's existence. If it is true that sin causes people to think *irrationally,* then these proofs are attempts to cause people to think *rationally* or correctly about the evidence for God's existence, in spite of the irrational tendencies caused by sin.

Most of the traditional proofs for the existence of God can be classified in four major types of argument:

1. The *cosmological argument* considers the fact that every known thing in the universe has a cause. Therefore, it reasons, the universe itself must also have a cause, and the cause of such a great universe can only be God.

2. The *teleological argument* is really a subcategory of the cosmological argument. It focuses on the evidence of harmony, order, and design in the universe, and argues that its design gives evidence of an intelligent purpose (the Greek word *telos* means "end" or "goal" or "purpose"). Since the universe appears to be designed with a purpose, there must be an intelligent and purposeful God who created it to function this way.

3. The *ontological argument* begins with the idea of God, who is defined as a being "greater than which nothing can be imagined." It then argues that the characteristic of existence must belong to such a being, since it is greater to exist than not to exist.[2]

4. The *moral argument* begins from man's sense of right and wrong, and of the need for justice to be done, and argues that there must be a God who is the source of right and wrong and who will someday mete out justice to all people.

---

[2]The stem *ont-* in "ontological" is derived from a Greek word that means "being."

Because all of these arguments are based on facts about the creation that are indeed true facts, we may say that all of these proofs (when carefully constructed) are, in an objective sense, valid proofs. They are valid in that they correctly evaluate the evidence and correctly reason to a true conclusion—in fact, the universe *does* have God as its cause, and it *does* show evidence of purposeful design, and God *does* exist as a being greater than which nothing can be imagined, and God *has* given us a sense of right and wrong and a sense that his judgment is coming someday. The *actual facts* referred to in these proofs, therefore, are *true,* and in that sense the proofs are valid, even though not all people are persuaded by them.

But in another sense, if "valid" means "able to compel agreement even from those who begin with false assumptions," then of course none of the proofs is valid because not one of them is able to *compel agreement* from *everyone who considers them.* Yet this is because many unbelievers either begin with invalid assumptions or do not reason correctly from the evidence. It is not because the proofs are invalid in themselves.

The value of these proofs, then, lies chiefly in overcoming some of the intellectual objections of unbelievers. They cannot bring unbelievers to saving faith, for that comes about through belief in the testimony of Scripture. But they can help overcome objections from unbelievers, and, for believers, they can provide further intellectual evidence for something they have already been persuaded of from their own inner sense of God and from the testimony of Scripture.

D. Only God Can Overcome Our Sin and Enable Us to Be Persuaded of His Existence

Finally, it must be remembered that in this sinful world *God must enable us to be persuaded* or we would never believe in him. We read that "the god of this world has *blinded the minds of the unbelievers,* to keep them from seeing the light of the gospel of the glory of Christ" (2 Cor. 4:4). Furthermore, Paul says that "since, in the wisdom of God, the world did not know God through wisdom, it pleased God through the folly of what we preach to save those who believe" (1 Cor. 1:21). In this sinful world, human wisdom is inadequate for coming to know God. Thus, Paul's preaching came "in demonstration of the Spirit and of power, *that your faith might not rest in the wisdom of men but in the power of God*" (1 Cor. 2:5). We are dependent upon God to remove the blindness and irrationality caused by sin and to enable us to evaluate the evidence rightly, believe what Scripture says, and come to saving faith in Christ.

QUESTIONS FOR PERSONAL APPLICATION

1. When the seraphim around God's throne cry out, "Holy, holy, holy is the Lord of hosts; *the whole earth is full of his glory*" (Isa. 6:3), do you think they are seeing the earth from a somewhat different perspective than ours? In what ways? How can we begin to see the world more from this perspective?

2. When is your inner sense of God's existence strongest? Weakest? Why? In which of these situations are you in a condition more like the one you will have in heaven? In which of these types of situations are your judgments more reliable?

3. Look at your hand. Is it more or less complex than a wristwatch? Is it logical to think that either one of them just came about by an accidental combination of elements?

4. Do most people today believe in the existence of God? Has this been true throughout history? If they believe that God exists, why have they not worshiped him rightly?

5. Why do some people deny the existence of God? Does Romans 1:18 suggest there is often a moral factor influencing their intellectual denial of God's existence (cf. Ps. 14:1–3)? What is the best way to approach someone who denies the existence of God?

SPECIAL TERMS

cosmological argument

inner sense of God

moral argument

ontological argument

teleological argument

BIBLIOGRAPHY

Brown, Colin. *Philosophy and the Christian Faith*. Downers Grove, Ill.: InterVarsity Press, 1968.

Charnock, Stephen. *The Existence and Attributes of God*. Repr. ed. Evansville, Ind.: Sovereign Grace Book Club, n.d., pp. 11–67 (first published 1655–80).

Clark, Gordon H. *Religion, Reason, and Revelation*. Nutley, N.J.: Craig Press, 1961.

France, R. T. *The Living God*. Downers Grove, Ill.: InterVarsity Press, 1970.

Geisler, Norman. *Christian Apologetics*. Grand Rapids: Baker, 1976.

_____, and Paul Feinberg. *Introduction to Philosophy: A Christian Perspective*. Grand Rapids: Baker, 1980.

Hackett, Stuart. *The Resurrection of Theism*. Chicago: Moody, 1957.

Hoover, A. J. "God, Arguments for the Existence of." In *EDT*, pp. 447–51.

Jastrow, Roberto. *God and the Astronomers*. 2nd ed. New York: Norton, 1992.

Lewis, Gordon R. *Testing Christianity's Truth Claims*. Chicago: Moody, 1976.

Mavrodes, George I. *Belief in God*. New York: Random House, 1970.

McDowell, Josh. *Evidence That Demands a Verdict*. San Bernardino, Calif.: Here's Life, 1972, 1979.

Packer, J. I. "God." In *NDT*, pp. 274–77.

Sire, James. *The Universe Next Door: A Basic World View Catalog*. Downers Grove, Ill.: InterVarsity Press, 1976.

Van Til, Cornelius. *The Defense of the Faith*. Philadelphia: Presbyterian and Reformed, 1955.

Yandell, Keith. *Christianity and Philosophy. Studies in a Christian World View*. Grand Rapids: Eerdmans, and Leicester: Inter-Varsity Press, 1984.

SCRIPTURE MEMORY PASSAGE

Romans 1:18–20: *For the wrath of God is revealed from heaven against all ungodliness and wickedness of men who by their wickedness suppress the truth. For what can be known about God is plain to them, because God has shown it to them. Ever since the creation of the world his invisible nature, namely, his eternal power and deity, has been clearly perceived in the things that have been made. So they are without excuse.*

HYMN

"The Spacious Firmament on High"

This hymn, based on Psalm 19:1–4, speaks of the testimony of the sun, moon, and stars to their Creator. The word *firmament* in the first verse refers to the expanse or open space that is visible to us as we look upward from earth; it is the place in which the sun, moon, and stars exist, and might be translated "sky" or "heavens." The third verse reminds us that though these heavenly bodies make no sounds that can be heard by our physical ears, they nonetheless proclaim, to all who think rightly about them, "The hand that made us is divine."

> The spacious firmament on high,
>   With all the blue ethereal sky,
> And spangled heav'ns, a shining frame,
>   Their great original proclaim.
> Th' unwearied sun, from day to day,
>   Does his Creator's pow'r display,
> And publishes to every land
>   The work of an Almighty hand.
>
> Soon as the evening shades prevail,
>   The moon takes up the wondrous tale,
> And nightly to the list'ning earth
>   Repeats the story of her birth;
> Whilst all the stars that round her burn,
>   And all the planets in their turn,
> Confirm the tidings as they roll,
>   And spread the truth from pole to pole.
>
> What though in solemn silence all
>   Move round this dark terrestrial ball?

What though nor real voice nor sound
    Amidst their radiant orbs be found?
In reason's ear they all rejoice,
    And utter forth a glorious voice;
For ever singing, as they shine,
    "The hand that made us is divine."

AUTHOR: JOSEPH ADDISON, 1712

Alternative hymns: "I Sing th' Almighty Power of God"; "This Is My Father's World"; or "Day Is Dying in the West"

Chapter 3

THE KNOWABILITY OF GOD

Can we really know God? How much of God can we know?

EXPLANATION AND SCRIPTURAL BASIS

A. The Necessity for God to Reveal Himself to Us

If we are to know God at all, it is necessary that he reveal himself to us. Even when discussing the revelation of God that comes through nature, Paul says that what can be known about God is plain to people "because *God has shown it to them*" (Rom. 1:19). The natural creation reveals God because he chose to have himself revealed in this way.

With regard to the personal knowledge of God that comes in salvation, this idea is even more explicit. Jesus says, "No one knows the Son except the Father, and no one knows the Father except the Son and *any one to whom the Son chooses to reveal him*" (Matt. 11:27). This kind of knowledge of God is not found through human effort or wisdom: "in the wisdom of God, *the world did not know God through wisdom*" (1 Cor. 1:21; cf. 1 Cor. 2:14; 2 Cor. 4:3–4; John 1:18).

The necessity for God to reveal himself to us also is seen in the fact that sinful people misinterpret the revelation about God found in nature. Those who "by their wickedness suppress the truth" are those who "became futile in their thinking and their senseless minds were darkened . . . they exchanged the truth about God for a lie" (Rom. 1:18, 21, 25). Therefore, we need Scripture if we are to interpret natural revelation rightly. Hundreds of false religions in the world are evidence of the way sinful people, without guidance from Scripture, will always misunderstand and distort the revelation about God found in nature. But the Bible alone tells us *how to understand the testimony about God from nature.* Therefore we depend on God's active communication to us in Scripture for our true knowledge of God.

B. We Can Never Fully Understand God

Because God is infinite and we are finite or limited, we can never fully understand God. In this sense God is said to be *incomprehensible*, where the term *incomprehensible* is used with an older and less common sense, "unable to be *fully* understood." This sense must be clearly distinguished from the more common meaning, "unable to be understood." It is not true to say that God is unable to be understood, but it is true to say that he cannot be understood fully or exhaustively.

Psalm 145 says, "Great is the LORD, and greatly to be praised, and *his greatness is unsearchable*" (Ps. 145:3). God's greatness is beyond searching out or discovering: it is too great ever to be fully known. Regarding God's understanding, Psalm 147 says, "Great is our LORD, and abundant in power; *his understanding is beyond measure*" (Ps. 147:5). We will never be able to measure or fully know the understanding of God: it is far too great for us to equal or to understand. Similarly, when thinking of God's knowledge of all his ways, David says, "*Such knowledge is too wonderful for me; it is high, I cannot attain it*" (Ps. 139:6; cf. v. 17).

Paul implies this incomprehensibility of God when he says that "the Spirit searches everything, even the depths of God," and then goes on to say that "no one comprehends the things[1] of God except the Spirit of God" (1 Cor. 2:10–12). At the end of a long discussion on the history of God's great plan of redemption, Paul breaks forth into praise: "O the depth of the riches and wisdom and knowledge of God! How unsearchable are his judgments and how inscrutable his ways!" (Rom. 11:33).

These verses allow us to take our understanding of the incomprehensibility of God one step further. It is not only true that we can never fully understand God; it is also true that *we can never fully understand any single thing about God.* His greatness (Ps. 145:3), his understanding (Ps. 147:5), his knowledge (Ps. 139:6), his riches, wisdom, judgments, and ways (Rom. 11:33) are *all* beyond our ability to understand fully. Other verses also support this idea: as the heavens are higher than the earth, so are God's ways higher than our ways and his thoughts than our thoughts (Isa. 55:9). Job says that God's great acts in creating and sustaining the earth are "but the outskirts of his ways," and exclaims, "how small a whisper do we hear of him! But the thunder of his power who can understand?" (Job 26:14; cf. 11:7–9; 37:5).

Thus, we may know *something* about God's love, power, wisdom, and so forth. But we can never know his love completely or *exhaustively.* We can never know his power exhaustively. We can never know his wisdom exhaustively, and so forth. In order to know any single thing about God exhaustively we would have to know it as he himself knows it. That is, we would have to know it in its relationship to everything else about God and in its relationship to everything else about creation throughout all eternity! We can only exclaim with David, "Such knowledge is too wonderful for me; it is high, I cannot attain it" (Ps. 139:6).

This doctrine of God's incomprehensibility has much positive application for our own lives. It means that we will never be able to know "too much" about God, for we will never run out of things to learn about him, and we will thus never tire in delighting in the discovery of more and more of his excellence and of the greatness of his works.

---

[1]So KJV, quite literally translating the Greek phrase *ta tou theou.* RSV, NIV, and NASB all supply the word *thoughts,* because the parallel expression in v. 11, *ta tou anthrōpou* ("the things of the man"), seems to require that we supply the word *thoughts* as necessary to the context. But Paul's mention of "the depths of God" in v. 10 suggests that not only God's thoughts but all of God's being is referred to in both v. 10 and v. 12.

Even in the age to come, when we are freed from the presence of sin, we will never be able fully to understand God or any one thing about him. This is seen from the fact that the passages cited above attribute God's incomprehensibility not to our sinfulness but to his infinite greatness. It is because we are finite and God is infinite that we will never be able to understand him fully.[2] For all eternity we will be able to go on increasing in our knowledge of God and delighting ourselves more and more in him, saying with David as we learn more and more of God's own thoughts, "How precious to me are your thoughts, O God! How vast is the sum of them! If I would count them, they are more than the sand" (Ps. 139:17–18).

But if this is so in eternity future, then it certainly must be so in this life. In fact, Paul tells us that if we are to lead a life "worthy of the Lord, fully pleasing to him," it must be one in which we are continually *increasing in the knowledge of God*" (Col. 1:10). We should be growing in our knowledge of God through our entire lives.

If we ever wished to make ourselves equal to God in knowledge, or if we wished to derive satisfaction from the sin of intellectual pride, the fact that we will never stop growing in knowledge of God would be a discouraging thing for us—we might become frustrated that God is a subject of study that we will never master! But if we rather delight in the fact that God alone is God, that he is always infinitely greater than we are, that we are his creatures who owe him worship and adoration, then this will be a very encouraging idea. Even though we spend time in Bible study and fellowship with God every day of our lives, there will always be more to learn about God and his relationships to us and the world, and thus there will always be more that we can be thankful for and for which we can give him praise. When we realize this, the prospect of a lifelong habit of regular Bible study, and even the prospect of a lifetime of study of theology (if it is theology that is solidly grounded in God's Word), should be a very exciting prospect to us. To study and to teach God's Word in both formal and informal ways will always be a great privilege and joy.

C. Yet We Can Know God Truly

Even though we cannot know God exhaustively, we can know *true* things about God. In fact, *all that Scripture tells us* about God is true. It is true to say that God is love (1 John 4:8), that God is light (1 John 1:5), that God is spirit (John 4:24), that God is just or righteous (Rom. 3:26), and so forth. To say this, does not imply or require that we know everything about God or about his love or his righteousness or any other attribute. When I say that I have three sons, that statement is entirely true, even though I do not know everything about my sons, nor even about myself. So it is in our knowledge of God: we have true knowledge of God from Scripture, even though we do not have exhaustive knowledge. We can know some of God's thoughts—even many of them—from Scripture, and when we know them, we, like David, find them to be "precious" (Ps. 139:17).

---

[2]This is not contradicted by 1 Cor. 13:12, "Now I know in part; then I shall understand fully, even as I have been fully understood." The phrase "know fully" is simply an attempt to translate the word *epiginōskō,* which suggests deeper or more accurate knowledge (or perhaps, in contrast with present partial knowledge, knowledge free from error or falsehood). Paul never says anything like, "Then I shall know all things," which would have been very easy to say in Greek (*tote epignōsomai ta panta*) if he had wished to do so.

Even more significantly, it is *God himself* whom we know, not simply facts about him or actions he does. We make a distinction between knowing *facts* and knowing *persons* in our ordinary use of English. It would be true for me to say that I know many facts about the president of the United States, but it would not be true for me to say that I know *him*. To say that I know him would imply that I had met him and talked with him, and that I had developed at least to some degree a personal relationship with him.

Now some people say that we cannot know God himself, but that we can only know facts about him or know what he does. Others have said that we cannot know God as he is in himself, but we can only know him as he relates to us (and there is an implication that these two are somehow different). But Scripture does not speak that way. Several passages speak of our *knowing God himself*. We read God's words in Jeremiah:

> Let not the wise man glory in his wisdom, let not the mighty man glory in his might, let not the rich man glory in his riches; but let him who glories glory in this, that he understands and *knows me,* that I am the LORD who practices stead-fast love, justice, and righteousness in the earth; for in these things I delight, says the LORD. (Jer. 9:23–24)

Here God says that the source of our joy and sense of importance ought to come not from our own abilities or possessions, but from the fact that we know him. Similarly, in praying to his Father, Jesus could say, "And this is eternal life, that *they know you* the only true God, and Jesus Christ whom you have sent" (John 17:3). The promise of the new covenant is that all shall know God, "from the least of them to the greatest" (Heb. 8:11), and John's first epistle tells us that the Son of God has come and given us under-standing "*to know him* who is true" (1 John 5:20; see also Gal. 4:9; Phil. 3:10; 1 John 2:3; 4:8). John can say, "I write to you, children, because *you know the Father*" (1 John 2:13).

The fact that we do know God himself is further demonstrated by the realization that the richness of the Christian life includes a personal relationship with God. As these passages imply, we have a far greater privilege than mere knowledge of facts about God. We speak to God in prayer, and he speaks to us through his Word. We commune with him in his presence, we sing his praise, and we are aware that he personally dwells among us and within us to bless us (John 14:23). Indeed, this personal relationship with God the Father, with God the Son, and with God the Holy Spirit may be said to be the greatest of all the blessings of the Christian life.

QUESTIONS FOR PERSONAL APPLICATION

1. Sometimes people say that heaven sounds boring. How does the fact that God is incomprehensible yet knowable help to answer that objection?

2. How can we be sure that when we reach heaven God will not tell us that most of what we had learned about him was wrong, and that we would have to forget what we had learned and begin to learn different things about him?

3. Do you want to go on knowing God more and more deeply for all eternity? Why or why not? Would you like sometime to be able to know God exhaustively? Why or why not?

4. Why do you think God decided to reveal himself to us? Do you learn more about God from his revelation in nature or his revelation in Scripture? Why do you think it is that God's thoughts are "precious" to us (Ps. 139:17)? Would you call your present relationship to God a personal relationship? How is it similar to your relationships with other people, and how is it different? What would make your relationship with God better?

SPECIAL TERMS

incomprehensible
knowable

BIBLIOGRAPHY

Bray, Gerald L. *The Doctrine of God.* Downers Grove, Ill.: InterVarsity Press, 1993.
Charnock, Stephen. *The Knowledge of God. The Complete Works of Stephen Charnock.* Vol. 4. Edinburgh: James Nichol, 1865. Repr. ed.: Edinburgh: Banner of Truth, 1985, esp. pp. 3–164.
Frame, John M. *The Doctrine of the Knowledge of God.* Phillipsburg, N.J.: Presbyterian and Reformed, 1987.
France, R. T. *The Living God.* Downers Grove, Ill.: InterVarsity Press, 1970.
Packer, J. I. "God." In *NDT,* pp. 274–77.
_____. *Knowing God.* London: Inter-Varsity Press, 1973, pp. 13–37.
Piper, John. *Desiring God.* Portland, Ore.: Multnomah, 1986.
Tozer, A. W. *The Knowledge of the Holy.* New York: Harper and Row, 1961.
Van Til, Cornelius. *In Defense of the Faith,* vol. 5: *An Introduction to Systematic Theology.* Phillipsburg, N. J.: Presbyterian and Reformed, 1976, pp. 159–99.

SCRIPTURE MEMORY PASSAGE

(Verse 3 of this passage tells us that God can never be fully known, but the fact that David is praising God and speaking to him shows also that he does know true things about God and does have a personal relationship to him.)

Psalm 145:1–3:

> *I will extol you, my God and King,*
>   *and bless your name for ever and ever.*
> *Every day I will bless you,*
>   *and praise your name for ever and ever.*
> *Great is the LORD, and greatly to be praised,*
>   *and his greatness is unsearchable.*

HYMN

"I Will Thee Praise, My God, O King"

Throughout the history of the church Christians have enjoyed rearranging the words of the psalms to fit some poetic meter and then setting these psalms to music for personal or group worship. This is an old metrical arrangement of the words to Psalm 145, set to the familiar melody of the hymn, "Jesus Shall Reign Where'er the Sun." Stanza 2 speaks of God's incomprehensibility ("The Lord is great; he praise exceeds; his greatness fully search can none"), and many of the other stanzas speak of various attributes of God that we know from Scripture. It should give us joy to sing this song, knowing both that we are singing absolutely true things about God, and that his greatness far exceeds any praise we will ever be able to sing to him.

> I will thee praise, my God, O King,
>   And I will ever bless thy name;
> I will extol thee every day
>   And evermore thy praise proclaim.
>
> The Lord is great; he praise exceeds;
>   His greatness fully search can none;
> Race shall to race extol thy deeds
>   And tell thy mighty acts each one.
>
> Upon thy glorious majesty
>   And wondrous works my mind shall dwell;
> Men shall recount thy dreadful acts,
>   And of thy greatness I will tell.
>
> They utter shall abundantly
>   The mem'ry of thy goodness great,
> And shall sing praises cheerfully
>   While they thy righteousness relate.
>
> Jehovah very gracious is;
>   In him compassions also flow;
> In lovingkindness he is great,
>   And unto anger he is slow.
>
> O'er all his works his mercies are;
>   The Lord is good to all that live.
> Praise, Lord, to thee thy works afford;
>   Thy saints to thee shall praises give.

FROM: *THE BOOK OF PSALMS WITH MUSIC*
(PITTSBURGH: REFORMED PRESBYTERIAN CHURCH OF NORTH AMERICA, 1973),
PSALM 145 (PP. 350–51)

Alternative hymn: "O Worship the King" (see this hymn at the end of chapter 5)

Chapter 4

THE CHARACTER OF GOD: "INCOMMUNICABLE" ATTRIBUTES

How is God different from us?

EXPLANATION AND SCRIPTURAL BASIS

A. Introduction to the Study of God's Character

1. Classifying God's Attributes. When we come to talk about the character of God, we realize that we cannot say everything the Bible teaches us about God's character at once. We need some way to decide which aspect of God's character to discuss first, which aspect to discuss second, and so forth. In other words, we need some way to categorize the attributes of God. This question is not as unimportant as it may seem. There is the possibility that we would adopt a misleading order of attributes or that we would emphasize some attributes so much that others would not be presented properly.

Several different methods of classifying God's attributes have been used. In this chapter we will adopt probably the most commonly used classification: the *incommunicable attributes* of God (that is, those attributes that God does not share or "communicate" to others) and the *communicable attributes* of God (those God shares or "communicates" with us).

Examples of the incommunicable attributes would be God's eternity (God has existed for all eternity, but we have not), unchangeableness (God does not change, but we do), or omnipresence (God is everywhere present, but we are present only in one place at one time). Examples of the communicable attributes would be love (God is love, and we are able to love as well), knowledge (God has knowledge, and we are able to have knowledge as well), mercy (God is merciful, and we are able to be merciful too), or justice (God is just and we, too, are able to be just). This classification of God's attributes into two major categories is helpful, and most people have an initial sense of which specific attributes should be called incommunicable and which should be called communicable. Thus it makes sense to say that God's love is communicable but his omnipresence is not.

However, upon further reflection we realize that this distinction, although helpful, is not perfect. That is because there is no attribute of God that is *completely* communicable, and there is no attribute of God that is *completely* incommunicable! This will be evident if we think for a moment about some things we already know about God.

For example, God's *wisdom* would usually be called a communicable attribute, because we also can be wise. But we will never be infinitely wise as God is. His wisdom is *to some extent* shared with us, but it is never *fully* shared with us. Similarly, we can share God's *knowledge* in part, yet we shall never share it fully, for God's thoughts are higher than ours "as the heavens are higher than the earth" (Isa. 55:9). We can imitate God's love and share in that attribute to some degree, but we will never be infinitely loving as God is. So it is with all the attributes that are normally called "communicable attributes": God does indeed share them with us *to some degree,* but none of these attributes is completely communicable. It is better to say that those attributes we call "communicable" are those that are *more shared* with us.

Those attributes we call "incommunicable" are better defined by saying that they are attributes of God that are *less shared* by us. Not one of the incommunicable attributes of God is completely without some likeness in the character of human beings. For example, God is unchangeable, while we change. But we do not change completely, for there are some aspects of our characters that remain largely unchanged: our individual identities, many of our personality traits, and some of our long-term purposes remain substantially unchanged over many years (and will remain largely unchanged once we are set free from sin and begin to live in God's presence forever).

Similarly, God is eternal, and we are subject to the limitations of time. However, we see *some* reflection of God's eternity in the fact that we will live with him forever and enjoy eternal life, as well as in the fact that we have the ability to remember the past and to have a strong sense of awareness of the future (unlike much of God's creation; cf. Eccl. 3:11). God's attributes of independence and omnipresence are perhaps those that are least easy to see reflected in our own natures, but even these can be seen to be faintly reflected in us when we compare ourselves with much of the rest of God's creation: as we grow to adulthood we attain some degree of independence from others for our existence; and, though we cannot be at more than one place at one time, we have the ability to act in ways that have effects in many different places at once (this again sets us apart from most of the rest of creation).

We will use the two categories of "incommunicable" and "communicable" attributes then, while realizing that they are not entirely precise classifications, and that there is in reality much overlap between the categories.

2. The Names of God in Scripture. In the Bible a person's name is a description of his or her character. Likewise, the names of God in Scripture are various descriptions of his character. In a broad sense, then, God's "name" is equal to all that the Bible and creation tell us about God. When we pray, "Hallowed be your *name*" as part of the Lord's Prayer (Matt. 6:9), we are praying that people would speak about God in a way that is honoring to him and that accurately reflects his character. This honoring of God's name can be done with actions as well as words, for our actions reflect the character of the Creator whom we serve (Matt. 5:16). To honor God's name is therefore to honor him. The command, "You shall not take the *name* of the LORD your God in vain" (Ex. 20:7) is a command that we not dishonor God's reputation either by words that speak of him in a foolish or misleading way, or by actions that do not reflect his true character.

Now the Bible does give many individual names to God, all of which reflect some true aspect of his character. Many of these names are taken from human experience or emotions in order to describe parts of God's character, while many other names are taken from the rest of the natural creation. In a sense, all of these expressions of God's character in terms of things found in the universe are "names" of God because they tell us something true about him.

Herman Bavinck, in *The Doctrine of God*,[1] gives a long list of such descriptions of God taken from creation: God is compared to a lion (Isa. 31:4), an eagle (Deut. 32:11), a lamb (Isa. 53:7), a hen (Matt. 23:37), the sun (Ps. 84:11), the morning star (Rev. 22:16), a light (Ps. 27:1), a torch (Rev. 21:23), a fire (Heb. 12:29), a fountain (Ps. 36:9), a rock (Deut. 32:4), a hiding place (Ps. 119:114), a tower (Prov. 18:10), a moth (Ps. 39:11), a shadow (Ps. 91:1), a shield (Ps. 84:11), a temple (Rev. 21:22), and so forth.

Taken from human experience, Bavinck finds an even more extensive list, which is reproduced here only in part: God is called bridegroom (Isa. 61:10), husband (Isa. 54:5), father (Deut. 32:6), judge and king (Isa. 33:22), man of war (Ex. 15:3), builder and maker (Heb. 11:10), shepherd (Ps. 23:1), physician (Ex. 15:26), and so forth. Furthermore, God is spoken of in terms of human actions such as knowing (Gen. 18:21), remembering (Gen. 8:1; Ex. 2:24), seeing (Gen. 1:10), hearing (Ex. 2:24), smelling (Gen. 8:21), tasting (Ps. 11:5), sitting (Ps. 9:7), rising (Ps. 68:1), walking (Lev. 26:12), wiping away tears (Isa. 25:8), and so forth. Human emotions are attributed to God, such as joy (Isa. 62:5), grief (Ps. 78:40; Isa. 63:10), anger (Jer. 7:18–19), love (John 3:16), hatred (Deut. 16:22), wrath (Ps. 2:5), and so forth.

Even though God does not have a physical body,[2] Scripture uses various parts of the human body to describe God's activities in a metaphorical way. Scripture can speak of God's face or countenance (Ex. 33:20, 23; Isa. 63:9; Ps. 16:11; Rev. 22:4), eyes (Ps. 11:4; Heb. 4:13), eyelids (Ps. 11:4), ears (Ps. 55:1; Isa. 59:1), nose (Deut. 33:10), mouth (Deut. 8:3), lips (Job 11:5), tongue (Isa. 30:27), neck (Jer. 18:17), arms (Ex. 15:16), hand (Num. 11:23), finger (Ex. 8:19), heart (Gen. 6:6), foot (Isa. 66:1), and so forth. Even terms describing personal characteristics such as good, merciful, gracious, righteous, holy, just, and many more, are terms whose meaning is familiar to us through an experience of these qualities in other human beings. And even those terms that seem least related to creation, such as eternity or unchangeableness, are understood by us not intuitively but by negating concepts that we know from our experience (eternity is not being limited by time and unchangeableness is not changing).

---

[1]Herman Bavinck, *The Doctrine of God*, trans. and ed. by William Hendriksen (Grand Rapids: Eerdmans, 1951), pp. 86–89.

[2]Although Jesus Christ now has a physical body as God-man, the Father and Holy Spirit do not, nor did the Son before he was conceived in Mary's womb. (In the Old Testament "theophanies," where God appeared in human form, these human bodies were only temporary appearances and did not belong to the person of God.)

The point of collecting all these passages is to show, first, that in one sense or another *all of creation reveals something about God to us,* and that the higher creation, especially man who is made in God's image, reveals him more fully.

The second reason for mentioning this long list is to show that all that we know about God from Scripture comes to us in terms that we understand because they describe events or things common to human experience. Using a more technical term, we can say that *all that Scripture says about God uses anthropomorphic language — that is, language that speaks of God in human terms.*[3] Sometimes people have been troubled by the fact that there is anthropomorphic language in Scripture. But this should not be troubling to us, for, if God is going to teach us about things we do not know by direct experience (such as his attributes), he has to teach us in terms of what we do know. This is why all that Scripture says about God is "anthropomorphic" in a broad sense (speaking of God either in human terms or in terms of the creation we know). This fact does not mean that Scripture gives us wrong or misleading ideas about God, for this is the way that God has chosen to reveal himself to us, and to reveal himself truly and accurately. Nonetheless, it should caution us not to take any one of these descriptions by itself and isolate it from its immediate context or from the rest of what Scripture says about God.[4] If we did that, we would run the risk of misunderstanding or of having an imbalanced or inadequate picture of who God is. Each description of one of God's attributes must be understood in the light of everything else that Scripture tells us about God. If we fail to remember this, we will inevitably understand God's character wrongly.

For example, we have an *idea* of love from human experience. That helps us to understand what Scripture means when it says that God is love, but our understanding of the meaning of "love" when applied to God is not identical with our experience of love in human relationships. So we must learn from observing how God acts in all of Scripture and from the other attributes of God that are given in Scripture, as well as from our own real-life experiences of God's love, if we are to refine our idea of God's love in an appropriate way and avoid misunderstanding. Thus, anthropomorphic language about God is *true* when it occurs in Scripture, but it can be understood rightly only by continual reading of Scripture throughout our lives in order that we may understand this language in the context of all of Scripture.

There is yet a third reason for pointing out the great diversity of descriptions about God taken from human experience and from the natural world. This language should remind us that *God made the universe so that it would show forth the excellence of his character,* that is, that it would show forth his glory. God is worthy to receive glory because he created all things (Rev. 4:11); therefore, all things should honor him.

Psalm 148 is an example of all creation being summoned to give praise to God:

---

[3]"Anthropomorphic" comes from two Greek words, *anthrōpos,* "man," and *morphē,* "form." An anthropomorphic description of God describes God in human forms or human terms.

[4]This mistake would be made, for example, by people who argue that God has a human body, because Scripture talks about his eyes, ears, mouth, etc. By the same reasoning they should say that God also looks like a lion, a lamb, an eagle, a fire, a rock, a hen, a fountain, the sun, a shield, a shadow, and a temple — all at once! The mistake is to fail to recognize that these are all metaphors that tell us about God's character, but that God himself is "spirit" (John 4:24) and has no material body.

> Praise him, sun and moon,
>> praise him, all you shining stars! . . .
>
> Praise the LORD from the earth,
>> you sea monsters and all deeps,
> fire and hail, snow and frost,
>> stormy wind fulfilling his command!
>
> Mountains and all hills,
>> fruit trees and all cedars! . . .
>
> Kings of the earth and all peoples . . .
>
> Let them praise the name of the Lord,
>> for his name alone is exalted;
>> his glory is above earth and heaven. (Ps. 148:3, 7–11, 13)

As we learn about God's character from Scripture, it should open our eyes and enable us to interpret creation rightly. As a result, we will be able to see reflections of the excellence of God's character everywhere in creation: "the whole earth is full of his glory" (Isa. 6:3).

It must be remembered that though all that Scripture tells us about God is true, it is not exhaustive. Scripture does not tell us everything about God's character. Thus, we will never know God's *full or complete "name"* in the sense that we will never understand God's character exhaustively. We will never know all there is to know about God. For this reason theologians have sometimes said, "God has many names, yet God has no name." God has many names in that we know many true descriptions of his character from Scripture, but God has no name in that we will never be able to describe or understand all of his character.

3. Balanced Definitions of God's Incommunicable Attributes. The incommunicable attributes of God are perhaps the most easily misunderstood, probably because they represent aspects of God's character that are least familiar to our experience. In this chapter, therefore, each of the incommunicable attributes of God is defined with a two-part sentence. The first part defines the attribute under discussion, and the second part guards against misunderstanding the attribute by stating a balancing or opposite aspect that relates to that attribute. For example, God's unchangeableness is defined as follows: "God is unchanging in his being, perfections, purposes, and promises, *yet* God does act, and he acts differently in response to different situations." The second half of the sentence guards against the idea that unchangeableness means inability to act at all. Some people do understand unchangeableness in this way, but such an understanding is inconsistent with the biblical presentation of God's unchangeableness.

B. The Incommunicable Attributes of God

1. Independence. God's independence is defined as follows: *God does not need us or the rest of creation for anything, yet we and the rest of creation can glorify him and bring him* *joy.* This attribute of God is sometimes called his self-existence or his *aseity* (from the Latin words *a se,* which mean "from himself").

Scripture in several places teaches that God does not need any part of creation in order to exist or for any other reason. God is absolutely independent and self-sufficient. Paul proclaims to the men of Athens, "The God who made the world and everything in it, being Lord of heaven and earth, does not live in shrines made by man, *nor is he served by human hands, as though he needed anything,* since he himself gives to all men life and breath and everything" (Acts 17:24–25). The implication is that God does not need anything from mankind.

God asks Job, "Who has given to me, that I should repay him? *Whatever is under the whole heaven is mine*" (Job 41:11). No one has ever contributed to God anything that did not first come from God who created all things. Similarly, we read God's word in Psalm 50, "every beast of the forest is mine, the cattle on a thousand hills. I know all the birds of the air, and all that moves in the field is mine. If I were hungry, I would not tell you; for *the world and all that is in it is mine*" (Ps. 50:10–12).

People have sometimes thought that God created human beings because he was lonely and needed fellowship with other persons. If this were true, it would certainly mean that God is not completely independent of creation. It would mean that God would *need* to create persons in order to be completely happy or completely fulfilled in his personal existence.

Yet there are some specific indications in Jesus' words that show this idea to be inaccurate. In John 17:5, Jesus prays, "Father, glorify me in your own presence with *the glory which I had with you before the world was made.*" Here is an indication that there was a sharing of glory between the Father and the Son before creation. Then in John 17:24, Jesus speaks to the Father of "my glory which you have given me *in your love for me before the foundation of the world.*" There was love and communication between the Father and the Son before creation.

These passages indicate explicitly what we can learn elsewhere from the doctrine of the Trinity, namely, that among the persons of the Trinity there has been perfect love and fellowship and communication for all eternity. The fact that God is three persons yet one God means that there was no loneliness or lack of personal fellowship on God's part before creation. In fact, the love and interpersonal fellowship, and the sharing of glory, have always been and will always be far more perfect than any communion we as finite human beings will ever have with God. And as the second verse quoted above speaks of the glory the Father gave to the Son, we should also realize that there is a giving of glory by the members of the Trinity to one another that far surpasses any bestowal of glory that could ever be given to God by all creation.

With regard to God's existence, this doctrine also reminds us that only God exists by virtue of his very nature, and that he was never created and never came into being. He always was. This is seen from the fact that all things that exist were made by him ("For you created *all things,* and by your will they existed and were created" [Rev. 4:11]; this is also affirmed in John 1:3; Rom. 11:35–36; 1 Cor. 8:6). Moses tells us that God existed before there was any creation: "*Before* the mountains were brought forth, or ever you had formed the earth and the world, from everlasting to everlasting *you are God*" (Ps. 90:2). God's independence is also seen in his self-designation in Exodus 3:14: "God said to Moses, '*I AM WHO I AM.*'" It is also possible to translate this statement "I will be what I will be," but in both cases the implication is that God's existence and character are determined by himself alone and are not dependent on anyone or anything else. This means that God's being has always been and will always be exactly what it is. God is not dependent upon any part of creation for his existence or his nature. Without creation, God would still be infinitely loving, infinitely just, eternal, omniscient, trinitarian, and so forth.

God's being is also something totally unique. It is not just that God *does not* need the creation for anything; God *could not* need the creation for anything. The difference between the creature and the Creator is an immensely vast difference, for God exists in a fundamentally different order of being. It is not just that we exist and God has always existed; it is also that God *necessarily* exists in an infinitely better, stronger, more excellent way. The difference between God's being and ours is more than the difference between the sun and a candle, more than the difference between the ocean and a raindrop, more than the difference between the arctic ice cap and a snowflake, more than the difference between the universe and the room we are sitting in: God's being is *qualitatively different.* No limitation or imperfection in creation should be projected onto our thought of God. He is the Creator; all else is creaturely. All else can pass away in an instant; he *necessarily exists* forever.

The balancing consideration with respect to this doctrine is the fact that *we and the rest of creation can glorify God and bring him joy.* This must be stated in order to guard against any idea that God's independence makes us meaningless. Someone might wonder, if God does not need us for anything, then are we important at all? Is there any significance to our existence or to the existence of the rest of creation? In response it must be said that we are in fact very meaningful because God has created us and he has determined that we would be *meaningful to him.* That is the final definition of genuine significance.

God speaks of his sons and daughters from the ends of the earth as "every one who is called by my name, whom I created *for my glory,* whom I formed and made" (Isa. 43:7). Although God did not have to create us, he chose to do so in a totally free choice. He decided that he would create us to glorify him (cf. Eph. 1:11–12; Rev. 4:11).

It is also true that we are able to bring real joy and delight to God. It is one of the most amazing facts in Scripture that God actually delights in his people and rejoices over them. Isaiah prophesies about the restoration of God's people:

> You shall be a crown of beauty in the hand of the LORD,
>   and a royal diadem in the hand of your God.
> You shall no more be termed Forsaken
>   and your land shall no more be termed Desolate;
> but you shall be called My delight is in her,
>   and your land Married;
> for *the LORD delights in you*
>   and your land shall be married. . . .
> *as the bridegroom rejoices over the bride,*
>   *so shall your God rejoice over you.* (Isa. 62:3–5)

Similarly, Zephaniah prophesies that the LORD "will rejoice over you with gladness, he will renew you in his love; *he will exult over you with loud singing* as on a day of festival" (Zeph. 3:17–18). God does not need us for anything, yet it is the amazing fact of our existence that he chooses to delight in us and to allow us to bring joy to his heart. This is the basis for personal significance in the lives of all God's people: to be significant to God is to be significant in the most ultimate sense. No greater personal significance can be imagined.

2. Unchangeableness. We can define the unchangeableness of God as follows: *God is unchanging in his being, perfections, purposes, and promises, yet God does act and feel emotions, and he acts and feels differently in response to different situations.*[5] This attribute of God is also called God's *immutability*.

a. Evidence in Scripture: In Psalm 102 we find a contrast between things that we may think to be permanent such as the earth or the heavens, on the one hand, and God, on the other hand. The psalmist says:

> Of old you laid the foundation of the earth,
> and the heavens are the work of your hands.
> They will perish, but you endure;
> they will all wear out like a garment.
> You change them like raiment, and they pass away;
> but *you are the same, and your years have no end.*
> (Ps. 102:25–27)[6]

God existed before the heavens and earth were made, and he will exist long after they have been destroyed. God causes the universe to change, but in contrast to this change he is "the same."

Referring to his own qualities of patience, long-suffering, and mercy, God says, "For *I the* LORD *do not change;* therefore you, O sons of Jacob, are not consumed" (Mal. 3:6). Here God uses a general statement of his unchangeableness to refer to some specific ways in which he does not change.

James reminds his readers that all good gifts come ultimately from God *"with whom there is no variation or shadow due to change"* (James 1:17). His argument is that since good gifts have always come from God, we can be confident that only good gifts will come from him in the future, because his character never changes in the slightest degree.

The definition given above specifies that God is unchanging—not in every way that we might imagine, but only in ways that Scripture itself affirms. The Scripture passages already cited refer either to God's own being or to some attribute of his character. From

---

[5]The four key words (*being, perfections, purposes, promises*) used as a summary of the ways in which God is unchanging are taken from Louis Berkhof, *Systematic Theology* (Grand Rapids: Eerdmans, 1939, 1941), p. 58.

[6]It is significant that this passage is quoted in Heb. 1:11–12 and applied to Jesus Christ. Heb. 13:8 also applies the attribute of unchangeableness to Christ: "Jesus Christ is the same yesterday and today and for ever." Thus, God the Son shares fully in this divine attribute.

these we can conclude that God is unchanging, at least with respect to his *"being,"* and with respect to his *"perfections"* (that is, his attributes or the various aspects of his character).

The great Dutch theologian Herman Bavinck notes that the fact that God is unchanging in his being is of the utmost importance for maintaining the Creator/creature distinction, and for our worship of God:

> The doctrine of God's immutability is of the highest significance for religion. The contrast between being and becoming marks the difference between the Creator and the creature. Every creature is continually becoming. It is changeable, constantly striving, seeks rest and satisfaction, and finds this rest in God, in him alone, for only he is pure being and no becoming. Hence, in Scripture God is often called the Rock. . . .[7]

The definition given above also affirms God's unchangeableness or immutability with respect to his *purposes.* "The counsel of the LORD stands for ever, the thoughts of his heart to all generations" (Ps. 33:11). This general statement about God's counsel is supported by several specific verses that talk about individual plans or purposes of God that he has had for all eternity (Matt. 13:35; 25:34; Eph. 1:4, 11; 3:9, 11; 2 Tim. 2:19; 1 Peter 1:20; Rev. 13:8). Once God has determined that he will assuredly bring something about, his purpose is unchanging, and it will be achieved. In fact, God claims through Isaiah that no one else is like him in this regard:

> I am God, and there is none like me,
> declaring the end from the beginning
>   and from ancient times things not yet done,
> saying, "My counsel shall stand,
>   and I will accomplish all my purpose" . . .
> I have spoken, and I will bring it to pass;
>   *I have purposed, and I will do it.* (Isa. 46:9–11)

Furthermore, God is unchanging in his *promises.* Once he has promised something, he will not be unfaithful to that promise: "God is not a man, that he should lie, or a son of man, that he should repent. Has he said, and will he not do it? Or has he spoken, and will he not fulfil it?" (Num. 23:19; cf. 1 Sam. 15:29).

b. Does God Sometimes Change His Mind? Yet when we talk about God being unchanging in his purposes, we may wonder about places in Scripture where God said he would judge his people and then because of prayer or the people's repentance (or both) God relented and did not bring judgment as he had said he would. Examples of such withdrawing from threatened judgment include the successful intervention of Moses in prayer to prevent the destruction of the people of Israel (Ex. 32:9–14), the adding of another fifteen years to the life of Hezekiah (Isa. 38:1–6), or the failure to bring

---

[7]Herman Bavinck, *The Doctrine of God,* trans. by William Hendriksen (Edinburgh: Banner of Truth, 1977, reprint of 1951 ed.), p. 149.

promised judgment upon Nineveh when the people repented (Jonah 3:4, 10). Are these not cases where God's purposes in fact did change? Then there are other passages where God is said to be sorry that he had carried out some previous action. One thinks of God being sorry that he had made man upon the earth (Gen. 6:6), or sorry that he had made Saul king (1 Sam. 15:10). Did not God's purposes change in these cases?

These instances should all be understood as true expressions of God's *present* attitude or intention *with respect to the situation as it exists at that moment.* If the situation changes, then of course God's attitude or expression of intention will also change. This is just saying that *God responds differently to different situations.* The example of Jonah preaching to Nineveh is helpful here. God sees the wickedness of Nineveh and sends Jonah to proclaim, "Yet forty days, and Nineveh shall be overthrown!" (Jonah 3:4). The possibility that God would withhold judgment if the people repented is not explicitly mentioned in Jonah's proclamation as recorded in Scripture, but it is of course *implicit* in that warning: the *purpose* for proclaiming a warning is to bring about repentance. Once the people repented, the situation was different, and God responded differently to that changed situation: "*When God saw what they did,* how they turned from their evil way, *God repented of the evil which he had said he would do to them;* and he did not do it" (Jonah 3:10).

The situations with Hezekiah and with the intercession of Moses are similar: God had said that he would send judgment, and that was a true declaration, *provided that the situation remained the same.* But then the situation changed: someone started to pray earnestly (Moses in one case and Hezekiah in the other). Here prayer itself was part of the new situation and was in fact what changed the situation. God responded to that changed situation by answering the prayer and withholding judgment.

In the cases of God being sorry that he had made man, or that he had made Saul king, these too can be understood as *expressions of God's present displeasure* toward the sinfulness of man. In neither case is the language strong enough to require us to think that if God could start again and act differently, he would in fact not create man or not make Saul king. It can instead imply that God's previous action led to events that, in the short term, caused him sorrow, but that nonetheless in the long term would ultimately achieve his good purposes. This is somewhat analogous to a human father who allows his child to embark on a course he knows will bring much sorrow, both to the parent and to the child, but who allows it nonetheless, because he knows that greater long-term good will come from it.

c. The Question of God's Impassibility: Sometimes in a discussion of God's attributes theologians have spoken of another attribute, namely, the *impassibility* of God. This attribute, if true, would mean that God does not have passions or emotions, but is "impassible," not subject to passions. In fact, chapter 2 of the Westminster Confession of Faith says that God is "without . . . passions." This statement goes beyond what we have affirmed in our definition above about God's unchangeableness, and affirms *more* than that God does not change in his being, perfections, purposes, or promises — it also affirms that God does not even feel emotions or "passions."

The Scripture proof given by the Westminster Confession of Faith is Acts 14:15, which in the King James Version reports Barnabas and Paul as rejecting worship from the people at Lystra, protesting that they are not gods but "men of *like passions* with you." The implication of the KJV translation might be that someone who is truly God would not have "like passions" as men do, or it might simply show that the apostles were responding to the false view of passionless gods assumed by the men of Lystra (see vv. 10–11). But if the verse is rightly translated, it certainly does not prove that God has no passions or emotions at all, for the Greek term here (*homoiopathēs*) can simply mean having similar circumstances or experiences, or being of a similar nature to someone else.[8] Of course, God does not have *sinful* passions or emotions. But the idea that God has no passions or emotions *at all* clearly conflicts with much of the rest of Scripture, and for that reason I have not affirmed God's impassibility in this book. Instead, quite the opposite is true, for God, who is the origin of our emotions and who created our emotions, certainly does feel emotions: God rejoices (Isa. 62:5). He is grieved (Ps. 78:40; Eph. 4:30). His wrath burns hot against his enemies (Ex. 32:10). He pities his children (Ps. 103:13). He loves with everlasting love (Isa. 54:8; Ps. 103:17). He is a God whose passions we are to imitate for all eternity as we like our Creator hate sin and delight in righteousness.

d. The Challenge From Process Theology: God's unchangeableness has been denied frequently in recent years by the advocates of *process theology,* a theological position that says that process and change are essential aspects of genuine existence, and that therefore God must be changing over time also, just like everything else that exists. In fact, Charles Hartshorne, the father of process theology, would say that God is continually adding to himself all the experiences that happen anywhere in the universe, and thus God is continually changing.[9] The real appeal of process theology comes from the fact that all people have a deep longing to mean something, to feel significant in the universe. Process theologians dislike the doctrine of God's immutability because they think it implies that nothing we do can really matter to God. If God is really unchangeable, process theologians will say, then nothing we do—in fact, nothing that happens in the universe—has any real effect on God, because God can never change. So what difference do we make? How can we have any ultimate meaning? In response to this question process theologians reject the doctrine of God's immutability and tell us that our actions are so significant that they have an influence on the very being of God himself! As we act, and as the universe changes, God is *truly* affected by these actions and the being of God changes—God *becomes* something other than what he was.[10]

---

[8]See *BAGD,* p. 566.

[9]Charles Hartshorne (born 1897) taught at the University of Chicago, Emory University, and the University of Texas. An introduction to process theology by two of its advocates is *Process Theology: An Introductory Exposition* by John B. Cobb, Jr., and David R. Griffin (Philadelphia: Westminster, 1976). Detailed evangelical analyses may be found in Carl F. H. Henry, "The Resurgence of Process Philosophy," in *God, Revelation, and Authority,* 6:52–75, and Royce Gruenler, *The Inexhaustible God: Biblical Faith and the Challenge of Process Theism* (Grand Rapids: Baker, 1983).

Two excellent recent articles from an evangelical perspective have been written by Bruce A. Ware: "An Exposition and Critique of the Process Doctrines of Divine Mutability and Immutability," *WTJ* 47 (1985): 175–96 (a critique of process theology), and "An Evangelical Reformulation of the Doctrine of the Immutability of God," *JETS* 29 (1986): 431–46 (a positive restatement of an orthodox view of God's immutability).

[10]See Ware's revealing discussion of Hartshorne's idea that we contribute value to God that he would otherwise lack: "Exposition and Critique," pp. 183–85.

Advocates of process theology often mistakenly accuse evangelical Christians (or the biblical writers themselves) of believing in a God who does not act in the world, or who cannot respond differently to different situations (errors we have discussed above). With regard to the idea that we must be able to influence the very being of God in order to be significant, we must respond that this is an *incorrect assumption* imported into the discussion, and that it is not consistent with Scripture. Scripture is clear that our ultimate significance comes not from being able to change the being of God, but from the fact that God has created us for his glory and that *he* counts us as significant. God alone gives the ultimate definition of what is significant and what is not significant in the universe, and if he counts us significant, then we are!

The other fundamental error in process theology is in assuming that God must be changeable like the universe he created. This is what Scripture explicitly denies: "You, Lord, did found the earth in the beginning, and the heavens are the work of your hands; they will perish, but you remain; they will all grow old like a garment . . . *they will be changed. But you are the same,* and your years will never end" (Heb. 1:10–12, quoting Ps. 102:25–27).

e. God Is Both Infinite and Personal: Our discussion of process theology illustrates a common difference between biblical Christianity and all other systems of theology. In the teaching of the Bible, God is both *infinite* and *personal:* he is infinite in that he is not subject to any of the limitations of humanity, or of creation in general. He is far greater than everything he has made, far greater than anything else that exists. But he is also personal: he interacts with us as a person, and we can relate to him as persons. We can pray to him, worship him, obey him, and love him, and he can speak to us, rejoice in us, and love us.

Apart from the true religion found in the Bible, no system of religion has a God who is both infinite and personal.[11] For example, the gods of ancient Greek and Roman mythology were *personal* (they interacted frequently with people), but they were not infinite: they had weaknesses and frequent moral failures, even petty rivalries. On the other hand, deism portrays a God who is *infinite* but far too removed from the world to be personally involved in it. Similarly, pantheism holds that God is infinite (since the whole universe is thought to be God), but such a God can certainly not be personal or relate to us as persons.

The error of process theology fits this general pattern. Its advocates are convinced that a God who is unchanging in his being is so different from the rest of creation—so infinite, so unlimited by the change that characterizes all of our existence—that he *cannot* also be personal in a way that we make a difference to him. So in order to gain a God who is personal, they think they have to give up a God who is infinite for a God who is continually in process of change. This kind of reasoning is typical of many (perhaps all) objections to the kind of God presented in the Bible. People say that if

---

[11]Technically speaking we must recognize that Judaism, so far as it is based on what we call the Old Testament, also has a view of God that shows him to be both infinite and personal, although Judaism has never recognized the indications of God's trinitarian nature that are present even in the Old Testament (see chapter 7, pp. 115–19).

God is infinite, he cannot be personal, or they say that if God is personal, he cannot be infinite. The Bible teaches that God is both infinite and personal. We must affirm both that God is infinite (or unlimited) with respect to change that occurs in the universe (nothing will change God's being, perfections, purposes, or promises), that God is *also* personal, and that he relates to us personally and counts us valuable.

f. The Importance of God's Unchangeableness: At first it may not seem very important to us to affirm God's unchangeableness. The idea is so abstract that we may not immediately realize its significance. But if we stop for a moment to imagine what it would be like if God *could* change, the importance of this doctrine becomes more clear. For example, if God *could* change (in his being, perfections, purposes, or promises), then any change would be either for the better or for the worse. But if God changed for the better, then he was not the best possible being when we first trusted him. And how could we be sure that he is the best possible being now? But if God could change for the worse (in his very *being*), then what kind of God might he become? Might he become, for instance, a little bit evil rather than wholly good? And if he could become a little bit evil, then how do we know he could not change to become largely evil—or *wholly* evil? And there would be not one thing we could do about it, for he is so much more powerful than we are. Thus, the idea that God could change leads to the horrible possibility that thousands of years from now we might come to live forever in a universe dominated by a wholly evil, omnipotent God. It is hard to imagine any thought more terrifying. How could we ever trust such a God who could change? How could we ever commit our lives to him?

Moreover, if God could change with regard to his *purposes,* then even though when the Bible was written he promised that Jesus would come back to rule over a new heaven and new earth, he has perhaps abandoned that plan now, and thus our hope in Jesus' return is in vain. Or, if God could change in regard to his *promises,* then how could we trust him completely for eternal life? Or for anything else the Bible says? Maybe when the Bible was written he promised forgiveness of sins and eternal life to those who trust in Christ, but (if God can change) perhaps he has changed his mind on those promises now—how could we be sure? Or perhaps his omnipotence will change someday, so that even though he wants to keep his promises, he will no longer be able to do so.

A little reflection like this shows how absolutely important the doctrine of God's unchangeableness is. If God is not unchanging, then the whole basis of our faith begins to fall apart, and our understanding of the universe begins to unravel. This is because our faith and hope and knowledge all ultimately depend on a *person* who is *infinitely worthy of trust*—because he is *absolutely* and *eternally* unchanging in his being, perfections, purposes, and promises.

3. Eternity. God's eternity may be defined as follows: *God has no beginning, end, or succession of moments in his own being, and he sees all time equally vividly, yet God sees events in time and acts in time.*

Sometimes this doctrine is called the doctrine of God's infinity with respect to time. To be "infinite" is to be unlimited, and this doctrine teaches that time does not limit God.

This doctrine is also related to God's unchangeableness. If it is true that God does not change, then we must say that *time* does not change God: it has no effect on his being, perfections, purposes, or promises. But that means that time has no effect on God's knowledge, for instance. God never learns new things or forgets things, for that would mean a change in his perfect knowledge. This implies also that the passing of time does not add to or detract from God's knowledge: he knows all things past, present, and future, and knows them all equally vividly.

a. God Is Timeless in His Own Being: The fact that God has no beginning or end is seen in Psalm 90:2: "Before the mountains were brought forth, or ever you had formed the earth and the world, *from everlasting to everlasting you are God.*" Similarly, in Job 36:26, Elihu says of God, "the number of his years is unsearchable."

God's eternity is also suggested by passages that talk about the fact that God always is or always exists. "'I am the Alpha and the Omega," says the Lord God, who is and who was and who is to come, the Almighty" (Rev. 1:8; cf. 4:8).[12]

It is also indicated in Jesus' bold use of a present tense verb that implies continuing present existence when he replied to his Jewish adversaries, "Before Abraham was, *I am*" (John 8:58). This statement is itself an explicit claiming of the name of God, "*I AM WHO I AM,*" from Exodus 3:14, a name that also suggests a continual present existence: God is the eternal "I AM," the one who eternally exists.

The fact that God never began to exist can also be concluded from the fact that God created all things, and that he himself is an immaterial spirit. Before God made the universe, there was no matter, but then he created all things (Gen. 1:1; John 1:3; 1 Cor. 8:6; Col. 1:16; Heb. 1:2). The study of physics tells us that matter and time and space must all occur together: if there is no matter, there can be no space or time either. Thus, before God created the universe, there was no "time," at least not in the sense of a succession of moments one after another. Therefore, when God created the universe, he also created time. When God began to create the universe, time began, and there began to be a succession of moments and events one after another.[13] But before there was a universe, and before there was time, God always existed, without beginning, and without being influenced by time. And time, therefore, does not have existence in itself, but, like the rest of creation, depends on God's eternal being and power to keep it existing.

The foregoing Scripture passages and the fact that God always existed before there was any time combine to indicate to us that God's own being does not have a succession of moments or any progress from one state of existence to another. To God himself, all of his existence is always somehow "present,"[14] though admittedly that idea is difficult for us to understand, for it is a kind of existence different from that which we experience.

---

[12]Alpha and omega are the first and last letters of the Greek alphabet, so when God says that he is the Alpha and the Omega he implies that he is before everything else and he is after everything else; he is the beginning of everything and will always be the end (or goal) of everything.

[13]In fact, the alternative to saying that time began when God created the universe is to say that time never began, but there has *always* been a succession of moments one after another,

extending infinitely far back into the past, but never having a starting point. But to have time without a beginning seems to many people to be absurd and is probably impossible. Bavinck says, "Eternal time in the sense of time without beginning is inconceivable" (*The Doctrine of God*, p. 157).

[14]As we shall see below, this does not mean that all events of history look to God as if they were present, for God sees events *in time* and acts *in time*.

b. God Sees All Time Equally Vividly: It is somewhat easier for us to understand that God sees all time equally vividly. We read in Psalm 90:4, "For a *thousand years* in your sight are but as *yesterday* when it is past, or as a *watch* in the night." It is sometimes difficult for us to remember events that occurred several weeks ago, or several months ago, or several years ago. We remember recent events more vividly, and the clarity of our memory fades with the passing of time. Even if it were possible for us to live "a thousand years," we would remember very few events from hundreds of years earlier, and the clarity of that memory would be very low. But here Scripture tells us that God views a thousand years "as yesterday." He can remember all the detailed events of a thousand years at least as clearly as we can remember the events of "yesterday." In fact, to him a thousand years is "as a watch in the night," a three- or four-hour period during which a guard would stand watch. Such a short period of time would pass quickly and all the events would be easily recalled. Yet this is how a thousand years seems to God.

When we realize that the phrase "a thousand years" does not imply that God forgets things after 1,100 or 1,200 years, but rather expresses as long a time as one might imagine, it becomes evident that *all of past history* is viewed by God with great clarity and vividness: all of time since the creation is to God as if it just happened. And it will always remain just that clear in his consciousness, throughout millions of years of eternity future.

In the New Testament, Peter tells us, "with the Lord one day is as a thousand years, and a thousand years as one day" (2 Peter 3:8). The second half of this statement had already been made in Psalm 90, but the first half introduces an additional consideration, "One day is as a thousand years"; that is, any one day from God's perspective seems to last for "a thousand years": it is as if that day never ends, but is always being experienced. Again, since "a thousand years" is a figurative expression for "as long a time as we can imagine," or "all history," we can say from this verse that any one day seems to God to be present to his consciousness forever.

Taking these two considerations together, we can say the following: in God's perspective, any extremely long period of time is as if it just happened. And any very short period of time (such as one day) seems to God to last forever: it never ceases to be "present" in his consciousness. Thus, God sees and knows all events past, present, and future with equal vividness. This should never cause us to think that God does not see events *in time* and act *in time* (see below), but just the opposite: God is the eternal Lord and Sovereign over history, and he sees it more clearly and acts in it more decisively than any other. But, once we have said that, we still must affirm that these verses speak of God's relationship to time in a way that we do not and cannot experience: God's experience of time is not just a patient endurance through eons of endless duration, but he has a *qualitatively different* experience of time than we do. This is consistent with the idea that in his own being, God is timeless; he does not experience a succession of moments. This has been the dominant view of Christian orthodoxy throughout the history of the church, though it has been frequently challenged, and even today many theologians deny it.[15]

---

[15]Carl F. H. Henry argues for God's timeless eternity as the historic position of Christian orthodoxy in *God, Revelation and Authority* (Waco, Tex.: Word, 1982), 5:235–67, and gives a detailed analysis of current challenges from both nonevangelical and evangelical theologians. A thorough recent philosophical defense of God's timeless eternity is Paul Helm, *Eternal God: A Study of God Without Time* (Oxford: Clarendon, 1988).

We can picture God's relationship to time as in figure 4.1. This diagram is meant to show that God created time and is Lord over time. Therefore he can see all events in time equally vividly, yet he also can see events in time and act in time.

The diagram also anticipates the following discussion, since it indicates that God knows events in the future, even the infinitely long eternal future. With regard to the future, God frequently claims through the Old Testament prophets that *he alone is the one who knows and can declare future events.* "Who told this long ago? Who declared it of old? Was it not I, the Lord? And there is no other god besides me, a righteous God and a Savior; there is none besides me" (Isa. 45:21). Similarly, we read:

> For I am God, and there is no other;
> I am God, and *there is none like me,*
> *declaring the end from the beginning*
> *and from ancient times things not yet done,*
> saying, "My counsel shall stand,
> and I will accomplish all my purpose." (Isa. 46:9–10)

Thus God somehow stands above time and is able to see it all as present in his consciousness. Although the analogy is not perfect, we might think of the moment we finish reading a long novel. Before putting it back on the shelf we might flip quickly through the pages once more, calling to mind the many events that had occurred in that novel. For a brief moment, things that transpired over a long period of time all seem to be "present" to our minds. Perhaps this is faintly analogous to God's experience of seeing all of history as equally present in his consciousness.

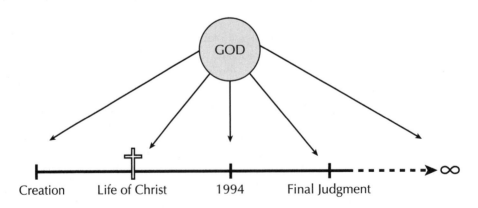

THE RELATIONSHIP OF GOD TO TIME
Figure 4.1

c. God Sees Events in Time and Acts in Time: Yet once all this has been said it is necessary to guard against misunderstanding by completing the definition of God's eternity: *"yet God sees events in time and acts in time."* Paul writes, *"when the time had fully come,*

God sent forth his Son, born of woman, born under the law, to redeem those who were under the law" (Gal. 4:4–5). God observed clearly and knew exactly what was happening with events in his creation as they occurred over time. We might say that God watched the progress of time as various events occurred within his creation. Then at the right time, "when the time had fully come," God sent forth his Son into the world.

It is evident throughout Scripture that God acts within time and acts differently at different points in time. For example, Paul tells the men of Athens, "The times of ignorance God overlooked, but *now* he commands all men everywhere to repent, because *he has fixed a day on which he will judge the world* in righteousness by a man whom he has appointed . . ." (Acts 17:30–31). This statement includes a description of a previous way in which God acted, God's present way of acting, and a future activity that he will carry out, all in time.

Indeed, the repeated emphasis on God's ability to predict the future in the Old Testament prophets requires us to realize that God predicts his actions at one point in time and then carries out his actions at a later point in time. And on a larger scale, the entire Bible from Genesis to Revelation is God's own record of the way he has acted over time to bring redemption to his people.

We must therefore affirm both that God has no succession of moments in his own being and sees all history equally vividly, and that in his creation he sees the progress of events over time and acts differently at different points in time; in short, he is the Lord who created time and who rules over it and uses it for his own purposes. God can act in time *because* he is Lord of time.[16] He uses it to display his glory. In fact, it is often God's good pleasure to fulfill his promises and carry out his works of redemption over a period of time so that we might more readily see and appreciate his great wisdom, his patience, his faithfulness, his lordship over all events, and even his unchangeableness and eternity.

---

[16]Sometimes theologians have objected that God cannot be "timelessly eternal" in the sense described above, because the moment he creates something, he is acting in time and therefore he must exist in time. (See, e.g., Stephen T. Davis, *Logic and the Nature of God* [Grand Rapids: Eerdmans, 1983], pp. 11–24.) But this objection fails to distinguish what God is in his own being (he exists without beginning, end, or succession of moments) from what God does outside of himself (he creates in time and acts in time in other ways). Davis says that we have no coherent notion of "causation in which an eternal cause produces a temporal effect" (p. 21), but that is simply to admit that *we do not understand* how a timelessly eternal God can act in time; it does *not* prove that God *cannot* be timeless and still act in time. Surely here, when talking about the relationship between God and time, it would be folly to say that what we cannot understand must be impossible!

Davis also falls into another form of the "if God is infinite he cannot be personal" mistake mentioned above (see note 12). He says, "A timeless being cannot be the personal, caring, involved God we read about in the Bible" (p. 14). But to prove this he just talks about God's actions in time, without ever showing why God cannot *both* act in time (be personally involved)

and be timeless in his own being (be infinite or unlimited with respect to time). Finally, while he mentions the possibility that time was created but will sometime cease to exist (p. 23), he fails to consider the alternative that seems much more likely in view of the Bible's promises of eternal life, namely, that time was once created but will never cease to exist in the future.

Those who, like Davis, deny that God is timelessly eternal, still say that God has eternally existed but that he has always existed in time and always experienced a succession of moments. But this position raises even more difficulties, because it requires that time never began, but stretches infinitely far into the past. However, that does not seem possible, because if the past is infinitely long, we could never have reached this moment. (This objection is one form of saying that an actual infinite cannot exist, a philosophical conception that is explained skillfully by William Lane Craig in *The Existence of God and the Beginning of the Universe* [San Bernardino, Calif.: Here's Life Publishers, 1979], pp. 35–53, and, with fuller reference to philosophical responses to this argument, by J. P. Moreland, *Scaling the Secular City: A Defense of Christianity* [Grand Rapids: Baker, 1987], pp. 15–34.)

d. We Will Always Exist in Time: Will we ever share in God's eternity? Specifically, in the new heaven and new earth which are yet to come, will time still exist? Some have thought that it would not. In fact, there is a hymn that begins, "When the trumpet of the Lord shall sound, and time shall be no more . . ." And we read in Scripture, "And the city has no need of sun or moon to shine upon it, for the glory of God is its light, and its lamp is the Lamb . . . and there shall be no night there" (Rev. 21:23, 25; cf. 22:5).

Nevertheless, it is not true to say that heaven will be "timeless," or without the presence of time or the passage of time. Rather, as long as we are finite creatures we will necessarily experience events one after another. Even the passage that talks about no night being in heaven also mentions the fact that the kings of the earth will bring into the heavenly city "the glory and the honor of the nations" (Rev. 21:26). We are told concerning the light of the heavenly city, "By its light shall the nations walk" (Rev. 21:24). These activities of bringing things into the heavenly city and walking by the light of the heavenly city imply that events are done one after another. Something is outside the heavenly city, and then at a later point in time this thing is part of the glory and honor of the nations that are brought into the heavenly city. To cast one's crown before the throne of God (Rev. 4:10) requires that at one moment the person has a crown and that at a later moment that crown is cast before the throne. To sing a new song of praise before God in heaven requires that one word be sung after another. In fact, the "tree of life" in the heavenly city is said to be *yielding its fruit each month* (Rev. 22:2), which implies a regular passage of time and the occurrence of events in time.[17]

Therefore, there will still be a succession of moments one after another and things happening one after another in heaven. We will experience eternal life not in an exact duplication of God's attribute of eternity, but rather in a duration of time that will never end: we, as God's people will experience fullness of joy in God's presence for all eternity—not in the sense that we will no longer experience time, but in the sense that our lives with him will go on forever: "And night shall be no more; they need no light of lamp or sun, for the Lord God will be their light, *and they shall reign for ever and ever*" (Rev. 22:5).

4. Omnipresence. Just as God is unlimited or infinite with respect to time, so God is unlimited with respect to space. This characteristic of God's nature is called God's omnipresence (the Latin prefix *omni-* means "all"). God's omnipresence may be defined as follows: *God does not have size or spatial dimensions and is present at every point of space with his whole being, yet God acts differently in different places.*

The fact that God is Lord of space and cannot be limited by space is evident first from the fact that he created it, for the creation of the material world (Gen. 1:1) implies the creation of space as well. Moses reminded the people of God's lordship over space: "Behold, to the LORD your God belong heaven and the heaven of heavens, the earth with all that is in it" (Deut. 10:14).

---

[17]Rev. 10:6 in the KJV reads, "that there should be time no longer," but "delay" is a better translation for the Greek term *chronos* in this context (as in the RSV, NASB, NIV, and NKJV). In fact, the next verse assumes the continuation of time, for it talks of events to be fulfilled "in the days of the trumpet call to be sounded by the seventh angel" (Rev. 10:7).

a. God Is Present Everywhere: Yet there are also specific passages that speak of God's presence in every part of space. We read in Jeremiah, "Am I a God at hand, says the Lord, and not a God afar off? Can a man hide himself in secret places so that I cannot see him? says the Lord. *Do I not fill heaven and earth? says the Lord*" (Jer. 23:23–24). God is here rebuking the prophets who think their words or thoughts are hidden from God. He is everywhere and fills heaven and earth.

God's omnipresence is beautifully expressed by David:

> Whither shall I go from your Spirit?
> > Or whither shall I flee from your presence?
> If I ascend to heaven, you are there!
> > If I make my bed in Sheol, you are there!
> If I take the wings of the morning
> > and dwell in the uttermost parts of the sea,
> even there your hand shall lead me,
> > and your right hand shall hold me. (Ps. 139:7–10)

There is nowhere in the entire universe, on land or sea, in heaven or in hell, where one can flee from God's presence.

We should note also that there is no indication that simply a *part* of God is in one place and a part of him in another. It is *God himself* who is present wherever David might go. We cannot say that some of God or just part of God is present, for that would be to think of his being in spatial terms, as if he were limited somehow by space. It seems more appropriate to say that God is present *with his whole being* in every part of space (cf. also Acts 17:28 where Paul affirms the correctness of the words, "In him we live and move and have our being," and Col. 1:17, which says of Christ, "in him all things hold together").

b. God Does Not Have Spatial Dimensions: While it seems necessary for us to say that God's whole being is present in every part of space, or at every point in space, it is also necessary to say that *God cannot be contained by any space,* no matter how large. Solomon says in his prayer to God, "But will God indeed dwell on the earth? Behold, *heaven and the highest heaven cannot contain you;* how much less this house which I have built!" (1 Kings 8:27). Heaven and the highest heaven cannot contain God; indeed, he cannot be contained by the largest space imaginable (cf. Isa. 66:1–2; Acts 7:48). While the thought that God is everywhere present with his whole being ought to encourage us greatly in prayer no matter where we are, the fact that no one place can be said to contain God should also discourage us from thinking that there is some special place of worship that gives people special access to God: he cannot be contained in any one place.

We should guard against thinking that God extends infinitely far in all directions so that he himself exists in a sort of infinite, unending space. Nor should we think that God is somehow a "bigger space" or bigger area surrounding the space of the universe as we know it. All of these ideas continue to think of God's being in spatial terms, as if he were simply an extremely large being. Instead, we should try to avoid thinking of God in terms of size or spatial dimensions. God is a being who exists *without* size or dimensions in space. In fact, before God created the universe, there was no matter or material so there was no space either. Yet God still existed. Where was God? He was not in a place that we could call a "where," for there was no "where" or space. But God still was! This fact makes us realize that God relates to space in a far different way than we do or than any created thing does. He exists as a kind of being that is far different and far greater than we can imagine.

We must also be careful not to think that God himself is equivalent to any part of creation or to all of it. A pantheist believes that everything is God, or that God is everything that exists. The biblical perspective is rather that God is *present* everywhere in his creation, but that he is also distinct from his creation. How can this be? The analogy of a sponge filled with water is not perfect, but it is helpful. Water is present everywhere in the sponge, but the water is still completely distinct from the sponge. Now this analogy breaks down at very small points within the sponge, where we could say that there is sponge at one point and not water, or water and not sponge. Yet this is because the analogy is dealing with two materials that have spatial characteristics and dimensions, while God does not.

c. God Can Be Present to Punish, to Sustain, or to Bless: The idea of God's omnipresence has sometimes troubled people who wonder how God can be present, for example, in hell. In fact, isn't hell the opposite of God's presence, or the absence of God? This difficulty can be resolved by realizing that *God is present in different ways in different places,* or that God acts differently in different places in his creation. Sometimes God is *present to punish.* A terrifying passage in Amos vividly portrays this presence of God in judgment:

> Not one of them shall flee away,
>   not one of them shall escape.
> Though they dig into Sheol,
>   from there shall my hand take them;
> though they climb up to heaven,
>   from there I will bring them down.
> Though they hide themselves on the top of Carmel,
>   from there I will search out and take them;
> and though they hide from my sight at the bottom of the sea,
>   there I will command the serpent, and it shall bite them.
> And though they go into captivity before their enemies,
>   there I will command the sword, and it shall slay them;
> and I will set my eyes upon them for evil and not for good.
>
> (Amos 9:1–4)

At other times God is present neither to punish nor to bless, but merely *present to sustain,* or to keep the universe existing and functioning in the way he intended it to function. In this sense the divine nature of Christ is everywhere present: "He is before all things, and in him all things hold together" (Col. 1:17). The author of Hebrews says of God the Son that he is (continually) "upholding the universe by his word of power" (Heb. 1:3).[18]

Yet at other times or in other places God is *present to bless.* David says, "*in your presence* there is fulness of joy, in your right hand are pleasures for evermore" (Ps. 16:11). Here David is speaking not of God's presence to punish or merely to sustain, but of God's presence to bless.

In fact, most of the time that the Bible talks about God's presence, it is referring to God's presence to bless. For example, it is in this way that we should understand God's presence above the ark of the covenant in the Old Testament. We read of "the ark of the covenant of the LORD of hosts, who is *enthroned on the cherubim*" (1 Sam. 4:4; cf. Ex. 25:22), a reference to the fact that God made his presence known and acted in a special way to bring blessing and protection to his people at the location he had designated as his throne, namely, the place above the two golden figures of heavenly beings ("cherubim") that were over the top of the ark of the covenant. It is not that God was not present elsewhere, but rather that here he especially made his presence known and here he especially manifested his character and brought blessing to his people.

In the new covenant, there is no one place on earth that God has chosen as his particular dwelling place, for we can worship him anywhere (see John 4:20). But now and for all eternity God has chosen the place the Bible calls "heaven" to be the focus of the manifestation of his character and the presence of his blessing and glory. So when the new Jerusalem comes down out of heaven from God, John in his vision hears a loud voice from God's throne saying, "Behold, the dwelling of God is with men. He will dwell with them, and they shall be his people, and God himself will be with them" (Rev. 21:3). We might find it misleading to say that God is "more present" in heaven than anywhere else, but it would not be misleading to say that God is present in a special way in heaven, present especially there to bless and to show forth his glory. We could also say that God manifests his presence more fully in heaven than elsewhere.

In this way also Paul's statement about Christ can be understood: "In him the whole fulness of deity dwells bodily" (Col. 2:9). In one sense of course we could say that God's whole being is present at every point in space and therefore at every point in every person, not only in Christ. But there are two difficulties with speaking this way: (1) The Bible never speaks about God's presence in unbelievers in a direct way, probably to avoid any connection between God and the responsibility or blame for evil deeds, and probably also to avoid any suggestion of God's presence to bless, since it is only a presence to sustain. (2) Furthermore, this sense of "present to sustain" is not the sense Paul has in mind in Colossians 2:9. In fact, there Paul does not even seem to mean simply "present to bless" in the same sense in which God is present to bless in the lives of all believers. Rather, Paul seems to mean that in Christ God's own nature is present to bless and to manifest his character in the fullest and most complete way possible.

Our difficulty in understanding how to express the way in which God is present in unbelievers, for example, leads us to realize that although the Bible *can* speak of God

---

[18]The present participle *pherōn,* "carrying along," in Heb. 1:3 implies that Christ's activity of "carrying along all things" (that is, keeping all things in the universe existing and functioning regularly) is a continual activity, one that never ceases.

as being present everywhere, when the Bible says that God is "present" it *usually* means "present to bless." That is, although there are a few references to God's presence to sustain or presence to punish, the vast majority of biblical references to God's presence are simply more brief ways of stating that he is *present to bless.* When we become more and more familiar with this biblical pattern of speech, it becomes more and more difficult to speak of God's presence in any other way. And perhaps it is even misleading to do so unless a clear explanation of our meaning can be given.

Some examples of the usual biblical means of expression are as follows: 2 Corinthians 3:17: "Where the Spirit of the Lord is, there is freedom"; Romans 8:9–10: "you are in the Spirit, if in fact the Spirit of God dwells in you. . . . if Christ is in you . . . your spirits are alive"; John 14:23: "If a man loves me, he will keep my word, and my Father will love him, and we will come to him and make our home with him," and so forth. All of these verses talk about God's presence and assume that we understand that they mean God's presence *to bless.*

In a parallel kind of expression, when the Bible talks about God being "far away" it usually means he is "not present to bless." For example, Isaiah 59:2 says, "Your iniquities have made a separation between you and your God," and Proverbs 15:29 declares: "The Lord is far from the wicked, but he hears the prayer of the righteous."

In summary, God is present in every part of space with his whole being, yet God acts differently in different places. Furthermore, when the Bible speaks of God's presence, it usually means his presence to bless, and it is only normal for our own speech to conform to this biblical usage.

Herman Bavinck, in *The Doctrine of God,* quotes a beautiful paragraph illustrating the practical application of the doctrine of God's omnipresence:

> When you wish to do something evil, you retire from the public into your house where no enemy may see you; from those places of your house which are open and visible to the eyes of men you remove yourself into your room; even in your room you fear some witness from another quarter; you retire into your heart, there you meditate: he is more inward than your heart. Wherever, therefore, you shall have fled, there he is. From yourself, whither will you flee? Will you not follow yourself wherever you shall flee? But since there is One more inward even than yourself, there is no place where you may flee from God angry but to God reconciled. There is no place at all whither you may flee. Will you flee from him? Flee unto him.[19]

5. Unity. The unity of God may be defined as follows: *God is not divided into parts, yet we see different attributes of God emphasized at different times.* This attribute of God has also been called *God's simplicity,* using *simple* in the less common sense of "not complex" or "not composed of parts." But since the word *simple* today has the more common sense of "easy to understand" and "unintelligent or foolish," it is more helpful now to speak of God's "unity" rather than his "simplicity."[20]

---

[19]Herman Bavinck, *The Doctrine of God,* p. 164. The citation is reproduced in the book with no indication of its source.

[20]Systematic theologians have often distinguished another aspect of God's unity at this point, namely the "unity" found

When Scripture speaks about God's attributes it never singles out one attribute of God as more important than all the rest. There is an assumption that every attribute is completely true of God and is true of all of God's character. For example, John can say that "God is light" (1 John 1:5) and then a little later say also that "God is love" (1 John 4:8). There is no suggestion that part of God is light and part of God is love, or that God is partly light and partly love. Nor should we think that God is more light than love or more love than light. Rather it is *God himself* who is light, and it is *God himself* who is also love.

The same is true of other descriptions of God's character, such as that in Exodus 34:6–7:

> The Lord passed before him and proclaimed, "The Lord, the Lord, a God merciful and gracious, slow to anger, and abounding in steadfast love and faithfulness, keeping steadfast love for thousands, forgiving iniquity and transgression and sin, but who will by no means clear the guilty, visiting the iniquity of the fathers upon the children and the children's children, to the third and the fourth generation."

We would not want to say that these attributes are only characteristic of some part of God, but rather that they are characteristic of God himself and therefore characteristic of all of God.

These considerations indicate that we should not think of God as some kind of collection of various attributes added together as in figure 4.2.

GOD'S BEING IS NOT A COLLECTION OF ATTRIBUTES ADDED TOGETHER
Figure 4.2

---

in the fact that God is one God, not many gods. This fact has been called the "unity of singularity," whereas what I have here called God's unity has then been called the "unity of simplicity."

While I agree that God is one God, it can be confusing to speak of two different kinds of unity in God. Therefore, I have not used the term "unity of singularity" or discussed the concept here, but have rather treated the question in chapter 14, on the Trinity.

Nor should we think of the attributes of God as something external from God's real being or real self, something added on to who God really is, after the analogy of figure 4.3.

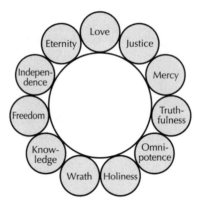

GOD'S ATTRIBUTES ARE NOT ADDITIONS TO HIS REAL BEING
Figure 4.3

Rather, we must remember that God's *whole being* includes all of his attributes: he is *entirely* loving, *entirely* merciful, *entirely* just, and so forth. Every attribute of God that we find in Scripture is true of *all* of God's being, and we therefore can say that *every attribute of God also qualifies every other attribute.*

Figure 4.4 may be helpful in understanding this doctrine of God's unity. In the diagram, let us assume that the horizontal lines represent the attribute of love, and that the vertical lines represent the aspect of God's justice.

GOD'S LOVE AND JUSTICE
Figure 4.4

Furthermore, let us understand the diagonal lines going from upper left to lower right as representing God's holiness and the diagonal lines going from upper right to lower left as representing God's wisdom, as in figure 4.5.

GOD'S LOVE, JUSTICE, HOLINESS, AND WISDOM
Figure 4.5

We could of course go on with different sorts of lines for each of the different attributes of God. But it should be clear that each attribute is simply a way of describing one aspect of God's total character or being. God himself is a *unity*, a unified and completely integrated whole person who is infinitely perfect in *all* of these attributes.

Why then does Scripture speak of these different attributes of God? It is probably because we are unable to grasp all of God's character at one time, and we need to learn of it from different perspectives over a period of time. Yet these perspectives should never be set in opposition to one another, for they are just different ways of looking at the totality of God's character.

In terms of practical application, this means that we should never think, for example, that God is a loving God at one point in history and a just or wrathful God at another point in history. He is the same God always, and everything he says or does is fully consistent with all his attributes. It is not accurate to say, as some have said, that God is a God of justice in the Old Testament and a God of love in the New Testament. God is and always has been infinitely just and infinitely loving as well, and everything he does in the Old Testament as well as the New Testament is completely consistent with both of those attributes.

Now it is true that some actions of God show certain of his attributes more prominently. Creation demonstrates his power and wisdom, the atonement demonstrates his love and justice, and the radiance of heaven demonstrates his glory and beauty. But all of these in some way or other *also* demonstrate his knowledge and holiness and mercy and truthfulness and patience and sovereignty, and so forth. It would be difficult indeed to find some attribute of God that is not reflected at least to some degree in any one of his acts of redemption. This is due to the fact mentioned above: God is a unity and everything he does is an act of the whole person of God.

Moreover, the doctrine of the unity of God should caution us against attempting to single out any one attribute of God as more important than all the others. At various times people have attempted to see God's holiness, or his love, or his self-existence, or his righteousness, or some other attribute as the most important attribute of his being. But all such attempts seem to misconceive of God as a combination of various parts, with some parts being somehow larger or more influential than others. Furthermore, it is hard to understand exactly what "most important" might mean. Does it mean that there are some actions of God that are not fully consistent with some of his other attributes?

That there are some attributes that God somehow sets aside at times in order to act in ways slightly contrary to those attributes? Certainly we cannot maintain either of these views, for that would mean that God is inconsistent with his own character or that he changes and becomes something different from what he was previously. Rather, when we see all the attributes as merely various aspects of the total character of God, then such a question becomes quite unnecessary and we discover that there is no attribute that can be singled out as more important. It is *God himself in his whole being* who is supremely important, and it is God himself in his whole being whom we are to seek to know and to love.

QUESTIONS FOR PERSONAL APPLICATION

1. As you think of God's independence, unchangeableness, eternity, omnipresence, and unity, can you see some faint reflections of these five incommunicable attributes in yourself as God created you to be? What would it mean to strive to become more like God in these areas? At what point would it be wrong to even want to be like God in each of these areas because it would be attempting to usurp his unique role as Creator and Lord?

2. Using each of these five incommunicable attributes, explain how we will be more like God in heaven than we are now, and also how we will for all eternity be unlike God in each of these five areas.

3. Explain how each aspect of the doctrine of God's independence makes you feel emotionally. Does this doctrine have a positive or negative effect on your spiritual life? Explain why.

4. Explain how the doctrine of God's immutability or unchangeableness helps to answer the following questions: Will we be able to do a good job of bringing up children in such an evil world as we have today? Is it possible to have the same close fellowship with God that people had during biblical times? What can we think or do to make Bible stories seem more real and less removed from our present life? Do you think that God is less willing to answer prayer today than he was in Bible times?

5. If you sin against God today, when would it start bringing sorrow to God's heart? When would it stop bringing sorrow to God's heart? Does this reflection help you understand why God's character requires that he punish sin? Why did God have to send his Son to bear the punishment for sin instead of simply forgetting about sin and welcoming sinners into heaven without having given the punishment for sin to anyone? Does God now think of your sins as forgiven or as unforgiven sins?

6. If you sing praise to God today, when will the sound of that praise cease being present in God's consciousness and bringing delight to his heart? Do songs of

praise to God have any ultimate meaning? What about trusting in him hour by hour or obeying him throughout each day?

7. Is control over the use of your time a struggle in your own life? As we grow toward maturity in the Christian life and toward conformity to the image of Christ, will we become more like God in our mastery over time? In what ways?

8. Explain how each of the five incommunicable attributes of God discussed in this chapter can be a help in your own prayer life.

SPECIAL TERMS

anthropomorphic language	infinity with respect to space
aseity	infinity with respect to time
communicable attributes	names of God
eternity	omnipresence
immutability	self-existence
incommunicable attributes	simplicity
independence	unchangeableness
infinite	unity

BIBLIOGRAPHY

Bromiley, G. W. "God." In *ISBE,* 2:493–503.
Charnock, Stephen. *The Existence and Attributes of God.* Repr. ed. Evansville, Ind.: Sovereign Grace Book Club, n.d., pp. 69–180 (first published 1655–1680).
Diehl, D. W. "Process Theology." In *EDT,* pp. 880–85.
Helm, Paul. *Eternal God: A Study of God Without Time.* Oxford: Clarendon, 1988.
Kaiser, Christopher B. *The Doctrine of God.* Westchester, Ill.: Good News, 1982.
Lewis, Gordon R. "God, Attributes of." In *EDT,* pp. 451–59.
McComiskey, Thomas E. "God, Names of." In *EDT,* pp. 464–68.
Packer, J. I. *Knowing God.* London: Hodder and Stoughton, 1973, pp. 67–79.
Saucy, R. H. "God, Doctrine of." In *EDT,* pp. 459–64.
Tozer, A. W. *The Knowledge of the Holy.* New York: Harper and Row, 1961.

SCRIPTURE MEMORY PASSAGE

Psalm 102:25–27:

> *Of old you laid the foundation of the earth,*
> *and the heavens are the work of your hands.*
> *They will perish, but you endure;*
> *they will all wear out like a garment.*
> *You change them like raiment, and they pass away;*
> *but you are the same, and your years have no end.*

HYMN

"Immortal, Invisible, God Only Wise"

In several lines of this hymn the various attributes of God are mentioned in such rapid succession that it is impossible for us to reflect on each one individually as we sing. That is not entirely a disadvantage of the hymn, however, for it makes us realize that when we finally see God in all his glory in heaven, the wonder of beholding him and all his perfections at once will overwhelm us far more completely than does this hymn, and we will find ourselves lost in praise.

> Immortal, invisible, God only wise,
>> In light inaccessible hid from our eyes,
> Most blessed, most glorious, the Ancient of Days,
>> Almighty, victorious, thy great name we praise.
>
> Unresting, unhasting, and silent as light,
>> Nor wanting, nor wasting, thou rulest in might;
> Thy justice like mountains high soaring above
>> Thy clouds which are fountains of goodness and love.
>
> Great Father of glory, pure Father of light,
>> Thine angels adore thee, all veiling their sight;
> All praise we would render; O help us to see
>> 'Tis only the splendor of light hideth thee!

AUTHOR: WALTER CHALMERS SMITH, 1867

Alternative hymn: "Have You Not Known, Have You Not Heard?"

Chapter 5

THE CHARACTER OF GOD: "COMMUNICABLE" ATTRIBUTES (PART 1)

How is God like us in his being and in mental and moral attributes?

EXPLANATION AND SCRIPTURAL BASIS

In this chapter we consider the attributes of God that are "communicable," or more shared with us than those mentioned in the previous chapter. It must be remembered that this division into "incommunicable" and "communicable" is not an absolute division and there is some room for difference of opinion concerning which attributes should fit into which categories.[1] The list of attributes here put in the category "communicable" is a common one, but understanding the definition of each attribute is more important than being able to categorize them in exactly the way presented in this book.

Furthermore, any list of God's attributes must be based on some understanding of how finely one wishes to make distinctions between various aspects of God's character. Are God's goodness and love two attributes or one? What about knowledge and wisdom, or spirituality and invisibility? In this chapter, each of these attributes is treated separately, and the result is a rather long list of various attributes. Yet in several cases it would not make much difference if someone were to treat these pairs as various aspects of the same attribute. If we remember that it is the entire and wholly integrated person of God about whom we are talking, it will be apparent that the division into various attributes is not a matter of great doctrinal significance but is something that must be based on one's judgment concerning the most effective way to present the biblical material.

---

[1]See discussion of communicable and incommunicable attributes in chapter 4, pp. 47–48.

This chapter divides God's "communicable" attributes into five major categories, with individual attributes listed under each category as follows:

A. Attributes Describing God's Being
    1. Spirituality
    2. Invisibility

B. Mental Attributes
    3. Knowledge (or Omniscience)
    4. Wisdom
    5. Truthfulness (and Faithfulness)

C. Moral Attributes
    6. Goodness
    7. Love
    8. Mercy (Grace, Patience)
    9. Holiness
    10. Peace (or Order)
    11. Righteousness (or Justice)
    12. Jealousy
    13. Wrath

D. Attributes of Purpose
    14. Will
    15. Freedom
    16. Omnipotence (or Power, and Sovereignty)

E. "Summary" Attributes
    17. Perfection
    18. Blessedness
    19. Beauty
    20. Glory

Because God's communicable attributes are to be imitated in our lives,[2] each of these sections will include a short explanation of the way in which the attribute in question is to be imitated by us.

A. Attributes Describing God's Being

1. Spirituality. People have often wondered, what is God made of? Is he made of flesh and blood like ourselves? Certainly not. What then is the material that forms his being? Is God made of matter at all? Or is God pure energy? Or is he in some sense pure thought?

The answer of Scripture is that God is none of these. Rather, we read that "God is *spirit*" (John 4:24). This statement is spoken by Jesus in the context of a discussion with

---

[2]Note that Eph. 5:1 tells us to "be imitators of God, as beloved children."

the woman at the well in Samaria. The discussion is about the *location* where people should worship God, and Jesus is telling her that true worship of God does not require that one be *present* either in Jerusalem or in Samaria (John 4:21), for true worship has to do not with physical location but with one's inner spiritual condition. This is because "God is spirit" and this apparently signifies that God is in no way limited to a spatial location.

Thus, we should *not* think of God as having *size* or *dimensions,* even infinite ones (see the discussion on God's omnipresence in the previous chapter). We should not think of God's existence as spirit as meaning that God is infinitely large, for example, for it is not *part* of God but *all* of God that is in every point of space (see Ps. 139:7 – 10). Nor should we think that God's existence as spirit means that God is infinitely small, for no place in the universe can surround him or contain him (see 1 Kings 8:27). Thus, God's being cannot be rightly thought of in terms of space, however we may understand his existence as "spirit."

We also find that God forbids his people to think of *his very being* as similar to *anything* else in the physical creation. We read in the Ten Commandments:

> You shall not make for yourself a graven image, or *any likeness of anything* that is in heaven above, or that is in the earth beneath, or that is in the water under the earth; you shall not bow down to them or serve them; *for I the Lord your God am a jealous God,* visiting the iniquity of the fathers upon the children to the third and the fourth generation of those who hate me, but showing steadfast love to thousands of those who love me and keep my commandments. (Ex. 20:4 – 6)

The creation language in this commandment ("heaven above, or . . . earth beneath, or . . . water under the earth") is a reminder that God's *being,* his essential mode of existence, is different from everything that he has created. To think of his being in terms of anything else in the created universe is to misrepresent him, to limit him, to think of him as less than he really is. To make a graven (or "carved" or "sculptured") image of God as a golden calf, for example, may have been an attempt to portray God as a God who is strong and full of life (like a calf), but to say that God was like a calf was a horribly false statement about God's knowledge, wisdom, love, mercy, omnipresence, eternity, independence, holiness, righteousness, justice, and so forth. Indeed, while we must say that God has made all creation so that each part of it reflects something of his own character, we must also now affirm that to picture God as *existing* in a form or *mode of being* that is like anything else in creation is to think of God in a horribly misleading and dishonoring way.

This is why God's jealousy is given as the reason for the prohibition against making images of him: "for I the Lord your God am a jealous God . . ." (Ex. 20:5). God is jealous to protect his own honor. He eagerly seeks for people to think of him as he is and to worship him for all his excellence, and he is angered when his glory is diminished or his character is falsely represented (cf. Deut. 4:23 – 24, where God's intense jealousy for his own honor is again given as the reason for a prohibition against making any images of him).

Thus, God does not have a physical body, nor is he made of any kind of matter like much of the rest of creation. Furthermore, God is not merely energy or thought or some other element of creation. He is also not like vapor or steam or air or space, all of which are created things: *God's being* is not like any of these. God's being is not even exactly like our own spirits, for these are created things that apparently are able to exist only in one place in one time.

Instead of all these ideas of God, we must say that God is *spirit*. Whatever this means, it is a kind of existence that is unlike anything else in creation. It is a kind of existence that is far superior to all our material existence. We might say that God is "pure being" or "the fullness or essence of being." Furthermore, this kind of existence is not less real or less desirable than our own existence. Rather, it is more real and more desirable than the material and immaterial existence of all creation. Before there was any creation, God existed as spirit. His own being is so very real that it was able to cause everything else to come into existence!

At this point we can define God's spirituality: *God's spirituality means that God exists as a being that is not made of any matter, has no parts or dimensions, is unable to be perceived by our bodily senses, and is more excellent than any other kind of existence.*

We may ask why God's being is this way. Why is God spirit? All that we can say is that this is the greatest, most excellent way to be! This is a form of existence far superior to anything we know. It is amazing to meditate on this fact.

These considerations make us wonder if God's spirituality should perhaps be called an "incommunicable" attribute. To do so would indeed be appropriate in some ways, since God's being is so different from ours. Nevertheless, the fact remains that God has given us spirits in which we worship him (John 4:24; 1 Cor. 14:14; Phil. 3:3), in which we are united with the Lord's spirit (1 Cor. 6:17), with which the Holy Spirit joins to bear witness to our adoption in God's family (Rom. 8:16), and in which we pass into the Lord's presence when we die (Luke 23:46; Eccl. 12:7; Heb. 12:23; cf. Phil. 1:23 – 24). Therefore there is clearly some communication from God to us of a spiritual nature that is something like his own nature, though certainly not in all respects. For this reason it also seems appropriate to think of God's spirituality as a communicable attribute.

2. Invisibility. Related to God's spirituality is the fact that God is invisible. Yet we also must speak of the visible ways in which God manifests himself. God's invisibility can be defined as follows: *God's invisibility means that God's total essence, all of his spiritual being, will never be able to be seen by us, yet God still shows himself to us through visible, created things.*

Many passages speak of the fact that God is not able to be seen. "No one has ever seen God" (John 1:18). Jesus says, "Not that any one has seen the Father except him who is from God; he has seen the Father" (John 6:46). Paul gives the following words of praise: "To the King of ages, immortal, *invisible,* the only God, be honor and glory for ever and ever. Amen" (1 Tim. 1:17). He speaks of God as one "who alone has immortality and dwells in unapproachable light, *whom no man has ever seen or can see*" (1 Tim. 6:16). John says, "No man has ever seen God" (1 John 4:12).

We must remember that these passages were all written after events in Scripture where people saw some outward manifestation of God. For example, very early in Scripture we read, "Thus the LORD used to speak to Moses face to face, as a man speaks to his friend" (Ex. 33:11). Yet God told Moses, "You cannot see my face; for man shall not see me and live" (Ex. 33:20). Nevertheless, God caused his glory to pass by Moses while he hid Moses in a cleft of the rock, and then God let Moses see his back after he had passed by, but said, "my face shall not be seen" (Ex. 33:21–23). This sequence of verses and others like it in the Old Testament indicate that there was a sense in which God could not be seen at all, but that there was also some outward form or manifestation of God which at least in part was able to be seen by man.

It is right, therefore, to say that although God's *total essence* will never be able to be seen by us, nevertheless, God still shows something of himself to us through visible, created things. This happens in a variety of ways.

If we are to *think* of God, we must think of him somehow. God understands this and gives us hundreds of different analogies taken from our human lives or from the creative world.[3] This huge diversity of analogies from all parts of creation reminds us that we should not focus overly much on any one of these analogies. Yet if we do not focus exclusively on any one of these analogies, all of them help to reveal God to us in a somewhat "visible" way (cf. Gen. 1:27; Ps. 19:1; Rom. 1:20).

The Old Testament also records a number of theophanies. A *theophany* is "an appearance of God." In these theophanies God took on various visible forms to show himself to people. God appeared to Abraham (Gen. 18:1–33), Jacob (Gen. 32:28–30), the people of Israel (as a pillar of cloud by day and fire by night: Ex. 13:21–22), the elders of Israel (Ex. 24:9–11), Manoah and his wife (Judg. 13:21–22), Isaiah (Isa. 6:1), and others.

A much greater visible manifestation of God than these Old Testament theophanies was found in the person of Jesus Christ himself. He could say, "He who has seen me has seen the Father" (John 14:9). And John contrasts the fact that no one has ever seen God with the fact that God's only Son has made him known to us: "No one has ever seen God; the only begotten God,[4] who is in the bosom of the Father, he has made him known" (John 1:18, author's translation). Furthermore, Jesus is "the image of the invisible God" (Col. 1:15), and is "the bright radiance of the glory of God" and is "the exact representation of his nature" (Heb. 1:3 author's translation). Thus, in the person of Jesus we have a unique visible manifestation of God in the New Testament that was not available to believers who saw theophanies in the Old Testament.

But how will we see God in heaven? We will never be able to see or know all of God, for "his greatness is unsearchable" (Ps. 145:3; cf. John 6:46; 1 Tim. 1:17; 6:16; 1 John 4:12, which were mentioned above). And we will not be able to see — at least with our physical eyes — the spiritual being of God. Nevertheless, Scripture says that we will see God himself. Jesus says, "Blessed are the pure in heart, for *they shall see God*" (Matt. 5:8).

---

[3]See the discussion of the names of God taken from creation in chapter 4, p. 49.

[4]There is a textual variant at this point, but "the only begotten God" (*monogenēs theos*) is better attested than "the only begotten Son," and this reading is not foreign to the context: see Leon Morris, *The Gospel According to John* (Grand Rapids: Eerdmans, 1971), pp. 113–14.

We will be able to see the human nature of Jesus, of course (Rev. 1:7). But it is not clear in exactly what sense we will be able to "see" the Father and the Holy Spirit, or the divine nature of God the Son (cf. Rev. 1:4; 4:2–3, 5; 5:6). Perhaps the nature of this "seeing" will not be known to us until we reach heaven.

Although what we see will not be an exhaustive vision of God, it will be a completely true and clear and real vision of God. We shall see "face to face" (1 Cor. 13:12) and "we shall see him as he is" (1 John 3:2). The most remarkable description of the open, close fellowship with God that we shall experience is seen in the fact that in the heavenly city "the throne of God and of the Lamb shall be in it, and his servants shall worship him; *they shall see his face,* and his name shall be on their foreheads" (Rev. 22:3–4).

When we realize that God is the perfection of all that we long for or desire, that he is the summation of everything beautiful or desirable, then we realize that the greatest joy of the life to come will be that we "shall see his face." This seeing of God "face to face" has been called the *beatific vision,* meaning "the vision that makes us blessed or happy" ("beatific" is from two Latin words, *beatus,* "blessed," and *facere,* "to make"). To look at God changes us and makes us like him: "We shall be like him, for *we shall see him as he is*" (1 John 3:2; cf. 2 Cor. 3:18). This vision of God will be the consummation of our knowing God and will give us full delight and joy for all eternity: "in your presence there is fulness of joy, in your right hand are pleasures for evermore" (Ps. 16:11).

B. Mental Attributes

3. Knowledge (Omniscience). God's knowledge may be defined as follows: *God fully knows himself and all things actual and possible in one simple and eternal act.*

Elihu says that God is the one "who is *perfect in knowledge*" (Job 37:16), and John says that God "*knows everything*" (1 John 3:20). The quality of knowing everything is called omniscience, and because God knows everything, he is said to be omniscient (that is, "all-knowing").

The definition given above explains omniscience in more detail. It says first that God fully knows himself. This is an amazing fact since God's own being is infinite or unlimited. Of course, only he who is infinite can fully know himself in every detail. This fact is implied by Paul when he says, "For the Spirit searches everything, even the depths of God. For what person knows a man's thoughts except the spirit of the man which is in him? So also no one comprehends the thoughts of God except the Spirit of God" (1 Cor. 2:10–11).

This idea is also suggested by John's statement that "God is light and in him is no darkness at all" (1 John 1:5). In this context "light" has a suggestion of both moral purity and full knowledge or awareness. If there is "no darkness at all" in God, but he is entirely "light," then God is himself both entirely holy and also entirely filled with self-knowledge.

The definition also says that God knows "all things *actual.*" This means all things that exist and all things that happen. This applies to creation, for God is the one before whom "no creature is hidden, but all are open and laid bare to the eyes of him with whom we have to do" (Heb. 4:13; cf. 2 Chron. 16:9; Job 28:24; Matt. 10:29–30). God also knows the future, for he is the one who can say, "I am God, and there is none like me, declaring the end from the beginning and from ancient times things not yet done" (Isa. 46:9–10; cf. 42:8–9 and frequent passages in the Old Testament prophets). He knows the tiny details of every one of our lives, for Jesus tells us, "Your Father knows what you need before you ask him" (Matt. 6:8), and, "Even the hairs of your head are all numbered" (Matt. 10:30).

In Psalm 139 David reflects on the amazing detail of God's knowledge of our lives. He knows our actions and thoughts: "O Lord, you have searched me and known me! You know when I sit down and when I rise up; you discern my thoughts from afar" (Ps. 139:1–2). He knows the words we will say before they are spoken: "Even before a word is on my tongue, lo, O Lord, you know it altogether" (Ps. 139:4). And he knows all the days of our lives even before we are born: "Your eyes beheld my unformed substance; in your book were written, every one of them, the days that were formed for me, when as yet there was none of them" (Ps. 139:16).

The definition of God's knowledge given above also specifies that God knows "all things *possible*." This is because there are some instances in Scripture where God gives information about events that might happen but that do not actually come to pass. For example, when David was fleeing from Saul he rescued the city of Keilah from the Philistines and then stayed for a time at Keilah. He decided to ask God whether Saul would come to Keilah to attack him and, if Saul came, whether the men of Keilah would surrender him into Saul's hand. David said:

> "Will Saul come down, as your servant has heard? O Lord, the God of Israel, I beseech you, tell your servant." And the Lord said, "He will come down." Then said David, "Will the men of Keilah surrender me and my men into the hand of Saul?" And the Lord said, "They will surrender you." Then David and his men, who were about six hundred, arose and departed from Keilah, and they went wherever they could go. When Saul was told that David had escaped from Keilah, he gave up the expedition. (1 Sam. 23:11–13)

Similarly, Jesus could state that Tyre and Sidon *would have* repented if Jesus' own miracles had been done there in former days: "Woe to you, Chorazin! woe to you, Bethsaida! for if the mighty works done in you had been done in Tyre and Sidon, they would have repented long ago in sackcloth and ashes" (Matt. 11:21). Similarly, he says, "And you, Capernaum, will you be exalted to heaven? You shall be brought down to Hades. For if the mighty works done in you had been done in Sodom, it would have remained until this day" (Matt. 11:23; cf. 2 Kings 13:19, where Elisha tells what would have happened if King Joash had struck the ground five or six times with the arrows).

The fact that God knows all things possible can also be deduced from God's full knowledge of himself. If God fully knows himself, he knows everything he is able to do, which includes all things that are possible. This fact is indeed amazing. God has made an incredibly complex and varied universe. But there are thousands upon thousands of other variations or kinds of things that God could have created but did not. God's infinite knowledge includes detailed knowledge of what each of those other possible creations would have been like and what would have happened in each of them! "Such knowledge is too wonderful for me; it is high, I cannot attain it" (Ps. 139:6). "For as the heavens are higher than the earth, so are my ways higher than your ways and my thoughts than your thoughts" (Isa. 55:9).

Our definition of God's knowledge speaks of God knowing everything in one "simple act." Here again the word *simple* is used in the sense "not divided into parts." This means that God is always fully aware of everything. If he should wish to tell us the number of grains of sand on the seashore or the number of stars in the sky, he would not have to count them all quickly like some kind of giant computer, nor would he have to call the number to mind because it was something he had not thought about for a time. Rather, he always knows all things at once. All of these facts and all other things that he knows are always fully present in his consciousness. He does not have to reason to conclusions or ponder carefully before he answers, for he knows the end from the beginning, and he never learns and never forgets anything (cf. Ps. 90:4; 2 Peter 3:8; and the verses cited above on God's perfect knowledge). Every bit of God's knowledge is always fully present in his consciousness; it never grows dim or fades into his nonconscious memory. Finally, the definition talks about God's knowledge as not only a simple act but also an "eternal act." This means that God's knowledge never changes or grows. If he were ever to learn something new, he would not have been omniscient beforehand. Thus, from all eternity God has known all things that would happen and all things that he would do.

Someone may object that God promises to forget our sins. For example, he says, "I will not remember your sins" (Isa. 43:25). Yet passages like this can certainly be understood to mean that God will never again let the knowledge of these sins play any part in the way he relates to us: he will "forget" them in his relationship to us. Another objection to the biblical teaching about God's omniscience has been brought from Jeremiah 7:31; 19:5; and 31:35, where God refers to the horrible practices of parents who burn to death their own children in the sacrificial fires of the pagan god Baal, and says, "which I did not command, *nor did it come into my mind*" (Jer. 7:31). Does this mean that before the time of Jeremiah God had never *thought* of the possibility that parents would sacrifice their own children? Certainly not, for that very practice had occurred a century earlier in the reigns of Ahaz (2 Kings 16:3) and Hoshea (2 Kings 17:17), and God himself had forbidden the practice eight hundred years earlier under Moses (Lev. 18:21). The verses in Jeremiah are probably better translated quite literally, "nor did it enter into my *heart*" (so KJV at Jer. 7:31, and the literal translation in the NASB mg.—the Hebrew word is *lēb*, most frequently translated "heart"), giving the sense, "nor did I wish for it, desire it, think of it in a positive way."[5]

Another difficulty that arises in this connection is the question of the relationship between God's knowledge of everything that will happen in the future and the reality and degree of freedom we have in our actions. If God knows everything that will happen, how can our choices be at all "free"? In fact, this difficulty has loomed so large that some theologians have concluded that God does not know all of the future. They

[5]The same phrase ("to have a thought enter into the heart") seems to have the sense "desire, wish for, long for" in all five of its occurrences in the Hebrew Old Testament: Isa. 65:17; Jer. 3:16 (where it cannot mean simply "have a factual knowledge of"); 7:31; 19:5; 32:35; as well as in the equivalent Greek phrase *anebē epi tēn kardian* in Acts 7:23.

have said that God does not know things that cannot (in their opinion) be known, such as the free acts of people that have not yet occurred (sometimes the phrase used is the "contingent acts of free moral agents," where "contingent" means "possible but not certain"). But such a position is unsatisfactory because it essentially denies God's knowledge of the future of human history at any point in time and thus is inconsistent with the passages cited above about God's knowledge of the future and with dozens of other Old Testament prophetic passages where God predicts the future far in advance and in great detail.[6]

How then are we to resolve this difficulty? Although this question will be treated in much more detail in chapter 9 on God's providence, it may be helpful at this point to note the suggestion of Augustine, who said that God has given us "reasonable self-determination." His statement does not involve the terms *free* or *freedom,* for these terms are exceptionally difficult to define in any way that satisfactorily accounts for God's complete knowledge of future events. But this statement does affirm what is important to us and what we sense to be true in our own experience, that our choices and decisions are "reasonable." That is, we think about what to do, consciously decide what we will do, and then we follow the course of action that we have chosen.

Augustine's statement also says that we have "self-determination." This is simply affirming that our choices really do determine what will happen. It is not as if events occur *regardless* of what we decide or do, but rather that they occur *because of* what we decide and do. No attempt is made in this statement to define the sense in which we are "free" or "not free," but that is not the really important issue: for us, it is important that we think, choose, and act, and that these thoughts, choices, and actions are real and actually have eternal significance. If God knows all our thoughts, words, and actions long before they occur, then there must be some sense in which our choices are not absolutely free. But further definition of this issue is better left until it can be treated more fully in chapter 9.

4. Wisdom. *God's wisdom means that God always chooses the best goals and the best means to those goals.* This definition goes beyond the idea of God knowing all things and specifies that God's decisions about what he will do are always wise decisions: that is, they always will bring about the best results (from God's ultimate perspective), and they will bring about those results through the best possible means.

Scripture affirms God's wisdom in general in several places. He is called "the only wise God" (Rom. 16:27). Job says that God "is wise in heart" (Job 9:4), and "With him are wisdom and might; he has counsel and understanding" (Job 12:13). God's wisdom is seen specifically in creation. The psalmist exclaims, "O LORD, how manifold are your works! In wisdom you have made them all; the earth is full of your creatures" (Ps. 104:24). As God created the universe, it was perfectly suited to bring him glory, both in its day-by-day processes and in the goals for which he created it. Even now, while we still see the effects of sin and the curse on the natural world, we should be amazed at how harmonious and intricate God's creation is.

---

[6]See additional discussion of this question in chapter 9, pp. 234–36.

God's wisdom is also seen in his great plan of redemption. Christ is "the wisdom of God" to those who are called (1 Cor. 1:24, 30), even though the word of the cross is "foolishness" to those who reject it and think themselves to be wise in this world (1 Cor. 1:18–20). Yet even this is a reflection of God's wise plan: "For since, in the wisdom of God, the world did not know God through wisdom, it pleased God through the folly of what we preach to save those who believe. . . . God chose what is foolish in the world to shame the wise . . . so that no human being might boast in the presence of God" (1 Cor. 1:21, 27, 29).

Paul knows that what we now think of as the "simple" gospel message, understandable even to the very young, reflects an amazing plan of God, which in its depths of wisdom surpasses anything man could ever have imagined. At the end of eleven chapters of reflection on the wisdom of God's plan of redemption, Paul bursts forth into spontaneous praise: "O the depth of the riches and wisdom and knowledge of God! How unsearchable are his judgments and how inscrutable his ways!" (Rom. 11:33).

When Paul preaches the gospel both to Jews and to Gentiles, and they become unified in the one body of Christ (Eph. 3:6), the incredible "mystery" that was "hidden for ages in God who created all things" (Eph. 3:9) is plain for all to see, namely, that in Christ such totally diverse people become united. When groups so different racially and culturally become members of the one body of Christ, then God's purpose is fulfilled, "that through the church the manifold *wisdom of God* might now be made known to the principalities and powers in the heavenly places" (Eph. 3:10).

Today this means that God's wisdom is shown even to angels and demons ("principalities and powers") when people from different racial and cultural backgrounds are united in Christ in the church. If the Christian church is faithful to God's wise plan, it will be always in the forefront in breaking down racial and social barriers in societies around the world, and will thus be a visible manifestation of God's amazingly wise plan to bring great unity out of great diversity and thereby to cause all creation to honor him.

God's wisdom is also shown in our individual lives. "We know that God works all things together for good for those who love him, who are called according to his purpose" (Rom. 8:28, author's translation). Here Paul affirms that God does work wisely in all the things that come into our lives, and that through all these things he advances us toward the goal of conformity to the image of Christ (Rom. 8:29). It should be our great confidence and a source of peace day by day to know that God causes all things to move us toward the ultimate goal he has for our lives, namely, that we might be like Christ and thereby bring glory to him. Such confidence enabled Paul to accept his "thorn in the flesh" (2 Cor. 12:7) as something that, though painful, God in his wisdom had chosen not to remove (2 Cor. 12:8–10).

Every day of our lives, we may quiet our discouragement with the comfort that comes from the knowledge of God's infinite wisdom: if we are his children, we can know that he is working wisely in our lives, even today, to bring us into greater conformity into the image of Christ.

God's wisdom is, of course, in part communicable to us. We can ask God confidently for wisdom when we need it, for he promises in his Word, "If any of you lacks wisdom, let him ask God, who gives to all men generously and without reproaching, and it will be given him" (James 1:5). This wisdom, or skill in living a life pleasing to God, comes primarily from reading and obeying his Word: "The testimony of the LORD is sure, making wise the simple" (Ps. 19:7; cf. Deut. 4:6–8).

"The fear of the LORD is the beginning of wisdom" (Ps. 111:10; Prov. 9:10; cf. Prov. 1:7), because if we fear dishonoring God or displeasing him, and if we fear his fatherly discipline, then we will have the motivation that makes us want to follow his ways and live according to his wise commands. Furthermore, the possession of wisdom from God will result not in pride but in humility (Prov. 11:2; James 3:13), not in arrogance but in a gentle and peaceful spirit (James 3:14–18). The person who is wise according to God's standards will continually walk in dependence on the Lord and with a desire to exalt him.

Yet we must also remember that God's wisdom is not entirely communicable: we can never fully share God's wisdom (Rom. 11:33). In practical terms, this means that there will frequently be times in this life when we will not be able to understand why God allowed something to happen. Then we have simply to trust him and go on obeying his wise commands for our lives: "Therefore let those who suffer according to God's will do right and entrust their souls to a faithful Creator" (1 Peter 4:19; cf. Deut. 29:29; Prov. 3:5–6). God is infinitely wise and we are not, and it pleases him when we have faith to trust his wisdom even when we do not understand what he is doing.

5. Truthfulness (and Faithfulness). *God's truthfulness means that he is the true God, and that all his knowledge and words are both true and the final standard of truth.*

The term *veracity,* which means "truthfulness" or "reliability," has sometimes been used as a synonym for God's truthfulness.

The first part of this definition indicates that the God revealed in Scripture is the true or real God and that all other so-called gods are idols. "The LORD is the true God; he is the living God and the everlasting King. . . . The gods who did not make the heavens and the earth shall perish from the earth and from under the heavens" (Jer. 10:10–11). Jesus says to his Father, "And this is eternal life, that they know you *the only true God,* and Jesus Christ whom you have sent" (John 17:3; cf. 1 John 5:20).

We might ask what it means to be the true God as opposed to other beings who are not God. It must mean that God in his own being or character is the one who fully conforms to the idea of what God should be: namely, a being who is infinitely perfect in power, in wisdom, in goodness, in lordship over time and space, and so forth. But we may further ask, *whose* idea of God is this? What idea of God must one conform to in order to be the true God?

At this point our train of thought becomes somewhat circular, for we must not say that a being must conform to *our* idea of what God should be like in order to be the true God! We are mere creatures! We cannot define what the true God must be like! So we must say that it is *God himself* who has the only perfect idea of what the true God should be like. And he himself is the true God because in his being and character he perfectly conforms to his own idea of what the true God should be. In addition, he has implanted in our minds a reflection of his own idea of what the true God must be, and this enables us to recognize him as God.

The definition given above also affirms that all of God's *knowledge* is true and is the final standard of truth. Job tells us that God is "perfect in knowledge" (Job 37:16; see also the verses cited above under the discussion of God's omniscience). To say that God knows all things and that his knowledge is perfect is to say that he is never mistaken in his perception or understanding of the world: all that he knows and thinks is true and is a correct understanding of the nature of reality. In fact, since God knows all things infinitely well, we can say that the standard of true knowledge is conformity to God's knowledge. If we think the same thing God thinks about anything in the universe, we are thinking truthfully about it.

Our definition also affirms that God's words are both *true* and the *final standard of truth*. This means that God is reliable and faithful in his words. With respect to his promises, God always does what he promises to do, and we can depend on him never to be unfaithful to his promises. Thus, he is "a God of faithfulness" (Deut. 32:4). In fact, this specific aspect of God's truthfulness is sometimes viewed as a distinct attribute: *God's faithfulness means that God will always do what he has said and fulfill what he has promised* (Num. 23:19; cf. 2 Sam. 7:28; Ps. 141:6, et al.). He can be relied upon, and he will never prove unfaithful to those who trust what he has said. Indeed, the essence of true faith is taking God at his word and relying on him to do as he has promised.

In addition to the fact that God is faithful to his promises, we must also affirm that all of God's *words* about himself and about his creation completely correspond to reality. That is, God always speaks truth when he speaks. He is "the unlying God" (Titus 1:2, author's translation), the God for whom it is impossible to lie (Heb. 6:18), the God whose every word is perfectly "pure" (Ps. 12:6), the one of whom it can be said, "Every word of God proves true" (Prov. 30:5). God's words are not simply true in the sense that they conform to some standard of truthfulness outside of God. Rather, they are truth itself; they are the final standard and definition of truth. So Jesus can say to the Father, "Your word is *truth*" (John 17:17). What was said about the truthfulness of God's knowledge can also be said about God's words, for they are based on his perfect knowledge and accurately reflect that perfect knowledge: God's words are "truth" in the sense that they are the final standard by which truthfulness is to be judged: whatever conforms to God's own words is also true, and what fails to conform to his words is not true.

The truthfulness of God is also communicable in that we can in part imitate it by striving to have true knowledge about God and about his world. In fact, as we begin to think true thoughts about God and creation, thoughts that we learn from Scripture and from allowing Scripture to guide us in our observation and interpretation of the natural world, we begin to think God's own thoughts after him! We can exclaim with the psalmist, "How precious to me are your thoughts, O God! How vast is the sum of them!" (Ps. 139:17).

This realization should encourage us in the pursuit of knowledge in all areas of the natural and social sciences and the humanities. Whatever the area of our investigation, when we discover more truth about the nature of reality, we discover more of the truth that God already knows. In this sense we can affirm that "all truth is God's truth"[7] and

---

[7]See *All Truth Is God's Truth* by Arthur Holmes (Grand Rapids: Eerdmans, 1977).

rejoice whenever the learning or discovery of this truth is used in ways pleasing to God. Growth in knowledge is part of the process of becoming more like God or becoming creatures who are more fully in God's image. Paul tells us that we have put on the "new nature," which, he says, "is being *renewed in knowledge* after the image of its creator" (Col. 3:10).

In a society that is exceedingly careless with the truthfulness of spoken words, we as God's children are to imitate our Creator and take great care to be sure that our words are always truthful. *"Do not lie to one another,* seeing that you have put off the old nature with its practices and have put on the new nature" (Col. 3:9–10). Again Paul admonishes, "Therefore, putting away falsehood, let every one *speak the truth* with his neighbor" (Eph. 4:25). In his own ministry, Paul says that he sought to practice absolute truthfulness: "We have renounced disgraceful, underhanded ways; we refuse to practice cunning or to tamper with God's word, but by the open statement of the truth we would commend ourselves to every man's conscience in the sight of God" (2 Cor. 4:2). God is pleased when his people put "devious talk" far from them (Prov. 4:24) and speak with words that are acceptable not only in the sight of people but also in the sight of the Lord himself (Ps. 19:14).

Furthermore, we should imitate God's truthfulness in our own reaction to truth and falsehood. Like God, we should *love* truth and *hate* falsehood. The commandment not to bear false witness against our neighbor (Ex. 20:16), like the other commandments, requires not merely outward conformity but also conformity in heart attitude. One who is pleasing to God "speaks truth from his heart" (Ps. 15:2), and strives to be like the righteous man who "hates falsehood" (Prov. 13:5). God commands his people through Zechariah, "Do not devise evil in your hearts against one another, and love no false oath, for all these things I hate, says the LORD" (Zech. 8:17).

These commands are given because God himself loves truth and hates falsehood: "Lying lips are an abomination to the LORD, but those who act faithfully are his delight" (Prov. 12:22; cf. Isa. 59:3–4). Falsehood and lying come not from God but from Satan, who delights in falsehood: "When he lies, he speaks according to his own nature, for he is a liar and the father of lies" (John 8:44). It is appropriate then that with "the cowardly, the faithless, the polluted" and the "murderers, fornicators, sorcerers, [and] idolaters" who are found in "the lake that burns with fire and sulphur" far from the heavenly city, are found also "all *liars*" (Rev. 21:8).

Thus, Scripture teaches us that lying is wrong not only because of the great harm that comes from it (and much more harm comes from lying than we often realize), but also for an even deeper and more profound reason: when we lie we dishonor God and diminish his glory, for we, as those created in God's image and created for the purpose of reflecting God's glory in our lives, are acting in a way that is contrary to God's own character.

C. Moral Attributes

6. Goodness. *The goodness of God means that God is the final standard of good, and that all that God is and does is worthy of approval.*

In this definition we find a situation similar to the one we faced in defining God as the true God. Here, "good" can be understood to mean "worthy of approval," but we have not answered the question, approval by whom? In one sense, we can say that anything that is truly good should be worthy of approval by us. But in a more ultimate sense, we are not free to decide by ourselves what is worthy of approval and what is not. Ultimately, therefore, God's being and actions are perfectly worthy of his own approval. He is therefore the final standard of good. Jesus implies this when he says, "No one is good but God alone" (Luke 18:19). The Psalms frequently affirm that "the LORD is good" (Ps. 100:5) or exclaim, "O give thanks to the LORD, for he is good" (Pss. 106:1; 107:1, et al.). David encourages us, "O taste and see that the LORD is good!" (Ps. 34:8).

But if God is himself good and therefore the ultimate standard of good, then we have a definition of the meaning of "good" that will greatly help us in the study of ethics and aesthetics. What is "good"? "Good" is what God approves. We may ask then, why is what God approves good? We must answer, "Because he approves it." That is to say, there is no higher standard of goodness than God's own character and his approval of whatever is consistent with that character. Nonetheless, God has given us some reflection of his own sense of goodness, so that when we evaluate things in the way God created us to evaluate them, we will also approve what God approves and delight in things in which he delights.

Our definition also states that all that God *does* is worthy of approval. We see evidence of this in the creation narrative: "And God saw everything that he had made, and behold, it was *very good*" (Gen. 1:31). The psalmist connects the goodness of God with the goodness of his actions: "You are good and you do *good;* teach me your statutes" (Ps. 119:68). Psalm 104 is an excellent example of praise to God for his goodness in creation, while many Psalms, such as Psalms 106 and 107, give thanks to God for his goodness in all his actions toward his people. And Paul encourages us to discover in practice how God's will for our lives is "*good* and acceptable and perfect" (Rom. 12:2).

Scripture also tells us that God is the source of all good in the world. "Every good endowment and every perfect gift is from above, coming down from the Father of lights with whom there is no variation or shadow due to change" (James 1:17; cf. Ps. 145:9; Acts 14:17). Moreover, God does only good things for his children. We read, "No good thing does the LORD withhold from those who walk uprightly" (Ps. 84:11). And in the same context in which Paul assures us that "in everything God works for good with those who love him" (Rom. 8:28), he also says, "He who did not spare his own Son but gave him up for us all, will he not also give us all things with him?" (Rom. 8:32). Much more than an earthly father, our heavenly Father will "give good things to those who ask him" (Matt. 7:11), and even his discipline is a manifestation of his love and is for our good (Heb. 12:10). This knowledge of God's great goodness should encourage us to "give thanks in all circumstances" (1 Thess. 5:18).

In imitation of this communicable attribute, we should ourselves do good (that is, we should do what God approves) and thereby imitate the goodness of our heavenly Father. Paul writes, "So then, as we have opportunity, let us do good to all men, and especially to those who are of the household of faith" (Gal. 6:10; cf. Luke 6:27, 33–35; 2 Tim. 3:17). Moreover, when we realize that God is the definition and source of all good, we will realize that God himself is the ultimate good that we seek. We will say with the psalmist,

"Whom have I in heaven but you? And there is nothing upon earth that I desire besides you. My flesh and my heart may fail, but God is the strength of my heart and my portion for ever" (Ps. 73:25–26; cf. 16:11; 42:1–2).

God's goodness is closely related to several other characteristics of his nature, among them love, mercy, patience, and grace. Sometimes these are considered separate attributes and are treated individually. At other times these are considered part of God's goodness and are treated as various aspects of God's goodness. In this chapter we will treat love as a separate attribute since it is so prominent in Scripture. The other three characteristics (mercy, patience, and grace), while also prominent in Scripture, will be treated together as aspects of God's goodness to individuals in specific situations. Thus, God's *mercy* is *his goodness toward those in distress*, his *grace* is *his goodness toward those who deserve only punishment*, and his *patience* is *his goodness toward those who continue to sin over a period of time* (see below, section C.8, on mercy, patience, and grace).

7. Love. *God's love means that God eternally gives of himself to others.*

This definition understands love as self-giving for the benefit of others. This attribute of God shows that it is part of his nature to give of himself in order to bring about blessing or good for others.

John tells us that "God is love" (1 John 4:8). We see evidence that this attribute of God was active even before creation among the members of the Trinity. Jesus speaks to his Father of "my glory which you have given me in your *love* for me *before the foundation of the world*" (John 17:24), thus indicating that there was love and a giving of honor from the Father to the Son from all eternity. It continues at the present time, for we read, "The Father loves the Son, and has given all things into his hand" (John 3:35).

This love is also reciprocal, for Jesus says, "I do as the Father has commanded me, so that the world may know that I love the Father" (John 14:31). The love between the Father and the Son also presumably characterizes their relationship with the Holy Spirit, even though it is not explicitly mentioned. This eternal love of the Father for the Son, the Son for the Father, and of both for the Holy Spirit makes heaven a world of love and joy because each person of the Trinity seeks to bring joy and happiness to the other two.

The self-giving that characterizes the Trinity finds clear expression in God's relationship to mankind, and especially to sinful men. "In this is love, not that we loved God but that he loved us and sent his Son to be the propitiation for our sins" (1 John 4:10, author's translation). Paul writes, "God shows his love for us in that while we were yet sinners Christ died for us" (Rom. 5:8). John also writes, "For God so loved the world that he gave his only Son, that whoever believes in him should not perish but have eternal life" (John 3:16). Paul also speaks of "the Son of God, who *loved me* and gave himself for me" (Gal. 2:20), thus showing an awareness of the directly personal application of Christ's love to individual sinners. It should cause us great joy to know that it is the purpose of God the Father, Son, and Holy Spirit to give of themselves to us to bring us true joy and happiness. It is God's nature to act that way toward those upon whom he has set his love, and he will continue to act that way toward us for all eternity.

We imitate this communicable attribute of God, first by loving God in return, and second by loving others in imitation of the way God loves them. All our obligations to

God can be summarized in this: "You shall love the Lord your God with all your heart, and with all your soul, and with all your mind. . . . You shall love your neighbor as yourself " (Matt. 22:37–38). If we love God, we will obey his commandments (1 John 5:3) and thus do what is pleasing to him. We will love God, not the world (1 John 2:15), and we will do all this because he first loved us (1 John 4:19).

It is one of the most amazing facts in all Scripture that just as God's love involves his giving of himself to make us happy, so we can in return give of ourselves and actually bring joy to God's heart. Isaiah promises God's people, "As the bridegroom rejoices over the bride, so *shall your God rejoice over you*" (Isa. 62:5), and Zephaniah tells God's people, "The Lord, your God, is in your midst . . . he will rejoice over you with gladness, he will renew you in his love; he will exult over you with loud singing as on a day of festival" (Zeph. 3:17–18).

Our imitation of God's love is also seen in our love for others. John makes this explicit: "Beloved, if God so loved us, we also ought to love one another" (1 John 4:11). In fact, our love for others within the fellowship of believers is so evidently an imitation of Christ that by it the world recognizes us as his: "By this all men will know that you are my disciples, if you have love for one another" (John 13:35; cf. 15:13; Rom. 13:10; 1 Cor. 13:4–7; Heb. 10:24). God himself gives us his love to enable us to love each other (John 17:26; Rom. 5:5). Moreover, our love for our enemies especially reflects God's love (Matt. 5:43–48).

8. Mercy, Grace, Patience. God's mercy, patience, and grace may be seen as three separate attributes, or as specific aspects of God's goodness. The definitions given here show these attributes as special examples of God's goodness when it is used for the benefit of specific classes of people.

God's *mercy* means God's goodness toward those in misery and distress.

God's *grace* means God's goodness toward those who deserve only punishment.

God's *patience* means God's goodness in withholding of punishment toward those who sin over a period of time.

These three characteristics of God's nature are often mentioned together, especially in the Old Testament. When God declared his name to Moses, he proclaimed, "The Lord, the Lord, a God merciful and gracious, slow to anger, and abounding in steadfast love and faithfulness" (Ex. 34:6). David says in Psalm 103:8, "The Lord is merciful and gracious, slow to anger and abounding in steadfast love."

Because these characteristics of God are often mentioned together, it may seem difficult to distinguish among them. Yet the characteristic of mercy is often emphasized where people are in misery or distress. David says, for example, "I am in great distress; let us fall into the hand of the Lord for his *mercy* is great . . ." (2 Sam. 24:14). The two blind men who wish Jesus to see their plight and heal them cry, "Have *mercy* on us, Son of David" (Matt. 9:27). When Paul speaks of the fact that God comforts us in affliction, he calls God the "Father of *mercies* and God of all comfort" (2 Cor. 1:3).[8] In time of need, we are to draw near to God's throne so that we might receive both mercy and grace

---

[8]This verse uses *oiktirmos*, "compassion, mercy," rather than *eleos*, "mercy," but the terms are closely related in meaning and both refer to compassion or goodness toward those in distress.

(Heb. 4:16; cf. 2:17; James 5:11). We are to imitate God's mercy in our conduct toward others: "Blessed are the merciful, for they shall obtain mercy" (Matt. 5:7; cf. 2 Cor. 1:3–4).

With respect to the attribute of *grace,* we find that Scripture emphasizes that God's grace, or his favor toward those who deserve no favor but only punishment, is never obligated but is always freely given on God's part. God says, "I will be gracious to whom I will be gracious, and will show mercy on whom I will show mercy" (Ex. 33:19; quoted in Rom. 9:15). Yet God is regularly gracious toward his people: "Turn to me and be *gracious* to me, *After Thy manner* with those who love Thy name" (Ps. 119:132 NASB). In fact, Peter can call God "the God of all grace" (1 Peter 5:10).

Grace as God's goodness especially shown to those who do not deserve it is seen frequently in Paul's writings. He emphasizes that salvation by grace is the opposite of salvation by human effort, for grace is a freely given gift. "Since all have sinned and fall short of the glory of God, they are justified by his *grace* as a gift, through the redemption which is in Christ Jesus" (Rom. 3:23–24). The distinction between grace and a salvation earned by works that merit a reward is also seen in Romans 11:6: "But if it is by grace, it is no longer on the basis of works; otherwise grace would no longer be grace." Grace, then, is God's favor freely given to those who do not deserve this favor.

Paul also sees that if grace is unmerited, then there is only one human attitude appropriate as an instrument for receiving such grace, namely, faith: "That is why it depends on faith, in order that the promise may rest on grace. . ." (Rom. 4:16). Faith is the one human attitude that is the opposite of depending on oneself, for it involves trust in or dependence upon another. Thus, it is devoid of self-reliance or attempts to gain righteousness by human effort. If God's favor is to come to us apart from our own merit, then it must come when we depend not on our own merit but on the merits of another, and that is precisely when we have faith.

In the New Testament, and especially in Paul, not only the forgiveness of sins, but also *the entire living of the Christian life* can be seen to result from God's continuous bestowal of grace. Paul can say, "by the grace of God I am what I am" (1 Cor. 15:10). Luke speaks of Antioch as the place where Paul and Barnabas "had been commended to the grace of God for the work which they had fulfilled" (Acts 14:26), indicating that the church there, in sending out Paul and Barnabas, saw the success of their ministry as dependent upon God's continuing grace. Furthermore, the blessing of "grace" upon Paul's readers is the most frequent apostolic blessing in his letters (see, e.g., Rom. 1:7; 16:20; 1 Cor. 1:3; 16:23; 2 Cor. 1:2; 13:14; Gal. 1:3; 6:18).

God's *patience,* similarly, was mentioned in some of the verses cited above in connection with God's mercy. The Old Testament frequently speaks of God as *"slow to anger"* (Ex. 34:6; Num. 14:18; Pss. 86:15; 103:8; 145:8; Jonah 4:2; Nah. 1:3, et al.). In the New Testament, Paul speaks about God's "kindness and forbearance and patience" (Rom. 2:4), and says that Jesus Christ displayed his "perfect patience" toward Paul himself as an example for others (1 Tim. 1:16; cf. Rom. 9:22; 1 Peter 3:20).

We are also to imitate God's patience and be "slow to anger" (James 1:19), and be patient in suffering as Christ was (1 Peter 2:20). We are to lead a life "with patience" (Eph. 4:2), and "patience" is listed among the fruit of the Spirit in Galatians 5:22 (see also Rom. 8:25; 1 Cor. 13:4; Col. 1:11; 3:12; 2 Tim. 3:10; 4:2; James 5:7–8; Rev. 2:2–3, et al.). As with most of the attributes of God that we are to imitate in our lives, patience requires a moment-by-moment trust in God to fulfill his promises and purposes in our lives at his chosen time. Our confidence that the Lord will soon fulfill his purposes for our good and his glory will enable us to be patient. James makes this connection when he says, "You also be patient. Establish your hearts, for the coming of the Lord is at hand" (James 5:8).

9. Holiness. *God's holiness means that he is separated from sin and devoted to seeking his own honor.* This definition contains both a relational quality (separation from) and a moral quality (the separation is from sin or evil, and the devotion is to the good of God's own honor or glory). The idea of holiness as including both separation from evil and devotion to God's own glory is found in a number of Old Testament passages. The word *holy* is used to describe both parts of the tabernacle, for example. The tabernacle itself was a place separate from the evil and sin of the world, and the first room in it was called the "holy place." It was dedicated to God's service. But then God commanded that there be a veil, "and the veil shall separate for you the holy place from the most holy" (Ex. 26:33). The most holy place, where the ark of the covenant was kept, was the place most separated from evil and sin and most fully devoted to God's service.

The place where God himself dwelt was itself holy: "Who shall ascend the hill of the LORD? And who shall stand in his holy place?" (Ps. 24:3). The element of dedication to God's service is seen in the holiness of the sabbath day: "the LORD blessed the sabbath day and made it holy" (or "hallowed it"; the verb is a Piel form of *qādash* and means "to make holy") (Ex. 20:11; cf. Gen. 2:3). The sabbath day was made holy because it was set apart from the ordinary activities of the world and dedicated to God's service. In the same way the tabernacle and the altar, as well as Aaron and his sons, were to be "made holy" (Ex. 29:44), that is, set apart from ordinary tasks and from the evil and sin of the world and dedicated to God's service (cf. Ex. 30:25–33).

God himself is the Most Holy One. He is called the "Holy One of Israel" (Pss. 71:22; 78:41; 89:18; Isa. 1:4; 5:19, 24, et al.). The seraphim around God's throne cry, "Holy, holy, holy is the LORD of hosts; the whole earth is full of his glory" (Isa. 6:3). "The LORD our God is holy!" exclaims the psalmist (Ps. 99:9; cf. 99:3, 5; 22:3).

God's holiness provides the pattern for his people to imitate. He commands them, "You shall be holy; for I the LORD your God am holy" (Lev. 19:2; cf. 11:44–45; 20:26; 1 Peter 1:16). When God called his people out of Egypt and brought them to himself and commanded them to obey his voice, then he said, "You shall be to me a kingdom of priests and a *holy nation*" (Ex. 19:4–6). In this case the idea of separation from evil and sin (which here included in a very striking way separation from life in Egypt) and the idea of devotion to God (in serving him and in obeying his statutes) are both seen in the example of a "holy nation."

New covenant believers are also to "strive . . . for the *holiness* without which no one will see the Lord" (Heb. 12:14) and to know that God's discipline is given to us "that we may share his holiness" (Heb. 12:10). Paul encourages Christians to be separate from the dominating influence that comes from close association with unbelievers (2 Cor. 6:14–18) and then encourages them, "Let us cleanse ourselves from every defilement of body and spirit, and *make holiness perfect in the fear of God*" (2 Cor. 7:1; cf. Rom.

12:1). The church itself is intended by God to grow "into a holy temple in the Lord" (Eph. 2:21), and Christ's present work for the church is "that he might sanctify her . . . that he might present the church to himself in splendor . . . that she might be holy and without blemish" (Eph. 5:26–27). Not only individuals but also the church itself must grow in holiness!

Zechariah prophesies a day when everything on earth will be "holy to the LORD." He says:

> And on that day there shall be inscribed on the bells of the horses, "Holy to the LORD." And the pots in the house of the LORD shall be as the bowls before the altar; and every pot in Jerusalem and Judah shall be sacred to the LORD of hosts. (Zech. 14:20–21)

At that time, everything on earth will be separated from evil, purified from sin, and devoted to the service of God in true moral purity.

10. Peace (or Order). In 1 Corinthians 14:33 Paul says, "God is not a God of confusion but of *peace.*" Although "peace" and "order" have not traditionally been classified as attributes of God, Paul here indicates another quality that we could think of as a distinct attribute of God. Paul says that God's actions are characterized by "peace" and not by "disorder" (Gk. *akatastasia,* a word meaning "disorder, confusion, unrest"). God himself is "the God of peace" (Rom. 15:33; 16:20; Phil. 4:9; 1 Thess. 5:23; Heb. 13:20; cf. Eph. 2:14; 2 Thess. 3:16). But those who walk in wickedness do not have peace: " 'There is no peace,' says the LORD, 'for the wicked' " (Isa. 48:22; 57:21; cf. 59:8).

However, when God looks with compassion upon the people whom he loves, he sees them as "afflicted . . . storm-tossed (LXX, *akatastatos,* "in disorder, in confusion"), and not comforted" (Isa. 54:11), and promises to establish their foundations with precious stones (Isa. 54:11–12) and lead them forth in "peace" (Isa. 55:12). The proclamation of God's plan of redemption contains the promise of peace to God's people (Pss. 29:11; 85:8; 119:165; Prov. 3:17; Isa. 9:6–7; 26:3; 57:19; John 14:27; Rom. 8:6; 2 Thess. 3:16, et al.). In fact, the third element that Paul lists as part of the fruit of the Spirit is "peace" (Gal. 5:22).

This peace certainly does not imply inactivity, for it was at a time of intense growth and activity that Luke could say that "the church throughout all Judea and Galilee and Samaria had peace and was built up" (Acts 9:31). Furthermore, although God is a God of peace, he is also the one who "will neither slumber nor sleep" (Ps. 121:4). He is the God who is continually working (John 5:17). And even though heaven is a place of peace, it is a place also of continual praise to God and service for him.

Thus, God's peace can be defined as follows: *God's peace means that in God's being and in his actions he is separate from all confusion and disorder, yet he is continually active in innumerable well-ordered, fully controlled, simultaneous actions.*

This definition indicates that God's peace does not have to do with inactivity, but with ordered and controlled activity. To engage in infinite activity of this sort, of course, requires God's infinite wisdom, knowledge, and power.

When we understand God's peace in this way we can see an imitation of this attribute of God not only in "peace" as part of the fruit of the Spirit in Galatians 5:22–23, but also in the last-mentioned element in the fruit of the Spirit, namely, "self-control"

(Gal. 5:23). When we as God's people walk in his ways, we come to know more and more fully by experience that the kingdom of God is indeed "righteousness and *peace* and joy in the Holy Spirit" (Rom. 14:17), and we can say of the path of God's wisdom, "Her ways are ways of pleasantness, and all her paths are *peace*" (Prov. 3:17).

11. Righteousness, Justice. In English the terms *righteousness* and *justice* are different words, but in both the Hebrew Old Testament and the Greek New Testament there is only one word group behind these two English terms. (In the Old Testament the terms primarily translate forms of the *tsedek* word group, and the New Testament members of the *dikaios* word group.) Therefore, these two terms will be considered together as speaking of one attribute of God.

God's righteousness means that God always acts in accordance with what is right and is himself the final standard of what is right.

Speaking of God, Moses says, "All his ways are *justice.* A God of faithfulness and without iniquity, *just* and *right* is he" (Deut. 32:4). Abraham successfully appeals to God's own character of righteousness when he says, "Shall not the Judge of all the earth do right?" (Gen. 18:25). God also speaks and commands what is right: "The precepts of the LORD are *right,* rejoicing the heart" (Ps. 19:8). And God says of himself, "I the LORD speak the truth, I declare what is *right*" (Isa. 45:19). As a result of God's righteousness, it is necessary that he treat people according to what they deserve. Thus, it is necessary that God punish sin, for it does not deserve reward; it is wrong and deserves punishment.

When God does not punish sin, it seems to indicate that he is unrighteous, unless some other means of punishing sin can be seen. This is why Paul says that when God sent Christ as a sacrifice to bear the punishment for sin, it "was to show God's righteousness, because in his divine forbearance he had passed over former sins; it was to prove at the present time that he himself is righteous and that he justifies him who has faith in Jesus" (Rom. 3:25–26). When Christ died to pay the penalty for our sins it showed that God was truly righteous, because he did give appropriate punishment to sin, even though he did forgive his people their sins.

With respect to the definition of righteousness given above, we may ask, what is "right"? In other words, what *ought* to happen and what *ought* to be? Here we must respond that *whatever conforms to God's moral character is right.* But why is whatever conforms to God's moral character right? It is right because it conforms to his moral character! If indeed God is the final standard of righteousness, then there can be no standard outside of God by which we measure righteousness or justice. He himself is the final standard. (This is similar to the situation we encountered with respect to truth and God being the ultimate standard of truth.) Whenever Scripture confronts the question of whether God himself is righteous or not, the ultimate answer is always that we as God's creatures have no right to say that God is unrighteous or unjust. The creature cannot say that of the Creator. Paul responds to a very difficult question about God's righteousness by saying, "But who are you, a man, to answer back to God? Will what is molded say to its molder, 'Why have you made me thus?' Has the potter no right over the clay, to make out of the same lump one vessel for beauty and another for menial use?" (Rom. 9:20–21).

In answer to Job's questioning about whether God has been righteous in his dealings with him, God answers Job, "Shall a faultfinder contend with the Almighty? . . . Will you even put me in the wrong? Will you condemn me that you may be justified?" (Job 40:2, 8). Then God answers *not* in terms of an explanation that would allow Job to *understand* why God's actions were right, but rather in terms of a statement of God's own majesty and power! God does not need to explain the rightness of his actions to Job, for God is the Creator and Job is the creature. "Have you an arm like God, and can you thunder with a voice like his?" (Job 40:9). "Have you commanded the morning since your days began, and caused the dawn to know its place . . . ?" (Job 38:12). "Can you lift up your voice to the clouds, that a flood of waters may cover you? Can you send forth lightnings, that they may go and say to you, 'Here we are'?" (Job 38:34–35). "Do you give the horse his might?" (Job 39:19). "Is it by your wisdom that the hawk soars, and spreads his wings toward the south?" (Job 39:26). Job answers, "Behold, I am of small account; what shall I answer you? I lay my hand on my mouth" (Job 40:4).

Nevertheless, it should be a cause for thanksgiving and gratitude when we realize that righteousness and omnipotence are both possessed by God. If he were a God of perfect righteousness without power to carry out that righteousness, he would not be worthy of worship and we would have no guarantee that justice will ultimately prevail in the universe. But if he were a God of unlimited power, yet without righteousness in his character, how unthinkably horrible the universe would be! There would be unrighteousness at the center of all existence and there would be nothing anyone could do to change it. Existence would become meaningless, and we would be driven to the most utter despair. We ought therefore continually to thank and praise God for who he is, "for *all his ways are justice. A God of faithfulness and without iniquity, just and right is he*" (Deut. 32:4).

12. Jealousy. Although the word *jealous* is frequently used in a negative sense in English, it also takes a positive sense at times. For example, Paul says to the Corinthians, "I feel a divine jealousy for you" (2 Cor. 11:2). Here the sense is "earnestly protective or watchful." It has the meaning of being deeply committed to seeking the honor or welfare of someone, whether oneself or someone else.

Scripture represents God as being jealous in this way. He continually and earnestly seeks to protect his own honor. He commands his people not to bow down to idols or serve them, saying, "for I the Lord your God am a *jealous* God" (Ex. 20:5). He desires that worship be given to himself and not to false gods. Therefore, he commands the people of Israel to tear down the altars of pagan gods in the land of Canaan, giving the following reason: "For you shall worship no other god, for the Lord, whose name is Jealous, is a jealous God" (Ex. 34:14; cf. Deut. 4:24; 5:9).

Thus, God's jealousy may be defined as follows: *God's jealousy means that God continually seeks to protect his own honor.*

People sometimes have trouble thinking that jealousy is a desirable attribute in God. This is because jealousy for our own honor as human beings is almost always wrong. We are not to be proud, but humble. Yet we must realize that the reason pride is wrong is a theological reason: it is that we do not deserve the honor that belongs to God alone (cf. 1 Cor. 4:7; Rev. 4:11).

It is not wrong for God to seek his own honor, however, for he deserves it fully. God freely admits that his actions in creation and redemption are done for his own honor.

Speaking of his decision to withhold judgment from his people, God says, "For my own sake, for my own sake, I do it. . . . *My glory I will not give to another*" (Isa. 48:11). It is healthy for us spiritually when we settle in our hearts the fact that God deserves all honor and glory from his creation, and that it is right for him to seek this honor. He alone is infinitely worthy of being praised. To realize this fact and to delight in it is to find the secret of true worship.

13. Wrath. It may surprise us to find how frequently the Bible talks about the wrath of God. Yet if God loves all that is right and good, and all that conforms to his moral character, then it should not be surprising that he would hate everything that is opposed to his moral character. God's wrath directed against sin is therefore closely related to God's holiness and justice. God's wrath may be defined as follows: *God's wrath means that he intensely hates all sin.*

Descriptions of God's wrath are found frequently in the narrative passages of Scripture, especially when God's people sin greatly against him. God sees the idolatry of the people of Israel and says to Moses, "I have seen this people . . . ; now therefore let me alone, that my *wrath* may burn hot against them and I may consume them" (Ex. 32:9–10). Later Moses tells the people, "Remember and do not forget how you provoked the LORD your God to *wrath* in the wilderness. . . . Even at Horeb you provoked the LORD to *wrath*, and the LORD was so angry with you that he was ready to destroy you" (Deut. 9:7–8; cf. 29:23; 2 Kings 22:13).

The doctrine of the wrath of God in Scripture is not limited to the Old Testament, however, as some have falsely imagined. We read in John 3:36, "He who believes in the Son has eternal life; he who does not obey the Son shall not see life, but *the wrath of God rests upon him.*" Paul says, "For the *wrath of God* is revealed from heaven against all ungodliness and wickedness of men" (Rom. 1:18; cf. 2:5, 8; 5:9; 9:22; Col. 3:6; 1 Thess. 1:10; 2:16; 5:9; Heb. 3:11; Rev. 6:16–17; 19:15). Many more New Testament verses also indicate God's wrath against sin.

As with the other attributes of God, this is an attribute for which we should thank and praise God. It may not immediately appear to us how this can be done, since wrath seems to be such a negative concept. Viewed alone, it would arouse only fear and dread. Yet it is helpful for us to ask what God would be like if he were a God that did not hate sin. He would then be a God who either delighted in sin or at least was not troubled by it. Such a God would not be worthy of our worship, for sin is hateful and it is *worthy* of being hated. Sin ought not to be. It is in fact a virtue to hate evil and sin (cf. Heb. 1:9; Zech. 8:17, et al.), and we rightly imitate this attribute of God when we feel hatred against great evil, injustice, and sin.[9]

Furthermore, we should feel no fear of God's wrath as Christians, for although "we were by nature children of wrath, like the rest of mankind" (Eph. 2:3), we now have trusted in Jesus, "who delivers us from the wrath to come" (1 Thess. 1:10; cf. Rom. 5:10). When we meditate on the wrath of God, we will be amazed to think that our Lord Jesus Christ bore the wrath of God that was due to our sin, in order that we might be saved (Rom. 3:25–26).

---

[9]It is appropriate for us in this regard to "hate the sin but love the sinner," as a popular slogan puts it.

Moreover, in thinking about God's wrath we must also bear in mind his patience. Both patience and wrath are mentioned together in Psalm 103: "The LORD is . . . *slow to anger* and abounding in steadfast love. He will not always chide, nor will he keep his anger for ever" (Ps. 103:8–9). In fact, the delay of the execution of God's wrath upon evil is for the purpose of leading people to repentance (see Rom. 2:4).

Thus, when we think of God's wrath to come, we should simultaneously be thankful for his patience in waiting to execute that wrath in order that yet more people may be saved: "The Lord is not slow about his promise as some count slowness, but is forbearing toward you, not wishing that any should perish, but that all should reach repentance. But the day of the Lord will come like a thief, and then the heavens will pass away with a loud noise . . ." (2 Peter 3:9–10). God's wrath should motivate us to evangelism and should also cause us to be thankful that God finally will punish all wrongdoing and will reign over new heavens and a new earth in which there will be no unrighteousness.

QUESTIONS FOR PERSONAL APPLICATION

Spirituality

1. Why is God so strongly displeased at carved idols, even those that are intended to represent him? How then shall we picture God or think of God in our minds when we pray to him?

2. What is it about our culture or our way of thinking today that makes us think of the physical world as more real and more permanent than the spiritual world? What can we do to change our intuitive perspective on the reality of the spiritual world?

Knowledge

3. When should we try to hide our thoughts and deeds from God? How is your answer to this question a blessing for your life?

4. With regard to the circumstances of your life, will God ever make a mistake, or fail to plan ahead, or fail to take into account all the eventualities that occur? How is the answer to this question a blessing in your life?

5. When did God learn that you would be at the location you are now in, reading this sentence, at this time on this day? How is the realization of your answer to this question a blessing to your life?

Wisdom

6. Do you really believe that God is working wisely today in your life? In the world? If you find this difficult to believe at times, what might you do to change your attitude?

Truthfulness

7. Why are people in our society, sometimes even Christians, quite careless with regard to truthfulness in speech? Why do we not very often realize that the greatest harm of all that comes from lying is the fact that God himself is dishonored?

Do you need to ask God's help to more fully reflect his truthfulness in speech in any of the following areas: promising to pray for someone; saying that you will be some place at a certain time; exaggerating events to make a more exciting story; taking care to remember and then be faithful to what you have said in business commitments; reporting what other people have said or what you think someone else is thinking; fairly representing your opponent's viewpoint in an argument?

Goodness

8. Remembering that every good and perfect gift is from God (James 1:17), see how many good gifts from God you can list on a piece of paper in five minutes. When you have finished, ask yourself how often you have an attitude of thankfulness to God for most of these gifts. Why do you think we tend to forget that these blessings come from God? What can we do to remember more frequently?

Love

9. Is it appropriate to define love as "self-giving" with respect to our own interpersonal relationships? In what ways could you imitate God's love specifically today?

10. Is it possible to decide to love someone and then to act on that decision, or does love between human beings simply depend on spontaneous emotional feelings?

Mercy

11. If you were to reflect God's mercy more fully, for whom among those you know would you show special care during the next week?

Holiness

12. Are there activities or relationships in your present pattern of life that are hindering your growth in holiness because they make it difficult for you to be separated from sin and devoted to seeking God's honor?

Peace

13. As you think about reflecting God's peace in your own life, think first about your own emotional, mental, and spiritual state. Can you say that by-and-large you have God's peace in the sense that your inner life is separate from confusion and disorder, and is frequently or continually active in well-ordered and well-controlled actions that further God's glory? Then ask the same questions concerning what may be called the "external circumstances" of your life, that is, your family relationships, your relationships with neighbors, your activities in studying or at your job, and your relationships in church activities. What about the overall picture of your life, viewed as a whole? Does it exhibit God's peace? What might you do to reflect God's peace more fully?

Righteousness

14. Do you ever find yourself wishing that some of God's laws were different than they are? If so, does such a wish reflect a dislike for some aspect of God's moral character? What passages of Scripture might you read to convince yourself more fully that God's character and his laws are right in these areas?

Jealousy

15. Do you reflect God's jealousy for his own honor instinctively when you hear him dishonored in conversation or on television or in other contexts? What can we do to deepen our jealousy for God's honor?

Wrath

16. Should we love the fact that God is a God of wrath who hates sin? In what ways is it right for us to imitate this wrath, and in what ways is it wrong for us to do so?

SPECIAL TERMS

attributes of being	jealousy	patience
beatific vision	justice	peace
communicable attributes	knowledge	reasonable self-
faithfulness	love	determination
good	mental attributes	righteousness
goodness	mercy	spirituality
grace	moral attributes	theophany
holiness	omniscience	truthfulness
impassible	one simple and eternal	veracity
invisibility	act	wisdom
	order	wrath

BIBLIOGRAPHY

Since chapters 5 and 6 are so closely related in subject matter, the bibliographic material for both is at the end of chapter 6.

SCRIPTURE MEMORY PASSAGE

Exodus 34:6–7: *The LORD passed before him, and proclaimed, "The LORD, the LORD, a God merciful and gracious, slow to anger, and abounding in steadfast love and faithfulness, keeping steadfast love for thousands, forgiving iniquity and transgression and sin, but who will by no means clear the guilty, visiting the iniquity of the fathers upon the children and the children's children, to the third and the fourth generation."*

Note: The last section of this passage speaks of God "visiting the iniquity of the fathers upon the children and the children's children." Some might want to stop short of this part in memorizing the passage, but we should remember that this, too, is Scripture and is written for our edification. This statement shows the horrible nature of sin in the way it has effects far beyond the individual sinner, also harming those around the sinner and harming future generations as well. We see this in tragic ways in ordinary life, where the children of alcoholics often become alcoholics and the children of abusive parents often become abusive parents.

Christians who are forgiven by Christ should not think of these phrases as applying to them, however, for they are in the other category of people mentioned just before this section on "the guilty": they are among the "thousands" to whom God continually shows "steadfast love," and is continually "forgiving iniquity and transgression and sin" (v. 7). When someone comes to Christ the chain of sin is broken. Here it is important to remember Peter's words: "You know that *you were ransomed from the futile ways inherited from your fathers,* not with perishable things such as silver or gold, but with the precious blood of Christ" (1 Peter 1:18 – 19).

HYMN

"O Worship the King"

Almost the entire hymnbook could be used to sing of one aspect or another of God's character. Literally hundreds of hymns would be appropriate. Yet this hymn contains a listing of many of God's attributes and combines them in such a way that the hymn is worthy of being sung again and again. Verse 1 speaks of God's glory, power, love; verse 2 speaks of his might, grace, wrath; and so forth. In verse 6, "ineffable" means "incapable of being expressed fully." The hymn is written as an encouragement for Christians to sing to one another, exhorting each other to "worship the King, all glorious above." Yet in the process of such exhortation the song itself also contains much high praise.

> O worship the King all glorious above,
> O gratefully sing his pow'r and his love;
> Our shield and defender, the Ancient of Days,
> Pavilioned in splendor, and girded with praise.
>
> O tell of his might, O sing of his grace,
> Whose robe is the light, whose canopy space.
> His chariots of wrath the deep thunder-clouds form,
> And dark is his path on the wings of the storm.
>
> The earth with its store of wonders untold,
> Almighty, your power has founded of old;
> Has 'stablished it fast by a changeless decree,
> And round it has cast, like a mantle, the sea.
>
> Your bountiful care what tongue can recite?
> It breathes in the air; it shines in the light;
> It streams from the hills; it descends to the plain;
> And sweetly distills in the dew and the rain.
>
> Frail children of dust, and feeble as frail,
> In you do we trust, nor find you to fail;
> Your mercies how tender, how firm to the end,
> Our maker, defender, redeemer, and friend!
>
> O measureless might! Ineffable love!
> While angels delight to hymn you above,
> The humbler creation, though feeble their ways,
> With true adoration shall lisp to your praise.

AUTHOR: SIR ROBERT GRANT, 1833 (BASED ON PSALM 104)

Alternative hymn: "Round the Lord in Glory Seated"

Chapter 6

THE CHARACTER OF GOD: "COMMUNICABLE" ATTRIBUTES (PART 2)

How is God like us in attributes of will and in attributes that summarize his excellence?

In the previous chapter we discussed the attributes of God that described his *being* (spirituality, invisibility), his *mental* attributes (knowledge, wisdom, and truthfulness), and his *moral* attributes (goodness, love, mercy, grace, patience, holiness, peace, righteousness, jealousy, and wrath). In this chapter we will examine God's attributes of *purpose*, that is, attributes that have to do with making and carrying out decisions (will, freedom, and omnipotence) and his *summary* attributes (perfection, blessedness, beauty, and glory).

D. Attributes of Purpose

In this category of attributes we will discuss first God's will in general, then the freedom of God's will, and finally the omnipotence (or infinite power) of God's will.

14. Will. *God's will is that attribute of God whereby he approves and determines to bring about every action necessary for the existence and activity of himself and all creation.*

This definition indicates that God's will has to do with deciding and approving the things that God is and does. It concerns God's choices of what to do and what not to do.

a. God's Will in General: Scripture frequently indicates God's will as the final or most ultimate reason for everything that happens. Paul refers to God as the one "who accomplishes all things *according to the counsel of his will*" (Eph. 1:11). The phrase here translated "all things" (*ta panta*) is used frequently by Paul to refer to everything that exists or everything in creation (see, for example, Eph. 1:10, 23; 3:9; 4:10; Col. 1:16 [twice], 17;

Rom. 11:36; 1 Cor. 8:6 [twice]; 15:27–28 [twice]).[1] The word translated "accomplishes" (*energeō*, "works, works out, brings about, produces") is a present participle and suggests continual activity. The phrase might more explicitly be translated, "who continually brings about everything in the universe according to the counsel of his will."

More specifically, all things were created by God's will: "For you created all things, and *by your will they existed and were created*" (Rev. 4:11). Both Old and New Testaments speak of human government as coming about according to God's will: the voice from heaven tells Nebuchadnezzar that he is to learn "that the Most High rules the kingdom of men and gives it to whom he will" (Dan. 4:32), and Paul says that "there is no authority except from God, and those that exist have been instituted by God" (Rom. 13:1).

All the events connected with the death of Christ were according to God's will, the church at Jerusalem believed, for in their prayer they said, "truly in this city there were gathered together against your holy servant Jesus, whom you anointed, both Herod and Pontius Pilate, with all the Gentiles and the peoples of Israel, to do *whatever your hand and your plan had predestined to take place*" (Acts 4:27–28). The specific mention of the various parties involved at different stages of the crucifixion, together with the indefiniteness of the plural relative pronoun "whatever" (Gk. *hosa*, "the things which") implies that not simply the fact of Jesus' death but all the detailed events connected with it are comprehended in this statement: God's hand and will had predestined that all those things would come about.

Sometimes it is God's will that Christians suffer, as is seen in 1 Peter 3:17, for example: "For it is better to suffer for doing right, *if that should be God's will,* than for doing wrong." Then in the next chapter Peter says, "Therefore let those who suffer *according to God's will* do right and entrust their souls to a faithful Creator" (1 Peter 4:19). In this verse, the phrase "according to God's will" cannot refer to the manner in which Christians endure suffering, for then it would make the verse say essentially, "Let those who suffer *while doing right, do right* and entrust their souls. . . ." This would make the phrase "according to God's will" redundant. Rather, the phrase "according to God's will" must refer to the fact that these Christians are suffering, just as "God's will" referred to suffering in the previous chapter (1 Peter 3:17).

James encourages us to see all the events of our lives as subject to God's will. To those who say, "Today or tomorrow we will go into such and such a town and spend a year there and trade and get gain," James says, "You do not know about tomorrow. . . . Instead you ought to say, '*if the Lord wills,* we shall live and we shall do this or that'" (James 4:13–15). To attribute so many events, even evil events, to the will of God often causes misunderstanding and difficulty for Christians. Some of the difficulties connected with this subject will be treated here and others will be dealt with in chapter 9 on God's providence.

b. Distinctions in Aspects of God's Will: (1) Necessary will and free will: Some distinctions made in the past may help us understand various aspects of God's will. Just as

---

[1]The phrase does not always carry that meaning (cf. Rom. 11:32; 1 Cor. 12:6; 2 Cor. 12:19), but in contexts where the scope of Paul's thought is cosmic or universal in nature (as in this passage), the phrase does seem quite clearly to refer to everything in all creation.

we can will or choose something eagerly or reluctantly, happily or with regret, secretly or publicly, so also God in the infinite greatness of his personality is able to will different things in different ways.

One helpful distinction applied to aspects of God's will is the distinction between God's *necessary will* and God's *free will*. God's necessary will includes everything that he must will according to his own nature. What does God will necessarily? He wills himself. God eternally wills to be, or wants to be, who he is and what he is. He says, "I AM WHO I AM" or, "I WILL BE WHAT I WILL BE" (Ex. 3:14). God *cannot* choose to be different than he is or to cease to exist.

God's *free will* includes all things that God decided to will but had no necessity to will according to his nature. Here we must put God's decision to create the universe, and all the decisions relating to the details of that creation. Here we must also place all God's acts of redemption. There was nothing in God's own nature that required him to decide to create the universe or to redeem out of sinful mankind a people for himself (see the discussion above concerning God's independence). However, God did decide to create and to redeem, and these were totally free choices on his part. Though within the members of the Trinity love and fellowship and glory exist in infinite measure for all eternity (see John 17:5, 24), nonetheless God decided to create the universe and to redeem us for his own glory (cf. Isa. 43:7; 48:9–11; Rom. 11:36; 1 Cor. 8:6; Eph. 1:12; Rev. 4:11). It would be wrong for us ever to try to find a necessary cause for creation or redemption in the being of God himself, for that would rob God of his total independence. It would be to say that without us God could not truly be God. God's decisions to create and to redeem were totally free decisions.

(2) Secret will and revealed will: Another helpful distinction applied to different aspects of God's will is the distinction between God's *secret will* and his *revealed will*. Even in our own experience we know that we are able to will some things secretly and then only later make this will known to others. Sometimes we tell others before the thing that we have willed comes about, and at other times we do not reveal our secret will until the event we willed has happened.

Surely a distinction between aspects of God's will is evident in many passages of Scripture. According to Moses, "The *secret things* belong to the LORD our God; but the *things that are revealed* belong to us and to our children for ever, that we may do all the words of this law" (Deut. 29:29). Those things that God has revealed are given for the purpose of obeying God's will: "that we may *do* all the words of this law." There were many other aspects of his plan, however, that he had not revealed to them: many details about future events, specific details of hardship or of blessing in their lives, and so forth. With regard to these matters, they were simply to trust him.

Because God's revealed will usually contains his commands or "precepts" for our moral conduct, God's revealed will is sometimes also called God's *will of precept* or will of command. This revealed will of God is God's declared will concerning *what we should do* or what God *commands* us to do.

On the other hand, God's secret will usually includes his hidden decrees by which he governs the universe and determines everything that will happen. He does not ordinarily reveal these decrees to us (except in prophecies of the future), so these decrees really are God's "secret" will. We find out what God has decreed when events actually happen. Because this secret will of God has to do with his decreeing of events in the world, this aspect of God's will is sometimes also called God's *will of decree*.[2]

There are several instances where Scripture mentions God's revealed will. In the Lord's prayer the petition, "*Your will be done,* On earth as it is in heaven" (Matt. 6:10) is a prayer that people would obey God's *revealed* will, his commands, on earth just as they do in heaven (that is, fully and completely). This could not be a prayer that God's secret will (that is, his decrees for events that he has planned) would in fact be fulfilled, for what God has decreed in his secret will shall certainly come to pass. To ask God to bring about what he has already decreed to happen would simply be to pray, "May what is going to happen happen." That would be a hollow prayer indeed, for it would not be asking for anything at all. Furthermore, since we do not know God's secret will regarding the future, the person praying a prayer for God's secret will to be done would never know for what he or she was praying. It would be a prayer without understandable content and without effect. Rather, the prayer "*Your will* be done" must be understood as an appeal for the *revealed* will of God to be followed on earth.

If the phrase is understood in this way, it provides a pattern for us to pray on the basis of God's commands in Scripture. In this sense, Jesus provides us with a guide for an exceedingly broad range of prayer requests. We are encouraged by Christ here to pray that people would obey God's laws, that they would follow his principles for life, that they would obey his commands to repent of sin and trust in Christ as Savior. To pray these things is to pray that God's will would be done on earth as it is in heaven.

A little later, Jesus says, "Not every one who says to me, 'Lord, Lord,' shall enter the kingdom of heaven, but he who does the *will* of my Father who is in heaven" (Matt. 7:21). Once again, the reference cannot be to God's secret will or will of decree (for all mankind follows this, even if unknowingly), but to God's *revealed* will, namely, the moral law of God that Christ's followers are to obey (cf. Matt. 12:50; probably also 18:14). When Paul commands the Ephesians to "understand *what the will of the Lord is*" (Eph. 5:17; cf. Rom. 2:18), he again is speaking of God's revealed will. So also is John when he says, "If we ask anything *according to his will* he hears us" (1 John 5:14).

It is probably best to put 1 Timothy 2:4 and 2 Peter 3:9 in this category as well. Paul says that God "*desires* [or 'wills, wishes,' Gk. *theleō*] all men to be saved and to come to the knowledge of the truth" (1 Tim. 2:4). Peter says that the Lord "is not slow about his promise as some count slowness, but is forbearing toward you, not wishing that any should perish, but that all should reach repentance" (2 Peter 3:9). In neither of these verses can God's will be understood to be his secret will, his decree concerning what will certainly occur. This is because the New Testament is clear that there will be a final judgment and not all will be saved. It is best therefore to understand these references as speaking of God's *revealed will,* his commands for mankind to obey and his declaration to us of what is pleasing in his sight.

On the other hand, many passages speak of God's secret will. When James tells us to say, "*If the Lord wills,* we shall live and we shall do this or that" (James 4:15), he cannot

---

[2]See the discussion of God's decrees in chapter 9, pp. 219–20.

be talking about God's revealed will or will of precept, for with regard to many of our actions we *know* that it is according to God's command that we do one or another activity that we have planned. Rather, to trust in the secret will of God overcomes pride and expresses humble dependence on God's sovereign control over the events of our lives.

Another instance is found in Genesis 50:20. Joseph says to his brothers, "As for you, you meant evil against me; but *God meant it for good,* to bring it about that many people should be kept alive, as they are today." Here God's *revealed* will to Joseph's brothers was that they should love him and not steal from him or sell him into slavery or make plans to murder him. But God's *secret* will was that in the disobedience of Joseph's brothers a greater good would be done when Joseph, having been sold into slavery into Egypt, gained authority over the land and was able to save his family.

When Paul says to the Corinthians, "I will come to you soon, *if the Lord wills*" (1 Cor. 4:19), he is not speaking of God's revealed will, for Paul has already determined, in obedience to God and in fulfillment of his apostolic office, to come to visit the Corinthians. He is speaking rather of God's secret will, his hidden plan for the future, which is unknown to Paul and which will be known only as it comes to pass (cf. Acts 21:14; Rom. 1:10; 15:32; Eph. 1:11; 1 Peter 3:17; 4:19).[3]

Both the revealing of the good news of the gospel to some and its hiding from others are said to be according to God's will. Jesus says, "I thank you, Father, Lord of heaven and earth, that you have hidden these things from the wise and understanding and revealed them to babes; yea, Father, *for such was your gracious will*" (Matt. 11:25–26). This again must refer to God's secret will, for his revealed will is that all come to salvation. Indeed, only two verses later, Jesus commands everyone, "Come to me, all who labor and are heavy laden, and I will give you rest" (Matt. 11:28). And both Paul and Peter tell us that God wills all people to be saved (see 1 Tim. 2:4; 2 Peter 3:9). Thus, the fact that some are not saved and some have the gospel hidden from them must be understood as happening according to God's secret will, unknown to us and inappropriate for us to seek to pry into. In the same way we must understand the mention of God's will in Romans 9:18 ("He has mercy upon whomever he wills, and he hardens the heart of whomever he wills") and Acts 4:28 ("to do whatever your hand and your plan had predestined to take place") as references to God's secret will.

There is danger in speaking about evil events as happening according to the will of God, even though we see Scripture speaking of them in this way. One danger is that we might begin to think that God takes pleasure in evil, which he does not do (see Ezek. 33:11), though he can use it for his good purposes (see chapter 9 for further discussion). Another danger is that we might begin to blame God for sin, rather than ourselves, or to think that we are not responsible for our evil actions. Scripture, however, does not hesitate to couple statements of God's sovereign will with statements of man's responsibility for evil. Peter could say in the same sentence that Jesus was "delivered up according to the definite plan and foreknowledge of God," and also that "this Jesus . . . *you crucified and killed* by the hands of *lawless men*" (Acts 2:23). Both God's hidden will of decree

---

[3]In Eph. 1:9–10 Paul says that God "has made known to us . . . the mystery of his will . . . to unite all things in him." Here he tells us that part of God's secret will has become God's revealed will because God made it known to the apostles and then to the church.

and the culpable wickedness of "lawless men" in carrying it out are affirmed in the same statement. However we may understand the secret workings of God's hidden will, we must never understand it to imply that we are freed from responsibility for evil, or that God is ever to be blamed for sin. Scripture never speaks that way, and we may not either, even though how this can be so may remain a mystery for us in this age.[4]

15. Freedom. *God's freedom is that attribute of God whereby he does whatever he pleases.* This definition implies that nothing in all creation can hinder God from doing his will. This attribute of God is therefore closely related to his will and his power. Yet this aspect of freedom focuses on the fact that God is not constrained by anything external to himself and that he is free to do whatever he wishes to do. There is no person or force that can ever dictate to God what he should do. He is under no authority or external restraint.

God's freedom is mentioned in Psalm 115, where his great power is contrasted with the weakness of idols: "Our God is in the heavens; *he does whatever he pleases*" (Ps. 115:3). Human rulers are not able to stand against God and effectively oppose his will, for "the king's heart is a stream of water in the hand of the LORD; he turns it wherever he will" (Prov. 21:1). Similarly, Nebuchadnezzar learns in his repentance that it is true to say of God, "*he does according to his will* in the host of heaven and among the inhabitants of the earth; and none can stay his hand or say to him, 'What are you doing?'" (Dan. 4:35).

Because God is free we should not try to seek any more ultimate answer for God's actions in creation than the fact that he willed to do something and that his will has perfect freedom (so long as the actions he takes are consistent with his own moral character). Sometimes people try to discover the reason why God had to do one or another action (such as create the world or save us). It is better simply to say that it was God's totally free will (working in a way consistent with his character) that was the final reason why he chose to create the world and to save sinners.

16. Omnipotence (Power, Sovereignty). *God's omnipotence means that God is able to do all his holy will.* The word *omnipotence* is derived from two Latin words, *omni,* "all," and *potens,* "powerful," and means "all-powerful." Whereas God's freedom referred to the fact that there are no external constraints on God's decisions, God's omnipotence has reference to his own power to do what he decides to do.

This power is frequently mentioned in Scripture. God is "The LORD, strong and mighty, the LORD, mighty in battle!" (Ps. 24:8). The rhetorical question, "Is anything too hard for the LORD?" (Gen. 18:14; Jer. 32:27) certainly implies (in the contexts in which it occurs) that nothing is too hard for the LORD. In fact, Jeremiah says to God, "*nothing* is too hard for you" (Jer. 32:17).

Paul says that God is "able to do far more abundantly than all that we ask or think" (Eph. 3:20), and God is called the "Almighty" (2 Cor. 6:18; Rev. 1:8), a term (Gk.

---

[4]See chapter 9, pp. 209–17, 230 for further discussion of the relationship between the will of God and evil. See also the excellent essay by John Piper, "Are There Two Wills in God? Divine Election and God's Desire for All to Be Saved," in *Still Sovereign,* ed. by Tom Schreiner and Bruce Ware (Grand Rapids: Baker, 2000).

pantokratōr) that suggests the possession of all power and authority. Furthermore, the angel Gabriel says to Mary, "With God nothing will be impossible" (Luke 1:37), and Jesus says, "With God *all things are possible*" (Matt. 19:26).

These passages indicate that God's power is infinite, and that he is therefore not limited to doing only what he actually has done. In fact, God is able to do more than he actually does. For example, John the Baptist says in Matthew 3:9, "God is able from these stones to raise up children to Abraham." God is one who "does whatever he pleases" (Ps. 115:3); he could have destroyed Israel and raised up a great nation from Moses (cf. Ex. 32:10), but he did not do so.

However, there are some things that God cannot do. God cannot will or do anything that would deny his own character. This is why the definition of omnipotence is stated in terms of God's ability to do "all his holy will." It is not absolutely everything that God is able to do, but everything that is consistent with his character. For example, God cannot lie. In Titus 1:2 he is called (literally) "the unlying God" or the "God who never lies." The author of Hebrews says that in God's oath and promise "it is impossible for God to lie" (Heb. 6:18, author's translation). Second Timothy 2:13 says of Christ, "He cannot deny himself." Furthermore, James says, "God cannot be tempted with evil and he himself tempts no one" (James 1:13). Thus, God cannot lie, sin, deny himself, or be tempted with evil. He cannot cease to exist, or cease to be God, or act in a way inconsistent with any of his attributes.

This means that it is not entirely accurate to say that God can do anything. Even the Scripture passages quoted above that use phrases similar to this must be understood in their contexts to mean that God can do anything he wills to do or anything that is consistent with his character. Although God's power is infinite, his use of that power is qualified by his other attributes (just as all God's attributes qualify all his actions). This is therefore another instance where misunderstanding would result if one attribute were isolated from the rest of God's character and emphasized in a disproportionate way.

God's exercise of power over his creation is also called God's *sovereignty*. God's sovereignty is his exercise of rule (as "sovereign" or "king") over his creation. This subject will be discussed in more detail in chapter 9, on God's providence.

As we conclude our treatment of God's attributes of purpose, it is appropriate to realize that he has made us in such a way that we show in our lives some faint reflection of each of them. God has made us as creatures with a *will*. We exercise choice and make real decisions regarding the events of our lives. Although our will is not absolutely free in the way God's is, God has nonetheless given us *relative freedom* within our spheres of activity in the universe he has created.

In fact, we have an intuitive sense that it is our ability to exercise our wills and make choices, and to do so in a relatively free way, that is one of the most significant marks of God-likeness in our existence. Of course our desire to exercise our wills and our desire to be free from restraint can show themselves in sinful ways. People can become proud and can desire a kind of freedom that involves rebellion against God's authority and a refusal to obey his will. Nonetheless, when we use our will and our freedom to make choices that are pleasing to God, we reflect his character and bring glory to him. When human beings are deprived of their ability to make free choices by evil governments or by other circumstances, a significant part of their God-likeness is suppressed. It is not surprising that they will pay almost any price to regain their freedom. American revolutionary Patrick Henry's cry, "Give me liberty or give me death!" finds an echo deep within every soul created in the image of God.

We do not of course have infinite power or omnipotence any more than we have infinite freedom or any of God's other attributes to an infinite degree. But even though we do not have omnipotence, God has given us *power* to bring about results, both physical power and other kinds of power: mental power, spiritual power, persuasive power, and power in various kinds of authority structures (family, church, civil government, and so forth). In all of these areas, the use of power in ways pleasing to God and consistent with his will is again something that brings him glory as it reflects his own character.

E. "Summary" Attributes

17. Perfection. *God's perfection means that God completely possesses all excellent qualities and lacks no part of any qualities that would be desirable for him.*

It is difficult to decide whether this should be listed as a separate attribute or simply be included in the description of the other attributes. Some passages say that God is "perfect" or "complete." Jesus tells us, "You, therefore, must be perfect, *as your heavenly Father is perfect*" (Matt. 5:48). And David says of God, "His way is *perfect*" (Ps. 18:30; cf. Deut. 32:4). There is some scriptural precedent, therefore, for stating explicitly that God lacks nothing in his excellence: he fully possesses all of his attributes and lacks nothing from any one of those attributes. Furthermore, there is no quality of excellence that it would be desirable for God to have that he does not have: he is "complete" or "perfect" in every way.

This attribute is the first of those classified as a "summary" attribute because it does not fit well into the other categories that have been listed. Even though all the attributes of God modify all the others in some senses, those that fit in this category seem more directly to apply to all the attributes or to describe some aspect of all of the attributes that it is worthwhile to state explicitly.

18. Blessedness. To be "blessed" is to be happy in a very full and rich sense. Often Scripture talks about the blessedness of those people who walk in God's ways. Yet in 1 Timothy Paul calls God "the *blessed* and only Sovereign" (1 Tim. 6:15) and speaks of "the glorious gospel of the *blessed* God" (1 Tim. 1:11). In both instances the word is not *eulogētos* (which is often translated "blessed"), but *makarios* (which means "happy").

Thus, God's blessedness may be defined as follows: *God's blessedness means that God delights fully in himself and in all that reflects his character.* In this definition the idea of God's happiness or blessedness is connected directly to his own person as the focus of all that is worthy of joy or delight. This definition indicates that God is perfectly happy, that he has fullness of joy in himself.

The definition reflects the fact that God takes pleasure in everything in creation that mirrors his own excellence. When he finished his work of creation, he looked at everything that he had made and saw that it was "very good" (Gen. 1:31). This indicates God's delight in and approval of his creation. Then in Isaiah we read a promise of God's future rejoicing over his people: "As the bridegroom rejoices over the bride, so shall your God rejoice over you" (Isa. 62:5; cf. Prov. 8:30–31; Zeph. 3:17).

It may at first seem strange or even somewhat disappointing to us that when God rejoices in his creation, or even when he rejoices in us, it is really the reflection of his own excellent qualities in which he is rejoicing. But when we remember that the sum of everything that is desirable or excellent is found in infinite measure in God himself, then we realize that it could not be otherwise: *whatever* excellence there is in the universe, *whatever* is desirable, must ultimately have come from him, for he is the Creator of all and he is the source of all good. "*Every* good endowment and *every* perfect gift is from above, coming down from the Father of lights with whom there is no variation or shadow due to change" (James 1:17).

We ought therefore to say to ourselves, as Paul says to the Corinthians, "What have you that you did not receive? If then you received it, why do you boast as if it were not a gift?" (1 Cor. 4:7). "For from him and through him and to him are all things. To him be glory for ever" (Rom. 11:36).

We imitate God's blessedness when we find delight and happiness in all that is pleasing to God, both those aspects of our own lives that are pleasing to God and the deeds of others. In fact, when we are thankful for and delight in the specific abilities, preferences, and other characteristics with which God has created us as individuals, then we also imitate his attribute of blessedness. Furthermore, we imitate God's blessedness by rejoicing in the creation as it reflects various aspects of his excellent character. And we find our greatest blessedness, our greatest happiness, in delighting in the source of all good qualities, God himself.

19. Beauty. *God's beauty is that attribute of God whereby he is the sum of all desirable qualities.* This attribute of God has been implicit in a number of the preceding attributes, and is especially related to God's perfection. However, God's perfection was defined in such a way as to show that he does not *lack* anything that would be desirable for him. This attribute, beauty, is defined in a positive way to show that God actually does possess all desirable qualities: "perfection" means that God doesn't lack anything desirable; "beauty" means that God has everything desirable. They are two different ways of affirming the same truth.

Nevertheless, there is value in affirming this positive aspect of God's possession of everything that is desirable. It reminds us that all of our good and righteous desires, all of the desires that really ought to be in us or in any other creature, find their ultimate fulfillment in God and in no one else.

David speaks of the beauty of the LORD in Psalm 27:4: "One thing have I asked of the LORD, that will I seek after; that I may dwell in the house of the LORD all the days of my life, to behold *the beauty of the LORD,* and to inquire in his temple." A similar idea is expressed in another psalm: "Whom have I in heaven but you? And there is nothing upon earth that I desire besides you" (Ps. 73:25). In both cases, the psalmist recognizes that his desire for God, who is the sum of everything desirable, far surpasses all other desires. This desire culminates in a longing to be near God and to enjoy his presence forevermore. Thus, the greatest blessing of the heavenly city shall be this: "They shall see his face" (Rev. 22:4).

Anne R. Cousin certainly had a proper perspective on heaven, for in the last stanza of her hymn, "The Sands of Time are Sinking" she wrote:

> The bride eyes not her garment,
>> But her dear bridegroom's face.
> I will not gaze at glory,
>> But on my King of grace;
> Not at the crown he giveth,
>> But on his pierced hand:
> The Lamb is all the glory
>> Of Emmanuel's land.

We reflect God's beauty in our own lives when we exhibit conduct that is pleasing to him. Thus, Peter tells wives in the churches to which he writes that their "adorning" (that is, their source of beauty) should be "the hidden person of the heart with the imperishable jewel of a gentle and quiet spirit, which in God's sight is very precious" (1 Peter 3:4). Similarly, Paul instructs servants that by their conduct they should "*adorn the doctrine of God our Savior*" (Titus 2:10).

The beauty of our lives is so important to Christ that his purpose now is to sanctify the entire church "that he might present the church to himself in splendor, without spot or wrinkle or any such thing, that she might be holy and without blemish" (Eph. 5:27). Thus, we individually and corporately reflect God's beauty in every way in which we exhibit his character. When we reflect his character, he delights in us and finds us beautiful in his sight.

But we also delight in God's excellence as we see it manifested in the lives of our brothers and sisters in the Lord. Therefore it is right that we feel joy and delight in the fellowship of one another, and that this joy deepens as our conformity to the life of Christ increases. It is right that we long to be in the fellowship of God's people in which God's character is manifested, for when we delight in the godliness of God's people, we are ultimately delighting in God himself as we see his character evidenced in the lives of his people.

20. Glory. In one sense of the word *glory* it simply means "honor" or "excellent reputation." This is the meaning of the term in Isaiah 43:7, where God speaks of his children, "whom I created for my *glory*," or Romans 3:23, which says that all "have sinned and fall short of the *glory* of God." It also has that meaning in John 17:5, where Jesus speaks to the Father of "the *glory* which I had with you before the world was made," and in Hebrews 1:3, which says that the Son "is the radiance of God's *glory*" (author's translation). In this sense, the glory of God is not exactly an attribute of his being but rather describes the superlative honor that should be given to God by everything in the universe (including, in Heb. 1:3 and John 17:5, the honor that is shared among the members of the Trinity). But that is not the sense of the word *glory* that we are concerned with in this section.

In another sense, God's "glory" means the bright light that surrounds God's presence. Since God is spirit, and not energy or matter, this visible light is not part of God's being but is something that was created. We may define it as follows: *God's glory is the created brightness that surrounds God's revelation of himself.*

This "attribute" of God is really not an attribute of God in the sense that the others were, for here we are speaking not of God's own character but of the *created* light or brilliance that surrounds God as he manifests himself in his creation. Thus, God's glory in this sense is not actually an attribute of God in himself. Nevertheless, God's glory is something that belongs to him alone and is the appropriate outward expression of his own excellence. It seems right therefore to treat it here immediately after the attributes of God.

Scripture often speaks of God's glory. David asks, "Who is this King of glory? The Lord of hosts, *he is the King of glory!*" (Ps. 24:10). We read in Psalm 104:1–2, "O Lord my God, you are very great! You are clothed with honor and majesty, you who cover yourself with light as with a garment. . . ." This glory of God is frequently mentioned in the Old Testament.

It is mentioned again in the New Testament in connection with the annunciation of Jesus' birth to the shepherds: "And an angel of the Lord appeared to them, and *the glory of the Lord shone around them,* and they were filled with fear" (Luke 2:9). God's glory was also evident at the transfiguration of Christ (cf. Matt. 17:2), and we find in the heavenly city yet to come that "the city has no need of sun or moon to shine upon it, for *the glory of God is its light,* and its lamp is the Lamb" (Rev. 21:23).

It is very appropriate that God's revelation of himself should be accompanied by such splendor and brightness, for this glory of God is the visible manifestation of the excellence of God's character. The greatness of God's being, the perfection of all his attributes, is something that we can never fully comprehend, but before which we can only stand in awe and worship. Thus, it is appropriate indeed that the visible manifestation of God be such that we would be unable to gaze fully upon it, and that it would be so bright that it would call forth both great delight and deep awe from us when we behold it only in part.

Quite amazingly, God made us to reflect his glory. Paul tells us that even now in our Christian lives we all are being "changed into his likeness from one degree of glory to another" (2 Cor. 3:18; cf. Matt. 5:16; Phil. 2:15). Though we do not now find ourselves surrounded by a visible light, there is a brightness, a splendor, or a beauty about the manner of life of a person who deeply loves God, and it is often evident to those around such a person. In the life to come, such brightness will be intensified, so that as we reign with Christ, it seems that we also will receive an outward appearance that is appropriate to that reign and to our status as image bearers of God and servants of the Lord Jesus Christ (cf. Prov. 4:18; Dan. 12:3; Matt. 13:43; 1 Cor. 15:43).

QUESTIONS FOR PERSONAL APPLICATION

Will, Freedom

1. As children grow toward adulthood, what are proper and improper ways for them to show in their own lives greater and greater exercise of individual will and freedom from parental control? Are these to be expected as evidence of our creation in the image of God?

Power

2. If God's power is his ability to do what he wills to do, then is power for us the ability to obey God's will and bring about results in the world that are pleasing to him? Name several ways in which we can increase in such power in our lives.

Perfection

3. How does God's attribute of perfection remind us that we can never be satisfied with the reflection of only some of God's character in our own lives? Can you describe some aspects of what it would mean to "be perfect" as our heavenly Father is perfect, with respect to your own life?

Blessedness

4. Are you happy with the way God created you — with the physical, emotional, mental, and relational traits he gave you? With the sex he gave you (whether masculine or feminine)? With the spiritual gifts he has given you? In what ways is it right to be happy or pleased with our own personalities, physical characteristics, abilities, positions, etc.? In what ways is it wrong to be pleased or happy about these things? Will we ever be fully "blessed" or happy? When will that be and why?

5. Think about the qualities that you admire in other people, both Christians and non-Christians. Which of these are right to admire and which are not? How can you decide? How can we come to delight more frequently and more fully in God himself?

Beauty

6. If we refuse to accept our society's definition of beauty, or even the definitions that we ourselves may have worked with previously, and decide that that which is truly beautiful is the character of God himself, then how will our understanding of beauty be different from the one we previously held? Will we still be able to rightly apply our new idea of beauty to some of the things we previously thought to be beautiful? Why or why not?

7. Can you understand why David's one desire above all others in life was "that I may dwell in the house of the LORD all the days of my life, to behold the beauty of the LORD, and to inquire in his temple" (Ps. 27:4)?

Glory

8. When the shepherds near Bethlehem experienced the glory of the Lord shining around them, "they were filled with fear" (Luke 2:9). Yet when we come to live forever in the heavenly city, we will continually be surrounded by the light of the glory of the Lord (Rev. 21:23). Will we then continually feel this same fear the shepherds felt? Why or why not? Would you like to live in the presence of this glory? Can we experience any of it in this life?

SPECIAL TERMS

attributes of purpose	perfection
beauty	power
blessedness	reasonable self-determination
freedom	revealed will
free will	secret will
glory	sovereignty
necessary will	"summary attributes"
omnipotence	will

BIBLIOGRAPHY

Bray, Gerald L. *The Doctrine of God.* Downers Grove, Ill.: InterVarsity Press, 1993.

Bromiley, G. W. "God." In *ISBE,* 2:493–503.

Charnock, Stephen. *The Existence and Attributes of God.* Repr. ed. Evansville, Ind.: Sovereign Grace Book Club, n.d., pp. 181–802 (first published 1655–1680).

Kaiser, Christopher B. *The Doctrine of God.* Westchester, Ill.: Good News, 1982.

Lewis, Gordon R. "God, Attributes of." In *EDT,* pp. 451–59.

_____. "Impassibility of God." In *EDT,* pp. 553–54.

Packer, J. I. "God." In *NDT,* pp. 274–77.

_____. *Knowing God.* London: Inter-Varsity Press, 1973, pp. 80–254.

Piper, John. *Desiring God.* Portland, Ore.: Multnomah, 1986.

_____. *The Pleasures of God.* Portland, Ore.: Multnomah, 1991.

Saucy, R. L. "God, Doctrine of." In *EDT,* pp. 459–64.

Tozer, A. W. *The Knowledge of the Holy.* New York: Harper and Row, 1961.

Van Til, Cornelius. *In Defense of the Faith,* vol. 5: *An Introduction to Systematic Theology.* Phillipsburg, N.J.: Presbyterian and Reformed, 1976, pp. 200–252.

Wenham, John W. *The Goodness of God.* London: Inter-Varsity Press, 1974.

SCRIPTURE MEMORY PASSAGE

Psalm 73:25–26: *Whom have I in heaven but you? And there is nothing upon earth that I desire besides you. My flesh and my heart may fail, but God is the strength of my heart and my portion for ever.*

HYMN

"If Thou but Suffer God to Guide Thee"

This is undoubtedly one of the most beautiful hymns ever written that expresses trust in God for his sovereignty.

> If thou but suffer God to guide thee,
> And hope in him through all thy ways,

He'll give thee strength, whate'er betide thee,
   And bear thee through the evil days:
Who trusts in God's unchanging love
   Builds on the rock that naught can move.

What can these anxious cares avail thee,
   These never-ceasing moans and sighs?
What can it help, if thou bewail thee
   O'er each dark moment as it flies?
Our cross and trials do but press
   The heavier for our bitterness.

Only be still, and wait his leisure
   In cheerful hope, with heart content
To take whate'er thy Father's pleasure
   And all-deserving love hath sent;
Nor doubt our inmost wants are known
   To him who chose us for his own.

All are alike before the highest;
   'Tis easy to our God, we know,
To raise thee up though low thou liest,
   To make the rich man poor and low;
True wonders still by him are wrought
   Who setteth up and brings to naught.

Sing, pray, and keep his ways unswerving,
   So do thine own part faithfully,
And trust his Word, though undeserving,
   Thou yet shalt find it true for thee;
God never yet forsook at need
   The soul that trusted him indeed.

AUTHOR: GEORG NEUMARK, 1641

Alternative hymns: "God Moves in a Mysterious Way" (printed at the end of chapter 9); "Crown Him With Many Crowns"

Chapter 7

GOD IN THREE PERSONS: THE TRINITY

How can God be three persons, yet one God?

The preceding chapters have discussed many attributes of God. But if we understood only those attributes, we would not rightly understand God at all, for we would not understand that God, in his very being, has always existed as more than one person. In fact, God exists as three persons, yet he is one God.

It is important to remember the doctrine of the Trinity in connection with the study of God's attributes. When we think of God as eternal, omnipresent, omnipotent, and so forth, we may have a tendency to think only of God the Father in connection with these attributes. But the biblical teaching on the Trinity tells us that all of God's attributes are true of all three persons, for each is fully God. Thus, God the Son and God the Holy Spirit are also eternal, omnipresent, omnipotent, infinitely wise, infinitely holy, infinitely loving, omniscient, and so forth.

The doctrine of the Trinity is one of the most important doctrines of the Christian faith. To study the Bible's teachings on the Trinity gives us great insight into the question that is at the center of all of our seeking after God: What is God like in himself? Here we learn that in himself, in his very being, God exists in the persons of Father, Son, and Holy Spirit, yet he is one God.

EXPLANATION AND SCRIPTURAL BASIS

We may define the doctrine of the Trinity as follows: *God eternally exists as three persons, Father, Son, and Holy Spirit, and each person is fully God, and there is one God.*

A. The Doctrine of the Trinity Is Progressively Revealed in Scripture

1. Partial Revelation in the Old Testament. The word *trinity* is never found in the Bible, though the idea represented by the word is taught in many places. The word *trinity* means "tri-unity" or "three-in-oneness." It is used to summarize the teaching of Scripture that God is three persons yet one God.

Sometimes people think the doctrine of the Trinity is found only in the New Testament, not in the Old. If God has eternally existed as three persons, it would be surprising to find no indications of that in the Old Testament. Although the doctrine of the Trinity is not explicitly found in the Old Testament, several passages suggest or even imply that God exists as more than one person.

For instance, according to Genesis 1:26, God said, "Let *us* make man in *our* image, after *our* likeness." What do the plural verb ("let us") and the plural pronoun ("our") mean? Some have suggested they are plurals of majesty, a form of speech a king would use in saying, for example, "We are pleased to grant your request."[1] However, in Old Testament Hebrew there are no other examples of a monarch using plural verbs or plural pronouns of himself in such a "plural of majesty," so this suggestion has no evidence to support it.[2] Another suggestion is that God is here speaking to angels. But angels did not participate in the creation of man, nor was man created in the image and likeness of angels, so this suggestion is not convincing. The best explanation is that already in the first chapter of Genesis we have an indication of a plurality of persons in God himself.[3] We are not told how many persons, and we have nothing approaching a complete doctrine of the Trinity, but it is implied that more than one person is involved. The same can be said of Genesis 3:22 ("Behold, the man has become like one of *us,* knowing good and evil"), Genesis 11:7 ("Come, let *us* go down, and there confuse their language"), and Isaiah 6:8 ("Whom shall I send, and who will go for *us*?"). (Note the combination of singular and plural in the same sentence in the last passage.)

Moreover, there are passages where one person is called "God" or "the Lord" and is distinguished from another person who is also said to be God. In Psalm 45:6–7 (NIV), the psalmist says, "Your throne, O God, will last for ever and ever. . . . You love righteousness and hate wickedness; therefore God, your God, has set you above your companions by anointing you with the oil of joy." Here the psalm passes beyond describing anything that could be true of an earthly king and calls the king "God" (v. 6), whose throne will last "forever and ever." But then, still speaking to the person called "God," the author says that "God, your God, has set you above your companions" (v. 7). So two separate persons are called "God" (Heb. *'Elōhîm*). In the New Testament, the author of

---

[1]Both Alexander the Great (in 152 B.C.) and King Demetrius (about 145 B.C.) refer to themselves in this way, for example, in the Septuagint text of 1 Macc. 10:19 and 11:31, but this is in Greek, not Hebrew, and it is written long after Genesis 1.

[2]See E. Kautzsch, ed., *Gesenius' Hebrew Grammar,* 2d ed. (Oxford: Clarendon Press, 1910), Section 124g, n. 2, with reference to the suggestion of a plural of majesty: "The plural used by God in Genesis 1:26, 11:7, Isaiah 6:8 has been incorrectly explained in this way." They understand Gen. 1:26 as "a plural of self-deliberation." My own extensive search of subsequent Jewish interpretation in the Babylonian Talmud, the targumim, and the midrashim showed only that later Rab-

binic interpreters were unable to reach agreement on any satisfactory interpretation of this passage, although the "plural of majesty" and "God speaking to angels" interpretations were commonly suggested.

[3]"The plural 'We' was regarded by the fathers and earlier theologians almost unanimously as indicative of the Trinity" [Keil and Delitzsch, *Old Testament Commentaries* (Grand Rapids: Associated Publishers and Authors, n.d.], 1:48, with objections to other positions and an affirmation that Gen. 1:26 contains "the truth that lies at the foundation of the Trinitarian view").

Hebrews quotes this passage and applies it to Christ: "Your throne, O God, is for ever and ever" (Heb. 1:8).[4]

Similarly, in Psalm 110:1, David says, "The LORD says to my lord: 'Sit at my right hand until I make your enemies a footstool for your feet' " (NIV). Jesus rightly understands that David is referring to two separate persons as "Lord" (Matt. 22:41–46), but who is David's "Lord" if not God himself? And who could be saying to God, "Sit at my right hand" except someone else who is also fully God? From a New Testament perspective, we can paraphrase this verse: "God the Father said to God the Son, 'Sit at my right hand.' " But even without the New Testament teaching on the Trinity, it seems clear that David was aware of a plurality of persons in one God. Jesus, of course, understood this, but when he asked the Pharisees for an explanation of this passage, "no one was able to answer him a word, nor from that day did any one dare to ask him any more questions" (Matt. 22:46). Unless they are willing to admit a plurality of persons in one God, Jewish interpreters of Scripture to this day will have no more satisfactory explanation of Psalm 110:1 (or of Gen. 1:26, or of the other passages just discussed) than they did in Jesus' day.

Isaiah 63:10 says that God's people "rebelled and grieved his Holy Spirit" (NIV), apparently suggesting both that the Holy Spirit is distinct from God himself (it is "his Holy Spirit"), and that this Holy Spirit can be "grieved," thus suggesting emotional capabilities characteristic of a distinct person. (Isa. 61:1 also distinguishes "The Spirit of the Lord GOD" from "the LORD," even though no personal qualities are attributed to the Spirit of the Lord in that verse.)

Similar evidence is found in Malachi, when the Lord says, "The Lord whom you seek will suddenly come to his temple; the messenger of the covenant in whom you delight, behold, he is coming, says the LORD of hosts. But who can endure the day of his coming, and who can stand when he appears?" (Mal. 3:1–2). Here again the one speaking ("the LORD of hosts") distinguishes himself from "the Lord whom you seek," suggesting two separate persons, both of whom can be called "Lord."

In Hosea 1:7, the Lord is speaking, and says of the house of Judah, "I will deliver them by the LORD their God," once again suggesting that more than one person can be called "Lord" (Heb. *Yahweh*) and "God" (*'Elōhîm*).

---

[4]The RSV translates Ps. 45:6, "Your divine throne endures forever and ever," but this is a highly unlikely translation because it requires understanding the Hebrew noun for "throne" in construct state, something extremely unusual when a noun has a pronominal suffix, as this one does. The RSV translation would only be adopted because of a theological assumption (that an Old Testament psalmist could not predict a fully divine messianic king), but not on the grounds of language or grammar. The KJV, NIV, and NASB all take the verse in its plain, straightforward sense, as do the ancient translations and Heb. 1:8. Derek Kidner, *Psalms 1-72*, TOTC (London: Inter-Varsity Press, 1973), p. 172, says this verse is "an example of Old Testament language bursting its banks, to demand a more than human fulfillment," and "this paradox is consistent with the Incarnation, but

mystifying in any other context."

Though some ancient kings, such as the Egyptian pharaohs, were sometimes addressed as "gods," this was part of the falsehood connected with pagan idolatry, and it should not be confused with Ps. 45, which is part of Scripture and therefore true.

The suggested translation of Heb. 1:8 in the RSV margin, "God is your throne forever and ever," while possible grammatically, is completely inconsistent with the thinking of both Old and New Testaments: the mighty God who created everything and rules supreme over the universe would never be merely a "throne" for someone else. The thought itself is dishonoring to God, and it should certainly not be considered as a possibly appropriate translation.

And in Isaiah 48:16, the speaker (apparently the servant of the Lord) says, "And now the Lord GOD has sent me and his Spirit."[5] Here the Spirit of the Lord, like the servant of the Lord, has been "sent" by the Lord GOD on a particular mission. The parallel between the two objects of sending ("me" and "his Spirit") would be consistent with seeing them both as distinct persons: it seems to mean more than simply "the Lord has sent me and his power."[6] In fact, from a full New Testament perspective (which recognizes Jesus the Messiah to be the true servant of the Lord predicted in Isaiah's prophecies), Isaiah 48:16 has trinitarian implications: "And now the Lord GOD has sent me and his Spirit," if spoken by Jesus the Son of God, refers to all three persons of the Trinity.

Furthermore, several Old Testament passages about "the angel of the LORD" suggest a plurality of persons in God. The word translated "angel" (Heb. *mal'ak*) means simply "messenger." If this angel of the LORD is a "messenger" of the LORD, he is then distinct from the LORD himself. Yet at some points the angel of the LORD is called "God" or "the LORD" (see Gen. 16:13; Ex. 3:2–6; 23:20–22 [note "my name is in him" in v. 21]; Num. 22:35 with 38; Judg. 2:1–2; 6:11 with 14). At other points in the Old Testament "the angel of the LORD" simply refers to a created angel, but at least at these texts the special angel (or "messenger") of the LORD seems to be a distinct person who is fully divine.

One of the most disputed Old Testament texts that could show distinct personality for more than one person is Proverbs 8:22–31. Although the earlier part of the chapter could be understood as merely a personification of "wisdom" for literary effect, showing wisdom calling to the simple and inviting them to learn, vv. 22–31, one could argue, say things about "wisdom" that seem to go far beyond mere personification. Speaking of the time when God created the earth, "wisdom" says, "Then I was the craftsman at his side. I was filled with delight day after day, rejoicing always in his presence, rejoicing in his whole world and delighting in mankind" (Prov. 8:30–31 NIV). To work as a "craftsman" at God's side in the creation suggests in itself the idea of distinct personhood, and the following phrases might seem even more convincing, for only real persons can be "filled with delight day after day" and can rejoice in the world and delight in mankind.[7]

But if we decide that "wisdom" here really refers to the Son of God before he became man, there is a difficulty. Verses 22–25 (RSV) seem to speak of the creation of this person who is called "wisdom":

> The LORD created me at the beginning of his work,
> the first of his acts of old.
> Ages ago I was set up,
> at the first, before the beginning of the earth.

---

[5]This RSV translation of Isa. 48:16 accurately reproduces both the literal sense of the Hebrew words and the word order in the Hebrew text.

[6]The NIV translation, "with his Spirit," is not required by the Hebrew text and tends to obscure the parallel thoughts of the Lord sending "me" and "his Spirit." The word *with* in the NIV is the translators' interpretation of the Hebrew conjunction *we* which most commonly means simply "and." The common Hebrew word for "with" (*'im*) is not in the text.

[7]In response to these arguments, one could argue that there are similarly detailed personifications of wisdom in Prov. 8:1–12 and 9:1–6, and of foolishness in Prov. 9:13–18, and no interpreter understands these to be actual persons. Therefore, Prov. 8:22–31 does not represent an actual person either. This argument seems convincing to me, but I have included the following paragraph because Prov. 8:22–31 has a long history of interpreters who think it refers to God the Son.

> When there were no depths I was brought forth,
>> when there were no springs abounding with water.
> Before the mountains had been shaped,
>> before the hills, I was brought forth.

Does this not indicate that this "wisdom" was created?

In fact, it does not. The Hebrew word that commonly means "create" (*bārā'*) is not used in verse 22; rather the word is *qānāh*, which occurs eighty-four times in the Old Testament and almost always means "to get, acquire." The NASB is most clear here: "The Lord possessed me at the beginning of his way" (similarly KJV). (Note this sense of the word in Gen. 39:1; Ex. 21:2; Prov. 4:5, 7; 23:23; Eccl. 2:7; Isa. 1:3 ["owner"].) This is a legitimate sense and, if wisdom is understood as a real person, would mean only that God the Father began to direct and make use of the powerful creative work of God the Son at the time creation began[8]: the Father summoned the Son to work with him in the activity of creation. The expression "brought forth" in verses 24 and 25 is a different term but could carry a similar meaning: the Father began to direct and make use of the powerful creative work of the Son in the creation of the universe.

2. More Complete Revelation of the Trinity in the New Testament. When the New Testament opens, we enter into the history of the coming of the Son of God to earth. It is to be expected that this great event would be accompanied by more explicit teaching about the trinitarian nature of God, and that is in fact what we find. Before looking at this in detail, we can simply list several passages where all three persons of the Trinity are named together.

When Jesus was baptized, "the heavens were opened and he saw the Spirit of God descending like a dove, and alighting on him; and lo, a voice from heaven, saying, 'This is my beloved Son, with whom I am well pleased'" (Matt. 3:16–17). Here at one moment we have three members of the Trinity performing three distinct activities. God the Father is speaking from heaven; God the Son is being baptized and is then spoken to from heaven by God the Father; and God the Holy Spirit is descending from heaven to rest upon and empower Jesus for his ministry.

At the end of Jesus' earthly ministry, he tells the disciples that they should go "and make disciples of all nations, baptizing them in the name of the Father and of the Son and of the Holy Spirit" (Matt. 28:19). The very names "Father" and "Son," drawn as they are from the family, the most familiar of human institutions, indicate very strongly the distinct personhood of both the Father and the Son. When "the Holy Spirit" is put in the same expression and on the same level as the other two persons, it is hard to avoid the conclusion that the Holy Spirit is also viewed as a person and of equal standing with the Father and the Son.

---

[8]The confusion surrounding the translation of the verse seems to have been caused by the unusual translation of the Septuagint, which used *ktizō* ("create") rather than the usual translation *ktaomai* ("acquire, take possession of") to translate the Hebrew term at this verse. *Qānāh* occurs eighty-four times in the Hebrew Old Testament and is translated more than seventy times by *ktaomai*, but only three times by *ktizō* (Gen. 14:19; Prov. 8:22; Jer. 39(32):15), all of which are questionable translations. The other Greek translations of the Old Testament by Aquila, Symmachus, and Theodotian all have *ktaomai* at Prov. 8:22.

When we realize that the New Testament authors generally use the name "God" (Gk. *theos*) to refer to God the Father and the name "Lord" (Gk. *kyrios*) to refer to God the Son, then it is clear that there is another trinitarian expression in 1 Corinthians 12:4–6: "Now there are varieties of gifts, but the same *Spirit;* and there are varieties of service, but the same *Lord;* and there are varieties of working, but it is the same *God* who inspires them all in every one."

Similarly, the last verse of 2 Corinthians is trinitarian in its expression: "The grace of the *Lord Jesus Christ* and the love of *God* and the fellowship of the *Holy Spirit* be with you all" (2 Cor. 13:14). We see the three persons mentioned separately in Ephesians 4:4–6 as well: "There is one body and one *Spirit,* just as you were called to the one hope that belongs to your call, one *Lord,* one faith, one baptism, one *God and Father* of us all, who is above all and through all and in all."

All three persons of the Trinity are mentioned together in the opening sentence of 1 Peter: "According to the foreknowledge of God the Father, by the sanctifying work of the Spirit, that you may obey Jesus Christ and be sprinkled with his blood" (1 Peter 1:2 NASB). And in Jude 20–21, we read: "But you, beloved, build yourselves up on your most holy faith; pray in the Holy Spirit; keep yourselves in the love of God; wait for the mercy of our Lord Jesus Christ unto eternal life."

However, the KJV translation of 1 John 5:7 should not be used in this connection. It reads, "For there are three that bear record in heaven, the Father, the Word, and the Holy Ghost: and these three are one."

The problem with this translation is that it is based on a very small number of unreliable Greek manuscripts, the earliest of which comes from the fourteenth century A.D. No modern translation (except NKJV) includes this KJV reading, but all omit it, as do the vast majority of Greek manuscripts from all major text traditions, including several very reliable manuscripts from the fourth and fifth century A.D., and also including quotations by church fathers such as Irenaeus (d. ca. A.D. 202), Clement of Alexandria (d. ca. A.D. 212), Tertullian (died after A.D. 220), and the great defender of the Trinity, Athanasius (d. A.D. 373).

B. Three Statements Summarize the Biblical Teaching

In one sense the doctrine of the Trinity is a mystery that we will never be able to understand fully. However, we can understand something of its truth by summarizing the teaching of Scripture in three statements:

1. God is three persons.
2. Each person is fully God.
3. There is one God.

The following section will develop each of these statements in more detail.

1. God Is Three Persons. The fact that God is three persons means that the Father is not the Son; they are distinct persons. It also means that the Father is not the Holy Spirit, but that they are distinct persons. And it means that the Son is not the Holy Spirit. These distinctions are seen in a number of the passages quoted in the earlier section as well as in many additional New Testament passages.

John 1:1–2 tells us: "In the beginning was the Word, and the Word was with God, and the Word was God. He was in the beginning with God." The fact that the "Word" (who is seen to be Christ in vv. 9–18) is "with" God shows distinction from God the Father. In John 17:24 (NIV), Jesus speaks to God the Father about "my glory, the glory you have given me because you loved me before the creation of the world," thus showing distinction of persons, sharing of glory, and a relationship of love between the Father and the Son before the world was created.

We are told that Jesus continues as our High Priest and Advocate before God the Father: "If any one does sin, we have an advocate with the Father, Jesus Christ the righteous" (1 John 2:1). Christ is the one who "is able for all time to save those who draw near to God through him, since he always lives to make intercession for them" (Heb. 7:25). Yet in order to intercede for us before God the Father, it is necessary that Christ be a person distinct from the Father.

Moreover, the Father is not the Holy Spirit, and the Son is not the Holy Spirit. They are distinguished in several verses. Jesus says, "But the Counselor, the Holy Spirit, whom the Father will send in my name, he will teach you all things, and bring to your remembrance all that I have said to you" (John 14:26). The Holy Spirit also prays or "intercedes" for us (Rom. 8:27), indicating a distinction between the Holy Spirit and God the Father to whom the intercession is made.

Finally, the fact that the Son is not the Holy Spirit is also indicated in the several trinitarian passages mentioned earlier, such as the Great Commission (Matt. 28:19), and in passages that indicate that Christ went back to heaven and then sent the Holy Spirit to the church. Jesus said, "It is to your advantage that I go away, for if I do not go away, the Counselor will not come to you; but if I go, I will send him to you" (John 16:7).

Some have questioned whether the Holy Spirit is indeed a distinct person, rather than just the "power" or "force" of God at work in the world. But the New Testament evidence is quite clear and strong.[9] First are the several verses mentioned earlier where the Holy Spirit is put in a coordinate relationship with the Father and the Son (Matt. 28:19; 1 Cor. 12:4–6; 2 Cor. 13:14; Eph. 4:4–6; 1 Peter 1:2): since the Father and Son are both persons, the coordinate expression strongly intimates that the Holy Spirit is a person also. Then there are places where the masculine pronoun *he* (Gk. *ekeinos*) is applied to the Holy Spirit (John 14:26; 15:26; 16:13–14), which one would not expect from the rules of Greek grammar, for the word "*spirit*" (Gk. *pneuma*) is neuter, not masculine, and would ordinarily be referred to with the neuter pronoun *ekeino*. Moreover, the name *counselor* or *comforter* (Gk. *paraklētos*) is a term commonly used to speak of a person who helps or gives comfort or counsel to another person or persons, but is used of the Holy Spirit in John's gospel (14:16, 26; 15:26; 16:7).

Other personal activities are ascribed to the Holy Spirit, such as teaching (John 14:26), bearing witness (John 15:26; Rom. 8:16), interceding or praying on behalf of

---

[9]The following section on the distinct personality of the Holy Spirit follows quite closely the excellent material in Louis Berkhof, *Systematic Theology* (Grand Rapids: Eerdmans, 1939, 1941), p. 96.

others (Rom. 8:26–27), searching the depths of God (1 Cor. 2:10), knowing the thoughts of God (1 Cor. 2:11), willing to distribute some gifts to some and other gifts to others (1 Cor. 12:11), forbidding or not allowing certain activities (Acts 16:6–7), speaking (Acts 8:29; 13:2; and many times in both Old and New Testaments), evaluating and approving a wise course of action (Acts 15:28), and being grieved by sin in the lives of Christians (Eph. 4:30).

Finally, if the Holy Spirit is understood simply to be the power of God, rather than a distinct person, then a number of passages would simply not make sense, because in them the Holy Spirit and his power or the power of God are both mentioned. For example, Luke 4:14, "And Jesus returned in the power of the Spirit into Galilee," would have to mean, "Jesus returned in the power of the power of God into Galilee." In Acts 10:38, "God anointed Jesus of Nazareth with the Holy Spirit and with power," would mean, "God anointed Jesus with the power of God and with power" (see also Rom. 15:13; 1 Cor. 2:4).

Although so many passages clearly distinguish the Holy Spirit from the other members of the Trinity, one puzzling verse has been 2 Corinthians 3:17: "Now the Lord is the Spirit, and where the Spirit of the Lord is, there is freedom." Interpreters often assume that "the Lord" here must mean Christ, because Paul frequently uses "the Lord" to refer to Christ. But that is probably not the case here, for a good argument can be made from grammar and context to say that this verse is better translated with the Holy Spirit as subject, "Now the Spirit is the Lord. . . ."[10] In this case, Paul would be saying that the Holy Spirit is also "Yahweh" (or "Jehovah"), the Lord of the Old Testament (note the clear Old Testament background of this context, beginning at v. 7). Theologically this would be quite acceptable, for it could truly be said that just as God the Father is "Lord" and God the Son is "Lord" (in the full Old Testament sense of "Lord" as a name for God), so also the Holy Spirit is the one called "Lord" in the Old Testament—and it is the Holy Spirit who especially manifests the presence of the Lord to us in the new covenant age.[11]

2. Each Person Is Fully God. In addition to the fact that all three persons are distinct, the abundant testimony of Scripture is that each person is fully God as well.

First, *God the Father is clearly God.* This is evident from the first verse of the Bible, where God created the heaven and the earth. It is evident through the Old and New Testaments, where God the Father is clearly viewed as sovereign Lord over all and where Jesus prays to his Father in heaven.

---

[10]Grammatically both "the Spirit" (*to pneuma*) and "the Lord" (*ho kyrios*) are in the nominative case, which is the case taken both by the subject and by the predicate noun in a sentence with the verb "to be." And word order does not indicate the subject in Greek as it does in English. The definite article (*ho,* "the") before "Lord" here is probably anaphoric (that is, it refers back to the previous mention of "Lord" in v. 16 and says that the Spirit is "the Lord" who was just mentioned in the previous sentence). (See Murray Harris, "2 Corinthians," in *EBC* 10:338–39.)

[11]Another possible interpretation is to say that this is speaking of the function of Christ and the function of the Holy Spirit as so closely related in the New Testament age that they can be spoken of as one in purpose. The verse would then mean something like "The Lord Jesus is in this age seen and known through the activity of the Holy Spirit, for the Holy Spirit's function is to glorify Christ." But this is a less persuasive interpretation, since it seems unlikely that Paul would speak of an identity of function in such an obscure way, or even that Paul would want to say that the work of Christ and the work of the Spirit are identical.

Next, *the Son is fully God.* Let us briefly note several explicit passages at this point. John 1:1–4 clearly affirms the full deity of Christ:

> In the beginning was the Word, and the Word was with God, and the Word was God. He was in the beginning with God; all things were made through him, and without him was not anything made that was made. In him was life, and the life was the light of men.

Here Christ is referred to as "the Word," and John says both that he was "with God" and that he "was God." The Greek text echoes the opening words of Genesis 1:1 ("In the beginning . . .") and reminds us that John is talking about something that was true before the world was made. God the Son was always fully God.

The translation "the Word was God" has been challenged by the Jehovah's Witnesses, who translate it "the Word was *a god*," implying that the Word was simply a heavenly being but not fully divine. They justify this translation by pointing to the fact that the definite article (Gk. *ho,* "the") does not occur before the Greek word *theos* ("God"). They say therefore that *theos* should be translated "a god." However, their interpretation has been followed by no recognized Greek scholar anywhere, for it is commonly known that the sentence follows a regular rule of Greek grammar, and the absence of the definite article merely indicates that "God" is the predicate rather than the subject of the sentence.[12] (A recent publication by the Jehovah's Witnesses now acknowledges the relevant grammatical rule but continues to affirm their position on John 1:1 nonetheless.)[13]

[12]This rule (called "Colwell's rule") is covered as early as chapter 6 of a standard introductory Greek grammar: See John Wenham, *The Elements of New Testament Greek* (Cambridge: Cambridge University Press, 1965), p. 35; also, *BDF,* 273. The rule is simply that in sentences with the linking verb "to be" (such as Gk. *eimi*), a definite predicate noun will usually drop the definite article when it precedes the verb, but the subject of the sentence, if definite, will retain the definite article. So if John had wanted to say, "The Word was God," John 1:1 is exactly the way he would have said it. (Recent grammatical study has confirmed and even strengthened Colwell's original rule: see Lane C. McGaughy, *Toward a Descriptive Analysis of EINAI as a Linking Verb in the New Testament* [SBLDS 6; Missoula, Mont.: SBL, 1972], esp. pp. 49–53, 73–77; and the important review of this book by E. V. N. Goetchius in *JBL* 95 [1976]: 147–49.)

Of course, if John had wanted to say, "The Word was a god" (with an indefinite predicate, "a god"), it would also have been written this way, since there would have been no definite article to drop in the first place. But if that were the case, there would have to be some clues in the context that John was using the word *theos* to speak of a heavenly being that was not fully divine. So the question becomes, what kind of God (or "god") is John talking about in this context? Is he speaking of the one true God who created the heavens and the earth? In that case, *theos* was definite and dropped the definite article to show

that it was the predicate noun. Or is he speaking about some other kind of heavenly being ("a god") who is not the one true God? In that case, *theos* was indefinite and never had a definite article in the first place.

The context decides this question clearly. From the other uses of the word *theos* to mean "God" in vv. 1, 2, 6, 12, 13, et al., and from the opening words that recall Gen. 1:1 ("In the beginning"), it is clear that John is speaking of the one true God who created the heavens and the earth. That means that *theos* in v. 2 must be understood to refer to that same God as well.

[13]The argument is found in a detailed, rather extensive attack on the doctrine of the Trinity: *Should You Believe in the Trinity?* (no author named; Brooklyn, N.Y.: Watchtower Bible and Tract Society, 1989). This group apparently deems this booklet a significant statement of their position, for page 2 states, "First printing in English: 5,000,000 copies." The booklet first advances the traditional argument that John 1:1 should be translated "a god" because of the absence on the definite article (p. 27). But then it later acknowledges that Colwell's rule is relevant for John 1:1 (p. 28) and there admits that the context, not the absence of the definite article, determines whether we should translate "the Word was God" (definite) or "the Word was a god" (indefinite). Then it argues as follows: ". . . when the context requires it, translators may insert an indefinite article in front of the noun in this type of sentence structure. Does the

The inconsistency of the Jehovah's Witnesses' position can further be seen in their translation of the rest of the chapter. For various other grammatical reasons the word *theos* also lacks the definite article at other places in this chapter, such as verse 6 ("There was a man sent from God"), verse 12 ("power to become children of God"), verse 13 ("but of God"), and verse 18 ("No one has ever seen God"). If the Jehovah's Witnesses were consistent with their argument about the absence of the definite article, they would have to translate all of these with the phrase "a god," but they translate "God" in every case.

John 20:28 in its context is also a strong proof for the deity of Christ. Thomas had doubted the reports of the other disciples that they had seen Jesus raised from the dead, and he said he would not believe unless he could see the nail prints in Jesus' hands and place his hand in his wounded side (John 20:25). Then Jesus appeared to the disciples when Thomas was with them. He said to Thomas, "Put your finger here, and see my hands; and put out your hand, and place it in my side; do not be faithless, but believing" (John 20:27). In response to this, we read, "Thomas answered him, 'My Lord and my God!'" (John 20:28). Here Thomas calls Jesus "my God." The narrative shows that both John in writing his gospel and Jesus himself approve of what Thomas has said and encourage everyone who hears about Thomas to believe the same things that Thomas did. Jesus immediately responds to Thomas, "Have you believed because you have seen me? Blessed are those who have not seen and yet believe" (John 20:29). As far as John is concerned, this is the dramatic high point of the gospel, for he immediately tells the reader—in the very next verse—that this was the reason he wrote it:

> Now Jesus did many other signs in the presence of the disciples, which are not written in this book; but these are written that you may believe that Jesus is the Christ, the Son of God, and that believing you may have life in his name. (John 20:30–31)

Jesus speaks of those who will not see him and will yet believe, and John immediately tells the reader that he recorded the events written in his gospel in order that they may believe in just this way, imitating Thomas in his confession of faith. In other words, the entire gospel is written to persuade people to imitate Thomas, who sincerely called Jesus "My Lord and my God." Because this is set out by John as the purpose of his gospel, the sentence takes on added force.[14]

---

context require an indefinite article at John 1:1? Yes, for the testimony of the entire Bible is that Jesus is not Almighty God" (p. 28).

We should note carefully the weakness of this argument: They admit that context is decisive, but then they quote not one shred of evidence from the context of John 1:1. Rather, they simply assert again their conclusion about "the entire Bible." If they agree that this context is decisive, but they can find nothing in this context that supports their view, they have simply lost the argument. Therefore, having acknowledged Colwell's rule, they still hold their view on John 1:1, but with no supporting evidence. To hold a view with no evidence to support it is simply irrationalism.

The booklet as a whole will give an appearance of scholarly work to laypersons, since it quotes dozens of theologians and academic reference works (always without adequate documentation). However, many quotations are taken out of context and made to say something the authors never intended, and others are from liberal Catholic or Protestant scholars who themselves are questioning both the doctrine of the Trinity and the truthfulness of the Bible.

[14]The Jehovah's Witnesses' booklet *Should You Believe in the Trinity?* offers two explanations for John 20:28: (1) "To Thomas, Jesus was like 'a god,' especially in the miraculous circumstances that prompted his exclamation" (p. 29). But this explanation is unconvincing, because Thomas did not say, "You

Other passages speaking of Jesus as fully divine include Hebrews 1:3, where the author says that Christ is the "exact representation" (Gk. *charaktēr*, "exact duplicate") of the nature or being (Gk. *hypostasis*) of God—meaning that God the Son exactly duplicates the being or nature of God the Father in every way: whatever attributes or power God the Father has, God the Son has them as well. The author goes on to refer to the Son as "God" in verse 8 ("But of the Son he says, 'Your throne, O God, is for ever and ever'"), and he attributes the creation of the heavens to Christ when he says of him, "You, Lord, did found the earth in the beginning, and the heavens are the work of your hands" (Heb. 1:10, quoting Ps. 102:25). Titus 2:13 refers to "our great *God* and Savior Jesus Christ," and 2 Peter 1:1 speaks of "the righteousness of our *God* and Savior Jesus Christ."[15] Romans 9:5, speaking of the Jewish people, says, "Theirs are the patriarchs, and from them is traced the human ancestry of Christ, who is God over all, forever praised! Amen" (NIV).[16]

In the Old Testament, Isaiah 9:6 predicts,

> "For to us a child is born,
>   to us a son is given;

---

are like a god," but rather called Jesus "my God." The Greek text has the definite article (it cannot be translated "a god") and is explicit: *ho theos mou* is not "a god of mine" but "my God."

(2) The second explanation offered is that "Thomas may simply have made an emotional exclamation of astonishment, spoken to Jesus but directed to God" (ibid.). The second part of this sentence, "spoken to Jesus but directed to God," is simply incoherent: it seems to mean, "spoken to Jesus but not spoken to Jesus," which is not only self-contradictory, but also impossible: if Thomas is speaking to Jesus he is also directing his words to Jesus. The first part of this sentence, the claim that Thomas is really not calling Jesus "God," but is merely swearing or uttering some involuntary words of exclamation, is without merit, for the verse makes it clear that Thomas was not speaking into the blue but was speaking directly to Jesus: "Thomas answered and said *to Him*, 'My Lord and my God!'-" (John 20:28, NASB). And immediately both Jesus and John in his writing commend Thomas, certainly not for swearing but for believing in Jesus as his Lord and his God.

[15]Both Titus 2:13 and 2 Peter 1:1 have marginal readings in the RSV whereby Jesus is referred to as a different person than "God" and therefore is not called God: "the great God and our Savior Jesus Christ" (Titus 2:13 mg.) and "our God and the Savior Jesus Christ" (2 Peter 1:1 mg.). These alternative translations are possible grammatically but are unlikely. Both verses have the same Greek construction, in which one definite article governs two nouns joined by the Greek word for *and* (*kai*). In all cases where this construction is found the two nouns are viewed as unified in some way, and often they are two separate names for the same person or thing. Especially significant is 2 Peter 1:1, for exactly the same construction is used by Peter three other times in this book to speak of "Our Lord and Savior Jesus Christ" (2 Peter 1:11; 2:20; 3:18).

In these three other verses, the Greek wording is exactly the same in every detail except that the word *Lord* (*kyrios*) is used instead of the word *God* (*theos*). If these other three instances are all translated "Our *Lord* and Savior Jesus Christ," as they are in all major translations, then consistency in translation would seem to require the translation of 2 Peter 1:1 as "Our *God* and Savior Jesus Christ," again referring to Christ as God. In Titus 2:13 Paul is writing about the hope of Christ's second coming, which the New Testament writers consistently speak of in terms that emphasize the manifestation of Jesus Christ in his glory, not in terms that emphasize the glory of the Father.

[16]The marginal reading in the NIV is similar to the reading in the main text of the RSV, which is, "and of their race, according to the flesh, is the Christ. God who is over all be blessed for ever. Amen" (Rom. 9:5 RSV). But this translation is far less likely on grammatical and contextual grounds and is justified primarily by arguing that Paul would not have referred to Christ as "God." The NIV translation, which refers to Christ as "God over all," is preferable because (1) Paul's normal pattern is to declare a word of blessing concerning the person about whom he has just been speaking, who in this case is Christ; (2) the Greek participle *ōn*, "being," which makes the phrase say literally, "who, being God over all is blessed forever," would be redundant if Paul were starting a new sentence as the RSV has it; (3) when Paul elsewhere begins a new sentence with a word of blessing to God, the word "blessed" comes first in the Greek sentence (see 2 Cor. 1:3; Eph. 1:3; cf. Peter's pattern in 1 Peter 1:3), but here the expression does not follow that pattern, making the RSV translation unlikely. See Donald Guthrie, *New Testament Theology* (Leicester: Inter-Varsity Press, 1981), pp. 339–40. For a definitive treatment of all the New Testament texts that refer to Jesus as "God," see Murray Harris, *Jesus as God* (Grand Rapids: Baker, 1992).

> and the government will be upon his shoulder,
>> and his name will be called
>> 'Wonderful Counselor, Mighty God.'"

As this prophecy is applied to Christ, it refers to him as "Mighty God." Note the similar application of the titles "Lord" and "God" in the prophecy of the coming of the Messiah in Isaiah 40:3, "In the wilderness prepare the way of the Lord, make straight in the desert a highway for our God," quoted by John the Baptist in preparation for the coming of Christ in Matthew 3:3.

There are other passages that deal with this, but these should be sufficient to demonstrate that the New Testament clearly refers to Christ as fully God. As Paul says in Colossians 2:9, "In him the whole fulness of deity dwells bodily."

Next, *the Holy Spirit is also fully God.* Once we understand God the Father and God the Son to be fully God, then the trinitarian expressions in verses like Matthew 28:19 ("baptizing them in the name of the Father and of the Son and of the Holy Spirit") assume significance for the doctrine of the Holy Spirit, because they show that the Holy Spirit is classified on an equal level with the Father and the Son. This can be seen if we recognize how unthinkable it would have been for Jesus to say something like, "baptizing them in the name of the Father and of the Son and of the archangel Michael"—this would give to a created being a status entirely inappropriate even to an archangel. Believers throughout all ages can only be baptized into the name (and thus into a taking on of the character) of God himself.[17] (Note also the other trinitarian passages mentioned above: 1 Cor. 12:4–6; 2 Cor. 13:14; Eph. 4:4–6; 1 Peter 1:2; Jude 20–21.)

In Acts 5:3–4, Peter asks Ananias, "Why has Satan filled your heart to lie to the Holy Spirit . . . ? You have not lied to men but *to God.*" According to Peter's words, to lie to the Holy Spirit is to lie to God. Paul says in 1 Corinthians 3:16, "Do you not know that you are God's temple and that God's Spirit dwells in you?" God's temple is the place where God himself dwells, which Paul explains by the fact that "God's Spirit" dwells in it, thus apparently equating God's Spirit with God himself.

David asks in Psalm 139:7–8, "Whither shall I go from your Spirit? Or whither shall I flee from your presence? If I ascend to heaven, you are there!" This passage attributes the divine characteristic of omnipresence to the Holy Spirit, something that is not true of any of God's creatures. It seems that David is equating God's Spirit with God's presence. To go from God's Spirit is to go from his presence, but if there is nowhere that David can flee from God's Spirit, then he knows that wherever he goes he will have to say, "You are there."

Paul attributes the divine characteristic of omniscience to the Holy Spirit in 1 Corinthians 2:10–11: "For the Spirit searches everything, even the depths of God. For what

---

[17]1 Tim. 5:21 should not be seen as a counter example to this claim, for there Paul is simply warning Timothy in the presence of a host of heavenly witnesses, both divine and angelic, who he knows are watching Timothy's conduct. This is similar to the mention of God and Christ and the angels of heaven and the "spirits of just men made perfect" in Heb. 12:22–24, where a great heavenly assembly is mentioned. 1 Tim. 5:21 should therefore be seen as significantly different from the trinitarian passages mentioned above, since those passages speak of uniquely divine activities, such as distributing gifts to every Christian (1 Cor. 12:4–6) or having the name into which all believers are baptized (Matt. 28:19).

person knows a man's thoughts except the spirit of the man which is in him? So also no one comprehends the thoughts of God [Gk., literally 'the things of God'] except the Spirit of God."

Moreover, the activity of giving new birth to everyone who is born again is the work of the Holy Spirit. Jesus said, "unless one is born of water and the Spirit, he cannot enter the kingdom of God. That which is born of the flesh is flesh, and that which is born of the Spirit is spirit. Do not marvel that I said to you, 'You must be born anew'" (John 3:5–7). But the work of giving new spiritual life to people when they become Christians is something that only God can do (cf. 1 John 3:9, "born of God"). This passage therefore gives another indication that the Holy Spirit is fully God.

Up to this point we have two conclusions, both abundantly taught throughout Scripture:

1. God is three persons.
2. Each person is fully God.

If the Bible taught only these two facts, there would be no logical problem at all in fitting them together, for the obvious solution would be that there are three Gods. The Father is fully God, the Son is fully God, and the Holy Spirit is fully God. We would have a system where there are three equally divine beings. Such a system of belief would be called polytheism—or, more specifically, "tritheism," or belief in three Gods. But that is far from what the Bible teaches.

3. There Is One God. Scripture is abundantly clear that there is one and only one God. The three different persons of the Trinity are one not only in purpose and in agreement on what they think, but they are one in essence, one in their essential nature. In other words, God is only one being. There are not three Gods. There is only one God.

One of the most familiar passages of the Old Testament is Deuteronomy 6:4–5 (NIV): "Hear, O Israel: The LORD our God, *the LORD is one.* Love the LORD your God with all your heart and with all your soul and with all your strength."

When Moses sings,

"Who is like you, O LORD, among the gods?
Who is like you, majestic in holiness,
terrible in glorious deeds, doing wonders?" (Ex. 15:11)

the answer obviously is "No one." God is unique, and there is no one like him and there can be no one like him. In fact, Solomon prays "that all the peoples of the earth may know that the LORD is God; there is no other" (1 Kings 8:60).

When God speaks, he repeatedly makes it clear that he is the only true God; the idea that there are three Gods to be worshiped rather than one would be unthinkable in the light of these extremely strong statements. God alone is the one true God and there is no one like him. When he speaks, he alone is speaking—he is not speaking as one God among three who are to be worshiped. He says:

"I am the LORD, and there is no other,
besides me there is no God;
I gird you, though you do not know me,

that men may know, from the rising of the sun
and from the west, that there is none besides me;
I am the LORD, and there is no other." (Isa. 45:5–6)

Similarly, he calls everyone on earth to turn to him:

"There is no other god besides me,
a righteous God and a Savior;
there is none besides me.

"Turn to me and be saved,
all the ends of the earth!
For I am God, and there is no other."
(Isa. 45:21–22; cf. 44:6–8)

The New Testament also affirms that there is one God. Paul writes, "For *there is one God,* and there is one mediator between God and men, the man Christ Jesus" (1 Tim. 2:5). Paul affirms that "God is one" (Rom. 3:30), and that "there is one God, the Father, from whom are all things and for whom we exist" (1 Cor. 8:6).[18] Finally, James acknowledges that even demons recognize that there is one God, even though their intellectual assent to that fact is not enough to save them: "You believe that God is one; you do well. Even the demons believe—and shudder" (James 2:19). But clearly James affirms that one "does well" to believe that "God is one."

4. Simplistic Solutions Must All Deny One Strand of Biblical Teaching. We now have three statements, all of which are taught in Scripture:

1. God is three persons.
2. Each person is fully God.
3. There is one God.

Throughout the history of the church there have been attempts to come up with a simple solution to the doctrine of the Trinity by denying one or another of these statements. If someone *denies the first statement,* then we are simply left with the fact that each of the persons named in Scripture (Father, Son, and Holy Spirit) is God, and there is one God. But if we do not have to say that they are distinct persons, then there is an easy solution: these are just different names for one person who acts differently at different times. Sometimes this person calls himself Father, sometimes he calls himself Son, and sometimes he calls himself Spirit.[19] We have no difficulty in understanding that, for in our own experience the same person can act at one time as a lawyer (for example), at another time as a father to his own children, and at another time as a son with respect

---

[18]1 Cor. 8:6 does not deny that God the Son and God the Holy Spirit are also "God," but here Paul says that God the Father is identified as this "one God." Elsewhere, as we have seen, he can speak of God the Son and God the Holy Spirit as also "God." Moreover, in this same verse, he goes on to speak of "one Lord, Jesus Christ, through whom are all things and through whom we exist." He is here using the word *Lord* in its full Old Testament sense of "Yahweh" as a name for God, and saying that this is the person through whom all things were created, thus affirming the full deity of Christ as well, but with a different name. Thus this verse affirms both the unity of God and the diversity of persons in God.

[19]The technical name for this view is modalism, a heresy condemned in the ancient church: see discussion below.

to his parents: The same person is a lawyer, a father, and a son. But such a solution would deny the fact that the three persons are distinct individuals, that God the Father sends God the Son into the world, that the Son prays to the Father, and that the Holy Spirit intercedes before the Father for us.

Another simple solution might be found by *denying the second statement,* that is, denying that some of the persons named in Scripture are really fully God. If we simply hold that God is three persons, and that there is one God, then we might be tempted to say that some of the "persons" in this one God are not fully God, but are only subordinate or created parts of God. This solution would be taken, for example, by those who deny the full deity of the Son (and of the Holy Spirit).[20] But, as we saw above, this solution would have to deny an entire category of biblical teaching.

Finally, as we noted above, a simple solution could come by *denying that there is one God.* But this would result in a belief in three Gods, something clearly contrary to Scripture.

Though the third error has not been common, as we shall see below, each of the first two errors has appeared at one time or another in the history of the church and they still persist today in some groups.

5. All Analogies Have Shortcomings. If we cannot adopt any of these simple solutions, then how can we put the three truths of Scripture together and maintain the doctrine of the Trinity? Sometimes people have used several analogies drawn from nature or human experience to attempt to explain this doctrine. Although these analogies are helpful at an elementary level of understanding, they all turn out to be inadequate or misleading on further reflection. To say, for example, that God is like a three-leaf clover, which has three parts yet remains one clover, fails because each leaf is only part of the clover, and any one leaf cannot be said to be the whole clover. But in the Trinity, each of the persons is not just a separate part of God, each person is fully God. Moreover, the leaf of a clover is impersonal and does not have distinct and complex personality in the way each person of the Trinity does.

Others have used the analogy of a tree with three parts: the roots, trunk, and branches all constitute one tree. But a similar problem arises, for these are only parts of a tree, and none of the parts can be said to be the whole tree. Moreover, in this analogy the parts have different properties, unlike the persons of the Trinity, all of whom possess all of the attributes of God in equal measure. And the lack of personality in each part is a deficiency as well.

The analogy of the three forms of water (steam, water, and ice) is also inadequate because (a) no quantity of water is ever all three of these at the same time,[21] (b) they have different properties or characteristics, (c) the analogy has nothing that corresponds to the fact that there is only one God (there is no such thing as "one water" or "all the water in the universe"), and (d) the element of intelligent personality is lacking.

---

[20]The technical name for this view is Arianism, another heresy condemned in the ancient church: see discussion below.

[21]There is a certain atmospheric condition (called the "triple point" by chemists) at which steam, liquid water, and ice can all exist simultaneously, but even then the quantity of water that is steam is not ice or liquid, the quantity that is liquid is not steam or ice, etc.

Other analogies have been drawn from human experience. It might be said that the Trinity is something like a man who is both a farmer, the mayor of his town, and an elder in his church. He functions in different roles at different times, but he is one man. However, this analogy is very deficient because there is only one person doing these three activities at different times, and the analogy cannot deal with the personal interaction among the members of the Trinity. (In fact, this analogy simply teaches the heresy called modalism, discussed below.)

Another analogy taken from human life is the union of the intellect, the emotions, and the will in one human person. While these are parts of a personality, however, no one factor constitutes the entire person. And the parts are not identical in characteristics but have different abilities.

So what analogy shall we use to teach the Trinity? Although the Bible uses many analogies from nature and life to teach us various aspects of God's character (God is like a rock in his faithfulness, he is like a shepherd in his care, etc.), it is interesting that Scripture nowhere uses any analogies to teach the doctrine of the Trinity. The closest we come to an analogy is found in the titles "Father" and "Son" themselves, titles that clearly speak of distinct persons and of the close relationship that exists between them in a human family. But on the human level, of course, we have two entirely separate human beings, not one being comprised of three distinct persons. It is best to conclude that no analogy adequately teaches about the Trinity, and all are misleading in significant ways.

6. God Eternally and Necessarily Exists as the Trinity. When the universe was created God the Father spoke the powerful creative words that brought it into being, God the Son was the divine agent who carried out these words (John 1:3; 1 Cor. 8:6; Col. 1:16; Heb. 1:2), and God the Holy Spirit was active "moving over the face of the waters" (Gen. 1:2). So it is as we would expect: if all three members of the Trinity are equally and fully divine, then they have all three existed for all eternity, and God has eternally existed as a Trinity (cf. also John 17:5, 24). Moreover, God cannot be other than he is, for he is unchanging (see chapter 4 above). Therefore it seems right to conclude that God necessarily exists as a Trinity—he cannot be other than he is.

C. Errors Have Come By Denying Any of the Three Statements Summarizing the Biblical Teaching

In the previous section we saw how the Bible requires that we affirm the following three statements:

1. God is three persons.
2. Each person is fully God.
3. There is one God.

Before we discuss further the differences between the Father, Son, and Holy Spirit, and the way they relate to one another, it is important that we recall some of the doctrinal errors about the Trinity that have been made in the history of the church. In this historical survey we will see some of the mistakes that we ourselves should avoid in any further thinking about this doctrine. In fact, the major trinitarian errors that have arisen have come through a denial of one or another of these three primary statements.[22]

1. Modalism Claims That There Is One Person Who Appears to Us in Three Different Forms (or "Modes"). At various times people have taught that God is not really three distinct persons, but only one person who appears to people in different "modes" at different times. For example, in the Old Testament God appeared as "Father." Throughout the Gospels, this same divine person appeared as "the Son" as seen in the human life and ministry of Jesus. After Pentecost, this same person then revealed himself as the "Spirit" active in the church.

This teaching is also referred to by two other names. Sometimes it is called Sabellianism, after a teacher named Sabellius who lived in Rome in the early third century A.D. Another term for modalism is "modalistic monarchianism," because this teaching not only says that God revealed himself in different "modes" but it also says that there is only one supreme ruler ("monarch") in the universe and that is God himself, who consists of only one person.

Modalism gains its attractiveness from the desire to emphasize clearly the fact that there is only one God. It may claim support not only from the passages talking about one God, but also from passages such as John 10:30 ("I and the Father are one") and John 14:9 ("He who has seen me has seen the Father"). However, the last passage can simply mean that Jesus fully reveals the character of God the Father, and the former passage (John 10:30), in a context in which Jesus affirms that he will accomplish all that the Father has given him to do and save all whom the Father has given to him, seems to mean that Jesus and the Father are one in purpose (though it may also imply oneness of essence).

The fatal shortcoming of modalism is the fact that it must deny the personal relationships within the Trinity that appear in so many places in Scripture (or it must affirm that these were simply an illusion and not real). Thus, it must deny three separate persons at the baptism of Jesus, where the Father speaks from heaven and the Spirit descends on Jesus like a dove. And it must say that all those instances where Jesus is praying to the Father are an illusion or a charade. The idea of the Son or the Holy Spirit interceding for us before God the Father is lost. Finally, modalism ultimately loses the heart of the doctrine of the atonement—that is, the idea that God sent his Son as a substitutionary sacrifice, and that the Son bore the wrath of God in our place, and that the Father, representing the interests of the Trinity, saw the suffering of Christ and was satisfied (Isa. 53:11).

Moreover, modalism denies the independence of God, for if God is only one person, then he has no ability to love and to communicate without other persons in his creation. Therefore it was necessary for God to create the world, and God would no longer be independent of creation (see chapter 5, above, on God's independence).

---

[22]An excellent discussion of the history and theological implications of the trinitarian heresies discussed in this section is found in Harold O. J. Brown, *Heresies: The Image* *of Christ in the Mirror of Heresy and Orthodoxy from the Apostles to the Present* (Garden City, N.Y.: Doubleday, 1984), pp. 95–157.

One present denomination within Protestantism (broadly defined), the United Pentecostal Church, is modalistic in its doctrinal position.[23]

2. Arianism Denies the Full Deity of the Son and the Holy Spirit.

a. The Arian Controversy: The term *Arianism* is derived from Arius, a Bishop of Alexandria whose views were condemned at the Council of Nicea in A.D. 325, and who died in A.D. 336. Arius taught that God the Son was at one point created by God the Father, and that before that time the Son did not exist, nor did the Holy Spirit, but the Father only. Thus, though the Son is a heavenly being who existed before the rest of creation and who is far greater than all the rest of creation, he is still not equal to the Father in all his attributes—he may even be said to be "like the Father" or "similar to the Father" in his nature, but he cannot be said to be "of the same nature" as the Father.

The Arians depended heavily on texts that called Christ God's *"only begotten"* Son (John 1:14; 3:16, 18; 1 John 4:9). If Christ were "begotten" by God the Father, they reasoned, it must mean that he was brought into existence by God the Father (for the word "beget" in human experience refers to the father's role in conceiving a child). Further support for the Arian view was found in Colossians 1:15, "He is the image of the invisible God, *the first-born of all creation.*" Does not "first-born" here imply that the Son was at some point brought into existence by the Father?[24] And if this is true of the Son, it must necessarily be true of the Holy Spirit as well.

But these texts do not require us to believe the Arian position. Colossians 1:15, which calls Christ "the first-born of all creation," is better understood to mean that Christ has the rights or privileges of the "first-born"—that is, according to biblical usage and custom, the right of leadership or authority in the family for one's generation. (Note Heb. 12:16 where Esau is said to have sold his "first-born status" or "birthright"—the Greek word *prototokia* is cognate to the term *prototokos,* "first-born" in Col. 1:15.) So

---

[23]Some of the leaders who formed this group had earlier been forced out of the Assemblies of God when the Assemblies decided to insist on a trinitarian statement of faith for its ministers in 1916. The United Pentecostal Church is sometimes identified with the slogan "Jesus only," and it insists that people should be baptized in the name of Jesus, not in the name of the Father, Son, and Holy Spirit. Because of its denial of the three distinct persons in God, the denomination should not be considered to be evangelical, and it is doubtful whether it should be considered genuinely Christian at all.

[24]Prov. 8:22 was also used by the Arians, who gained support from the fact that the Septuagint misleadingly translated it, "The Lord created me" (Gk. *ktizō*) rather than "The Lord acquired me or possessed me" (Gk. *ktaomai*). See discussion of this verse above, pp. 118–19.

The Jehovah's Witnesses, who are modern-day Arians, also point to Rev. 3:14, where Jesus calls himself "the beginning of God's creation," and take it to mean that "Jesus was created by God as the beginning of God's invisible creations" (no author named, *Should You Believe in the Trinity?* [Brooklyn,

N.Y.: Watch Tower Bible and Tract Society, 1989], p. 14). But this verse does not mean that Jesus was the first being created, for the same word for "beginning" (Gk. archem) is used by Jesus when he says that he is "the Alpha and the Omega, the first and the last, the beginning and the end" (Rev. 22:13), and "beginning" here is a synonym for "Alpha" and "first." God the Father similarly says of himself, "I am the Alpha and the Omega" (Rev. 1:8). In both cases, to be "the Alpha" or "the beginning" means to be the one who was there before anything else existed. The word does not imply that the Son was created or that there was a time when he began to be, for both the Father and the Son have always been "the Alpha and the Omega" and "the beginning and the end," since they have existed eternally. (The Jewish historian Josephus uses this same word to call God the "beginning (archem)" of "all things," but certainly he does not think that God himself was created: see Against Apion 2.190.)

The NIV translates this verse differently: "the ruler of God's creation." This is an acceptable alternative sense for *archē:* see the same meaning in Luke 12:11; Titus 3:1.

Colossians 1:15 means that Christ has the privileges of authority and rule, the privileges belonging to the "first-born," but with respect to the whole creation. The NIV translates it helpfully, "the firstborn *over all creation.*"

As for the texts that say that Christ was God's "only begotten Son," the early church felt so strongly the force of many other texts showing that Christ was fully and completely God, that it concluded that, whatever "only begotten" meant, it did not mean "created." Therefore the Nicene Creed in 325 affirmed that Christ was "begotten, not made":

> We believe in one God, the Father Almighty, Maker of all things visible and invisible. And in one Lord Jesus Christ, the Son of God, begotten of the Father, the only-begotten; that is, of the essence of the Father, God of God, Light of Light, very God of very God, begotten, not made, being of one substance (*homoousion*) with the Father. . . .[25]

This same phrase was reaffirmed at the Council of Constantinople in 381. In addition, the phrase "before all ages" was added after "begotten of the Father," to show that this "begetting" was eternal. It never began to happen, but is something that has been eternally true of the relationship between the Father and the Son. However, the nature of that "begetting" has never been defined very clearly, other than to say that it has to do with the relationship between the Father and the Son, and that in some sense the Father has eternally had a primacy in that relationship.

In further repudiation of the teaching of Arius, the Nicene Creed insisted that Christ was "of the same substance as the Father." The dispute with Arius concerned two words that have become famous in the history of Christian doctrine, *homoousios* ("of the same nature") and *homoiousios* ("of a similar nature").[26] The difference depends on the different meaning of two Greek prefixes, *homo-,* meaning "same," and *homoi-,* meaning "similar." Arius was happy to say that Christ was a supernatural heavenly being and that he was created by God before the creation of the rest of the universe, and even that he was "similar" to God in his nature. Thus, Arius would agree to the word *homoiousios.* But the Council of Nicea in 325 and the Council of Constantinople in 381 realized that this did not go far enough, for if Christ is not of exactly the same nature as the Father, then he is not fully God. So both councils insisted that orthodox Christians confess Jesus to be *homoousios,* of the *same* nature as God the Father. The difference between the two words was only one letter, the Greek letter iota, and some have criticized the church for allowing a doctrinal dispute over a single letter to consume so much attention for most of the fourth century A.D. Some have wondered, "Could anything be more foolish than arguing over a single letter in a word?" But the difference between the two words was profound, and the presence or absence of the iota really did mark the difference between biblical Christianity, with a true doctrine of the Trinity, and a heresy that did not accept the full deity of Christ and therefore was nontrinitarian and ultimately destructive to the whole Christian faith.

---

[25]This is the original form of the Nicene Creed, but it was later modified at the Council of Constantinople in 381 and there took the form that is commonly called the "Nicene Creed" by churches today. This text is taken from Philip Schaff, *Creeds of Christendom,* 3 vols. (Grand Rapids: Baker, 1983 reprint of 1931 edition), 1:28–29.

[26]Older translations of *homoousios* sometimes use the term "consubstantial," an uncommon English word simply meaning "of the same substance or nature."

b. Subordinationism: In affirming that the Son was of the same nature as the Father, the early church also excluded a related false doctrine, subordinationism. While Arianism held that the Son was created and was not divine, subordinationism held that the Son was eternal (not created) and divine, but still not equal to the Father in being or attributes—the Son was inferior or "subordinate" in being to God the Father.[27] The early church father Origen (c. 185 – c. A.D. 254) advocated a form of subordinationism by holding that the Son was inferior to the Father in being, and that the Son eternally derives his being from the Father. Origen was attempting to protect the distinction of persons and was writing before the doctrine of the Trinity was clearly formulated in the church. The rest of the church did not follow him but clearly rejected his teaching at the Council of Nicea.

Although many early church leaders contributed to the gradual formulation of a correct doctrine of the Trinity, the most influential by far was Athanasius. He was only twenty-nine years old when he came to the Council of Nicea in A.D. 325, not as an official member but as secretary to Alexander, the Bishop of Alexandria. Yet his keen mind and writing ability allowed him to have an important influence on the outcome of the Council, and he himself became Bishop of Alexandria in 328. Though the Arians had been condemned at Nicea, they refused to stop teaching their views and used their considerable political power throughout the church to prolong the controversy for most of the rest of the fourth century. Athanasius became the focal point of Arian attack, and he devoted his entire life to writing and teaching against the Arian heresy. "He was hounded through five exiles embracing seventeen years of flight and hiding," but, by his untiring efforts, "almost single-handedly Athanasius saved the Church from pagan intellectualism."[28] The "Athanasian Creed" which bears his name is not today thought to stem from Athanasius himself, but it is a very clear affirmation of trinitarian doctrine that gained increasing use in the church from about A.D. 400 onward and is still used in Protestant and Catholic churches today.

c. Adoptionism: Before we leave the discussion of Arianism, one related false teaching needs to be mentioned. "Adoptionism" is the view that Jesus lived as an ordinary man until his baptism, but then God "adopted" Jesus as his "Son" and conferred on him supernatural powers. Adoptionists would not hold that Christ existed before he was born as a man; therefore, they would not think of Christ as eternal, nor would they think of him as the exalted, supernatural being created by God that the Arians held him to be. Even after Jesus' "adoption" as the "Son" of God, they would not think of him as divine in nature, but only as an exalted man whom God called his "Son" in a unique sense.

Adoptionism never gained the force of a movement in the way Arianism did, but there were people who held adoptionist views from time to time in the early church, though their views were never accepted as orthodox. Many modern people who think of

---

[27]The heresy of subordinationism, which holds that the Son is inferior in being to the Father, should be clearly distinguished from the orthodox doctrine that the Son is eternally subordinate to the Father in role or function: without this truth, we would lose the doctrine of the Trinity, for we would not have any eternal personal distinctions between the Father and the Son, and they would not eternally be Father and Son. (See section D below on the differences between the Father, Son, and Holy Spirit.)

[28]S. J. Mikolaski, "Athanasius," *NIDCC*, 81.

Jesus as a great man and someone especially empowered by God, but not really divine, would fall into the adoptionist category. We have placed it here in relation to Arianism because it, too, denies the deity of the Son (and, similarly, the deity of the Holy Spirit).

The controversy over Arianism was drawn to a close by the Council of Constantinople in A.D. 381. This council reaffirmed the Nicene statements and added a statement on the deity of the Holy Spirit, which had come under attack in the period since Nicea. After the phrase, "And in the Holy Spirit," Constantinople added, "the Lord and Giver of Life; who proceeds from the Father; who with the Father and the Son together is worshipped and glorified; who spake by the Prophets." The version of the creed that includes the additions at Constantinople is what is commonly known as the Nicene Creed today.

d. The Filioque Clause: In connection with the Nicene Creed, one unfortunate chapter in the history of the church should be briefly noted, namely the controversy over the insertion of the filioque clause into the Nicene Creed, an insertion that eventually led to the split between western (Roman Catholic) Christianity and eastern Christianity (consisting today of various branches of eastern orthodox Christianity, such as the Greek Orthodox Church, the Russian Orthodox Church, etc.) in A.D. 1054.

The word *filioque* is a Latin term that means "and from the Son." It was not included in the Nicene Creed in either the first version of A.D. 325 or the second version of A.D. 381. Those versions simply said that the Holy Spirit "proceeds from the Father." But in A.D. 589, at a regional church council in Toledo (in what is now Spain), the phrase "and the Son" was added, so that the creed then said that the Holy Spirit "proceeds from the Father *and the Son (filioque)*." In the light of John 15:26 and 16:7, where Jesus said that he would send the Holy Spirit into the world, it seems there could be no objection to such a statement if it referred to the Holy Spirit proceeding from the Father and the Son at a point in time (particularly at Pentecost). But this was a statement about the nature of the Trinity, and the phrase was understood to speak of the *eternal* relationship between the Holy Spirit and the Son, something Scripture never explicitly discusses.[29] The form of the Nicene Creed that had this additional phrase gradually gained in general use and received an official endorsement in A.D. 1017. The entire controversy was complicated by ecclesiastical politics and struggles for power, and this apparently very insignificant doctrinal point was the main doctrinal issue in the split between eastern and western Christianity in A.D. 1054. (The underlying political issue, however, was the relation of the Eastern church to the authority of the Pope.) The doctrinal controversy and the split between the two branches of Christianity have not been resolved to this day.

Is there a correct position on this question? The weight of evidence (slim though it is) seems clearly to favor the western church. In spite of the fact that John 15:26 says that the Spirit of truth "proceeds from the Father," this does not deny that he proceeds also from the Son (just as John 14:26 says that the Father will send the Holy Spirit, but John 16:7 says that the Son will send the Holy Spirit). In fact, in the same sentence in John 15:26 Jesus speaks of the Holy Spirit as one "whom I shall send to you from the Father." And

---

[29]The word *proceeds* was not understood to refer to a creating of the Holy Spirit, or any deriving of his being from the Father and Son, but to indicate the way the Holy Spirit eternally relates to the Father and Son.

if the Son together with the Father sends the Spirit into the world, by analogy it would seem appropriate to say that this reflects eternal ordering of their relationships. This is not something that we can clearly insist on based on any specific verse, but much of our understanding of the *eternal* relationships among the Father, Son, and Holy Spirit comes by analogy from what Scripture tells us about the way they relate to the creation *in time*. Moreover, the eastern formulation runs the danger of suggesting an unnatural distance between the Son and the Holy Spirit, leading to the possibility that even in personal worship an emphasis on more mystical, Spirit-inspired experience might be pursued to the neglect of an accompanying rationally understandable adoration of Christ as Lord. Nevertheless, the controversy was ultimately over such an obscure point of doctrine (essentially, the relationship between the Son and Spirit before creation) that it certainly did not warrant division in the church.

e. The Importance of the Doctrine of the Trinity: Why was the church so concerned about the doctrine of the Trinity? Is it really essential to hold to the full deity of the Son and the Holy Spirit? Yes it is, for this teaching has implications for the very heart of the Christian faith. First, the atonement is at stake. If Jesus is merely a created being, and not fully God, then it is hard to see how he, a creature, could bear the full wrath of God against all of our sins. Could any creature, no matter how great, really save us? Second, justification by faith alone is threatened if we deny the full deity of the Son. (This is seen today in the teaching of the Jehovah's Witnesses, who do not believe in justification by faith alone.) If Jesus is not fully God, we would rightly doubt whether we can really trust him to save us completely. Could we really depend on any creature fully for our salvation? Third, if Jesus is not infinite God, should we pray to him or worship him? Who but an infinite, omniscient God could hear and respond to all the prayers of all God's people? And who but God himself is worthy of worship? Indeed, if Jesus is merely a creature, no matter how great, it would be idolatry to worship him — yet the New Testament commands us to do so (Phil. 2:9–11; Rev. 5:12–14). Fourth, if someone teaches that Christ was a created being but nonetheless one who saved us, then this teaching wrongly begins to attribute credit for salvation to a creature and not to God himself. But this wrongfully exalts the creature rather than the Creator, something Scripture never allows us to do. Fifth, the independence and personal nature of God are at stake: If there is no Trinity, then there were no interpersonal relationships within the being of God before creation, and, without personal relationships, it is difficult to see how God could be genuinely personal or be without the need for a creation to relate to. Sixth, the unity of the universe is at stake: If there is not perfect plurality and perfect unity in God himself, then we have no basis for thinking there can be any ultimate unity among the diverse elements of the universe either. Clearly, in the doctrine of the Trinity, the heart of the Christian faith is at stake. Herman Bavinck says that "Athanasius understood better than any of his contemporaries that Christianity stands or falls with the confession of the deity of Christ and of the Trinity."[30] He adds, "In the confession of the Trinity throbs the heart of the Christian religion: every error results from, or upon deeper reflection may be traced to, a wrong view of this doctrine."[31]

---

[30]Bavinck, *The Doctrine of God*, p. 281.   [31]Ibid., p. 285.

3. Tritheism Denies That There Is Only One God. A final possible way to attempt an easy reconciliation of the biblical teaching about the Trinity would be to deny that there is only one God. The result is to say that God is three persons and each person is fully God. Therefore, there are three Gods. Technically this view would be called "tritheism."

Few persons have held this view in the history of the church. It has similarities to many ancient pagan religions that held to a multiplicity of gods. This view would result in confusion in the minds of believers. There would be no absolute worship or loyalty or devotion to one true God. We would wonder to which God we should give our ultimate allegiance. And, at a deeper level, this view would destroy any sense of ultimate unity in the universe: even in the very being of God there would be plurality but no unity.

Although no modern groups advocate tritheism, perhaps many evangelicals today unintentionally tend toward tritheistic views of the Trinity, recognizing the distinct personhood of the Father, the Son, and the Holy Spirit, but seldom being aware of the unity of God as one undivided being.

D. What Are the Distinctions Between the Father, the Son, and the Holy Spirit?

After completing this survey of errors concerning the Trinity, we may now go on to ask if anything more can be said about the distinctions between the Father, Son, and Holy Spirit. If we say that each member of the Trinity is fully God, and that each person fully shares in all the attributes of God, then is there any difference at all among the persons? We cannot say, for example, that the Father is more powerful or wiser than the Son, or that the Father and Son are wiser than the Holy Spirit, or that the Father existed before the Son and Holy Spirit existed, for to say anything like that would be to deny the full deity of all three members of the Trinity. But what then are the distinctions between the persons?

1. The Persons of the Trinity Have Different Primary Functions in Relating to the World. When Scripture discusses the way in which God relates to the world, both in creation and in redemption, the persons of the Trinity are said to have different functions or primary activities. Sometimes this has been called the "economy of the Trinity," using *economy* in an old sense meaning "ordering of activities." (In this sense, people used to speak of the "economy of a household" or "home economics," meaning not just the financial affairs of a household, but all of the "ordering of activities" within the household.) The "economy of the Trinity" means the different ways the three persons act as they relate to the world and (as we shall see in the next section) to each other for all eternity.

We see these different functions in the work of creation. God the Father spoke the creative words to bring the universe into being. But it was God the Son, the eternal Word of God, who carried out these creative decrees. "All things were made through him, and without him was not anything made that was made" (John 1:3). Moreover, "in him all things were created, in heaven and on earth, visible and invisible, whether thrones or dominions or principalities or authorities—all things were created through him and for him" (Col. 1:16; see also Ps. 33:6, 9; 1 Cor. 8:6; Heb. 1:2). The Holy Spirit was active as well in a different way, in "moving" or "hovering" over the face of the waters (Gen. 1:2), apparently sustaining and manifesting God's immediate presence in his creation (cf. Ps. 33:6, where "breath" should perhaps be translated "Spirit"; see also Ps. 139:7).

In the work of redemption there are also distinct functions. God the Father planned redemption and sent his Son into the world (John 3:16; Gal. 4:4; Eph. 1:9–10). The Son obeyed the Father and accomplished redemption for us (John 6:38; Heb. 10:5–7, et al.). God the Father did not come and die for our sins, nor did God the Holy Spirit. That was the particular work of the Son. Then, after Jesus ascended back into heaven, the Holy Spirit was sent by the Father and the Son to apply redemption to us. Jesus speaks of "the Holy Spirit, whom the Father will send in my name" (John 14:26), but also says that he himself will send the Holy Spirit, for he says, "If I go, I will send him to you" (John 16:7), and he speaks of a time "when the Counselor comes, whom I shall send to you from the Father, even the Spirit of truth" (John 15:26). It is especially the role of the Holy Spirit to give us regeneration or new spiritual life (John 3:5–8), to sanctify us (Rom. 8:13; 15:16; 1 Peter 1:2), and to empower us for service (Acts 1:8; 1 Cor. 12:7–11). In general, the work of the Holy Spirit seems to be to bring to completion the work that has been planned by God the Father and begun by God the Son.

So we may say that the role of the Father in creation and redemption has been to plan and direct and send the Son and Holy Spirit. This is not surprising, for it shows that the Father and the Son relate to one another as a father and son relate to one another in a human family: the father directs and has authority over the son, and the son obeys and is responsive to the directions of the father. The Holy Spirit is obedient to the directives of both the Father and the Son.

Thus, while the persons of the Trinity are equal in all their attributes, they nonetheless differ in their relationships to the creation. The Son and Holy Spirit are equal in deity to God the Father, but they are subordinate in their roles.

Moreover, these differences in role are not temporary but will last forever: Paul tells us that even after the final judgment, when the "last enemy," that is, death, is destroyed and when all things are put under Christ's feet, "then the Son himself will also be subjected to him who put all things under him, that God may be everything to every one" (1 Cor. 15:28).

2. The Persons of the Trinity Eternally Existed as Father, Son, and Holy Spirit. But why do the persons of the Trinity take these different roles in relating to creation? Was it accidental or arbitrary? Could God the Father have come instead of God the Son to die for our sins? Could the Holy Spirit have sent God the Father to die for our sins, and then sent God the Son to apply redemption to us?

No, it does not seem that these things could have happened, for the role of commanding, directing, and sending is appropriate to the position of the Father, after whom all human fatherhood is patterned (Eph. 3:14–15). And the role of obeying, going as the Father sends, and revealing God to us is appropriate to the role of the Son, who is also called the Word of God (cf. John 1:1–5, 14, 18; 17:4; Phil. 2:5–11). These roles could not have been reversed or the Father would have ceased to be the Father and the Son would have ceased to be the Son. And by analogy from that relationship, we may conclude that the role of the Holy Spirit is similarly one that was appropriate to the relationship he had with the Father and the Son before the world was created.

Second, before the Son came to earth, and even before the world was created, for all eternity the Father has been the Father, the Son has been the Son, and the Holy Spirit has been the Holy Spirit. These relationships are eternal, not something that occurred only in time. We may conclude this first from the unchangeableness of God (see chapter 4): if God now exists as Father, Son, and Holy Spirit, then he has always existed as Father, Son, and Holy Spirit. We may also conclude that the relationships are eternal from other verses in Scripture that speak of the relationships the members of the Trinity had to one another before the creation of the world. For instance, when Scripture speaks of God's work of election before the creation of the world, it speaks of the Father choosing us "in" the Son: "Blessed be the God and Father of our Lord Jesus Christ . . . *he chose us in him before the foundation of the world,* that we should be holy and blameless before him" (Eph. 1:3–4). The initiatory act of choosing is attributed to God the Father, who regards us as united to Christ or "in Christ" before we ever existed. Similarly, of God the Father, it is said that "those whom he foreknew he also predestined to be conformed to the image of his Son" (Rom. 8:29). We also read of the "foreknowledge of God the Father" in distinction from particular functions of the other two members of the Trinity (1 Peter 1:2 NASB; cf. 1:20).[32] Even the fact that the Father "gave his only Son" (John 3:16) and "sent the Son into the world" (John 3:17) indicate that there was a Father-Son relationship before Christ came into the world. The Son did not become the Son when the Father sent him into the world. Rather, the great love of God is shown in the fact that the one who was *always* Father gave the one who was *always* his only Son: "For God so loved the world that he gave his only Son . . ." (John 3:16). "But when the time had fully come, God sent forth his Son" (Gal. 4:4).

When Scripture speaks of creation, once again it speaks of the Father creating *through* the Son, indicating a relationship prior to when creation began (see John 1:3; 1 Cor. 8:6; Heb. 1:2; also Prov. 8:22–31). But nowhere does it say that the Son or Holy Spirit created through the Father. These passages again imply that there was a relationship of Father (as originator) and Son (as active agent) before creation, and that this relationship made it appropriate for the different persons of the Trinity to fulfill the roles they actually did fulfill.

Therefore, the different functions that we see the Father, Son, and Holy Spirit performing are simply outworkings of an eternal relationship between the three persons, one that has always existed and will exist for eternity. God has always existed as three distinct persons: Father, Son, and Holy Spirit. These distinctions are essential to the very nature of God himself, and they could not be otherwise.

Finally, it may be said that there are no differences in deity, attributes, or essential nature between the Father, Son, and Holy Spirit. Each person is fully God and has all the attributes of God. *The only distinctions between the members of the Trinity are in the*

---

[32]Another passage that may suggest such a distinction in function is John 17:5: When Jesus asks the Father, "glorify me in your own presence with the glory which I had with you before the world was made" (John 17:5), he suggests that it is the Father's right to give glory to whom he will and that this glory had been given to the Son by the Father because the Father loved the Son before the foundation of the world.

ways they relate to each other and to the creation. In those relationships they carry out roles that are appropriate to each person.

This truth about the Trinity has sometimes been summarized in the phrase "ontological equality but economic subordination," where the word *ontological* means "being."[33] Another way of expressing this more simply would be to say "equal in being but subordinate in role." Both parts of this phrase are necessary to a true doctrine of the Trinity: If we do not have ontological equality, not all the persons are fully God. But if we do not have economic subordination,[34] then there is no inherent difference in the way the three persons relate to one another, and consequently we do not have the three distinct persons existing as Father, Son, and Holy Spirit for all eternity. For example, if the Son is not eternally subordinate to the Father in role, then the Father is not eternally "Father" and the Son is not eternally "Son." This would mean that the Trinity has not eternally existed.

This is why the idea of eternal equality in being but subordination in role has been essential to the church's doctrine of the Trinity since it was first affirmed in the Nicene Creed, which said that the Son was "begotten of the Father before all ages" and that the Holy Spirit "proceeds from the Father and the Son." Surprisingly, some recent evangelical writings have denied an eternal subordination in role among the members of the Trinity,[35] but it has clearly been part of the church's doctrine of the Trinity (in Catholic, Protestant, and Orthodox expressions), at least since Nicea (A.D. 325). So Charles Hodge says:

> The Nicene doctrine includes, (1) the principle of the subordination of the Son to the Father, and of the Spirit to the Father and the Son. But this subordination does not imply inferiority. . . . The subordination intended is only that which concerns the mode of subsistence and operation. . . .
>
> The creeds are nothing more than a well-ordered arrangement of the facts of Scripture which concern the doctrine of the Trinity. They assert the distinct personality of the Father, Son, and Spirit . . . and their consequent perfect equality; and the subordination of the Son to the Father, and of the Spirit to the Father and the Son, as to the mode of subsistence and operation. These are

---

[33]See section D.1, above, where *economy* was explained to refer to different activities or roles.

[34]Economic subordination should be carefully distinguished from the error of "subordinationism," which holds that the Son or Holy Spirit are inferior in being to the Father (see section C.2, above).

[35]See, for example, Richard and Catherine Kroeger, in the article "Subordinationism" in *EDT:* They define subordinationism as "a doctrine which assigns an inferiority of being, status, *or role* to the Son or the Holy Spirit within the Trinity. Condemned by numerous church councils, this doctrine has continued in one form or another throughout the history of the church" (p. 1058, emphasis mine). When the Kroegers speak of "inferiority of . . . role" they apparently mean to say that any affirmation of eternal subordination in role belongs to the heresy of subordinationism. But if this is what they are saying, then they are condemning all orthodox Christology

from the Nicene Creed onward and thereby condemning a teaching that Charles Hodge says has been a teaching of "the Church universal."

Similarly, Millard Erickson, in his *Christian Theology* (Grand Rapids: Baker, 1983–85), pp. 338 and 698, is willing only to affirm that Christ had a temporary subordination in function for the period of ministry on earth, but nowhere affirms an eternal subordination in role of the Son to the Father or the Holy Spirit to the Father and the Son. (Similarly, his *Concise Dictionary of Christian Theology,* p. 161.)

Robert Letham, in "The Man-Woman Debate: Theological Comment," *WTJ* 52:1 (Spring 1990), pp. 65–78, sees this tendency in recent evangelical writings as the outworking of an evangelical feminist claim that a subordinate role necessarily implies lesser importance or lesser personhood. Of course, if this is not true among members of the Trinity, then it is not necessarily true between husband and wife either.

scriptural facts, to which the creeds in question add nothing; *and it is in this sense they have been accepted by the Church universal.*[36]

Similarly, A. H. Strong says:

> Father, Son, and Holy Spirit, while equal in essence and dignity, stand to each other in an order of personality, office, and operation. . . .
>
> The subordination of the *person* of the Son to the *person* of the Father, or in other words an order of personality, office, and operation which permits the Father to be officially first, the Son second, and the Spirit third, is perfectly consistent with equality. Priority is not necessarily superiority. . . . *We frankly recognize an eternal subordination of Christ to the Father,* but we maintain at the same time that this subordination is a subordination of order, office, and operation, not a subordination of essence.[37]

3. What Is the Relationship Between the Three Persons and the Being of God? After the preceding discussion, the question that remains unresolved is, What is the difference between "person" and "being" in this discussion? How can we say that God is one undivided being, yet that in this one being there are three persons?

First, it is important to affirm that each person is completely and fully God; that is, that each person has the whole fullness of God's being in himself. The Son is not partly God or just one-third of God, but the Son is wholly and fully God, and so is the Father and the Holy Spirit. Thus, it would not be right to think of the Trinity according to figure 7.1, with each person representing only one-third of God's being.

Rather, we must say that the person of the Father possesses the *whole being* of God in himself. Similarly, the Son possesses the *whole being* of God in himself, and the Holy Spirit possesses the *whole being* of God in himself. When we speak of the Father, Son, and Holy Spirit together we are not speaking of any greater being than when we speak of the Father alone, or the Son alone, or the Holy Spirit alone. The Father is *all* of God's being. The Son also is *all* of God's being. And the Holy Spirit is *all* of God's being.

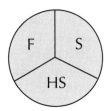

GOD'S BEING IS NOT DIVIDED INTO THREE EQUAL PARTS
BELONGING TO THE THREE MEMBERS OF THE TRINITY
Figure 7.1

[36]*Systematic Theology* (3 vols.; Grand Rapids: Eerdmans, 1970 [reprint; first published 1871–73]), 1:460–62 (italics mine).

[37]*Systematic Theology* (Valley Forge, Pa.: Judson, 1907), p. 342 (third italics mine).

This is what the Athanasian Creed affirmed in the following sentences:

> And the Catholic Faith is this: That we worship one God in Trinity, and Trinity in Unity; Neither confounding the Persons: nor dividing the Substance [Essence]. For there is one Person of the Father: another of the Son: and another of the Holy Spirit. But the Godhead of the Father, of the Son, and of the Holy Spirit, is all one: the Glory equal, the Majesty coeternal. Such as the Father is: such is the Son: and such is the Holy Spirit. . . . For like as we are compelled by the Christian verity: to acknowledge every Person by himself to be God and Lord: So are we forbidden by the Catholic Religion: to say, There be [are] three Gods, or three Lords.

But if each person is fully God and has all of God's being, then we also should not think that the personal distinctions are any kind of additional attributes added on to the being of God, something after the pattern of figure 7.2.

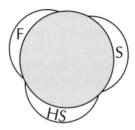

THE PERSONAL DISTINCTIONS IN THE TRINITY ARE NOT
SOMETHING ADDED ONTO GOD'S REAL BEING
Figure 7.2

Rather, each person of the Trinity has all of the attributes of God, and no one person has any attributes that are not possessed by the others.

On the other hand, we must say that the persons are real, that they are not just different ways of looking at the one being of God. (This would be modalism or Sabellianism, as discussed above.) So figure 7.3 would not be appropriate.

Rather, we need to think of the Trinity in such a way that the reality of the three persons is maintained, and each person is seen as relating to the others as an "I" (a first person) and a "you" (a second person) and a "he" (a third person).

The only way it seems possible to do this is to say that the distinction between the persons is not a difference in "being" but a difference in "relationships." This is something far removed from our human experience, where every different human "person" is a different being as well. Somehow God's being is so much greater than ours that within his one undivided being there can be an unfolding into interpersonal relationships, so that there can be three distinct persons.

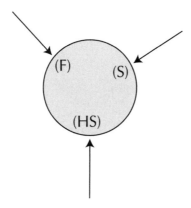

THE PERSONS OF THE TRINITY ARE NOT JUST THREE DIFFERENT
WAYS OF LOOKING AT THE ONE BEING GOD
Figure 7.3

What then are the differences between Father, Son, and Holy Spirit? There is no difference in attributes at all. The only difference between them is the way they relate to each other and to the creation. The unique quality of the Father is the way he *relates as Father* to the Son and Holy Spirit. The unique quality of the Son is the way he *relates as Son.* And the unique quality of the Holy Spirit is the way he *relates as Spirit.*[38]

While the three diagrams given above represented erroneous ideas to be avoided, the following diagram may be helpful in thinking about the existence of three persons in the one undivided being of God.

In this diagram, the Father is represented as the section of the circle designated by F, and also the rest of the circle, moving around clockwise from the letter F; the Son is represented as the section of the circle designated by S, and also the rest of the circle, moving around clockwise from the letter S; and the Holy Spirit is represented as the section of the circle marked HS and also the rest of the circle, moving around clockwise from the HS. Thus, there are three distinct persons, but each person is fully and wholly God. Of course the representation is imperfect, for it cannot represent God's infinity, or personality, or indeed any of his attributes. It also requires looking at the circle in more than one way in order to understand it: the dotted lines must be understood to indicate personal relationship, not any division in the one being of God. Thus, the circle itself represents God's being while the dotted lines represent a form of personal existence other than a difference in being. But the diagram may nonetheless help guard against some misunderstanding.

---

[38]Some systematic theologies give names to these different relationships: "paternity" (or "generation") for the Father, "begottenness" (or "filiation") for the Son, and "procession" (or "spiration") for the Holy Spirit, but the names do not mean anything more than "relating as a Father," and "relating as a Son," and "relating as Spirit." In an attempt to avoid the proliferation of technical terms that do not exist in contemporary English, or whose meaning differs from their ordinary English sense, I have not used these terms in this chapter.

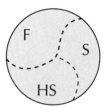

THERE ARE THREE DISTINCT PERSONS, AND THE BEING OF
EACH PERSON IS EQUAL TO THE WHOLE BEING OF GOD
Figure 7.4

Our own human personalities provide another faint analogy that can provide some help in thinking about the Trinity. A man can think about different objects outside of himself, and when he does this he is the subject who does the thinking. He can also think about himself, and then he is the object who is being thought about: then he is both subject and object. Moreover, he can reflect on his ideas about himself as a third thing, neither subject nor object, but *thoughts* that he as a subject has about himself as an object. When this happens, the subject, object, and thoughts are three distinct things. Yet each thing in a way includes his whole being: All of the man is the subject, and all of the man is the object, and the thoughts (though in a lesser sense) are thoughts about all of himself as a person.[39]

But if the unfolding of human personality allows this kind of complexity, then the unfolding of God's personality must allow for far greater complexity than this. Within the one being of God the "unfolding" of personality must allow for the existence of three distinct persons, while each person still has the whole of God's being in himself. The difference in persons must be one of relationship, not one of being, and yet each person must really exist. This tri-personal form of being is far beyond our ability to comprehend. *It is a kind of existence far different from anything we have experienced,* and far different from anything else in the universe.

Because the existence of three persons in one God is something beyond our understanding, Christian theology has come to use the word *person* to speak of these differences in relationship, not because we fully understand what is meant by the word *person* when referring to the Trinity, but rather so that we might say something instead of saying nothing at all.

4. Can We Understand the Doctrine of the Trinity? We should be warned by the errors that have been made in the past. They have all come about through attempts to simplify the doctrine of the Trinity and make it completely understandable, removing all mystery from it. This we can never do. However, it is not correct to say that we cannot under-

---

[39]We said above that no analogy teaches the Trinity perfectly, and this one has several shortcomings as well: this man remains as one person; he is not three persons. And his "thoughts" do not equal all of him as a person. But the analogy is helpful in hinting at something of the complexity even of human personality and suggesting that the complexity of divine personality is something far greater than this.

stand the doctrine of the Trinity at all. Certainly we can understand and know that God is three persons, and that each person is fully God, and that there is one God. We can know these things because the Bible teaches them. Moreover, we can know some things about the way in which the persons relate to each other (see the section above). But what we cannot understand fully is how to fit together those distinct biblical teachings. We wonder how there can be three distinct persons, and each person have the whole being of God in himself, and yet God is only one undivided being. This we are unable to understand. In fact, it is spiritually healthy for us to acknowledge openly that God's very being is far greater than we can ever comprehend. This humbles us before God and draws us to worship him without reservation.

But it should also be said that Scripture does not ask us to believe in a contradiction. A contradiction would be "There is one God and there is not one God," or "God is three persons and God is not three persons," or even (which is similar to the previous statement) "God is three persons and God is one person." But to say that "God is three persons and there is one God" is not a contradiction. It is something we do not understand, and it is therefore a mystery or a paradox, but that should not trouble us as long as the different aspects of the mystery are clearly taught by Scripture, for as long as we are finite creatures and not omniscient deity, there will always (for all eternity) be things that we do not fully understand. Louis Berkhof wisely says:

> The Trinity is a mystery . . . man cannot comprehend it and make it intelligible. It is intelligible in some of its relations and modes of manifestation, but unintelligible in its essential nature. . . . The real difficulty lies in the relation in which the persons in the Godhead stand to the divine essence and to one another; and this is a difficulty which the Church cannot remove, but only try to reduce to its proper proportion by a proper definition of terms. It has never tried to explain the mystery of the Trinity but only sought to formulate the doctrine of the Trinity in such a manner that the errors which endangered it were warded off.[40]

Berkhof also says, "It is especially when we reflect on the relation of the three persons to the divine essence that all analogies fail us and we become deeply conscious of the fact that the Trinity is a mystery far beyond our comprehension. It is the incomprehensible glory of the Godhead."[41]

E. Application

Because God in himself has both unity and diversity, it is not surprising that unity and diversity are also reflected in the human relationships he has established. We see this first in marriage. When God created man in his own image, he did not create merely isolated individuals, but Scripture tells us, "male and female he created them" (Gen. 1:27). And in the unity of marriage (see Gen. 2:24) we see, not a triunity as with God, but at least a remarkable unity of two persons, persons who remain distinct individuals yet also become

---

[40]Berkhof, *Systematic Theology*, p. 89.　　[41]Ibid., p. 88.

one in body, mind, and spirit (cf. 1 Cor. 6:16–20; Eph. 5:31). In fact, in the relationship between man and woman in marriage we see also a picture of the relationship between the Father and Son in the Trinity. Paul says, "But I want you to understand that the head of every man is Christ, the head of a woman is her husband, and the head of Christ is God" (1 Cor. 11:3). Here, just as the Father has authority over the Son in the Trinity, so the husband has authority over the wife in marriage. The husband's role is parallel to that of God the Father and the wife's role is parallel to that of God the Son. Moreover, just as Father and Son are equal in deity and importance and personhood, so the husband and wife are equal in humanity and importance and personhood. And, although it is not explicitly mentioned in Scripture, the gift of children within marriage, coming from both the father and the mother, and subject to the authority of both father and mother, is analogous to the relationship of the Holy Spirit to the Father and Son in the Trinity.

But the human family is not the only way in which God has ordained that there would be both diversity and unity in the world that reflect something of his own excellence. In the church we have "many members" yet "one body" (1 Cor. 12:12). Paul reflects on the great diversity among members of the human body (1 Cor. 12:14–26) and says that the church is like that: We have many different members in our churches with different gifts and interests, and we depend on and help each other, thereby demonstrating great diversity and great unity at the same time. When we see different people doing many different things in the life of a church we ought to thank God that this allows us to glorify him by reflecting something of the unity and diversity of the Trinity.

We should also notice that God's purpose in the history of the universe has frequently been to display unity in diversity, and thus to display his glory. We see this not only in the diversity of gifts in the church (1 Cor. 12:12–26), but also in the unity of Jews and Gentiles, so that all races, diverse as they are, are united in Christ (Eph. 2:16; 3:8–10; see also Rev. 7:9). Paul is amazed that God's plans for the history of redemption have been like a great symphony so that his wisdom is beyond finding out (Rom. 11:33–36). Even in the mysterious unity between Christ and the church, in which we are called the bride of Christ (Eph. 5:31–32), we see unity beyond what we ever would have imagined, unity with the Son of God himself. Yet in all this we never lose our individual identity but remain distinct persons always able to worship and serve God as unique individuals.

Eventually the entire universe will partake of this unity of purpose with every diverse part contributing to the worship of God the Father, Son, and Holy Spirit, for one day, at the name of Jesus every knee will bow "in heaven and on earth and under the earth, and every tongue confess that Jesus Christ is Lord, to the glory of God the Father" (Phil. 2:10–11).

On a more everyday level, there are many activities that we carry out as human beings (in the labor force, in social organizations, in musical performances, and in athletic teams, for example) in which many distinct individuals contribute to a unity of purpose or activity. As we see in these activities a reflection of the wisdom of God in allowing us both unity and diversity, we can see a faint reflection of the glory of God in his trinitarian existence. Though we will never fully comprehend the mystery of the Trinity, we can worship God for who he is both in our songs of praise, and in our words and actions as they reflect something of his excellent character.

QUESTIONS FOR PERSONAL APPLICATION

1. Why is God pleased when people exhibit faithfulness, love, and harmony within a family? What are some ways in which members of your family reflect the diversity found in the members of the Trinity? How does your family reflect the unity found among members of the Trinity? What are some ways in which your family relationships could reflect the unity of the Trinity more fully? How might the diversity of persons in the Trinity encourage parents to allow their children to develop different interests from each other, and from their parents, without thinking that the unity of the family will be damaged?

2. Have you ever thought that if your church allows new or different kinds of ministries to develop, that it might hinder the unity of the church? Or have you thought that encouraging people to use other gifts for ministry than those that have been used in the past might be divisive in the church? How might the fact of unity and diversity in the Trinity help you to approach those questions?

3. Do you think that the trinitarian nature of God is more fully reflected in a church in which all the members have the same racial background, or one in which the members come from many different races (see Eph. 3:1–10)?

4. In addition to our relationships within our families, we all exist in other relationships to human authority in government, in employment, in voluntary societies, in educational institutions, and in athletics, for example. Sometimes we have authority over others, and sometimes we are subject to the authority of others. Whether in the family or one of these other areas, give one example of a way in which your use of authority or your response to authority might become more like the pattern of relationships in the Trinity.

5. If we see the trinitarian existence of God as the fundamental basis for all combinations of unity and diversity in the universe, then what are some other parts of creation that show both unity and diversity (for example: the interdependency of environmental systems on the earth, or the fascinating activity of bees in a hive, or the harmonious working of the various parts of the human body)? Do you think God has made us so that we take spontaneous delight in demonstrations of unity in diversity, such as a musical composition that manifests great unity and yet great diversity of various parts at the same time, or in the skillful execution of some planned strategy by members of an athletic team working together?

6. In the being of God we have infinite unity combined with the preservation of distinct personalities belonging to the members of the Trinity. How can this fact reassure us if we ever begin to fear that becoming more united to Christ as we grow in the Christian life (or becoming more united to one another in the church) might tend to obliterate our individual personalities? In heaven, do you think you will be exactly like everyone else, or will you have a personality that is distinctly your own? How do eastern religions (such as Buddhism) differ from Christianity in this regard?

SPECIAL TERMS

adoptionism

Arianism

economic subordination

eternal begetting of the Son

eternal generation of the Son

filioque

homoiousios

homoousios

modalism

modalistic monarchianism

only-begotten

ontological equality

Sabellianism

subordinationism

Trinity

tritheism

BIBLIOGRAPHY

Augustine. *On the Trinity*. NPNF, First Series, 3:1–228. (This is considered the most thorough development of the orthodox doctrine of the Trinity in the history of the church.)

Bavinck, Herman. *The Doctrine of God*. Trans. by William Hendriksen (Edinburgh and Carlisle, Pa.: Banner of Truth, 1977 [reprint of 1951 edition]), pp. 255–334. (This is one of the most thorough modern discussions of the Trinity.)

Beisner, Calvin. *God in Three Persons*. Wheaton, Ill.: Tyndale Press, 1984.

Bickersteth, Edward H. *The Trinity*. Grand Rapids: Kregel, 1957 reprint.

Bloesch, Donald G. *The Battle for the Trinity: The Debate Over Inclusive God-Language*. Ann Arbor, Mich.: Servant, 1985.

Bowman, Robert M., Jr. *Why You Should Believe in the Trinity: An Answer to Jehovah's Witnesses*. Grand Rapids: Baker, 1989.

Bray, G. L. "Trinity." In *NDT*, pp. 691–94.

_____. "Tritheism." In *NDT*, p. 694.

Brown, Harold O. J. *Heresies: The Image of Christ in the Mirror of Heresy and Orthodoxy From the Apostles to the Present*. Garden City, N.Y.: Doubleday, 1984, pp. 95–157.

Davis, Stephen T. *Logic and the Nature of God*. Grand Rapids: Eerdmans, 1983, pp. 132–44.

Gruenler, Royce Gordon. *The Trinity in the Gospel of John*. Grand Rapids: Baker, 1986.

Harris, Murray. *Jesus as God*. Grand Rapids: Baker, 1992.

Kaiser, Christopher B. *The Doctrine of God: An Historical Survey*. Westchester, Ill.: Crossway, 1982, pp. 23–71.

McGrath, Alister E. *Understanding the Trinity*. Grand Rapids: Zondervan, 1988.

Mikolaski, S. J. "The Triune God." In *Fundamentals of the Faith*. Ed. by C. F. H. Henry. Grand Rapids: Zondervan, 1969, pp. 59–76.

Packer, J. I. "God." *NDT*, 274–77.

_____. *Knowing God*. Downers Grove, Ill.: InterVarsity Press, 1973, pp. 57–63.

Wright, D. F. "Augustine." In *NDT*, pp. 58–61.

SCRIPTURE MEMORY PASSAGE

Matthew 3:16–17: *And when Jesus was baptized, he went up immediately from the water, and behold, the heavens were opened and he saw the Spirit of God descending like a dove, and alighting on him; and lo, a voice from heaven, saying, "This is my beloved Son, with whom I am well pleased."*

HYMN

"Holy, Holy, Holy"

> Holy, holy, holy, Lord God Almighty!
>   Early in the morning our song shall rise to thee;
> Holy, holy, holy! Merciful and mighty!
>   God in three persons, blessed Trinity!
>
> Holy, holy, holy! All the saints adore thee,
>   Casting down their golden crowns around the glassy sea;
> Cherubim and seraphim falling down before thee,
>   Who wert, and art, and evermore shalt be.
>
> Holy, holy, holy! Though the darkness hide thee,
>   Though the eye of sinful man thy glory may not see,
> Only thou art holy; there is none beside thee
>   Perfect in pow'r, in love, and purity.
>
> Holy, holy, holy! Lord God Almighty!
>   All thy works shall praise thy name, in earth and sky and sea;
> Holy, holy, holy! Merciful and mighty!
>   God in three persons, blessed Trinity!

AUTHOR: REGINALD HEBER, 1826

Chapter 8

CREATION

Why, how, and when did God create the universe?

EXPLANATION AND SCRIPTURAL BASIS[1]

How did God create the world? Did he create every different kind of plant and animal directly, or did he use some kind of evolutionary process, guiding the development of living things from the simplest to the most complex? And how quickly did God bring about creation? Was it all completed within six twenty-four-hour days, or did he use thousands or perhaps millions of years? How old is the earth, and how old is the human race?

These questions face us when we deal with the doctrine of creation. Unlike most of the earlier material in this book, this chapter treats several questions on which evangelical Christians have differing viewpoints, sometimes very strongly held ones.

This chapter is organized to move from those aspects of creation that are most clearly taught in Scripture, and on which almost all evangelicals would agree (creation out of nothing, special creation of Adam and Eve, and the goodness of the universe), to other aspects of creation about which evangelicals have had disagreements (whether God used a process of evolution to bring about much of creation, and how old the earth and the human race are).

We may define the doctrine of creation as follows: *God created the entire universe out of nothing; it was originally very good; and he created it to glorify himself.*

A. God Created the Universe Out of Nothing

1. Biblical Evidence for Creation Out of Nothing. The Bible clearly requires us to believe that God created the universe out of nothing. (Sometimes the Latin phrase *ex nihilo,* "out of nothing" is used; it is then said that the Bible teaches creation *ex nihilo.*)

---

[1]I am grateful for many helpful comments on this chapter made by friends with specialized knowledge about some aspects of it, especially Steve Figard, Doug Brandt, and Terry Mortenson.

This means that before God began to create the universe, nothing else existed except God himself.[2]

This is the implication of Genesis 1:1, which says, "In the beginning God created the heavens and the earth." The phrase "the heavens and the earth" includes the entire universe. Psalm 33 also tells us, "By the word of the LORD the heavens were made, and all their host by the breath of his mouth. . . . For he spoke, and it came to be; he commanded, and it stood forth" (Ps. 33:6, 9). In the New Testament, we find a universal statement at the beginning of John's gospel: "*All things* were made through him, and without him was not anything made that was made" (John 1:3). The phrase "all things" is best taken to refer to the entire universe (cf. Acts 17:24; Heb. 11:3). Paul is quite explicit in Colossians 1 when he specifies all the parts of the universe, both visible and invisible things: "For in him *all things* were created, in heaven and on earth, *visible and invisible,* whether thrones or dominions or principalities or authorities—all things were created through him and for him" (Col. 1:16). The song of the twenty-four elders in heaven likewise affirms this truth:

> "You are worthy, our Lord and God,
> to receive glory and honor and power,
> for you created *all things,*
> and by your will they existed and were created." (Rev. 4:11)

In the last phrase God's will is said to be the reason why things even "existed" at all and why they "were created."

That God created both the heavens and the earth and everything in them is affirmed several other times in the New Testament. For instance, Acts 4:24 speaks of God as the "Sovereign Lord, who made *the heaven and the earth and the sea and everything in them.*" One of the first ways of identifying God is to say that he is the one who created all things. Barnabas and Paul explain to the pagan audience at Lystra that they are messengers of "a living God who made the heaven and the earth and the sea and all that is in them" (Acts 14:15). Similarly, when Paul is speaking to pagan Greek philosophers in Athens, he identifies the true God as "The God who made the world and everything in it" and says that this God "gives to all men life and breath and everything" (Acts 17:24–25; cf. Isa. 45:18; Rev. 10:6).

Hebrews 11:3 says, "By faith we understand that the worlds were prepared by the word of God, so that what is seen was not made out of things which are visible" (NASB). This translation (as well as the NIV) most accurately reflects the Greek text.[3] Though the text does not quite teach the doctrine of creation out of nothing, it comes close to doing

---

[2]When we say that the universe was created "out of nothing," it is important to guard against a possible misunderstanding. The word *nothing* does not imply some kind of existence, as some philosophers have taken it to mean. We mean rather that God did not use any previously existing materials when he created the universe.

[3]The RSV translation ("so that what is seen was made out of things which do not appear") apparently affirms that God made the universe out of invisible matter of some sort, but the word order of the Greek text (*mē ek phainomenōn*) shows that the word "not" negates the phrase "out of appearing things." The RSV translation reads as if the word "not" negated the participle "appearing," but it would need to appear immediately before it in order to do that. See discussion in Philip Hughes, *A Commentary on the Epistle to the Hebrews* (Grand Rapids: Eerdmans, 1977), pp. 443–52.

so, since it says that God did not create the universe out of anything that is visible. The somewhat strange idea that the universe might have been created out of something that was invisible is probably not in the author's mind. He is contradicting the idea of creation out of previously existing matter, and for that purpose the verse is quite clear.

Romans 4:17 also implies that God created out of nothing, even if it does not exactly state it. The Greek text literally speaks of God as one who "calls things not existing as existing." The RSV translation, "calls into existence the things that do not exist" (similarly NASB) is unusual but possible grammatically,[4] and it makes an explicit affirmation of creation out of nothing. Yet even if we translate it so that the Greek word *hos* takes its common sense "as," the verse says that God "calls the things which do not exist as existing" (NASB mg.). But if God speaks to or calls something that does not exist, as if in fact it did exist, then what is implied? If he calls things that do not exist as though they existed, it must mean that they will soon exist, irresistibly called into existence.

Because God created the entire universe out of nothing there is no matter in the universe that is eternal. All that we see—the mountains, the oceans, the stars, the earth itself—all came into existence when God created them. There was a time when they did not exist:

> "Before the mountains were brought forth,
>   or ever you had formed the earth and the world,
>   from everlasting to everlasting you are God." (Ps. 90:2)

This reminds us that God rules over all the universe and that nothing in creation is to be worshiped instead of God or in addition to him. However, were we to deny creation out of nothing, we would have to say that some matter has always existed and that it is eternal like God. This idea would challenge God's independence, his sovereignty, and the fact that worship is due to him alone: if matter existed apart from God, then what inherent right would God have to rule over it and use it for his glory? And what confidence could we have that every aspect of the universe will ultimately fulfill God's purposes, if some parts of it were not created by him?

The positive side of the fact that God created the universe out of nothing is that it has meaning and a purpose. God, in his wisdom, created it for something. We should try to understand that purpose and use creation in ways that fit that purpose, namely, to bring glory to God himself.[5] Moreover, whenever the creation brings us joy (cf. 1 Tim. 6:17), we should give thanks to the God who made it all.

2. The Creation of the Spiritual Universe. This creation of the entire universe includes the creation of an unseen, spiritual realm of existence: God created the angels and other kinds of heavenly beings as well as animals and man. He also created heaven as a place where his presence is especially evident. The creation of the spiritual realm is certainly implied in all the verses above that speak of God creating not only the earth but also "heaven and what is in it" (Rev. 10:6; cf. Acts 4:24), but it is also explicitly affirmed in

---

[4]See C. E. B. Cranfield, *A Critical and Exegetical Commentary on the Epistle to the Romans,* ICC, vol. 1 (Edinburgh: T. & T. Clark, 1975), p. 244: Greek *hos* as expressing consequence.
[5]See section C below on God's purpose for creation.

a number of other verses. The prayer of Ezra says very clearly: "You are the LORD, you alone; you have made heaven, the heaven of heavens, with all their host, the earth and all that is on it, the seas and all that is in them; and you preserve all of them; and the host of heaven worships you" (Neh. 9:6). The "host of heaven" in this verse seems to refer to the angels and other heavenly creatures, since Ezra says that they engage in the activity of worshiping God (the same term *host* is used to speak of angels who worship God in Ps. 103:21 and 148:2).[6]

In the New Testament, Paul specifies that in Christ "all things were created, in heaven and on earth, visible *and invisible,* whether thrones or dominions or principalities or authorities—all things were created through him and for him" (Col. 1:16; cf. Ps. 148:2–5). Here the creation of invisible heavenly beings is also explicitly affirmed.

3. The Direct Creation of Adam and Eve. The Bible also teaches that God created Adam and Eve in a special, personal way. "The LORD God formed man of dust from the ground, and breathed into his nostrils the breath of life; and man became a living being" (Gen. 2:7). After that, God created Eve from Adam's body: "So the LORD God caused a deep sleep to fall upon the man, and while he slept took one of his ribs and closed up its place with flesh; and the rib which the LORD God had taken from the man he made into a woman and brought her to the man" (Gen. 2:21–22). God apparently let Adam know something of what had happened, for Adam said,

> "This at last is bone of my bones
> > and flesh of my flesh;
> she shall be called Woman,
> > because she was taken out of Man." (Gen. 2:23)

As we shall see below, Christians differ on the extent to which evolutionary developments may have occurred after creation, perhaps (according to some) leading to the development of more and more complex organisms. While there are sincerely held differences on that question among some Christians with respect to the plant and animal kingdoms, these texts are so explicit that it would be very difficult for someone to hold to the complete truthfulness of Scripture and still hold that human beings are the result of a long evolutionary process. This is because when Scripture says that the Lord "formed man of dust from the ground" (Gen. 2:7), it does not seem possible to understand that to mean that he did it over a process that took millions of years and employed the random development of thousands of increasingly complex organisms.[7] Even more impossible to reconcile with an evolutionary view is the fact that this narrative clearly portrays Eve as having no female parent: she was created directly from Adam's rib while Adam slept (Gen. 2:21). But on a purely evolutionary view, this would not be possible, for

---

[6]The word translated "host" (Heb. *tsābā'*) is sometimes used to refer to the planets and stars (Deut. 4:19; Isa. 34:4; 40:26), but none of the examples cited in BDB, p. 839 (1.c) speak of the stars worshiping God, and most speak of the heavenly bodies as "the host of heaven" who are wrongly worshiped by pagans (Deut. 17:3; 2 Kings 17:16; 21:3; Jer. 8:2, et al.).

[7]In spite of this explicit statement in Gen. 2:7, Derek Kid-ner (who holds a view of the truthfulness of Scripture compatible with that advocated in this book) does advocate the possibility of evolutionary development of a long line of pre-Adamite creatures into one of whom God finally "breathed human life" (*Genesis: An Introduction and Commentary,* TOTC [London and Chicago: InterVarsity Press, 1967], p. 28). But he then affirms a special creation of Eve (p. 29).

even the very first female "human being" would have been descended from some nearly human creature that was still an animal. The New Testament reaffirms the historicity of this special creation of Eve from Adam when Paul says, "For man was not made from woman, but *woman from man*. Neither was man created for woman, but woman for man" (1 Cor. 11:8–9).

The special creation of Adam and Eve shows that, though we may be like animals in many respects in our physical bodies, nonetheless we are very different from animals. We are created "in God's image," the pinnacle of God's creation, more like God than any other creature, appointed to rule over the rest of creation. Even the brevity of the Genesis account of creation places a wonderful emphasis on the importance of man in distinction from the rest of the universe. It thus resists modern tendencies to see man as meaningless against the immensity of the universe. Derek Kidner notes that Scripture stands

> against every tendency to empty human history of meaning. . . . in presenting the tremendous acts of creation as a mere curtain-raiser to the drama that slowly unfolds throughout the length of the Bible. The prologue is over in a page; there are a thousand to follow.

By contrast, Kidner notes that the modern scientific account of the universe, true though it may be,

> overwhelms us with statistics that reduce our apparent significance to a vanishing-point. Not the prologue, but the human story itself, is now the single page in a thousand, and the whole terrestrial volume is lost among uncataloged millions.[8]

Scripture gives us the perspective on human significance that God intends us to have.

4. The Creation of Time. One other aspect of God's creation is the creation of time (the succession of moments one after another). This idea was discussed with respect to God's attribute of eternity in chapter 4, and we need only summarize it here. When we speak of God's existence "before" the creation of the world, we should not think of God as existing in an unending extension of time. Rather, God's eternity means that he has a different kind of existence, an existence without the passage of time, a kind of existence that is difficult for us even to imagine. (See Job 36:26; Ps. 90:2, 4; John 8:58; 2 Peter 3:8; Rev. 1:8.) The fact that God created time reminds us of his lordship over it and our obligation to use it for his glory.

5. The Work of the Son and of the Holy Spirit in Creation. God the Father was the primary agent in initiating the act of creation. But the Son and the Holy Spirit were also active. The Son is often described as the one "through" whom creation came about. "All things were made *through* him, and without him was not anything made that was made" (John 1:3). Paul says there is "one Lord, Jesus Christ, *through* whom are all things and *through* whom we exist" (1 Cor. 8:6), and, "all things were created *through* him and for

---

[8]Kidner, *Genesis*, p. 57.

him" (Col. 1:16). We read also that the Son is the one "through whom" God "created the world" (Heb. 1:2). These passages give a consistent picture of the Son as the active agent carrying out the plans and directions of the Father.

The Holy Spirit was also at work in creation. He is generally pictured as completing, filling, and giving life to God's creation. In Genesis 1:2, "the Spirit of God was moving over the face of the waters," indicating a preserving, sustaining, governing function. Job says, "The spirit of God has made me, and the breath of the Almighty gives me life" (Job 33:4). In a number of Old Testament passages, it is important to realize that the same Hebrew word (*rûach*) can mean, in different contexts, "spirit," or "breath," or "wind." But in many cases there is not much difference in meaning, for even if one decided to translate some phrases as the "breath of God" or even the "wind of God," it would still seem to be a figurative way of referring to the activity of the Holy Spirit in creation. So the psalmist, in speaking of the great variety of creatures on the earth and in the sea, says, "When you send forth your Spirit, they are created" (Ps. 104:30; note also, on the Holy Spirit's work, Job 26:13; Isa. 40:13; 1 Cor. 2:10). However, the testimony of Scripture to the specific activity of the Holy Spirit in creation is scarce. The work of the Holy Spirit is brought into much greater prominence in connection with the inspiring of the authors of Scripture and the applying of Christ's redemptive work to the people of God.

B. Creation Is Distinct From God Yet Always Dependent on God

The teaching of Scripture about the relationship between God and creation is unique among the religions of the world. The Bible teaches that God is distinct from his creation. He is not part of it, for he has made it and rules over it. The term often used to say that God is much greater than creation is the word *transcendent*. Very simply, this means that God is far "above" the creation in the sense that he is greater than the creation and he is independent of it.

God is also very much involved in creation, for it is continually dependent on him for its existence and its functioning. The technical term used to speak of God's involvement in creation is the word *immanent*, meaning "remaining in" creation. The God of the Bible is no abstract deity removed from, and uninterested in his creation. The Bible is the story of God's involvement with his creation, and particularly the people in it. Job affirms that even the animals and plants depend on God: "In his hand is the life of every living thing and the breath of all mankind" (Job 12:10). In the New Testament, Paul affirms that God "gives to all men life and breath and everything" and that "in him we live and move and have our being" (Acts 17:25, 28). Indeed, in Christ "all things hold together" (Col. 1:17), and he is continually "upholding the universe by his word of power" (Heb. 1:3). God's transcendence and immanence are both affirmed in a single verse when Paul speaks of "one God and Father of us all, who is above all and through all and in all" (Eph. 4:6).

The fact that creation is distinct from God yet always dependent on God, that God is far above creation yet always involved in it (in brief, that God is both transcendent and immanent), may be represented as in figure 8.1.

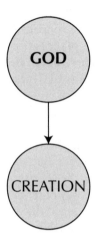

CREATION IS DISTINCT FROM GOD YET ALWAYS DEPENDENT ON GOD
(GOD IS BOTH TRANSCENDENT AND IMMANENT)
Figure 8.1

This is clearly distinct from *materialism,* which is the most common philosophy of unbelievers today, and which denies the existence of God altogether. Materialism would say that the material universe is all there is. It may be represented as in figure 8.2.

MATERIALISM
Figure 8.2

Christians today who focus almost the entire effort of their lives on earning more money and acquiring more possessions become "practical" materialists in their activity, since their lives would be not much different if they did not believe in God at all.

The scriptural account of God's relation to his creation is also distinct from pantheism. The Greek word *pan* means "all" or "every," and *pantheism* is the idea that everything, the whole universe, is God, or is part of God. This can be pictured as in figure 8.3.

Pantheism denies several essential aspects of God's character. If the whole universe is God, then God has no distinct personality. God is no longer unchanging, because as the universe changes, God also changes. Moreover, God is no longer holy, because the evil in the universe is also part of God. Another difficulty is that ultimately most panthe-

PANTHEISM
Figure 8.3

istic systems (such as Buddhism and many other eastern religions) end up denying the importance of individual human personalities: since everything is God, the goal of an individual should be to blend in with the universe and become more and more united with it, thus losing his or her individual distinctiveness. If God himself (or itself) has no distinct personal identity separate from the universe, then we should certainly not strive to have one either. Thus, pantheism destroys not only the personal identity of God, but also, ultimately, of human beings as well.

Any philosophy that sees creation as an "emanation" out of God (that is, something that comes out of God but is still part of God and not distinct from him) would be similar to pantheism in most or all of the ways in which aspects of God's character are denied.

The biblical account also rules out *dualism*. This is the idea that both God and the material universe have eternally existed side by side. Thus, there are two ultimate forces in the universe, God and matter. This may be represented as in figure 8.4.

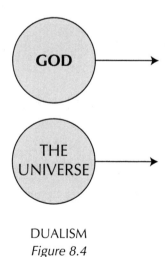

DUALISM
Figure 8.4

The problem with dualism is that it indicates an eternal conflict between God and the evil aspects of the material universe. Will God ultimately triumph over evil in the universe? We cannot be sure, because both God and evil have apparently always existed side by side. This philosophy would deny both God's ultimate lordship over creation and also that creation came about because of God's will, that it is to be used solely for his purposes, and that it is to glorify him. This viewpoint would also deny that all of the universe was created inherently good (Gen. 1:31) and would encourage people to view material reality as somewhat evil in itself, in contrast with a genuine biblical account of a creation that God made to be good and that he rules over for his purposes.

One recent example of dualism in modern culture is the series of *Star Wars* movies, which postulate the existence of a universal "Force" that has both a good and an evil side. There is no concept of one holy and transcendent God who rules over all and will certainly triumph over all. When non-Christians today begin to be aware of a spiritual aspect to the universe, they often become dualists, merely acknowledging that there are good and evil aspects to the supernatural or spiritual world. Most "New Age" religion is dualistic. Of course, Satan is delighted to have people think that there is an evil force in the universe that is perhaps equal to God himself.

The Christian view of creation is also distinct from the viewpoint of *deism*. Deism is the view that God is not now directly involved in the creation. It may be represented as in figure 8.5.

DEISM
Figure 8.5

Deism generally holds that God created the universe and is far greater than the universe (God is "transcendent"). Some deists also agree that God has moral standards and will ultimately hold people accountable on a day of judgment. But they deny God's present involvement in the world, thus leaving no place for his immanence in the created order. Rather, God is viewed as a divine clock maker who wound up the "clock" of creation at the beginning but then left it to run on its own.

While deism does affirm God's transcendence in some ways, it denies almost the entire history of the Bible, which is the history of God's active involvement in the world. Many "lukewarm" or nominal Christians today are, in effect, practical deists, since they live lives almost totally devoid of genuine prayer, worship, fear of God, or moment-by-moment trust in God to care for needs that arise.

C. God Created the Universe to Show His Glory

It is clear that God created his people for his own glory, for he speaks of his sons and daughters as those "whom I created *for my glory,* whom I formed and made" (Isa. 43:7). But it is not only human beings that God created for this purpose. The entire creation is intended to show God's glory. Even the inanimate creation, the stars and sun and moon and sky, testify to God's greatness, "The heavens are telling the glory of God; and the firmament proclaims his handiwork. Day to day pours forth speech, and night to night declares knowledge" (Ps. 19:1–2). The song of heavenly worship in Revelation 4 connects God's creation of all things with the fact that he is worthy to receive glory from them:

"You are worthy, our Lord and God,
    to receive glory and honor and power,
for you have created all things,
    and by your will they existed and were created." (Rev. 4:11)

What does creation show about God? Primarily it shows his great power and wisdom, far above anything that could be imagined by any creature. "It is he who made the earth by his power, who established the world by his wisdom, and by his understanding stretched out the heavens" (Jer. 10:12). In contrast to ignorant men and the "worthless" idols they make, Jeremiah says, "Not like these is he who is the portion of Jacob, for he is the one who formed all things . . . the LORD of hosts is his name" (Jer. 10:16). One glance at the sun or the stars convinces us of God's infinite power. And even a brief inspection of any leaf on a tree, or of the wonder of the human hand, or of any one living cell, convinces us of God's great wisdom. Who could make all of this? Who could make it out of nothing? Who could sustain it day after day for endless years? Such infinite power, such intricate skill, is completely beyond our comprehension. When we meditate on it, we give glory to God.

When we affirm that God created the universe to show his glory, it is important that we realize that he did not need to create it. We should not think that God needed more glory than he had within the Trinity for all eternity, or that he was somehow incomplete without the glory that he would receive from the created universe. This would be to deny God's independence and imply that God needed the universe in order to be fully God.[9] Rather, we must affirm that the creation of the universe was a *totally free act of God.* It was not a necessary act but something that God chose to do. "You created all things, and *by your will* they existed and were created" (Rev. 4:11). God desired to create the universe to demonstrate his excellence. The creation shows his great wisdom and power, and ultimately it shows all of his other attributes as well.[10] It seems that God created the universe,

[9]See the discussion of God's independence in chapter 4, pp. 51–54.

[10]See the discussion in chapter 4, pp. 49–51, on the ways in which all of creation reveals various aspects of God's character.

then, to take delight in his creation, for as creation shows forth various aspects of God's character, to that extent he takes delight in it.

This explains why we take spontaneous delight in all sorts of creative activities ourselves. People with artistic or musical or literary skills enjoy creating things and seeing, hearing, or pondering their creative work. God has so made us to enjoy imitating, in a creaturely way, his creative activity. And one of the amazing aspects of humanity—in distinction from the rest of creation—is our ability to create new things. This also explains why we take delight in other kinds of "creative" activity: many people enjoy cooking, or decorating their home, or working with wood or other materials, or producing scientific inventions, or devising new solutions to problems in industrial production. Even children enjoy coloring pictures or building houses out of blocks. In all of these activities we reflect in small measure the creative activity of God, and we should delight in it and thank him for it.

D. The Universe God Created Was "Very Good"

This point follows from the previous point. If God created the universe to show his glory, then we would expect that the universe would fulfill the purpose for which he created it. In fact, when God finished his work of creation, he did take delight in it. At the end of each stage of creation God saw that what he had done was "good" (Gen. 1:4, 10, 12, 18, 21, 25). Then at the end of the six days of creation, "God saw everything that he had made, and behold, it was very good" (Gen. 1:31). God delighted in the creation that he had made, just as he had purposed to do.

Even though there is now sin in the world, the material creation is still good in God's sight and should be seen as "good" by us as well. This knowledge will free us from a false asceticism that sees the use and enjoyment of the material creation as wrong. Paul says that those who "forbid marriage," and "enjoin abstinence from foods which God created to be received with thanksgiving by those who believe and know the truth" (1 Tim. 4:1–3) are giving heed to "doctrines of demons." The apostle takes such a firm line because he understands that "everything created by God is good, and nothing is to be rejected if it is received with thanksgiving; for then it is consecrated by the word of God and prayer" (1 Tim. 4:4–5). Paul's mention of "the word of God" that consecrates or "sanctifies" the foods and other things we enjoy in the material creation is probably a reference to the blessing of God spoken in Genesis 1:31, "It was very good."

Though the created order can be used in sinful or selfish ways and can turn our affections away from God, nonetheless we must not let the danger of the abuse of God's creation keep us from a positive, thankful, joyful use of it for our own enjoyment and for the good of his kingdom. Shortly after Paul has warned against the desire to be rich and the "love of money" (1 Tim. 6:9–10), he affirms that it is God himself "who richly furnishes us with everything to enjoy" (1 Tim. 6:17). This fact gives warrant for Christians to encourage proper industrial and technological development (together with care for the environment), and joyful and thankful use of all the products of the abundant earth that God has created—both by ourselves and by those with whom we are to share generously of our possessions (note 1 Tim. 6:18). Yet in all of this we are to remember that material possessions are only temporary, not eternal. We are to set our hopes on God (see Ps. 62:10; 1 Tim. 6:17) and on receiving a kingdom that cannot be shaken (Col. 3:1–4; Heb. 12:28; 1 Peter 1:4).

E. The Relationship Between Scripture and the Findings of Modern Science

At various times in history, Christians have found themselves dissenting from the accepted findings of contemporary science. In the vast majority of cases, sincere Christian faith and strong trust in the Bible have led scientists to the discovery of new facts about God's universe, and these discoveries have changed scientific opinion for all of subsequent history. The lives of Isaac Newton, Galileo Galilei, Johannes Kepler, Blaise Pascal, Robert Boyle, Michael Faraday, James Clerk Maxwell, and many others are examples of this.[11]

On the other hand, there have been times when accepted scientific opinion has been in conflict with people's understanding of what the Bible said. For example, when the Italian astronomer Galileo (1564–1642) began to teach that the earth was not the center of the universe but that the earth and other planets revolved around the sun (thus following the theories of the Polish astronomer Copernicus [1472–1543]), he was criticized, and eventually his writings were condemned by the Roman Catholic Church. This was because many people thought that the Bible taught that the sun revolved about the earth. In fact, the Bible does not teach that at all, but it was Copernican astronomy that made people look again at Scripture to see if it really taught what they thought it taught. In fact, descriptions of the sun rising and setting (Eccl. 1:5, et al.) merely portray events as they appear from the perspective of the human observer, and, from that perspective, they give an accurate description. But they imply nothing about the relative motion of the earth and the sun, and nowhere does the Bible explain what makes the sun go "down" in the viewpoint of a human observer. Scripture says nothing at all about whether the earth or the sun or some other body is the "center" of the universe or the solar system—that is not a question Scripture addresses. Yet the lesson of Galileo, who was forced to recant his teachings and who had to live under house arrest for the last few years of his life, should remind us that careful observation of the natural world can cause us to go back to Scripture and reexamine whether Scripture actually teaches what we think it teaches. Sometimes, on closer examination of the text, we may find that our previous interpretations were incorrect.

Scientific investigation has helped Christians reevaluate what earlier generations thought about the age of the earth, for example, so that no evangelical scholar today would hold that the world was created in 4004 B.C. Yet that date was once widely believed to be the date of the creation because of the writings of Irish Archbishop James Ussher (1581–1656), one of the great scholars of his day, who carefully added together the dates in the genealogies of the Bible to find when Adam was created. Today it is widely

[11]See August J. Kling, "Men of Science/ Men of Faith," *HIS*, May 1976, pp. 26–31, for a brief survey of the life and work of several of these scientists.

acknowledged that the Bible does not tell us the precise date of the creation of the earth or of the human race (see below).

On the other hand, many people in the Christian community have steadfastly refused to agree with the dominant opinion of scientists today regarding evolution. On this matter, thousands of Christians have examined Scripture again and again in great detail, and many have concluded that Scripture is not silent on the process by which living organisms came into being. Moreover, careful observation of the facts of the created universe has produced widespread disagreement regarding theories of evolution (both from scientists who are Christians and from a number of non-Christian scientists as well).[12] So on both biblical and scientific grounds, theories of evolution have been challenged by Christians.

We should also remember that the question of the creation of the universe is unlike many other scientific questions because creation is not something that can be repeated in a laboratory experiment, nor were there any human observers of it. Therefore pronouncements by scientists about creation and the early history of the earth are at best educated speculation. If we are convinced, however, that the only observer of these events (God himself) has told us about them in the reliable words of the Bible, then we should pay careful attention to the biblical account.

In the following section, we have listed some principles by which the relationship between creation and the findings of modern science can be approached.

1. When All the Facts Are Rightly Understood, There Will Be "No Final Conflict" Between Scripture and Natural Science. The phrase "no final conflict" is taken from a very helpful book by Francis Schaeffer, *No Final Conflict*.[13] Regarding questions about the creation of the universe, Schaeffer lists several areas where, in his judgment, there is room for disagreement among Christians who believe in the total truthfulness of Scripture:

1. There is a possibility that God created a "grown-up" universe.
2. There is a possibility of a break between Genesis 1:1 and 1:2 or between 1:2 and 1:3.
3. There is a possibility of a long day in Genesis 1.
4. There is a possibility that the flood affected the geological data.
5. The use of the word "kinds" in Genesis 1 may be quite broad.
6. There is a possibility of the death of animals before the fall.
7. Where the Hebrew word *bārā'* is not used there is the possibility of sequence from previously existing things.[14]

Schaeffer makes clear that he is not saying that any of those positions is his own; only that they are theoretically possible. Schaeffer's major point is that in both our understanding of the natural world and our understanding of Scripture, our knowledge is not perfect. But we can approach both scientific and biblical study with the confidence that

---

[12]For analysis of the increasingly large body of scientific evidence against evolution, see especially the books by Michael Denton and Phillip E. Johnson cited in the bibliography to this chapter and discussed on pp. 168–72 below.

[13]Downers Grove, Ill.: InterVarsity Press, 1975.

[14]Ibid., pp. 25–33.

when all the facts are correctly understood, and when we have understood Scripture rightly, our findings will never be in conflict with each other: there will be "no final conflict." This is because God, who speaks in Scripture, knows all facts, and he has not spoken in a way that would contradict any true fact in the universe.

This is a very helpful perspective with which the Christian should begin any study of creation and modern science. We should not fear to investigate scientifically the facts of the created world but should do so eagerly and with complete honesty, confident that when facts are rightly understood, they will always turn out to be consistent with God's inerrant words in Scripture. Similarly, we should approach the study of Scripture eagerly and with confidence that, when rightly understood, Scripture will never contradict facts in the natural world.

Someone may object that this whole discussion is inappropriate, for the Bible is given to us to teach religious and ethical matters; it is not intended to teach "science." However, Scripture itself places no such restriction on the subjects to which it can speak. Although the Bible is of course not a "textbook" of science in a formal sense, it does nonetheless contain many affirmations about the natural world — its origin, its purposes, its ultimate destiny — and many statements about how it functions from day to day. If we take seriously the idea that it is God himself (as well as the human authors) who speaks all the words of Scripture, then we must take these statements seriously and believe them as well. Indeed, Scripture says that our understanding of some "scientific" facts is a matter of our faith! Hebrews 11:3 tells us, *"By faith we understand that the worlds were prepared by the word of God, so that what is seen was not made out of things which are visible"* (NASB).

2. Some Theories About Creation Seem Clearly Inconsistent With the Teachings of Scripture. In this section we will examine three types of explanation of the origin of the universe that seem clearly inconsistent with Scripture.

a. Secular Theories: For the sake of completeness we mention here only briefly that any purely secular theories of the origin of the universe would be unacceptable for those who believe in Scripture. A "secular" theory is any theory of the origin of the universe that does not see an infinite-personal God as responsible for creating the universe by intelligent design. Thus, the "big bang" theory (in a secular form in which God is excluded), or any theories that hold that matter has always existed, would be inconsistent with the teaching of Scripture that God created the universe out of nothing, and that he did so for his own glory. (When Darwinian evolution is thought of in a totally materialistic sense, as it most often is, it would belong in this category also.)[15]

b. Theistic Evolution: Ever since the publication of Charles Darwin's book *Origin of Species by Means of Natural Selection* (1859), some Christians have proposed that living organisms came about by the process of evolution that Darwin proposed, but that God guided that process so that the result was just what he wanted it to be. This view is called

---

[15]See pp. 167–75 below, for a discussion of Darwinian evolution.

theistic evolution because it advocates belief in God (it is "theistic") and in evolution too. Many who hold to theistic evolution would propose that God intervened in the process at some crucial points, usually (1) the creation of matter at the beginning, (2) the creation of the simplest life form, and (3) the creation of man. But, with the possible exception of those points of intervention, theistic evolutionists hold that evolution proceeded in the ways now discovered by natural scientists, and that it was the process that God decided to use in allowing all of the other forms of life on earth to develop. They believe that the random mutation of living things led to the evolution of higher life forms through the fact that those that had an "adaptive advantage" (a mutation that allowed them to be better fitted to survive in their environment) lived when others did not.

Theistic evolutionists are quite prepared to change their views of the way evolution came about, because, according to their standpoint, the Bible does not specify how it happened. It is therefore up to us to discover this through ordinary scientific investigation. They would argue that as we learn more and more about the way in which evolution came about, we are simply learning more and more about the process that God used to bring about the development of life forms.

The objections to theistic evolution are as follows:

1. The clear teaching of Scripture that there is purposefulness in God's work of creation seems incompatible with the randomness demanded by evolutionary theory. When Scripture reports that God said, "Let the earth bring forth living creatures according to their kinds: cattle and creeping things and beasts of the earth according to their kinds" (Gen. 1:24), it pictures God as doing things intentionally and with a purpose for each thing he does. But this is the opposite of allowing mutations to proceed entirely *randomly,* with no purpose for the millions of mutations that would have to come about, under evolutionary theory, before a new species could emerge.

The fundamental difference between a biblical view of creation and theistic evolution lies here: the driving force that brings about change and the development of new species in all evolutionary schemes is *randomness.* Without the random mutation of organisms you do not have evolution in the modern scientific sense at all. Random mutation is the underlying force that brings about eventual development from the simplest to the most complex life forms. But the driving force in the development of new organisms according to Scripture is God's *intelligent design.* God created "the great creatures of the sea and every living and moving thing with which the water teems, according to their kinds, and every winged bird according to its kind" (Gen. 1:21 NIV). "God made the wild animals according to their kinds, the livestock according to their kinds, and all the creatures that move along the ground according to their kinds. And God saw that it was good" (Gen. 1:25 NIV). These statements seem inconsistent with the idea of God creating or directing or observing millions of random mutations, none of which were "very good" in the way he intended, none of which really were the kinds of plants or animals he wanted to have on the earth. Instead of the straightforward biblical account of God's creation, the theistic evolution view has to understand events to have occurred something like this:

> And God said, "Let the earth bring forth living creatures according to their kinds." And after three hundred eighty-seven million four hundred ninety-two thousand eight hundred seventy-one attempts, God finally made a mouse that worked.

That may seem a strange explanation, but it is precisely what the theistic evolutionist must postulate for each of the hundreds of thousands of different kinds of plants and animals on the earth: they all developed through a process of random mutation over millions of years, gradually increasing in complexity as occasional mutations turned out to be advantageous to the creature.

A theistic evolutionist may object that God intervened in the process and guided it at many points in the direction he wanted it to go. But once this is allowed then there is purpose and intelligent design in the process—we no longer have evolution at all, because there is no longer random mutation (at the points of divine interaction). No secular evolutionist would accept such intervention by an intelligent, purposeful Creator. But once a Christian agrees to some active, purposeful design by God, then there is no longer any need for randomness or any development emerging from random mutation. Thus we may as well have God immediately creating each distinct creature without thousands of attempts that fail.

2. Scripture pictures God's creative word as bringing immediate response. When the Bible talks about God's creative word it emphasizes the power of his word and its ability to accomplish his purpose.

> By the word of the LORD the heavens were made,
>   and all their host by the breath of his mouth.
> . . . For he spoke, and it came to be;
>   he commanded, and it stood forth. (Ps. 33:6, 9)

This kind of statement seems incompatible with the idea that God spoke and after millions of years and millions of random mutations in living things his power brought about the result that he had called for. Rather, as soon as God says, "Let the earth put forth vegetation," the very next sentence tells us, "And it was so" (Gen. 1:11).

3. When Scripture tells us that God made plants and animals to reproduce *according to their kinds*" (Gen. 1:11, 24), it suggests that God created many different types of plants and animals and that, though there would be some differentiation among them (note many different sizes, races, and personal characteristics among human beings!), nonetheless there would be some narrow limits to the kind of change that could come about through genetic mutations.[16]

4. God's present active role in creating or forming every living thing that now comes into being is hard to reconcile with the distant "hands off" kind of oversight of evolution

[16]We do not need to insist that the Hebrew word *min* ("kind") corresponds exactly with the biological category "species," for that is simply a modern means of classifying different living things. But the Hebrew word does seem to indicate a narrow specification of various types of living things. It is used, for example, to speak of several very specific types of animals that bear young and are distinguished according to their "kind." Scripture speaks of "the falcon according to its kind," "every raven according to its kind," "the hawk according to its kind," "the heron according to its kind," and "the locust according to its kind" (Lev. 11:14, 15, 16, 19, 22). Other animals that exist according to an individual "kind" are the cricket, grasshopper, great lizard, buzzard, kite, sea gull, and stork (Lev. 11:22, 29; Deut. 14:13, 14, 15, 18). These are very specific kinds of animals, and God created them so that they would reproduce only according to their own "kinds." It seems that this would allow only for diversification within each of these types of animals (larger or smaller hawks, hawks of different color and with different shapes of beaks, etc.), but certainly not any "macroevolutionary" change into entirely different kinds of birds. (Frair and Davis, *A Case for Creation* [Norcross, Ga.: CRS Books, 1983], p. 129, think that "kind" may correspond to family or order today, or else to no precise twentieth-century equivalent.)

that is proposed by theistic evolution. David is able to confess, "You formed my inward parts, you knit me together in my mother's womb" (Ps. 139:13). And God said to Moses, "Who has made man's mouth? Who makes him dumb, or deaf, or seeing, or blind? Is it not I, the LORD?" (Ex. 4:11). God makes the grass grow (Ps. 104:14; Matt. 6:30) and feeds the birds (Matt. 6:26) and the other creatures of the forest (Ps. 104:21, 27–30). If God is so involved in causing the growth and development of every step of every living thing even now, does it seem consistent with Scripture to say that these life forms were originally brought about by an evolutionary process directed by random mutation rather than by God's direct, purposeful creation, and that only after they had been created did he begin his active involvement in directing them each moment?

5. The special creation of Adam, and Eve from him, is a strong reason to break with theistic evolution. Those theistic evolutionists who argue for a special creation of Adam and Eve because of the statements in Genesis 1–2 have really broken with evolutionary theory at the point that is of most concern to human beings anyway. But if, on the basis of Scripture, we insist upon God's special intervention at the point of the creation of Adam and Eve, then what is to prevent our allowing that God intervened, in a similar way, in the creation of living organisms?

We must realize that the special creation of Adam and Eve as recorded in Scripture shows them to be far different from the nearly animal, just barely human creatures that evolutionists would say were the first humans, creatures who descended from ancestors that were highly developed nonhuman apelike creatures. Scripture pictures the first man and woman, Adam and Eve, as possessing highly developed linguistic, moral, and spiritual abilities from the moment they were created. They can talk with each other. They can even talk with God. They are very different from the nearly animal first humans, descended from nonhuman apelike creatures, of evolutionary theory.

Some may object that Genesis 1–2 does not intend to portray Adam and Eve as literal individuals, but (a) the historical narrative in Genesis continues without a break into the obviously historical material about Abraham (Gen. 12), showing that the author intended the entire section to be historical,[17] and (b) in Romans 5:12–21 and 1 Corinthians 15:21–22, 45–49, Paul affirms the existence of the "one man" Adam through whom sin came into the world, and bases his discussion of Christ's representative work of earning salvation on the previous historical pattern of Adam being a representative for mankind as well. Moreover, the New Testament elsewhere clearly understands Adam and Eve to be historical figures (cf. Luke 3:38; Acts 17:26; 1 Cor. 11:8–9; 2 Cor. 11:3; 1 Tim. 2:13–14). The New Testament also assumes the historicity of the sons of Adam and Eve, Cain (Heb. 11:4; 1 John 3:12; Jude 11) and Abel (Matt. 23:35; Luke 11:51; Heb. 11:4; 12:24).

---

[17]Note the phrase "These are the generations of " introducing successive sections in the Genesis narrative at Gen. 2:4 (heavens and the earth); 5:1 (Adam); 6:9 (Noah); 10:1 (the sons of Noah); 11:10 (Shem); 11:27 (Terah, the father of Abraham); 25:12 (Ishmael); 25:19 (Isaac); 36:1 (Esau); and 37:2 (Jacob). The translation of the phrase may differ in various English versions, but the Hebrew expression is the same and literally says, "These are the generations of. . . ." By this literary device the author has introduced various sections of his historical narrative, tying it all together in a unified whole, and indicating that it is to be understood as history-writing of the same sort throughout. If the author intends us to understand Abraham, Isaac, and Jacob as historical figures, then he also intends us to understand Adam and Eve as historical figures.

6. There are many scientific problems with evolutionary theory (see the following section). The increasing number of questions about the validity of the theory of evolution being raised even by non-Christians in various scientific disciplines indicates that anyone who claims to be forced to believe in evolution because the "scientific facts" leave no other option has simply not considered all the evidence on the other side. The scientific data do not force one to accept evolution, and if the scriptural record argues convincingly against it as well, it does not seem to be a valid theory for a Christian to adopt.

It seems most appropriate to conclude in the words of geologist Davis A. Young, "The position of theistic evolutionism as expressed by some of its proponents is not a consistently Christian position. It is not a truly biblical position, for it is based in part on principles that are imported into Christianity."[18] According to Louis Berkhof "theistic evolution is really a child of embarrassment, which calls God in at periodic intervals to help nature over the chasms that yawn at her feet. It is neither the biblical doctrine of creation, nor a consistent theory of evolution."[19]

c. Notes on the Darwinian Theory of Evolution: The word *evolution* can be used in different ways. Sometimes it is used to refer to "micro-evolution"—small developments within one species, so that we see flies or mosquitoes becoming immune to insecticides, or human beings growing taller, or different colors and varieties of roses being developed. Innumerable examples of such "micro-evolution" are evident today, and no one denies that they exist.[20] But that is not the sense in which the word *evolution* is usually used when discussing theories of creation and evolution.

The term *evolution* is more commonly used to refer to "macro-evolution"—that is, the "general theory of evolution" or the view that "nonliving substance gave rise to the first living material, which subsequently reproduced and diversified to produce all extinct and extant organisms."[21] In this chapter, when we use the word *evolution* it is used to refer to macro-evolution or the general theory of evolution.

(1) Current Challenges to Evolution: Since Charles Darwin first published his *Origin of Species by Means of Natural Selection* in 1859, there have been challenges to his theory by Christians and non-Christians alike. Current neo-Darwinian theory is still foundationally similar to Darwin's original position, but with refinements and modifications due to over a hundred years of research. In modern Darwinian evolutionary theory, the

---

[18]Davis A. Young, *Creation and the Flood: An Alternative to Flood Geology and Theistic Evolution* (Grand Rapids: Baker, 1977), p. 38. Young includes a discussion of the views of Richard H. Bube, one of the leading proponents of theistic evolution today (pp. 33–35).

[19]Berkhof, *Systematic Theology,* pp. 139–40.

[20]Phillip E. Johnson, *Darwin on Trial* (Downers Grove, Ill.: InterVarsity Press, 1991), points out that some studies frequently claimed as evidence of evolution are really just temporary population differences with no genetic change. For example, he mentions Kettlewell's observation of "industrial melanism" in the peppered moth, whereby the prevailing color of the moths changed from white to black and back to

white again when leaves on trees were light colored, then covered with soot from pollution, then again light colored when the pollution ended. But at every stage, both black and white moths were present, even though in differing proportions (moths that did not match the leaf color were more easily seen and eaten by predators). No evolutionary change occurred at all, for both black and white moths were still industrial moths, just as black and white horses are both still horses. In fact, the moth functioned to preserve its genetic identity in differing circumstances, rather than evolving or becoming extinct (see pp. 26–28, 160–61).

[21]Frair and Davis, *A Case for Creation,* p. 25.

history of the development of life began when a mix of chemicals present on the earth spontaneously produced a very simple, probably one-celled life form. This living cell reproduced itself, and eventually there were some mutations or differences in the new cells produced. These mutations led to the development of more complex life forms. A hostile environment meant that many of them would perish, but those that were better suited to their environment would survive and multiply. Thus, nature exercised a process of "natural selection" in which the differing organisms most fitted to the environment survived. More and more mutations eventually developed into more and more varieties of living things, so that from the very simplest organism all the complex life forms on earth eventually developed through this process of mutation and natural selection.

The most recent, and perhaps most devastating, critique of current Darwinian theory comes from Phillip E. Johnson, a law professor who specializes in analyzing the logic of arguments. In his book *Darwin on Trial*,[22] he quotes extensively from current evolutionary theorists to demonstrate that:

1. After more than one hundred years of experimental breeding of various kinds of animals and plants, the amount of variation that can be produced (even with intentional, not random, breeding) is extremely limited, due to the limited range of genetic variation in each type of living thing: dogs who are selectively bred for generations are still dogs, fruit flies are still fruit flies, etc. And when allowed to return to the wild state, "the most highly specialized breeds quickly perish and the survivors revert to the original wild type." He concludes that "natural selection," claimed by Darwinists to account for the survival of new organisms, is really a conservative force that works to preserve the genetic fitness of a population, not to change its characteristics.[23]

2. In current evolutionary arguments, the idea of "survival of the fittest" (or "natural selection") is popularly thought to mean that those animals whose different characteristics give them a comparative advantage will survive, and others will die out. But in actual practice almost any characteristic can be argued to be either an advantage or a disadvantage.[24] So how do Darwinists know which characteristics have given an advantage in survival to certain animals? By observing which kinds survive. But this means that natural selection is often at bottom not a powerful new insight into what happens in nature but simply a tautology (a meaningless repetition of the same idea), since it boils down to saying that the "fittest" animals are those who have the most offspring. In this sense, natural selection means: animals who have the most offspring have the most

---

[22]Downers Grove, Ill.: InterVarsity Press, 1991.

[23]Johnson, pp. 15–20 (quotation from p. 18). Johnson notes that in a few cases new "species" have been produced, in the sense of a part of a population that is incapable of inter-breeding with another part: this has happened with fruit flies and with some plant hybrids (p. 19). But even though incapable of interbreeding with some other fruit flies, the new fruit flies still are fruit flies, not some other kind of creature: the amount of variation the fruit fly is capable of is inherently limited by the range of variability in its gene pool.

[24]Johnson notes (pp. 29–30) that Darwinists have even accounted for obviously disadvantageous characteristics by invoking pleiotropy, the idea that several genetic changes may occur all at once, so that the negative ones come along with the positive ones. On this basis no existing characteristic in any animal could be cited to disprove the claim that the fittest survive, for it really becomes a claim that those that have survived have survived. But then how do we really know that survival of the fittest has been the mechanism that has led to current diversity of life forms?

offspring.[25] But this proves nothing about any supposed mutations to produce different, more fit offspring over the course of many generations.

3. The vast and complex mutations required to produce complex organs such as an eye or a bird's wing (or hundreds of other organs) could not have occurred in tiny mutations accumulating over thousands of generations, because the individual parts of the organ are useless (and give no "advantage") unless the entire organ is functioning. But the mathematical probability of such random mutations happening together in one generation is effectively zero. Darwinists are left saying that it must have happened because it happened.[26]

An amusing example of the need for all the parts of a complex organic system to be put in place at once is pointed out by Robert Kofahl and Kelly Segraves in their book, *The Creation Explanation: A Scientific Alternative to Evolution*.[27] They describe the "Bombardier beetle," which repels enemies by firing a hot charge of chemicals from two swivel tubes in its tail. The chemicals fired by this beetle will spontaneously explode when mixed together in a laboratory, but apparently the beetle has an inhibitor substance that blocks the explosive reaction until the beetle squirts some of the liquid into its "combustion chambers," where an enzyme is added to catalyze the reaction. An explosion takes place and the chemical repellent is fired at a temperature of 212°F at the beetle's enemies. Kofahl and Segraves rightly ask whether any evolutionary explanation can account for this amazing mechanism:

> Note that a rational evolutionary explanation for the development of this creature must assign some kind of adaptive advantage to each of the millions of hypothetical intermediate stages in the construction process. But would the stages of one-fourth, one-half, or two-thirds completion, for example, have conferred any advantage? After all, a rifle is useless without all of its parts functioning. . . . Before this defensive mechanism could afford any protection to the beetle, all of its parts, together with the proper explosive mixture of chemicals, plus the instinctive behavior required for its use, would have to be assembled in the insect. The partially developed set of organs would be useless. Therefore, according to the principles of evolutionary theory, there would be no selective pressure to cause the system to evolve from a partially completed stage toward the final completed system. . . . If a theory fails to explain the data in any science, that theory should be either revised or replaced with a theory that is in agreement with the data.[28]

In this case, of course, the amusing question is, What would happen if the explosive chemical mixture developed in the beetle without the chemical inhibitor?

4. The fossil record was Darwin's greatest problem in 1859, and it has simply become a greater problem since then. In Darwin's time, hundreds of fossils were available showing

[25]Johnson does not say that all evolutionists argue this way, but he quotes several who do (pp. 20–23).

[26]Johnson, pp. 32–44.

[27]Robert E. Kofahl and Kelly L. Segraves, *The Creation Explanation: A Scientific Alternative to Evolution* (Wheaton,

Ill.: Harold Shaw, 1975). This book is a fascinating collection of scientific evidence favoring creation by intelligent design.

[28]Kofahl and Segraves, *The Creation Explanation*, pp. 2–3. They give many other similar examples.

the existence of many distinct kinds of animals and plants in the distant past. But Darwin was unable to find any fossils from "intermediate types" to fill in the gaps between distinct kinds of animals—fossils showing some characteristics of one animal and a few characteristics of the next developmental type, for example. In fact, many ancient fossils exactly resembled present-day animals—showing that (according to the chronological assumptions of his view) numerous animals have persisted for millions of years essentially unchanged. Darwin realized that the absence of "transitional types" in the fossil record weakened his theory, but he thought it was due to the fact that not enough fossils had been discovered, and was confident that further discoveries would unearth many transitional types of animals. However, the subsequent 130 years of intensive archaeological activity has still failed to produce one convincing example of a needed transitional type.[29]

Johnson quotes noted evolutionist Stephen Jay Gould of Harvard as saying that there are two characteristics of the fossil record that are inconsistent with the idea of gradual change through generations:

1. Stasis. Most species exhibit no directional change during their tenure on earth. They appear in the fossil record looking pretty much the same as when they disappear; morphological change is usually limited and directionless.

2. Sudden appearance. In any local area, a species does not arise gradually by the steady transformation of its ancestors; it appears all at once and "fully formed."[30]

So difficult is this problem for Darwinian evolution that many evolutionary scientists today propose that evolution came about in sudden jumps to new life forms—so that each of the thirty-two known orders of mammals, for example, appeared quite suddenly in the history of Europe.[31]

But how could hundreds or thousands of genetic changes come about all at once? No explanation has been given other than to say that it must have happened, because it happened. (A glance at the dotted lines in any current biology textbook, showing the supposed transitions from one kind of animal to another, will indicate the nature of the gaps still unfilled after 130 years of investigation.) The significance of this problem is

---

[29]Johnson, pp. 73–85, discusses the two examples sometimes claimed out of perhaps 100 million fossils that have been discovered, Archaeopteryx (a bird with some characteristics that resemble reptiles), and some ape-like examples thought to be prehuman hominids. Archaeopteryx is still very much a bird, not a near-reptile, and studies of the characteristics of the supposedly prehuman fossils include large amounts of subjective speculation, resulting in strong differences among experts who have examined them.

A helpful discussion of the gaps that remain in the fossil record is found in Frair and Davis, *A Case for Creation*, pp. 55–65. They note that the continued discovery and classification of fossils since Darwin's time has resulted in the fact that "on the whole, the discontinuities have been emphasized with increased collecting. There appears to be little question that the gaps are real, and it seems increasingly less likely that they will be filled" (p. 57).

[30]Johnson, p. 50, apparently quoting a paper by Gould and Niles Eldredge, "Punctuated Equilibria, an Alternative to Phyletic Gradualism," printed as a appendix to Eldredge's book, *Time Frames* (Johnson, p. 167).

[31]This view is called "punctuated equilibrium," meaning that the ordinary equilibrium of the natural world was occasionally interrupted (punctuated) by the sudden appearance of new life forms.

demonstrated forcefully in a recent book by a non-Christian writer, Michael Denton, *Evolution: A Theory in Crisis.*[32] Denton himself proposes no alternative explanation for the emergence of life in its present form upon the earth, but he notes that since Darwin's time,

> neither of the two fundamental axioms of Darwin's macroevolutionary theory—the concept of the continuity of nature, that is the idea of a functional continuum of all life forms linking all species together and ultimately leading back to a primeval cell, and the belief that all the adaptive design of life has resulted from a blind random process—have been validated by one single empirical discovery or scientific advance since 1859.[33]

5. The molecular structures of living organisms do show relationships, but Darwinists simply assume that relationships imply common ancestry, a claim that certainly has not been proven. Moreover, there are amazing molecular differences between living things, and no satisfactory explanation for the origin of those differences has been given.[34]

Of course, similarity of design at any level (including levels above the molecular level) has often been used as a argument for evolution. The assumption of evolutionists is that similarity of design between two species implies that the "lower" species evolved into the "higher" species, but the proof for that assumption has never been given. Gleason Archer illustrates this well by supposing that one visits a museum of science and industry and finds a display of how human beings evolved from earlier apelike creatures into progressively more human-looking beings and finally into modern man. But he rightly notes that

> a continuity of basic design furnishes no evidence whatever that any "lower" species phased into the next "higher" species by any sort of internal dynamic, as evolution demands. For if the museum visitor were to go to another part of that museum of science and industry, he would find a completely analogous series of automobiles, commencing with 1900 and extending up until the present decade. Stage by stage, phase by phase, he could trace the development of the Ford from its earliest Model-T prototype to the large and luxurious LTD of the 1970's.[35]

Of course, a much better explanation for the similarities in various models of Ford automobiles is the fact that an intelligent designer (or group of designers) used similar structures in successively more complex automobiles—if a steering mechanism works well in one model, there is no need to invent a different kind of steering mechanism for another model. In the same way, similarities in design among all living things can equally well be taken as evidence of the work of an intelligent master craftsman, the Creator himself.

---

[32]Bethesda, Md.: Adler and Adler, 1986.

[33]Denton, p. 345. An earlier analysis of evolution by a respected British biologist who is himself an evolutionist is G. A. Kerkut, *Implications of Evolution* (New York: Pergamon, 1960). This is a very technical study pointing out numerous remaining difficulties in the theory of evolution.

[34]Johnson, pp. 86–99.

[35]Gleason L. Archer, *Encyclopedia of Bible Difficulties* (Grand Rapids: Zondervan, 1982), p. 57.

6. Probably the greatest difficulty of all for evolutionary theory is explaining how any life could have begun in the first place. The spontaneous generation of even the simplest living organism capable of independent life (the prokaryote bacterial cell) from inorganic materials on the earth could not happen by random mixing of chemicals: it requires intelligent design and craftsmanship so complex that no advanced scientific laboratory in the world has been able to do it. Johnson quotes a now-famous metaphor: "That a living organism emerged by chance from a pre-biotic soup is about as likely as that 'a tornado sweeping through a junkyard might assemble a Boeing 747 from the materials therein.' Chance assembly is just a naturalistic way of saying 'miracle.'"[36]

At a common-sense level, a simple illustration will show this. If I were to take my digital watch, hand it to someone, and say that I found it near an iron mine in northern Minnesota, and that it was my belief that the watch had come together by itself simply through the operation of random movement and environmental forces (plus some energy from a few bolts of lightning, perhaps), I would quickly be written off as mad. Yet any one living cell on the leaf of any tree, or any one cell in the human body, is thousands of times more complex than my digital watch. Even given 4.5 billion years the "chance" of even one living cell arising spontaneously is, for all practical purposes, zero.

In fact, some attempts have been made to calculate the probability of life arising spontaneously in this way. Kofahl and Segraves give a statistical model in which they begin with a very generous assumption: that every square foot of the earth's surface was somehow covered with 95 pounds of protein molecules that could mix freely, and that are all replaced with fresh protein every year for one billion years. They then estimate the probability that even one enzyme molecule would develop in each one billion years of the earth's history. The probability is 1.2 times 10^{-11} or one chance in 80 billion. They note, however, that even with the generous assumptions and starting with fresh protein every year for a billion years, finding one enzyme molecule—for all practical purposes an impossible task—would not solve the problem at all:

> The probability of finding two of the active molecules would be about 10^{22}, and the probability that they would be identical would be 10^{70}. And could life start with just a single enzyme molecule? Furthermore, what is the possibility that an active enzyme molecule, once formed, could find its way through thousands of miles and millions of years to that randomly formed RNA or DNA molecule which contains the code for that particular enzyme molecule's amino acid sequence, so that new copies of itself could be produced? Zero for all practical purposes.[37]

Kofahl and Segraves report a study by an evolutionary scientist who formulates a model to calculate the probability for the formation, not just of one enzyme molecule but the smallest likely living organism by random processes. He comes up with a probability

---

[36]Johnson, p. 104, quoting Fred Hoyle. In fact, one could argue that the 747 is more likely to occur accidentally, because intelligent human designers have been able to make a 747, but they have not been able to make one living cell.

[37]Kofahl and Segraves, *The Creation Explanation*, pp. 99–100.

of one chance in $10^{340,000,000}$ — that is, one chance in 10 with 340 million zeros after it! But Kofahl and Segraves note, "Yet Dr. Morowitz and his fellow evolutionary scientists still believe that it happened!"[38]

If someone were to ask me to entrust my life to ride on an airplane, and then explained that the airline company completed its flights safely once in every $10^{340,000,000}$ times — or even one in every 80 billion flights — I certainly would not get on board, nor would anyone else in his or her right mind. Yet it is tragic that the common opinion, perpetuated in many science textbooks today, that evolution is an established "fact," has continued to persuade many people that they should not consider the total truthfulness of the Bible to be an intellectually acceptable viewpoint for responsible, thinking individuals to hold today. The myth that "evolution has disproved the Bible" persists and keeps many from considering Christianity as a valid option.

But what if some day life were actually "created" in the laboratory by scientists? Here it is important to understand what is meant. First, this would not be "creation" in the pure sense of the word, since all laboratory experiments begin with some kinds of previously existing matter. It would not give an explanation of the origin of matter itself, nor would it be the kind of creating that the Bible says God did. Second, most contemporary attempts to "create life" are really just very small steps in the gigantic process of moving from nonliving materials to an independently living organism, even one consisting of only one cell. The construction of a protein molecule or an amino acid nowhere approaches the complexity of a single living cell. But most importantly, what would it demonstrate if the collective work of thousands of the most intelligent scientists in the world, with the most expensive and complex laboratory equipment available, working over the course of several decades, actually did produce a living organism? Would that "prove" that God did not create life? Quite the opposite: it would demonstrate that life simply does not come about by chance but must be intentionally created by an intelligent designer. In theory at least, it is not impossible that human beings, created in the image of God and using their God-given intelligence could someday create a living organism out of nonliving substances (though the complexity of the task far surpasses any technology that exists today). But that would only show that God made us to be "God-like" — that in biological research as in many other areas of life we in a very small way can imitate God's activity. All such scientific research in this direction really ought to be done out of reverence for God and with gratitude for the scientific capability with which he has endowed us.

Many unbelieving scientists have been so influenced by the cumulative force of the objections brought against evolution that they have openly advocated novel positions for one part or another of the proposed evolutionary development of living things. Francis Crick, who won the Nobel Prize for helping to discover the structure of DNA molecules, proposed in 1973 that life may have been sent here by a spaceship from a distant planet,

---

[38]Ibid., p. 101, quoting Harold J. Morowitz, *Energy Flow in Biology* (New York: Academic Press, 1968), p. 99. The classic study of the mathematical improbability of evolution is P. S. Moorehead and M. M. Kaplan, eds., *Mathematical Challenges to the Neo-Darwinian Interpretation of Evolution* (Philadelphia: The Wistar Institute Symposium Monograph, no. 5, 1967). See also the article "Heresy in the Halls of Biology: Mathematicians Question Darwinism," *Scientific Research* (November 1987), pp. 59–66, and I. L. Cohen, *Darwin Was Wrong — A Study in Probabilities* (Greenvale, N.Y.: New Research Publications, 1984).

a theory that Crick calls "Directed Panspermia."[39] To the present author, it seems ironic that brilliant scientists could advocate so fantastic a theory without one shred of evidence in its favor, all the while rejecting the straightforward explanation given by the one book in the history of the world that has never been proven wrong, that has changed the lives of millions of people, that has been believed completely by many of the most intelligent scholars of every generation, and that has been a greater force for good than any other book in the history of the world. Why will otherwise intelligent people commit themselves to beliefs that seem so irrational? It seems as though they will believe in anything, so long as it is not belief in the personal God of Scripture, who calls us to forsake our pride, humble ourselves before him, ask his forgiveness for failure to obey his moral standards, and submit ourselves to his moral commands for the rest of our lives. To refuse to do this is irrational, but all sin is ultimately irrational at its root.

Other challenges to the theory of evolution have been published in the last twenty or thirty years, and no doubt many more will be forthcoming. One only hopes it will not be too long before the scientific community publicly acknowledges the implausibility of evolutionary theory, and textbooks written for high school and college students openly acknowledge that evolution simply is not a satisfactory explanation for the origin of life on the earth.

(2) The Destructive Influences of Evolutionary Theory in Modern Thought: It is important to understand the incredibly destructive influences that evolutionary theory has had on modern thinking. If in fact life was not created by God, and if human beings in particular are not created by God or responsible to him, but are simply the result of random occurrences in the universe, then of what significance is human life? We are merely the product of matter plus time plus chance, and so to think that we have any eternal importance, or really any importance at all in the face of an immense universe, is simply to delude ourselves. Honest reflection on this notion should lead people to a profound sense of despair.

Moreover, if all of life can be explained by evolutionary theory apart from God, and if there is no God who created us (or at least if we cannot know anything about him with certainty), then there is no supreme Judge to hold us morally accountable. Therefore there are no moral absolutes in human life, and people's moral ideas are only subjective preferences, good for them perhaps but not to be imposed on others. In fact, in such a case the only thing forbidden is to say that one knows that certain things are right and certain things are wrong.

There is another ominous consequence of evolutionary theory: If the inevitable processes of natural selection continue to bring about improvement in life forms on earth through the survival of the fittest, then why should we hinder this process by caring for those who are weak or less able to defend themselves? Should we not rather allow them to die without reproducing so that we might move toward a new, higher form of

---

[39]*Time*, September 10, 1973, p. 53, summarizing the article "Directed Panspermia," by F. H. C. Crick and L. E. Orgel in *Icarus* 19 (1973): 341–46.

humanity, even a "master race"? In fact, Marx, Nietzsche, and Hitler all justified war on these grounds.[40]

Moreover, if human beings are continually evolving for the better, then the wisdom of earlier generations (and particularly of earlier religious beliefs) is not likely to be as valuable as modern thought. In addition, the effect of Darwinian evolution on the people's opinions of the trustworthiness of Scripture has been a very negative one.

Contemporary sociological and psychological theories that see human beings as simply higher forms of animals are another outcome of evolutionary thought. And the extremes of the modern "animal rights" movement that oppose all killing of animals (for food, or for leather coats, or for medical research, for example) also flow naturally out of evolutionary thought.

d. The Theory of a "Gap" Between Genesis 1:1 and 1:2: Some evangelicals have proposed that there is a gap of millions of years between Genesis 1:1 ("In the beginning God created the heavens and the earth") and Genesis 1:2 ("The earth was without form and void, and darkness was upon the face of the deep"). According to this theory, God made an earlier creation, but there was eventually a rebellion against God (probably in connection with Satan's own rebellion), and God judged the earth so that "it became without form and void" (an alternative, but doubtful, translation proposed for Gen. 1:2).[41] What we read of in Genesis 1:3–2:3 is really the *second* creation of God, in six literal twenty-four-hour days, which occurred only recently (perhaps 10,000 to 20,000 years ago). The ancient fossils found on the earth, many of which are said to be millions of years old, stem from the *first* creation (4,500,000,000 years ago), which is mentioned only in Genesis 1:1.

The primary biblical argument for this theory is that the words "without form and void" and "darkness" in Genesis 1:2 picture an earth that has suffered the effects of judgment by God: darkness elsewhere in the Old Testament is frequently a sign of God's judgment, and the Hebrew words *tohû* ("without form") and *bohû* ("void, empty") in verses such as Isaiah 34:11 and Jeremiah 4:23 refer to places such as deserts that have suffered the desolating consequences of God's judgment.

But these arguments do not seem strong enough to persuade us that Genesis 1:2 pictures the earth as desolate after God's judgment. If God first forms the earth (v. 1) and then later creates light (v. 3), there would have to be darkness over the earth in

---

[40]See *NIDCC*, p. 283.

[41]This "gap theory" is given as one possible interpretation of Gen. 1:1–2 in *The New Scofield Reference Bible* (Oxford: Oxford University Press, 1967), in notes to Gen. 1:2 and Isa. 45:18. It also remains commonplace in much popular Bible teaching. An extensive defense of this theory is found in Arthur C. Custance, *Without Form and Void: A Study of the Meaning of Genesis 1:2* (Brockville, Ontario: Doorway Papers, 1970). An extensive critique is in Weston W. Fields, *Unformed and Unfilled* (Nutley, N.J.: Presbyterian and Reformed, 1976). A substantial critique of the lexical and grammatical arguments used in the gap theory is also found in Oswald T. Allis, *God Spake by Moses* (Philadelphia:

Presbyterian and Reformed, 1951), pp. 153–59.

Some readers may wonder why I have classified this view along with secular views and theistic evolution as a theory that seems "clearly inconsistent with the teachings of Scripture." I should note here that I am doing this only because the arguments for this position seem to me to be based on highly unlikely interpretations of the biblical text, and I do not wish to imply that those who hold to the gap theory are unbelievers, or that they are like many theistic evolutionists who think the Bible cannot teach us about science. On the contrary, advocates of the gap theory have uniformly been believers in the total truthfulness of Scripture on whatever subject it speaks to.

verse 2—this indicates that creation is in progress, not that any evil is present. In addition, each day there is an "evening," and there is "darkness" present during the six days of creation (vv. 5, 8, 13, 18–19, et al.), with no suggestion of evil or of God's disapproval (cf. Ps. 104:20). As far as the phrase "without form and void," the sense is just that it is not yet fit for habitation: God's preparatory work has not yet been done. Of course, when God curses a desert, it does become unfit for habitation, but we should not read the cause of that unfitness in one case (God's curse on a desert) into another case, the creation, where the cause of unfitness for habitation is simply that God's work is still in progress; the preparation for man is not yet complete.[42] (It is not proper to read the circumstances that surround a word in one place into the use of that word in another place when the meaning of the word and its use in the second context do not require those same circumstances.)

In addition to the fact that Genesis 1:2 does not give support to this view, there are some other arguments that weigh strongly against the gap theory:

1. There is no verse in Scripture that explicitly talks about an earlier creation. So this theory is lacking even one verse of Scripture to give it explicit support.

2. In Genesis 1:31, when God finished his work of creation, we read, "And God saw everything that he had made, and behold, it was very good." But according to the gap theory, God would be looking at an earth full of the results of rebellion, conflict, and terrible divine judgment. He would also be looking at all the demonic beings, the hosts of Satan who had rebelled against him, and yet be calling everything "very good." It is difficult to believe that there was so much evil and so many evidences of rebellion and judgment on the earth, and that God could still say that creation was very good.

Moreover, Genesis 2:1 says, in an apparent summary of all that has happened in Genesis 1, "Thus the heavens and the earth were finished, and all the host of them." Here it is not just God's work on the earth, but all that he made in the heavens, that is said to have been completed in the narrative in Genesis 1. This would not allow for large parts of heaven and earth to have been finished long before the six creation days.

3. In a later description of God's work of creation found in the Ten Commandments, we read, "for *in six days the LORD made heaven and earth, the sea, and all that is in them,* and rested the seventh day; therefore the LORD blessed the sabbath day and hallowed it" (Ex. 20:11). Here the creation of both the heaven and the earth, and the making of "all that is in them," is attributed to God's work in the six days of creation. Whether we take these to be twenty-four-hour days or longer periods of time, on either view the making of the entire heavens and earth and *everything in them* is put within these six days. But the proponents of the gap theory would have to say that there are many things in the earth (such as fossil remains of dead animals, and the earth itself) and in the heavens (such as

---

[42]The second word, *bohû,* "void," only occurs two other times in Scripture (Isa. 34:11; Jer. 4:23), both picturing desolate lands that have experienced God's judgment. But the first word, *tohû,* which can mean "formlessness, confusion, unreality, emptiness" (*BDB,* p. 1062), occurs nineteen other times, sometimes to refer to a desolate place resulting from judgment (Isa. 34:11 and Jer. 4:23, both with *bohû*), and sometimes just to refer to an empty place, with no sense of evil or judgment implied (Job 26:7, of "space" over which God stretches the north, parallel to the "nothingness" in which he hangs the earth; also Deut. 32:10; Job 12:24; Ps. 107:40). The sense "uninhabitable" is especially appropriate in Isa. 45:18, speaking of God's creation of the earth: "He did not create it to be empty [*tohû*], but formed it to be inhabited" (NIV). (The fact that God did not create the earth to be "empty" but "formed it to be inhabited" [Isa. 45:18] speaks of God's completed work of creation and does not deny that it was "without form and void" at the earliest stage of creation.)

the stars) that God did not make in the six days specified in Exodus 20:11, a view that seems exactly contrary to what is affirmed in the verse.

Moreover, while some passages of Scripture do speak of God's judgment on rebellious angels or his judgment on the earth at various times (see Isa. 24:1; Jer. 4:23–26; 2 Peter 2:4), none of the passages places this judgment at a time before the creation narrative in Genesis 1:2–31.

4. This theory must assume that all of the fossils of animals from millions of years ago that resemble very closely animals from today indicate that God's first creation of the animal and plant kingdom resulted in a failure. These animals and plants did not fulfill God's original purpose, so he destroyed them, but in the second creation he made others that were exactly like them. Moreover, since Adam and Eve were the first man and woman, this theory must assume that there was a prior creation of God that existed for millions of years but lacked the highest aspect of God's creative work, namely, man himself. But both the failure of God to accomplish his purposes with the original plant and animal kingdoms, and the failure of God to crown creation with his highest creature, man, seem inconsistent with the biblical picture of God as one who always accomplishes his purposes in whatever he does. So the gap theory does not seem an acceptable alternative for evangelical Christians today.

3. The Age of the Earth: Some Preliminary Considerations. Up to this point, the discussions in this chapter have advocated conclusions that we hope will find broad assent among evangelical Christians. But now at last we come to a perplexing question about which Bible-believing Christians have differed for many years, sometimes very sharply. The question is simply this: How old is the earth?

It is appropriate to treat this question after all the earlier matters, because it is really much less important than the doctrines considered above. These earlier matters may be summarized as follows: (1) God created the universe out of nothing; (2) creation is distinct from God, yet always dependent on God; (3) God created the universe to show his glory; (4) the universe God created was very good; (5) there will be no final conflict between Scripture and science; (6) secular theories that deny God as Creator, including Darwinian evolution, are clearly incompatible with belief in the Bible.

The question of the age of the earth is also less important than other matters, that is, (7) the creation of the angelic world (chapter 12), and (8) the creation of man in the image of God. It is important to keep these things in mind, because there is a danger that Christians will spend too much time arguing over the age of the earth and neglect to focus on much more important and much clearer aspects of the overall teaching of the Bible on creation.

The two options to choose from for a date of the earth are the "old earth" position, which agrees with the consensus of modern science that the earth is 4,500,000,000 years old, and the "young earth" position, which says that the earth is 10,000 to 20,000 years old, and that secular scientific dating schemes are incorrect. The difference between these two views is enormous: 4,499,980,000 years!

Before considering the specific arguments for both positions, we will examine some preliminary questions about the genealogies in the Bible, current estimates for the age of the human race, differing views on the date of dinosaurs, and the length of the six creation days in Genesis 1.

a. There Are Gaps in the Genealogies of the Bible: When one reads the list of names in Scripture together with their ages, it might seem as though we could add together the ages of all the people in the history of redemption from Adam to Christ and come up with an approximate date for the creation of the earth. Certainly this would give a very recent date for creation (such as Archbishop Ussher's date of 4004 B.C.). But closer inspection of the parallel lists of names in Scripture will show that Scripture itself indicates the fact that the genealogies list only those names the biblical writers thought it important to record for their purposes. In fact, some genealogies include names that are left out by other genealogies in Scripture itself.

For instance, Matthew 1:8–9 tells us that Asa was "the father of Jehoshaphat, and Jehoshaphat the father of Joram, and Joram the father of Uzziah, and Uzziah the father of Jotham, and Jotham the father of Ahaz." But from 1 Chronicles 3:10–12 (which uses the alternate name Ahaziah for Uzziah), we learn that three generations have been omitted by Matthew: Joash, Amaziah, and Azariah. So these texts can be compared in the following table:

Example of gaps in genealogies

1 Chronicles 3:10–12	Matthew 1:8–9
Asa	Asa
Jehoshaphat	Jehoshaphat
Joram	Joram
Ahaziah (Uzziah)	Uzziah
Joash	
Amaziah	
Azariah	
Jotham	Jotham
Ahaz	Ahaz
Hezekiah	Hezekiah
(etc.)	(etc.)

Therefore, when Matthew says that Uzziah was "the father of Jotham," it can mean that he was the father of someone who led to Jotham. Matthew has selected those names that he wants to emphasize for his own purposes.[43] A similar phenomenon is evident in Matthew 1:20 where the angel of the Lord speaks to Joseph and calls him, "Joseph, son of David." Now Joseph is not directly the son of David (for David lived around 1000 B.C.), but Joseph is the descendant of David and is therefore called his "son."

Another example is found in 1 Chronicles 26:24 in a list of officers appointed by King David near the end of his life. We read that "Shebuel the son of Gershom, son of Moses, was chief officer in charge of the treasuries" (1 Chron. 26:24). Now we know from Exodus

---

[43]See a fuller discussion of the gaps in genealogies in Francis Schaeffer, *No Final Conflict*, pp. 37–43.

2:22 that Gershom was the son born to Moses before the Exodus, sometime around 1480 B.C. (or, on a late date for the exodus, around 1330 B.C.). But these officials mentioned in 1 Chronicles 26 were appointed at the time that David made Solomon king over Israel, around 970 B.C. (see 1 Chron. 23:1). That means that in 1 Chronicles 26:24 Shebuel is said to be "the son of Gershom," who was born 510 (or at least 360) years earlier. Ten or more generations have been omitted in this designation "son of."[44]

It seems only fair to conclude that the genealogies of Scripture have some gaps in them, and that God only caused to be recorded those names that were important for his purposes. How many gaps there are and how many generations are missing from the Genesis narratives, we do not know. The life of Abraham may be placed at approximately 2000 B.C., because the kings and places listed in the stories of Abraham's life (Gen. 12ff.) can be correlated with archaeological data that can be dated quite reliably,[45] but prior to Abraham the setting of dates is very uncertain. In view of the exceptionally long life spans reported for people prior to the flood, it would not seem unreasonable to think that a few thousand years have been passed over in the narrative. This gives us some flexibility in our thinking about the date that man first appeared on the earth. (It would seem to be quite another thing, however, and quite foreign to the sense of continuity in the narrative, to think that *millions* of years have been omitted, but that names and details of the lives of key persons have been remembered and passed down over such a long period of time.)

b. The Age of the Human Race: While current scientific estimates say that man first appeared on the earth about 2.5 million years ago, it is important to recognize what kind of "man" this is claimed to be. The following table is a rough guide to current scientific opinion:[46]

homo habilis ("skillful man") stone tools	2–3.5 million years B.C.

homo erectus
     variety of stone tools,
     used fire by 500,000 B.C.,
     hunted large animals
	1.5 million years B.C.

homo sapiens ("wise man" or
     "thinking man")
     buried their dead
     (example: Neanderthal man)
	40,000–150,000 B.C.
	     (or perhaps 300,000 B.C.)

[44]The NIV translates the verse, "Shubael, *a descendant of* Gershom," but this is simply an interpretation, for the Hebrew text simply has the word *ben*, "son." It should not be objected that Gershom may have lived over 500 years, for such long life spans are not found after the flood (note Gen. 6:3); in fact, Abraham was miraculously given a son when he was almost 100 (cf. Rom. 4:19; Heb. 11:12); and Moses, long before David or Solomon, counted man's life as 70 or 80 years: "The years of our life are threescore and ten, or even by reason of strength fourscore" (Ps. 90:10).

[45]See "Chronology of the Old Testament" in *IBD*, esp. pp. 268–70.

[46]This table was adapted from Frair and Davis, *A Case for Creation*, pp. 122–26, and Karl W. Butzer, "Prehistoric People," in *World Book Encyclopedia* (Chicago: World Book, 1974), 15:666–74.

homo sapiens sapiens	90,000 B.C.
("wise, wise man")	
(example: Cro-Magnon man)	18,000–35,000 B.C.
cave paintings	
(example: Neolithic man)	19,000 B.C.
cattle raising, agriculture,	
metalwork	

Whether Christians hold to a young earth or old earth view, they will agree that man is certainly on the earth by the time of the cave paintings by Cro-Magnon man, paintings which date from about 10,000 B.C. There is some variation in the date of Cro-Magnon man, however, since the dating of a Cro-Magnon burial site in Siberia is approximately 20,000 to 35,000 B.C. according to the geological evidence found there, but the Carbon-14 dating method gives a date of only 9,000 B.C., or 11,000 years ago.[47] Earlier than the paintings by Cro-Magnon man, there is disagreement. Was Neanderthal man really a man, or just a human-like creature?[48] How human were earlier man-like creatures? (Higher forms of animals, such as chimpanzees, can use tools, and burial of one's dead is not necessarily a uniquely human trait.) Moreover, dating methods used for earlier periods are very approximate with results that often conflict.[49]

So how long ago did man first appear on the earth? Certainly by 10,000 B.C., if the Cro-Magnon cave paintings have been dated correctly. But before that it is difficult to say.

c. Did Animals Die Before the Fall? For young earth advocates, there is no need to ask whether animals died before the fall, because animals and man were both created on the sixth day, and there may have been only a short time before Adam and Eve sinned. This could have introduced death into the animal kingdom as well, as part of the curse of the fall (Gen. 3:17–19; Rom. 8:20–23).

But for old earth advocates, this is an important question. There are millions of apparently ancient fossils in the earth. Might they have come from animals who lived and died for long ages before Adam and Eve were created? Might God have created an animal kingdom that was subject to death from the moment of creation? This is quite possible. There was no doubt death in the plant world, if Adam and Eve were to eat plants; and if God had made an original creation in which animals would reproduce and also live forever, the earth would soon be overcrowded with no hope of relief. The warning to Adam in Genesis 2:17 was only that *he* would die if he ate of the forbidden fruit, not that animals would also begin to die. When Paul says, "Sin came into the world through one man and death through sin" (Rom. 5:12a), the following phrase makes clear that he is talking about death for human beings, not for plants and animals, for he immediately adds, "and so death spread to all men because all men sinned" (Rom. 5:12b).

[47]Kofahl and Segraves, *The Creation Explanation*, p. 207.
[48]Two helpful discussions of the various proposed human ancestors are found in Frair and Davis, *A Case for Creation*, pp. 122–26, and Davis A. Young, *Creation and the Flood*, pp. 146–55. Frair and Davis think that Neanderthal man was "entirely human" although "racially distinct" (p. 125).

[49]Philip Johnson notes that a recent theory that has received support from several molecular biologists is that all humans descended from a "mitochondrial Eve" who lived in Africa less than 200,000 years ago (*Darwin on Trial*, pp. 83, 177–78).

From the information we have in Scripture, we cannot now know whether God created animals subject to aging and death from the beginning, but it remains a real possibility.

d. What About Dinosaurs?: Current scientific opinion holds that dinosaurs became extinct about 65 million years ago, millions of years before human beings appeared on the earth. But those who hold to six twenty-four-hour days of creation and a young earth would say that dinosaurs were among the creatures created by God on the same day he created man (the sixth day). They would therefore say that dinosaurs and human beings lived on the earth at the same time and that dinosaurs subsequently became extinct (perhaps in the flood). Young earth advocates of course would differ with the methods used to arrive at such ancient dates for dinosaurs.

Among those who hold to an old earth view, some would want to say that dinosaurs were among the creatures that Adam named in Genesis 2:19–20, and that they subsequently perished (perhaps in the flood). They would admit that dinosaurs may have existed earlier, but would say that they did not become extinct until after the time of Adam and Eve. Others would say that the sixth day of creation was millions of years long, and that dinosaurs had already become extinct by the time Adam was created and named the animals. In this case, Adam did not name dinosaurs (the Bible does not say that he did), but he only named all the creatures that were living at the time God brought him all the animals to name (Gen. 2:19–20; see NIV). Of course, this view would require that there was death in the animal world before there was sin (see previous section).

e. Are the Six Days of Creation Twenty-four-Hour Days?: Much of the dispute between "young earth" and "old earth" advocates hinges on the interpretation of the length of "days" in Genesis 1. Old earth supporters propose that the six "days" of Genesis 1 refer not to periods of twenty-four hours, but rather to long periods of time, millions of years, during which God carried out the creative activities described in Genesis 1. This proposal has led to a heated debate with other evangelicals, which is far from being settled decisively one way or another.

In favor of viewing the six days as long periods of time is the fact that the Hebrew word *yôm*, "day," is sometimes used to refer not to a twenty-four-hour literal day, but to a longer period of time. We see this when the word is used in Genesis 2:4, for example: "In the *day* that the LORD God made the earth and the heavens," a phrase that refers to the entire creative work of the six days of creation. Other examples of the word *day* to mean a period of time are Job 20:28 ("the *day* of God's wrath"); Psalm 20:1 ("The LORD answer you in the *day* of trouble!"); Proverbs 11:4 ("Riches do not profit in the *day* of wrath"); 21:31 ("The horse is made ready for the *day* of battle"); 24:10 ("If you faint in the *day* of adversity, your strength is small"); 25:13 ("the *time* [*yôm*] of harvest"); Ecclesiastes 7:14 ("In the *day* of prosperity be joyful, and in the *day* of adversity consider; God has made the one as well as the other"); many passages referring to "the *day* of the LORD" (such as Isa. 2:12; 13:6, 9; Joel 1:15; 2:1; Zeph. 1:14); and many other Old Testament passages predicting times of judgment or blessing. A concordance will show that this is a frequent sense for the word *day* in the Old Testament.

An additional argument for a long period of time in these "days" is the fact that the sixth day includes so many events that it must have been longer than twenty-four hours.

The sixth day of creation (Gen. 1:24–31) includes the creation of animals and the creation of man and woman both ("male and female he created them," Gen. 1:27). It was also on the sixth day that God blessed Adam and Eve and said to them, "Be fruitful and multiply, and fill the earth and subdue it; and have dominion over the fish of the sea and over the birds of the air and over every living thing that moves upon the earth" (Gen. 1:28). But that means that the sixth day included God's creation of Adam, God's putting Adam in the Garden of Eden to till it and keep it, and giving Adam directions regarding the tree of the knowledge of good and evil (Gen. 2:15–17), his bringing all the animals to man for them to be named (Gen. 2:18–20), finding no helper fit for Adam (Gen. 2:20), and then causing a deep sleep to fall upon Adam and creating Eve from his rib (Gen. 2:21–25). The finite nature of man and the incredibly large number of animals created by God would by itself seem to require that a much longer period of time than part of one day would be needed to include so many events—at least that would be an "ordinary" understanding of the passage for an original reader, a consideration that is not unimportant in a debate that often emphasizes what an ordinary reading of the text by the original readers would lead them to conclude.[50] If the sixth day is shown by contextual considerations to be considerably longer than an ordinary twenty-four-hour day, then does not the context itself favor the sense of *day* as simply a "period of time" of unspecified length?

Related to this is one more consideration. The seventh day, it should be noted, is not concluded with the phrase "and there was evening and there was morning, a seventh day." The text just says that God "rested on the seventh day from all his work which he had done" and that "God blessed the seventh day and hallowed it" (Gen. 2:2–3). The possibility, if not the implication, suggested by this is that the seventh day is still continuing. It never ended but is also a "day" that is really a long period of time (cf. John 5:17; Heb. 4:4, 9–10).

Some have objected that whenever the word *day* refers to a period of time other than a twenty-four-hour day in the Old Testament the context makes it clear that this is the case, but since the context does not make this clear in Genesis 1 we must assume that normal days are meant. But to this we may answer that whenever the word *day* means a twenty-four-hour day, the context makes this clear as well. Otherwise, we could not know that a twenty-four-hour day is meant in that context. So this is not a persuasive objection. It simply affirms what everyone agrees to, namely, that the context enables us to determine which sense a word will take when it has various possible meanings.

Another objection is that the Bible could have used other words if a period longer than a twenty-four-hour day was intended. However, if (as is clearly the case) the original readers knew that the word *day* could mean a long period of time, then there was no need to use some other word, for the word *yôm* conveyed the intended meaning quite well. Furthermore, it was a very appropriate word to use when describing six successive periods of work plus a period of rest that would set the pattern for the seven days of the week in which people would live.

---

[50]Advocates of a twenty-four-hour day can give scenarios whereby Adam only named representative types of animals or named them rapidly without any observation of their activities or abilities, but both suggestions are much less likely interpretations in view of the importance attached to naming in the Old Testament.

That brings us back to the original question, namely, what does the word *day* mean in the context of Genesis 1? The fact that the word must refer to a longer period of time just a few verses later in the same narrative (Gen. 2:4) should caution us against making dogmatic statements that the original readers would have certainly known that the author was talking about twenty-four-hour days. In fact, both senses were commonly known meanings in the minds of the original readers of this narrative.[51]

It is important to realize that those who advocate long periods of time for the six "days" of creation are not saying that the context *requires* that these be understood as periods of time. They are simply saying that the context does not clearly specify for us one meaning of *day* or another, and if convincing scientific data about the age of the earth, drawn from many different disciplines and giving similar answers, convinces us that the earth is billions of years old, then this possible interpretation of *day* as a long period of time may be the best interpretation to adopt. In this way, the situation is something like that faced by those who first held that the earth rotates on its axis and revolves about the sun. They would not say that the passages about the sun "rising" or "going down" *require* us, in their contexts, to believe in a heliocentric (sun-centered) solar system, but that this is a *possible* understanding of the texts, seeing them as only speaking from the standpoint of the observer. Observational evidence taken from science informs us that this is in fact the correct way to interpret those texts.

On the other side of this question are the arguments in favor of understanding "day" as a twenty-four-hour day in Genesis 1:

1. It is significant that each of the days of Genesis 1 ends with an expression such as, "And there was evening, and there was morning—the first day" (Gen. 1:5 NIV). The phrase "And there was evening, and there was morning" is repeated in verses 8, 13, 19, 23, and 31. This seems to imply the sequence of events marking a literal twenty-four-hour day and suggests that the readers should understand it in that way.

This is a strong argument from context, and many have found it persuasive. Yet those who hold to a long period of time for these "days" could respond (a) that even evening and morning do not constitute an entire day, but only the end of one day and the beginning of another, so the expression itself may be simply part of the author's way of telling us that the end of the first creative day (that is, long period of time) occurred, and the beginning of the next creative "day" had come;[52] and also (b) that the first three creative "days" could not have been marked by evening and morning as caused by the sun shining on the earth, for the sun was not created until the fourth day (Gen. 1:14–19); thus, the very context shows that "evening and morning" in this chapter does not refer to the ordinary evening and morning of days as we know them now. So the argument from "evening and morning," though it may give some weight to the twenty-four-hour view, does not seem to tip the balance decisively in its favor.

2. The third day of creation cannot be very long, because the sun does not come into being until the fourth day, and plants cannot live long without light. In response to this, it

might be said that the light that God created on the first day energized the plants for millions of years. But that would suppose God to have created a light that is almost exactly like sunlight in brightness and power, but still not sunlight—an unusual suggestion.

3. It is hard to avoid the conclusion that in the Ten Commandments the word *day* is used to mean a twenty-four-hour day:

> Remember the sabbath day, to keep it holy. Six *days* you shall labor, and do all your work; but the seventh *day* is a sabbath to the LORD your God; . . . for in six *days* the LORD made heaven and earth, the sea, and all that is in them, and rested the seventh day; therefore the LORD blessed the sabbath day and hallowed it." (Ex. 20:8–11)

Certainly in that text the sabbath "day" is a twenty-four-hour day. And must we not say that verse 11, which in the same sentence says that the Lord made heaven and earth in "six days," uses "day" in the same sense? This is again a weighty argument, and on balance it gives additional persuasiveness to the twenty-four-hour day position. But once again it is not quite conclusive in itself, for one could respond that the readers were aware (from a careful reading of Gen. 1–2) that the days there were unspecified periods of time, and that the sabbath commandment merely told God's people that, just as he followed a six-plus-one pattern in creation (six periods of work followed by a period of rest), so they were to follow a six-plus-one pattern in their lives (six days of work followed by a day of rest; also six years of work followed by a sabbath year of rest, as in Ex. 23:10–11). In fact, in the very next sentence of the Ten Commandments, "day" means "a period of time": "Honor your father and your mother, that your *days* may be long in the land which the LORD your God gives you" (Ex. 20:12). Certainly here the promise is not for "long" literal days (such as twenty-five- or twenty-six-hour days!), but rather that the period of one's life may be lengthened upon the earth.[53]

4. Those who argue for "day" as a twenty-four-hour day also ask whether anywhere else in the Hebrew Bible the word "days" in the plural, especially when a number is attached (such as "six days"), ever refers to anything but twenty-four-hour days. This argument is not compelling, however, because (a) a plural example of "days" to mean periods of time is found in Exodus 20:12, discussed in the previous paragraph and (b) if the word clearly takes the sense "period of time" in the singular (which it does, as all admit), then to speak of six such "periods" of time would certainly be understandable to the readers, even if the Old Testament did not elsewhere have examples of such a meaning. The fact that such an expression does not appear elsewhere may mean nothing more than that there was no occasion to use it elsewhere.

5. When Jesus says, "But from the beginning of creation, 'God made them male and female'" (Mark 10:6), he implies that Adam and Eve were not created billions of years after the beginning of creation, but at the beginning of creation. This argument also has

---

[53]The Hebrew text does not say "that your days may be *many* (Heb. *rab*)" which is a common Hebrew expression (Gen. 21:34; 37:34; Ex. 2:23; Num. 9:19, et al.), but "that your days may be *long*" (Heb. *'arak*, "be long," used also as physical length in 1 Kings 8:8; Ps. 129:3; Isa. 54:2 ["lengthen your cords"]; Ezek. 31:5).

some force, but old earth advocates may respond that Jesus is just referring to the whole of Genesis 1–2 as the "beginning of creation," in contrast to the argument from the laws given by Moses that the Pharisees were depending on (v. 4).

I have given an answer to each of the five arguments for a twenty-four-hour day, but these answers may not persuade its advocates. They would respond to the "period of time" position as follows: (1) Of course, it is true that *day* may mean "period of time" in many places in the Old Testament, but that does not demonstrate that *day* must have that meaning in Genesis 1. (2) The sixth day of creation need not have been longer than twenty-four hours, especially if Adam only named major representative kinds of birds and of "every beast of the field" (Gen. 2:20). (3) Though there was no sun to mark the first three days of creation, nonetheless, the earth was still rotating on its axis at a fixed speed, and there was "light" and "darkness" that God created on the first day (Gen. 1:3–4), and he called the light "day" and the darkness "night" (Gen. 3:5). So God in some way caused an alternation between day and night from the very first day of creation, according to Genesis 1:3–5.

What shall we conclude about the length of days in Genesis 1? It does not seem at all easy to decide with the information we now have. It is not simply a question of "believing the Bible" or "not believing the Bible," nor is it a question of "giving in to modern science" or "rejecting the clear conclusions of modern science." Even for those who believe in the complete truthfulness of Scripture (such as the present author), and who retain some doubt about the exceptionally long periods of time scientists propose for the age of the earth (such as the present author), the question does not seem to be easy to decide. At present, considerations of the power of God's creative word and the immediacy with which it seems to bring response, the fact that "evening and morning" and the numbering of days still suggest twenty-four-hour days, and the fact that God would seem to have no purpose for delaying the creation of man for thousands or even millions of years, seem to me to be strong considerations in favor of the twenty-four-hour day position. But even here there are good arguments on the other side: To the one who lives forever, for whom "one day is as a thousand years, and a thousand years as one day" (2 Peter 3:8), who delights in gradually working out all his purposes over time, perhaps 15 billion years is just the right amount of time to take in preparing the universe for man's arrival and 4.5 billion years in preparing the earth. The evidence of incredible antiquity in the universe would then serve as a vivid reminder of the even more amazing nature of God's eternity, just as the incredible size of the universe causes us to wonder at God's even greater omnipresence and omnipotence.

Therefore, with respect to the length of days in Genesis 1, the possibility must be left open that God has chosen not to give us enough information to come to a clear decision on this question, and the real test of faithfulness to him may be the degree to which we can act charitably toward those who in good conscience and full belief in God's Word hold to a different position on this matter.

4. Both "Old Earth" and "Young Earth" Theories Are Valid Options for Christians Who Believe the Bible Today. After discussing several preliminary considerations regarding the age of the earth, we come finally to the specific arguments for old earth and young earth views.

a. "Old Earth" Theories of Creation: In this first category we list two viewpoints held by those who believe in an old earth with an age of about 4.5 billion years and a universe about 15 billion years old.

(1) Day-Age View: Many who believe that the earth is many millions of years old maintain that the days of Genesis 1 are extremely long "ages" of time.[54] The arguments given above for long days in Genesis 1 will apply here, and, as we argued above, the words of the Hebrew text do allow for the days to be long periods of time. The evident advantage of this view is that, if the current scientific estimate for an earth 4.5 billion years old is correct, it explains how the Bible is consistent with this fact. Among evangelicals who hold to an old earth view, this is a common position. This view is sometimes called a "concordist" view because it seeks agreement or "concord" between the Bible and scientific conclusions about dating.

Many have been attracted to this position because of scientific evidence regarding the age of the earth. A very helpful survey of the views of theologians and scientists regarding the age of the earth, from ancient Greece to the twentieth century, is found in a book by a professional geologist who is also an evangelical Christian, Davis A. Young, *Christianity and the Age of the Earth*.[55] Young demonstrates that in the nineteenth and twentieth centuries, many Christian geologists, under the weight of apparently overwhelming evidence, have concluded that the earth is about 4.5 billion years old. Although some "young earth" proponents (see discussion below) have claimed that radiometric dating techniques are inaccurate because of changes that occurred on the earth at the time of the flood, Young notes that radiometric dating of rocks from the moon and of meteorites recently fallen to the earth, which could not have been affected by Noah's flood, coincide with many other radiometric evidences from various materials on the earth, and that the results of these tests are "remarkably consistent in pointing to about 4.5–4.7 billion years."[56]

Some of Young's most forceful arguments for an old earth, in addition to those from radiometric dating, include the time required for liquid magma to cool (about 1 million years for a large formation in southern California), the time and pressure required for the formation of many metamorphic rocks that contain small fossils (some apparently could only be formed by the pressure of being buried twelve to eighteen miles under ground and later brought to the surface—but when could this have happened on a young earth view?), continental drift (fossil-bearing rock fields near the coasts of Africa and South America were apparently previously joined together, then separated by continental

---

[54]One variation of this view would say that the six days were twenty-four-hour days, but there were millions of years between each day and the following one. This is certainly possible, but the difficulty with this view is that it seems to be importing "gaps" between all the days simply to account for scientific chronology, with no clear evidence in the text to support it. This view is defended by Robert C. Newman and Herman J. Eckelmann, Jr., *Genesis One and the Origin of the Earth* (Downers Grove, Ill.: InterVarsity Press, 1977).

[55]Grand Rapids: Zondervan, 1982, pp. 13–67.

[56]*Christianity and the Age of the Earth*, p. 63; see also the detailed discussion on pp. 93–116, and *Creation and the Flood*, pp. 185–93.

drift, something that could not have happened in 20,000 years at the present rate of two centimeters per year),[57] and coral reefs (some of which apparently would have required hundreds of thousands of years of gradual deposits to attain their present state).[58] Several other arguments, especially from astronomy, have been summarized by Robert C. Newman and Herman J. Eckelmann, Jr., in *Genesis One and the Origin of the Earth*.[59] These arguments favor an old earth view, and the day-age theory is an attractive position for old earth advocates.

The day-age view is certainly possible, but it has several difficulties: (1) The sequence of events in Genesis 1 does not exactly correspond to current scientific understanding of the development of life, which puts sea creatures (Day 5) before trees (Day 3), and insects and other land animals (Day 6), as well as fish (Day 5), before birds (Day 5).[60] (2) The greatest difficulty for this view is that it puts the sun, moon, and stars (Day 4) millions of years *after* the creation of plants and trees (Day 3). That makes no sense at all according to current scientific opinion, which sees the stars as formed long before the earth or any living creatures on the earth. It also makes no sense in terms of the way the earth now operates, for plants do not grow without sunlight, and there are many plants (Day 3) that do not pollinate without birds or flying insects (Day 5), and there are many birds (Day 5) that live off creeping insects (Day 6). Moreover, how would the waters on the earth keep from freezing for millions of years without the sun?

In response, those who hold the concordist view say that the sun, moon, and stars were created on Day 1 (the creation of light) or before Day 1, when "in the beginning God created the heavens and the earth" (Gen. 1:1), and that the sun, moon, and stars were only *made visible* or *revealed* on Day 4 (Gen. 1:14–19). But this argument is not very convincing, because all the other five days of creation involve not *revealing* something that was previously created but actually *creating* things for the first time. Moreover, the creative statements are similar to those of other days, "And God said, 'Let there be lights in the firmament of the heavens to separate the day from the night . . . to give light upon the earth.' And it was so" (Gen. 1:14–15). This is the form of language used in verses 3, 6, 11, 20, and 24 for creating things, not revealing them. Furthermore, the creation (not the revealing) of the sun, moon, and stars is made explicit in the next sentence: "And

---

[57]See *Creation and the Flood*, pp. 171–210, for these examples. A continental drift of 2 cm. per year x 20,000 years = 40,000 cm. or 400 m. (about 437 yd. or 1/4 mile). This hardly accounts for the present distance between South America and Africa.

[58]*Christianity and the Age of the Earth*, pp. 84–86. Coral reefs are not formed by the immense pressure of a flood, but by tiny sea creatures (called coral polyps) who attach themselves to each other and build colorful limestone formations by removing calcium carbonate from seawater and depositing it around the lower half of their body. When they die, their limestone "skeletons" remain behind, and, over tens of thousands of years, huge coral reefs are formed. This can only happen in water warmer than 65° F (18° C), and in water clear and shallow enough for photosynthesis to occur in algae, which the coral polyps need to produce their skeletons. (See Robert D. Barnes, "Coral," in *World Book Encyclopedia* [Chicago: World

Book, 1983], 4:828.)

[59]Downers Grove, Ill.: InterVarsity Press, 1977, pp. 15–34, 89–103. They show that the length of time required for light to reach the earth is not the only astronomical evidence for a very old universe: measurements of star movements show the universe has apparently been expanding for over 15 billion years; background radiation in the universe gives a similar age; and the kind of light coming from certain stars shows that many stars have an age consistent with this estimate. Young earth proponents (see below) may say that God created the light rays in place so Adam and Eve could see stars, but it is much harder to explain why God would have created these other evidences so consistent with a universe about 15 billion years old.

[60]Of course, current scientific hypotheses of these sequences may be incorrect.

God made the two great lights, the greater light to rule the day, and the lesser light to rule the night; he made the stars also" (Gen. 1:16). Here the word "made" (Heb. *'āsāh*) is the same word used when God *made* the firmament, the beasts of the earth, and man (Gen. 1:7, 25, 26)—in none of these cases is it used to speak of revealing something previously made. The Hebrew *'āsāh* is also the word used in the summary in verse 31: "And God saw everything that he had made, and behold, it was very good." This frequent use throughout Genesis 1 makes it very unlikely that Genesis 1:16 merely refers to the revealing of the sun, moon, and stars.

But a modification of the day-age view in response to these objections seems possible. The verbs in Genesis 1:16 can be taken as perfects, indicating something that God had done before: "And God *had made* the two great lights, the greater light to rule the day, and the lesser light to rule the night; he *had made*[61] the stars also." Grammatically this is possible (this is how the NIV translates the same verb form in 2:8 and 2:19, for example). This view would imply that God had made the sun, moon, and stars earlier (in v. 1, the creation of heavens and earth, or in v. 3, the creation of light) but only placed them near the earth on Day 4, or allowed them to be seen from the earth on Day 4 (vv. 14–15, 17–18). This allows the word *made* (*'āsāh*) to mean "created" and thus avoids the difficulty mentioned above with the view that it means "revealed" in verse 16. This option remains as a genuine possibility for the day-age view, and in fact this view is the one that seems most persuasive to the present author, if an old earth position is to be adopted. With regard to light needed for the plants and warmth needed for the waters, there was light available from Day 1—even if we are not sure whether this light was light from the sun and stars or the light of God's glory (which will replace the sun in the New Jerusalem, Rev. 21:23).[62]

Another answer from the day-age view might be that the fourth day is not exactly in sequence, though an overall outline of progressive work of God is given. Yet once we begin changing the sequence of events that is so prominent in this progression of six creative days, it is doubtful that we need to allow the text to tell us anything other than the bare fact that God created things—but in that case, the whole inquiry about the age of the earth is unnecessary. (Further discussion of disruption in the sequence of days is given in the next section.)

(2) Literary Framework View: Another way of interpreting the days of Genesis 1 has gained a significant following among evangelicals. Since it argues that Genesis 1 gives us no information about the age of the earth, it would be compatible with current scientific estimates of a very old earth. This view argues that the six days of Genesis 1 are not intended to indicate a chronological sequence of events, but are rather a literary "framework," which the author uses to teach us about God's creative activity. The framework is

---

[61]The second verb is implied by the direct object marker but is not expressed in the Hebrew text; it would take the same form as the first verb in the sentence.

[62]The question of pollination without birds and insects remains a difficulty for this view, though it should be noted that even today many plants self-pollinate or are cross-pollinated by the wind, and we cannot be sure that pollination by flying insects was required before the fall and before creation was complete. Similarly, the need for some birds to live off creeping insects is a difficulty, but they possibly ate only plants and seeds before the fall.

skillfully constructed so that the first three days and the second three days correspond to each other.[63]

Days of forming	Days of filling
Day 1: Light and darkness separated	Day 4: Sun, moon, and stars (lights in the heaven)
Day 2: Sky and waters separated	Day 5: Fish and birds
Day 3: Dry land and seas separated, plants and trees	Day 6: Animals and man

In this way a parallel construction is seen. On Day 1 God separates light and darkness, while on Day 4 he puts the sun, moon, and stars in the light and in the darkness. On Day 2 he separates the waters and the sky, while on Day 5 he puts the fish in the waters and the birds in the sky. On Day 3 he separates the dry land and the seas and makes plants to grow, while on Day 6 he puts the animals and man on the dry land and gives the plants to them for food.

According to the "framework" view, Genesis 1 should not be read as though the author wanted to inform us about the sequence of days or the order in which things were created, nor did he intend to tell us about the length of time the creation took. The arrangement of six "days" is a literary device the author uses to teach that God created everything. The six "days," which are neither twenty-four-hour days nor long periods of time, give us six different "pictures" of creation, telling us that God made all aspects of the creation, that the pinnacle of his creative activity was man, and that over all creation is God himself, who rested on the seventh day and who calls man therefore to worship him on the sabbath day as well.[64]

In the words of a recent advocate of this position, "Chronology has no place here."[65] The attractions in favor of this hypothesis are (1) the neat correspondence between the pairs of days as shown in the table above, (2) the fact that it avoids any conflict with modern science over the age of the earth and the age of living creatures (since no chronology at all is implied), (3) the way it avoids the conflict of sequence between Genesis 1 and 2 in which man (Gen. 2:7) seems to be formed before plants (Gen. 2:8) and animals (Gen. 2:19), a sequence different from Genesis 1, and (4) the fact that Genesis 2:5 shows that the "days" of creation were not literal twenty-four-hour days, for it says that there were no plants on the earth because it had not yet rained, something that would not make sense in a six day creation, since plants can certainly survive three or four days without rain.

Several points may be made against the framework theory.

---

[63]The following table is adapted from *The NIV Study Bible,* ed. by Kenneth Barker et al. (Grand Rapids: Zondervan, 1985), p. 6 (note to Gen. 1:11). A forceful defense of the "framework" view is found in Henri Blocher, *In the Beginning: The Opening Chapters of Genesis,* trans. by David G. Preston (Leicester: Inter-Varsity Press, 1984), pp. 49–59. Blocher mentions several other evangelical scholars who hold this position, which he calls the "literary interpretation": N. H. Ridderbos, Bernard Ramm, Meredith G. Kline, D. F. Payne, and J. A. Thompson. This "framework" view is called the "pictorial day" view in Millard Erickson, *Christian Theology* (Grand Rapids: Baker, 1983–85), p. 381.

[64]This framework view is also defended by Ronald Youngblood, *How It All Began* (Ventura, Calif.: Regal, 1980), pp. 25–33.

[65]Henri Blocher, *In the Beginning,* p. 52.

1. First, the proposed correspondence between the days of creation is not nearly as exact as its advocates have supposed. The sun, moon, and stars created on the fourth day as "lights in the firmament of the heavens" (Gen. 1:14) are placed not in any space created on Day 1 but in the "firmament" (Heb. *raqia'*) that was created on the second day. In fact, the correspondence in language is quite explicit: this "firmament" is not mentioned at all on Day 1 but five times on Day 2 (Gen. 1: 6–8) and three times on Day 4 (Gen. 1:14–19). Of course Day 4 also has correspondences with Day 1 (in terms of day and night, light and darkness), but if we say that the second three days show the creation of things to fill the forms or spaces created on the first three days, then Day 4 overlaps at least as much with Day 2 as it does with Day 1.

Moreover, the parallel between Days 2 and 5 is not exact, because in some ways the preparation of a space for the fish and birds of Day 5 does not come in Day 2 but in Day 3. It is not until Day 3 that God gathers the waters together and calls them "seas" (Gen. 1:10), and on Day 5 the fish are commanded to "fill the waters in the *seas*" (Gen. 1:22). Again in verses 26 and 28 the fish are called "fish of the *sea*," giving repeated emphasis to the fact that the sphere the fish inhabit was specifically formed on Day 3. Thus, the fish formed on Day 5 seem to belong much more to the place prepared for them on Day 3 than to the widely dispersed waters below the firmament on Day 2. Establishing a parallel between Day 2 and Day 5 faces further difficulties in that nothing is created on Day 5 to inhabit the "waters above the firmament," and the flying things created on this day (the Hebrew word would include flying insects as well as birds) not only fly in the sky created on Day 2, but also live and multiply on the "earth" or "dry land" created on Day 3. (Note God's command on Day 5: "Let birds multiply on the earth" [Gen. 1:22].) Finally, the parallel between Days 3 and 6 is not precise, for nothing is created on Day 6 to fill the seas that were gathered together on Day 3. With all of these points of imprecise correspondence and overlapping between places and things created to fill them, the supposed literary "framework," while having an initial appearance of neatness, turns out to be less and less convincing upon closer reading of the text.

2. Since all proposals for understanding Genesis 1 attempt to provide explanations for scientific data about the age of the earth, this is not a unique argument in favor of the framework theory. However, we must recognize that one aspect of the attractiveness of this theory is the fact that it relieves evangelicals of the burden of even trying to reconcile scientific findings with Genesis 1. Yet, in the words of one advocate of this theory, "So great is the advantage, and for some the relief, that it could constitute a temptation." He wisely adds, "We must not espouse the theory on grounds of its convenience but only if the text leads us in that direction."[66]

3. Those who have not adopted the framework theory have seen no conflict in sequence between Genesis 1 and 2, for it has been commonly understood that Genesis 2 implies no description of sequence in the original creation of the animals or plants, but simply recapitulates some of the details of Genesis 1 as important for the specific account of the creation of Adam and Eve in Genesis 2. The NIV avoids the appearance of conflict by translating, "Now the LORD God *had planted* a garden in the East, in Eden" (Gen. 2:8)

[66]Ibid., p. 50.

and "Now the LORD God *had formed out* of the ground all the beasts of the field and all the birds of the air" (Gen. 2:19).

4. Genesis 2:5 does not really say that plants were not on the earth because the earth was too dry to support them. If we adopt that reasoning we would also have to say there were no plants because "there was no man to till the ground" (Gen. 2:5), for that is the second half of the comment about no rain coming on the earth. Moreover, the remainder of the sentence says that the earth was the opposite of being too dry to support plants: "streams came up from the earth and watered the whole surface of the ground" (Gen. 2:6 NIV). The statement in Genesis 2:5 is simply to be understood as an explanation of the general time frame in which God created man. Genesis 2:4–6 sets the stage, telling us that "no plant of the field was yet in the earth and no herb of the field had yet sprung up — for the LORD God had not caused it to rain upon the earth, and there was no man to till the ground; but a mist went up from the earth and watered the whole face of the ground." The statements about lack of rain and no man to till the ground do not give the *physical reason* why there were no plants, but only explain that God's work of creation was not complete. This introduction puts us back into the first six days of creation as a general setting — into "the day that the LORD God made the earth and the heavens" (Gen. 2:4). Then in that setting it abruptly introduces the main point of chapter 2 — the creation of man. The Hebrew text does not include the word "then" at the beginning of verse 7, but simply begins, "And the LORD God formed man" (Gen. 2:7 KJV).[67]

5. Finally, the strongest argument against the framework view, and the reason why comparatively few evangelicals have adopted it, is that the whole of Genesis 1 strongly suggests not just a literary framework but a chronological sequence of events. When the narrative proceeds from the less complex aspects of creation (light and darkness, waters, sky, and dry land) to the more complex aspects (fish and birds, animals and man), we see a progressive build-up and an ordered sequence of events that are entirely understandable chronologically. When a sequence of numbers (1-2-3-4-5-6) is attached to a set of days that correspond exactly to the ordinary week human beings experience (Day 1, Day 2, Day 3, Day 4, Day 5, Day 6, Day 7, with rest on Day 7), the implication of chronological sequence in the narrative is almost inescapable. The sequence of days seems more clearly intended than a literary framework which is nowhere made explicit in the text, and in which many details simply do not fit. As Derek Kidner observes:

> The march of the days is too majestic a progress to carry no implication of ordered sequence; it also seems over-subtle to adopt a view of the passage which discounts one of the primary impressions it makes on the ordinary reader. It is a story, not only a statement.[68]

6. A sequence of days is also implied in God's command to human beings to imitate his pattern of work plus rest: "Remember the sabbath day, to keep it holy. Six days you shall labor, and do all your work; but the seventh day is a sabbath to the LORD your God . . . for in six days the LORD made heaven and earth, the sea, and all that is in them, and rested

---

[67]For further discussion on Gen. 2:5, see Meredith G. Kline, "Because It Had Not Rained," *WTJ* 20 (1957–58): 146–57; and, in response, Derek Kidner, "Genesis 2:5, 6: Wet or Dry?" *TB* 17 (1966): 109–14.

[68]D. Kidner, *Genesis: An Introduction and Commentary,* TOTC (Chicago: InterVarsity Press, 1967), pp. 54–55.

the seventh day" (Ex. 20:8–11). But if God did not create the earth by working for six days and resting on the seventh, then the command to imitate him would be misleading or make no sense.

In conclusion, while the "framework" view does not deny the truthfulness of Scripture, it adopts an interpretation of Scripture which, upon closer inspection, seems very unlikely.

b. "Young Earth" Theories of Creation: Another group of evangelical interpreters rejects the dating systems that currently give an age of millions of years to the earth and argue instead that the earth is quite young, perhaps 10,000 to 20,000 years old. Young earth advocates have produced a number of scientific arguments for a recent creation of the earth.[69] Those who hold to a young earth generally advocate one or both of the following positions:

(1) Creation With an Appearance of Age (Mature Creationism): Many who hold to a young earth point out that the original creation must have had an "appearance of age" even from the first day. (Another term for this view is "mature creationism," since it affirms that God created a mature creation.) The appearance of Adam and Eve as full-grown adults is an obvious example. They appeared as though they had lived for perhaps twenty or twenty-five years, growing up from infancy as human beings normally do, but in fact they were less than a day old. Similarly, they probably saw the stars the first night that they lived, but the light from most stars would take thousands or even millions of years to reach the earth. This suggests that God created the stars with light beams already in place. And full-grown trees would probably have had rings (Adam and Eve would not have had to wait years before God told them which trees of the garden they could eat from and which they could not, nor would they have had to wait weeks or months before edible plants grew large enough to provide them food). Following this line of reasoning, might we go further and suppose that many geological formations, when originally created, had a similar appearance to formations that would now take thousands or even millions of years to complete by present "slow" processes?

This suggestion has currently found many supporters, and, initially at least, it seems to be an attractive proposal. Those who hold this position often combine it with certain objections to current scientific dating processes. They question how we can be certain of the reliability of radiometric dating beyond a few thousand years, for example, and how scientists can know that the rates of decay of certain elements have been constant

---

[69]Several scientific arguments pointing to a young earth (about 10,000–20,000 years old) are given in Henry M. Morris, ed., *Scientific Creationism* (San Diego, Calif.: Creation-Life, 1974), esp. pp. 131–69; also Kofahl and Segraves, *The Creation Explanation*, pp. 181–213.

A response to most of these arguments, from an "old earth" perspective, is given by Davis A. Young in *Christianity and the Age of the Earth*, pp. 71–131, and, specifically in response to "flood geology," in *Creation and the Flood*, pp. 171–213. Another book, *Science Held Hostage: What's Wrong With Creation Science and Evolutionism*, by Howard J. Van Till, Davis A. Young, and Clarence Menninga (Downers Grove, Ill.: InterVarsity Press, 1988), raises serious objections against the evaluation and use of scientific research materials by some prominent young earth advocates (see pp. 45–125). A preliminary young earth response to Young's arguments is found in a thirty-four-page pamphlet by Henry M. Morris and John D. Morris, *Science, Scripture, and the Young Earth* (El Cajon, Calif.: Institute for Creation Research, 1989).

since creation. They also suggest that events such as the fall and the subsequent cursing of nature (which altered the productivity and ecological balance of the earth, and caused man himself to begin to age and decay, Gen. 3:17–19), or the flood in Noah's time (Gen. 6–9), may have brought about significant differences in the amount of radioactive material in living things. This would mean that estimates of the age of the earth using present methods of measurement would not be accurate.

A common objection to this "appearance of age" view is that it "makes God an apparent deceiver,"[70] something that is contrary to his nature. But is God a "deceiver" if he creates a mature man and woman in a day and then tells us explicitly that he did it? Or if he creates mature fish and animals and full-grown trees and tells us that he did it? Or if he allows Adam and Eve to see the stars, which he created in order that people might see them and give glory to him, on the first night that they lived? Rather than manifesting deception, it seems that these actions point to God's infinite wisdom and power. This is particularly so if God explicitly tells us that he created everything in "six days." According to this position, those who are deceived are those who refuse to hear God's own explanation of how the creation came about.

The real problem with the appearance of age view is that there are some things in the universe that it cannot easily account for. Everyone will agree that Adam and Eve were created as adults, not newborn infants, and therefore had an appearance of age. Most who hold to twenty-four-hour days in Genesis 1 would also say there was an appearance of age with plants and trees, and with all the animals when they were first created (the chicken came before the egg!), and probably with light from the stars. But the creation of fossils presents a real problem, for responsible Christians would not want to suggest that God scattered fossils throughout the earth to give an added appearance of age! This would not be creating something "in process" or in a state of maturity; it would be creating the remains of a dead animal, not so that the animal could serve Adam and Eve, but simply to make people think the earth was older than it really was. Furthermore, one would have to say that God created all these dead animals and called them "very good."[71]

While the creation of stars with light beams in place or trees that are mature would be for the purpose of enabling human beings to glorify God for the excellence of his creation, the depositing of fossils in the earth could only be for the purpose of misleading or deceiving human beings regarding the earlier history of the world. More problematic is that Adam, the plants, the animals, and the stars all would have appeared to have different ages (because they were created with mature functions in place), whereas modern geological research gives approximately the same age estimates from radiometric dating, astronomical estimates, rock formations, samples of moon rocks and meteorites, etc. Why would God create so many different indications of an earth that is 4.5 billion years old if this were not true? Would it not be better to conclude that the earth is 4.5 billion

---

[70]Millard Erickson, *Christian Theology*, p. 382.

[71]We should note that old earth advocates must also have God speaking in Gen. 1:31 and calling the old fossils "very good." This is not a decisive objection if the death of animals before the fall did not result from sin, but it is a difficulty.

Only flood geology advocates (see below) will say that no fossils existed at Gen. 1:31, but that they were deposited suddenly by the flood in Gen. 6–9. This perhaps is a consideration in favor of the flood geology position.

years old, and that God left many indications there to show us this fact rather than in any way imply that he deceived us? So it seems the only credible explanations for the fossil record that Christians can adopt are: (a) current dating methods are incorrect by colossal proportions because of flawed assumptions or because of changes brought about by the fall or the flood; or (b) current dating methods are approximately correct and the earth is many millions or even billions of years old.

(2) Flood Geology: Another common view among evangelicals is what may be called "flood geology." This is the view that the tremendous natural forces unleashed by the flood at the time of Noah (Gen. 6–9) significantly altered the face of the earth, causing the creation of coal and diamonds, for example, within the space of a year rather than hundreds of millions of years, because of the extremely high pressure exerted by the water on the earth. This view also claims that the flood deposited fossils in layers of incredibly thick sediment all over the earth.[72] The flood geology view is also called "neo-catastrophism" because its advocates attribute most of the present geological status of the earth to the immense catastrophe of the flood.

The geological arguments put forth by advocates of this view are technical and difficult for the nonspecialist to evaluate. Personally, though I think the flood of Genesis 6–9 was world-wide, and that it did have a significant impact on the face of the earth, and that all living people and animals outside the ark perished in the flood, I am not persuaded that all of the earth's geological formations were caused by Noah's flood rather than by millions of years of sedimentation, volcanic eruptions, movement of glaciers, continental drift, and so forth. The controversy over flood geology is strikingly different from the other areas of dispute regarding creation, for its advocates have persuaded almost no professional geologists, even those who are Bible-believing evangelical Christians. By contrast, the books objecting to evolution that we mentioned above chronicle 130 years of cogent objections to Darwinian evolution that have been raised by a significant number of biologists, biochemists, zoologists, anthropologists, and paleontologists, both Christian and non-Christian, because evolution has so many problems in explaining facts evident from observation of the created world. If present geological formations could only be explained as the result of a universal flood, then would this not be evident even to non-Christians who look at the evidence? Would not the hundreds of Christians who are professional geologists be prepared to acknowledge the evidence if it were there? It may be that the flood geologists are right, but if they are, we would expect to see more progress in persuading some professional geologists that their case is a plausible one.[73]

5. Conclusions on the Age of the Earth. How old is the earth then? Where does this discussion leave us? Young's arguments for an old earth based on many kinds of scientific

---

[72]See Henry M. Morris and John C. Whitcomb, *The Genesis Flood* (Philadelphia: Presbyterian and Reformed, 1961); John C. Whitcomb, *The World That Perished* (Grand Rapids: Baker, 1988); Stephen A. Austin, *Catastrophes in Earth History* (El Cajon, Calif.: Institute for Creation Research, 1984). Other studies by flood geology advocates have been published in the *CRSQ*, though by no means all articles in that journal advocate the flood geology perspective, nor do all members of the Creation Research Society hold to flood geology.

[73]The arguments against flood geology have been marshalled by an evangelical who is also a professional geologist; see Davis A. Young, *Creation and the Flood.*

data from different disciplines seem (to the present writer at least) to be very strong. This is particularly true of arguments based on fossil-bearing rocks, coral reefs, continental drift, and the similarity of results from different kinds of radiometric dating. Newman and Eckelmann's arguments from astronomy indicating a very old universe give significant added weight. It is understandable, on the one hand, that God may have created a universe in which stars appeared to have been shining for 15 billion years, Adam appeared to have been living for 25 years, some trees appeared to have been living for 50 years, and some animals appeared to have been living for 1 to 10 years. But, on the other hand, it is difficult to understand why God would have created dozens or perhaps hundreds of different kinds of rocks and minerals on the earth, all of which actually were only one day old, but all of which had an appearance of being exactly 4.5 billion years old—exactly the apparent age that he also gave the moon and the meteorites when they, too, were only one day old. And it is difficult to understand why the evidence of star life cycles and the expansion of the universe would make the universe appear to be 15 billion years old if it were not. It is possible, but it seems unlikely, almost as if God's only purpose in giving these uniform apparent ages was to mislead us rather than simply to have a mature, functioning universe in place. So the old earth advocates seem to me to have a greater weight of scientific evidence on their side, and it seems that the weight of evidence is increasing yearly.

On the other hand, the interpretations of Genesis 1 presented by old earth advocates, while possible, do not seem as natural to the sense of the text. Davis Young's own solution of "seven successive figurative days of indeterminate duration"[74] really does not solve the problem, for he is willing to spread God's creative activities around on the various days as needed in order to make the sequence scientifically possible. For example, he thinks that some birds were created before Day 5:

> We may also suggest that even though birds were created on the fifth day, nevertheless, the most primitive birds or original bird ancestors were miraculously formed on a day prior to the fifth day. Hence the data of Genesis 1 actually allow for some overlap of the events of the days. If such overlap exists, then all apparent discrepancies between Genesis 1 and science would fall away (p. 131).

But this procedure allows us to say that the events of creation occurred at almost any time, no matter whether Scripture says they occurred then or not. Once this procedure is adopted, then ultimately we can know little if anything about the sequence of creation events from Genesis 1, because any of the events narrated there may have had precursors at previous periods of time. This can hardly be the impression the original readers were intended to get from the text. (Much more likely, however, is the modified day-age view presented on pp. 186–88 above.)

6. The Need for Further Understanding. Although our conclusions are tentative, at this point in our understanding, Scripture seems to be more easily understood to *suggest* (but not to require) a young earth view, while the observable facts of creation seem increasingly to favor an old earth view. Both views are possible, but neither one is certain. And we must

---

[74]*Creation and the Flood*, p. 89.

say very clearly that the age of the earth is a matter that is not directly taught in Scripture, but is something we can think about only by drawing more or less probable inferences from Scripture. Given this situation, it would seem best (1) to admit that God may not allow us to find a clear solution to this question before Christ returns, and (2) to encourage evangelical scientists and theologians who fall in both the young earth and old earth camps to begin to work together with much less arrogance, much more humility, and a much greater sense of cooperation in a common purpose.

There are difficulties with both old earth and young earth viewpoints, difficulties that the proponents of each view often seem unable to see in their own positions. Progress will certainly be made if old earth and young earth scientists who are Christians will be more willing to talk to each other without hostility, *ad hominem* attacks, or highly emotional accusations, on the one hand, and without a spirit of condescension or academic pride on the other. These attitudes are not becoming to the body of Christ, nor are they characteristic of the way of wisdom, which is "first pure, then peaceable, gentle, open to reason, full of mercy and good fruits, without uncertainty or insincerity," and full of the recognition that "the harvest of righteousness is sown in peace by those who make peace" (James 3:17–18).

As for evangelism and apologetics done in publications designed to be read outside the evangelical world, young earth and old earth proponents could cooperate much more in amassing the extremely strong arguments for creation by intelligent design, and in laying aside their differences over the age of the earth. Too often young earth proponents have failed to distinguish scientific arguments for creation by design from scientific arguments for a young earth, and have therefore prevented old earth advocates from joining them in a battle for the minds of an unbelieving scientific community. Moreover, young earth proponents have sometimes failed to recognize that scientific arguments for a young earth (which seem to them to be very persuasive) are not nearly as strong as the overwhelming scientific arguments for creation by intelligent design. As a result, young earth proponents have too often given the impression that the only true "creationists" are those who believe not only in creation by God but also in a young earth. The result has been unfortunate divisiveness and lack of community among scientists who are Christians—to the delight of Satan and the grieving of God's Holy Spirit.

Finally, we can view this controversy with some expectancy that there will be further progress in scientific understanding of the age of the earth. It is likely that scientific research in the next ten or twenty years will tip the weight of evidence decisively toward either a young earth or an old earth view, and the weight of Christian scholarly opinion (from both biblical scholars and scientists) will begin to shift decisively in one direction or another. This should not cause alarm to advocates of either position, because the truthfulness of Scripture is not threatened (our interpretations of Genesis 1 have enough uncertainty that either position is possible). Both sides need to grow in knowledge of the truth, even if this means abandoning a long-held position.

F. Application

The doctrine of creation has many applications for Christians today. It makes us realize that the material universe is good in itself, for God created it good and wants us to use it in ways pleasing to him. Therefore we should seek to be like the early Christians, who "partook of food with glad and generous hearts" (Acts 2:46), always with thanksgiving to God and trust in his provisions. A healthy appreciation of creation will keep us from false asceticism that denies the goodness of creation and the blessings that come to us through it. It will also encourage some Christians to do scientific and technological research into the goodness of God's abundant creation, or to support such research.[75] The doctrine of creation will also enable us to recognize more clearly that scientific and technological study in itself glorifies God, for it enables us to discover how incredibly wise, powerful, and skillful God was in his work of creation. "Great are the works of the Lord, studied by all who have pleasure in them" (Ps. 111:2).

The doctrine of creation also reminds us that God is sovereign over the universe he created. He made it all, and he is Lord of all of it. We owe all that we are and have to him, and we may have complete confidence that he will ultimately defeat all his enemies and be manifested as Sovereign King to be worshiped forever. In addition, the incredible size of the universe and the amazing complexity of every created thing will, if our hearts are right, draw us continually to worship and praise him for his greatness.

Finally, as we indicated above, we can wholeheartedly enjoy creative activities (artistic, musical, athletic, domestic, literary, etc.) with an attitude of thanksgiving that our Creator God enables us to imitate him in our creativity.

QUESTIONS FOR PERSONAL APPLICATION

1. Are there ways in which you could be more thankful to God for the excellence of his creation? Look around you and give some examples of the goodness of the creation that God has allowed you to enjoy. Are there ways in which you could be a better steward of parts of God's creation of which he has entrusted to your care?

2. Might the goodness of all that God created encourage you to try to enjoy different kinds of foods than those you normally prefer? Can children be taught to thank God for variety in the things God has given us to eat? Does the doctrine of creation provide an answer to some strict animal rights advocates who say we should not eat steak or chicken or other meat, or wear clothing made from animal skins, since we are simply another form of animal ourselves? (See Gen. 3:21.)

3. In order to understand something of the despair felt by contemporary non-Christians, just try to imagine for a moment that you believe that there is no God and that you are just a product of matter plus time plus chance, the spontaneous result of random variation in organisms over millions of years. How would you feel differently about yourself? About other people? About the future? About right and wrong?

[75]Frair and Davis, *A Case for Creation*, pp. 135–40, have many specific practical challenges to scientists who believe in creation to do specific kinds of greatly needed research.

4. Why do we feel joy when we are able to "subdue" even a part of the earth and make it useful for serving us—whether it be in growing vegetables, developing a better kind of plastic or metal, or using wool to knit a piece of clothing? Should we feel joy at the accomplishment of these and other tasks? What other attitudes of heart should we feel as we do them?

5. When you think about the immensity of the stars, and that God put them in place to show us his power and glory, how does it make you feel about your place in the universe? Is this different from the way a non-Christian would feel?

6. Before reading this chapter, what did you think about the theory of evolution? How has your view changed, if at all?

7. What are some things that Christians can learn about theological discussion in general from observing the current controversy over the age of the earth? What significance do you see in this controversy for your own Christian faith?

SPECIAL TERMS

concordist theory
creation *ex nihilo*
Cro-Magnon man
day-age theory
deism
dualism
flood geology
gap theory
homo sapiens

immanent
literary framework
  theory
macro-evolution
materialism
mature creationism
micro-evolution
neo-catastrophism
old-earth theory

pantheism
pictorial-day theory
progressive creationism
theistic evolution
transcendent
twenty-four-hour day
  theory
young earth theory

BIBLIOGRAPHY

Several of these titles have been taken from an extensive bibliography on creation and evolution prepared by a professional biologist, Dr. Wayne Frair of The King's College, Briarcliff Manor, New York.

Anderson, J. Kerby, and Harold G. Coffin. *Fossils in Focus.* Grand Rapids: Zondervan, 1977.

Austin, Stephen A. *Catastrophes in Earth History.* El Cajon, Calif.: Institute of Creation Research, 1984. (young earth view)

Barclay, D. R. "Creation." In *NDT,* pp. 177–79.

Blocher, Henri. *In the Beginning: The Opening Chapters of Genesis.* Trans. by David G. Preston. Leicester: Inter-Varsity Press, 1984.

Cameron, Nigel M. de S. *Evolution and the Authority of the Bible.* Exeter: Paternoster, 1983.

_____, ed. *In the Beginning. . . .: A Symposium on the Bible and Creation.* Glasgow: The Biblical Creation Society, 1980.

Clotz, J. W. *Genes, Genesis and Evolution.* St. Louis, Mo.: Concordia Publishing House, 1970.

_____. *Studies in Creation.* St. Louis, Mo.: Concordia Publishing House, 1985.

Custance, Arthur C. *Evolution or Creation.* Grand Rapids: Zondervan, 1976.

_____. *Without Form and Void: A Study of the Meaning of Genesis 1:2.* Brockville, Ontario: Doorway Papers, 1970.

Davidheiser, Bolton. *Evolution and the Christian Faith.* Grand Rapids: Baker, 1969.

Denton, Michael. *Evolution: A Theory in Crisis.* Bethesda, Md.: Adler and Adler, 1986.

De Young, Donald B. *Astronomy and the Bible: Questions and Answers.* Grand Rapids: Baker, 1989. (young earth view)

Fields, Weston W. *Unformed and Unfilled.* Nutley, N.J.: Presbyterian and Reformed, 1976.

Frair, Wayne, and Percival Davis. *A Case for Creation.* Norcross, Ga.: CRS Books, 1983.

Gange, Robert. *Origins and Destiny: A Scientist Examines God's Handiwork.* Waco, Tex.: Word, 1986.

Geisler, Norman L. and J. Kerby Anderson. *Origin Science: A Proposal for the Creation-Evolution Controversy.* Foreword by Walter L. Bradley. Grand Rapids: Baker, 1987.

Gentry, R. V. *Creation's Tiny Mystery.* Knoxville, Tenn.: Earth Science Associates, 1986.

Gish, D. T. *Evolution: The Challenge of the Fossil Record.* El Cajon, Calif.: Master Books, 1985. (young earth view)

Houston, James. *I Believe in the Creator.* Grand Rapids: Eerdmans, 1980.

Hummel, Charles E. *Creation or Evolution? Resolving the Crucial Issues.* Downers Grove, Ill.: InterVarsity Press, 1989.

Johnson, Phillip E. *Darwin on Trial.* Downers Grove, Ill.: InterVarsity Press, 1991.

Kaiser, Christopher B. *Creation and the History of Science.* Grand Rapids: Eerdmans, 1991.

Kerkut, G. A. *Implications of Evolution.* New York: Pergamon, 1960.

Kofahl, Robert E., and Kelly L. Segraves. *The Creation Explanation: A Scientific Alternative to Evolution.* Wheaton, Ill.: Harold Shaw, 1975. (young earth view)

Lester, L. P., and R. G. Bohlin. *The Natural Limits to Biological Change.* Grand Rapids: Zondervan, 1984.

Maatman, Russell. *The Bible, Natural Science and Evolution.* Grand Rapids: Reformed Fellowship, 1970.

Morris, Henry M., ed. *Scientific Creationism.* San Diego, Calif.: Creation-Life, 1974. (young earth view)

_____, and John C. Whitcomb. *The Genesis Flood.* Philadelphia: Presbyterian and Reformed, 1961. (young earth view)

_____, and John D. Morris. *Science, Scripture, and the Young Earth: An Answer to Current Arguments Against the Biblical Doctrine of Recent Creation.* El Cajon, Calif.: Institute for Creation Research, 1989. (young earth view)

Newman, Robert C., and Herman J. Eckelmann. *Genesis One and the Origin of the Earth.* Downers Grove, Ill.: InterVarsity Press, 1977. (argues against young earth view)

Pitman, M. *Adam and Evolution*. Grand Rapids: Baker, 1984.

Ramm, Bernard. *The Christian View of Science and Scripture*. Grand Rapids: Eerdmans, 1954.

Ross, Hugh. *Creation and Time: A Biblical and Scientific Perspective on the Creation-Date Controversy*. Colorado Springs: NavPress, 1994. (an articulate and highly trained scientist who argues against the young earth view on the basis of recent scientific evidence)

Rusch, W. H., Sr. *The Argument—Creationism vs. Evolutionism*. Norcross, Ga: CRS Books, 1984.

Schaeffer, Francis. *No Final Conflict*. Downers Grove, Ill.: InterVarsity Press, 1975.

Thaxton, C. B., W. L. Bradley, and R. L. Olsen. *The Mystery of Life's Origin: Reassessing Current Theories*. New York: Philosophical Library, 1984.

Van Till, Howard J., Davis A. Young, and Clarence Menninga. *Science Held Hostage: What's Wrong With Creation Science and Evolutionism?* Downers Grove, Ill.: InterVarsity Press, 1988. (argues against young earth view)

Whitcomb, John C. *The World That Perished*. Grand Rapids: Baker, 1988. (young earth view)

_____. *The Early Earth*. Revised edition. Grand Rapids: Baker, 1986. (young earth view)

Wilder-Smith, A. E. *The Natural Sciences Know Nothing of Evolution*. El Cajon, Calif.: Master Books, 1981.

Young, Davis A. *Christianity and the Age of the Earth*. Grand Rapids: Zondervan, 1982. (argues against young earth view)

_____. *Creation and the Flood: An Alternative to Flood Geology and Theistic Evolution*. Grand Rapids: Baker, 1977. (argues against young earth view)

Youngblood, Ronald. *How It All Began*. Ventura, Calif.: Regal, 1980.

SCRIPTURE MEMORY PASSAGE

Nehemiah 9:6: *And Ezra said: "You are the Lord, you alone; you have made heaven, the heaven of heavens, with all their host, the earth and all that is on it, the seas and all that is in them; and you preserve all of them; and the host of heaven worships you.*

HYMN

"Hallelujah, Praise Jehovah!"

This hymn contains the entire content of Psalm 148 set to music. It summons all creation, including "things visible and things invisible," to worship God our Creator.

> Hallelujah, praise Jehovah, from the heavens praise his name;
> Praise Jehovah in the highest, all his angels, praise proclaim.
> All his hosts, together praise him, sun and moon and stars on high;
> Praise him, O ye heav'ns of heavens, and ye floods above the sky.

Refrain:
Let them praises give Jehovah, for his name alone is high,
    And his glory is exalted, and his glory is exalted, and his glory
      is exalted
Far above the earth and sky.

Let them praises give Jehovah, they were made at his command;
    Them for ever he established, his decree shall ever stand.
From the earth, O praise Jehovah, all ye seas, ye monsters all,
    Fire and hail and snow and vapors, stormy winds that hear his call.

All ye fruitful trees and cedars, all ye hills and mountains high,
    Creeping things and beasts and cattle, birds that in the heavens fly,
Kings of earth, and all ye people, princes great, earth's judges all;
    Praise his name, young men and maidens, aged men,
      and children small.

AUTHOR: WILLIAM J. KIRKPATRICK, 1838–1921

Chapter 9

GOD'S PROVIDENCE

If God controls all things, how can our actions have real meaning? What are the decrees of God?

EXPLANATION AND SCRIPTURAL BASIS

Once we understand that God is the all-powerful Creator (see chapter 8), it seems reasonable to conclude that he also preserves and governs everything in the universe as well. Though the term *providence* is not found in Scripture, it has been traditionally used to summarize God's ongoing relationship to his creation. When we accept the biblical doctrine of providence, we avoid four common errors in thinking about God's relationship to creation. The biblical doctrine is not *deism* (which teaches that God created the world and then essentially abandoned it), nor *pantheism* (which teaches that the creation does not have a real, distinct existence in itself, but is only part of God), but *providence*, which teaches that though God is actively related to and involved in the creation at each moment, creation is distinct from him. Moreover, the biblical doctrine does not teach that events in creation are determined by *chance* (or randomness), nor are they determined by impersonal *fate* (or determinism), but by God, who is the personal yet infinitely powerful Creator and Lord.

We may define God's providence as follows: *God is continually involved with all created things in such a way that he (1) keeps them existing and maintaining the properties with which he created them; (2) cooperates with created things in every action, directing their distinctive properties to cause them to act as they do; and (3) directs them to fulfill his purposes.*

Under the general category of providence we have three subtopics, according to the three elements in the definition above: (1) Preservation, (2) Concurrence, and (3) Government.

We shall examine each of these separately, then consider differing views and objections to the doctrine of providence. It should be noted that this is a doctrine on which there has been substantial disagreement among Christians since the early history of the church, particularly with respect to God's relationship to the willing choices of moral creatures. In this chapter we will first present a summary of the position favored in this textbook (what is commonly called the "Reformed" or "Calvinist" position),[1] then consider arguments that have been made from another position (what is commonly called the "Arminian" position).

A. Preservation

God keeps all created things existing and maintaining the properties with which he created them.

Hebrews 1:3 tells us that Christ is "upholding the universe by his word of power." The Greek word translated "upholding" is *phero*, "carry, bear." This is commonly used in the New Testament for carrying something from one place to another, such as bringing a paralyzed man on a bed to Jesus (Luke 5:18), bringing wine to the steward of the feast (John 2:8), or bringing a cloak and books to Paul (2 Tim. 4:13). It does not mean simply "sustain," but has the sense of active, purposeful control over the thing being carried from one place to another. In Hebrews 1:3, the use of the present participle indicates that Jesus is "*continually* carrying along all things" in the universe by his word of power. Christ is actively involved in the work of providence.

Similarly, in Colossians 1:17, Paul says of Christ that "in him all things hold together." The phrase "all things" refers to every created thing in the universe (see v. 16), and the verse affirms that Christ keeps all things existing—in him they continue to exist or "endure" (NASB mg.). Both verses indicate that if Christ were to cease his continuing activity of sustaining all things in the universe, then all except the triune God would instantly cease to exist. Such teaching is also affirmed by Paul when he says, "In him we live and move and *have our being*" (Acts 17:28), and by Ezra: "You are the LORD, you alone; you have made heaven, the heaven of heavens, with all their host, the earth and all that is on it, the seas and all that is in them; *and you preserve all of them;* and the host of heaven worships you" (Neh. 9:6). Peter also says that "the heavens and earth that now exist" are "being *kept* until the day of judgment" (2 Peter 3:7).

One aspect of God's providential preservation is the fact that he continues to give us breath each moment. Elihu in his wisdom says of God, "If he should take back his spirit to himself, and gather to himself his breath, all flesh would perish together, and man would return to dust" (Job 34:14–15; cf. Ps. 104:29).

God, in preserving all things he has made, also causes them to maintain the properties with which he created them. God preserves water in such a way that it continues to

---

[1]Though philosophers may use the term *determinism* (or *soft determinism*) to categorize the position I advocate in this chapter, I do not use that term because it is too easily misunderstood in everyday English: (1) It suggests a system in which human choices are not real and make no difference in the outcome of events; and (2) it suggests a system in which the ultimate cause of events is a mechanistic universe rather than a wise and personal God. Moreover, (3) it too easily allows critics to group the biblical view with non-Christian deterministic systems and blur the distinctions between them.

The view advocated in this chapter is also sometimes called "compatibilism," because it holds that absolute divine sovereignty is compatible with human significance and real human choices. I have no objection to the nuances of this term, but I have decided not to use it because (1) I want to avoid the proliferation of technical terms in studying theology, and (2) it seems preferable simply to call my position a traditional Reformed view of God's providence, and thereby to place myself within a widely understood theological tradition represented by John Calvin and the other systematic theologians listed in the "Reformed" category at the end of this chapter.

act like water. He causes grass to continue to act like grass, with all its distinctive characteristics. He causes the paper on which this sentence is written to continue to act like paper so that it does not spontaneously dissolve into water and float away or change into a living thing and begin to grow! Until it is acted on by some other part of creation and thereby its properties are changed (for instance, until it is burned with fire and it becomes ash), this paper will continue to act like paper so long as God preserves the earth and the creation that he has made.

We should not, however, think of God's preservation as a continuous new creation: he does not continuously create new atoms and molecules for every existing thing every moment. Rather, he *preserves* what has already been created: he "carries along all things" by his word of power (Heb. 1:3, author's translation). We must also appreciate that created things are *real* and that their characteristics are *real*. I do not just imagine that the rock in my hand is hard—it is hard. If I bump it against my head, I do not just imagine that it hurts—it *does* hurt! Because God keeps this rock maintaining the properties with which he created it, the rock has been hard since the day it was formed, and (unless something else in creation interacts with it and changes it) it will be hard until the day God destroys the heavens and the earth (2 Peter 3:7, 10–12).

God's providence provides a basis for science: God has made and continues to sustain a universe that acts in predictable ways. If a scientific experiment gives a certain result today, then we can have confidence that (if all the factors are the same) it will give the same result tomorrow and a hundred years from tomorrow. The doctrine of providence also provides a foundation for technology: I can be confident that gasoline will make my car run today just as it did yesterday, not simply because "it has always worked that way," but because God's providence sustains a universe in which created things maintain the properties with which he created them. The *result* may be similar in the life of an unbeliever and the life of a Christian: we both put gasoline in our cars and drive away. But he will do so without knowing the ultimate reason why it works that way, and I will do so with knowledge of the actual final reason (God's providence) and with thanks to my Creator for the wonderful creation that he has made and preserves.

B. Concurrence

God cooperates with created things in every action, directing their distinctive properties to cause them to act as they do.

This second aspect of providence, *concurrence,* is an expansion of the idea contained in the first aspect, *preservation.* In fact, some theologians (such as John Calvin) treat the fact of concurrence under the category of preservation, but it is helpful to treat it as a distinct category.

In Ephesians 1:11 Paul says that God "accomplishes all things according to the counsel of his will." The word translated "accomplishes" (*energeō*) indicates that God "works" or "brings about" *all things* according to his own will. No event in creation falls outside of his providence. Of course this fact is hidden from our eyes unless we read it in Scripture. Like preservation, God's work of concurrence is not clearly evident from observation of the natural world around us.

In giving scriptural proof for concurrence, we will begin with the inanimate creation, then move to animals, and finally to different kinds of events in the life of human beings.

1. Inanimate Creation. There are many things in creation that we think of as merely "natural" occurrences. Yet Scripture says that God causes them to happen. We read of "fire and hail, snow and frost, stormy wind fulfilling his command!" (Ps. 148:8). Similarly,

> To the *snow* he says, "Fall on the earth";
>> and to the shower and the *rain,* "Be strong." . . .
> By the breath of God *ice* is given,
>> and the broad waters are frozen fast.
> He loads the thick cloud with moisture;
>> the clouds scatter his *lightning.*
> They turn round and round by his guidance,
>> to accomplish all that he commands them
>> on the face of the habitable world.
> Whether for correction, or for his land,
>> or for love, he causes it to happen.
> (Job 37:6–13; cf. similar statements in 38:22–30)

Again, the psalmist declares that "Whatever the LORD pleases he does, in heaven and on earth, in the seas and all deeps" (Ps. 135:6), and then in the next sentence he illustrates God's doing of his will in the weather: "He it is who makes the clouds rise at the end of the earth, who makes lightnings for the rain and brings forth the wind from his storehouses" (Ps. 135:7; cf. 104:4).

God also causes the grass to grow: "*You cause the grass to grow* for the cattle, and plants for man to cultivate, that he may bring forth food from the earth" (Ps. 104:14). God directs the stars in the heavens, asking Job, "Can you bring forth the constellations in their seasons or lead out the Bear with its cubs?" (Job 38:32 NIV; "the Bear" or Ursa Major is commonly called the Big Dipper; v. 31 refers to the constellations Pleiades and Orion). Moreover, God continually directs the coming of the morning (Job 38:12), a fact Jesus affirmed when he said that God "*makes his sun rise* on the evil and on the good, and *sends rain* on the just and on the unjust" (Matt. 5:45).

2. Animals. Scripture affirms that God feeds the wild animals of the field, for, "These all look to you, to give them their food in due season. When you give to them, they gather it up; when you open your hand, they are filled with good things. When you hide your face, they are dismayed" (Ps. 104:27–29; cf. Job 38:39–41). Jesus also affirmed this when he said, "Look at the *birds* of the air . . . your heavenly Father *feeds them*" (Matt. 6:26). And he said that not one sparrow "will fall to the ground without your Father's will" (Matt. 10:29).

3. Seemingly "Random" or "Chance" Events. From a human perspective, the casting of lots (or its modern equivalent, the rolling of dice or flipping of a coin) is the most typical of random events that occur in the universe. But Scripture affirms that the outcome of such an event is from God: "The lot is cast into the lap, but the decision is wholly from the LORD" (Prov. 16:33).[2]

4. Events Fully Caused by God and Fully Caused by the Creature as Well. For any of these foregoing events (rain and snow, grass growing, sun and stars, the feeding of animals, or casting of lots), we could (at least in theory) give a completely satisfactory "natural" explanation. A botanist can detail the factors that cause grass to grow, such as sun, moisture, temperature, nutrients in the soil, etc. Yet Scripture says that *God* causes the grass to grow. A meteorologist can give a complete explanation of factors that cause rain (humidity, temperature, atmospheric pressure, etc.), and can even produce rain in a weather laboratory. Yet Scripture says that *God* causes the rain. A physicist with accurate information on the force and direction a pair of dice was rolled could fully explain what caused the dice to give the result they did — yet Scripture says that *God* brings about the decision of the lot that is cast.

This shows us that it is incorrect for us to reason that if we know the "natural" cause of something in this world, then God did not cause it. Rather, if it rains we should thank him. If crops grow we should thank him. In all of these events, it is not as though the event was partly caused by God and partly by factors in the created world. If that were the case, then we would always be looking for some small feature of an event that we could not explain and attribute that (say 1 percent of the cause) to God. But surely this is not a correct view. Rather, these passages affirm that such events are entirely caused by God. Yet we know that (in another sense) they are entirely caused by factors in the creation as well.

The doctrine of concurrence affirms that God *directs,* and *works through,* the distinctive properties of each created thing, so that these things themselves bring about the results that we see. In this way it is possible to affirm that in one sense events are fully (100 percent) caused by God and fully (100 percent) caused by the creature as well. However, divine and creaturely causes work in different ways. The divine cause of each event works as an invisible, behind-the-scenes, directing cause and therefore could be called the "primary cause" that plans and initiates everything that happens. But the created thing brings about actions in ways consistent with the creature's own properties, ways that can often be described by us or by professional scientists who carefully observe the processes. These creaturely factors and properties can therefore be called the "secondary" causes of everything that happens, even though they are the causes that are evident to us by observation.

5. The Affairs of Nations. Scripture also speaks of God's providential control of human affairs. We read that God "makes nations great, and he destroys them: he enlarges nations, and leads them away" (Job 12:23). "Dominion belongs to the LORD, and he rules over

---

[2]It is true that Eccl. 9:11 says that "the race is not to the swift, nor the battle to the strong, nor bread to the wise, nor riches to the intelligent, nor favor to the men of skill; but time and *chance* happen to them all." But Michael Eaton correctly observes, "On the lips of an Israelite 'chance' means what is unexpected, not what is random" (*Ecclesiastes,* TOTC [Leicester and Downers Grove, Ill.: InterVarsity Press, 1983], p. 70). The rare word here translated "chance" (Heb., *pega'*) occurs only once more in the Bible (1 Kings 5:4[18], of an evil *event*).

the nations" (Ps. 22:28). He has determined the time of existence and the place of every nation on the earth, for Paul says, "he made from one every nation of men to live on all the face of the earth, having determined allotted periods and the boundaries of their habitation" (Acts 17:26; cf. 14:16). And when Nebuchadnezzar repented, he learned to praise God,

> For his dominion is an everlasting dominion,
>   and his kingdom endures from generation to generation;
> all the inhabitants of the earth are accounted as nothing;
>   and *he does according to his will in the host of heaven*
>   *and among the inhabitants of the earth;*
> and none can stay his hand or say to him,
>   "What are you doing?" (Dan. 4:34–35)

6. All Aspects of Our Lives. It is amazing to see the extent to which Scripture affirms that God brings about various events in our lives. For example, our dependence on God to give us food each day is affirmed every time we pray, "Give us this day our daily bread" (Matt. 6:11), even though we work for our food and (as far as mere human observation can discern) obtain it through entirely "natural" causes. Similarly, Paul, looking at events with the eye of faith, affirms that "my God will supply every need" of his children (Phil 4:19), even though God may use "ordinary" means (such as other people) to do so.

God plans our days before we are born, for David affirms, "In your book were written, every one of them, the days that were formed for me, when as yet there was none of them" (Ps. 139:16). And Job says that man's "days are determined, and the number of his months is with you, and you have appointed his bounds that he cannot pass" (Job 14:5). This can be seen in the life of Paul, who says that God "had set me apart before I was born" (Gal. 1:15), and Jeremiah, to whom God said, "Before I formed you in the womb I knew you, and before you were born I consecrated you; I appointed you a prophet to the nations" (Jer. 1:5).

All our actions are under God's providential care, for "in him we live and *move*" (Acts 17:28). The individual steps we take each day are directed by the Lord. Jeremiah confesses, "I know, O Lord, that the way of man is not in himself, that it is not in man who walks to direct his steps" (Jer. 10:23). We read that "a man's steps are ordered by the Lord" (Prov. 20:24), and that "a man's mind plans his way, but the Lord directs his steps" (Prov. 16:9). Similarly, Proverbs 16:1 affirms, "The plans of the mind belong to man, but the answer of the tongue is from the Lord."[3]

[3]David J. A. Clines, "Predestination in the Old Testament," in *Grace Unlimited,* ed. by Clark H. Pinnock (Minneapolis: Bethany House, 1975), pp. 116–17, objects that these verses simply affirm that "when it comes to conflict between God and man, undoubtedly it cannot be man who wins the day." He says that these verses do not describe life in general, but describe unusual situations where God overcomes man's will in order to bring about his special purposes. Clines denies that these verses mean that God always acts this way or that these verses represent God's control of human conduct generally. Yet no such restriction is seen in these passages (see Prov. 16:1, 9). The verses do not say that God directs a man's steps in rare instances where God needs to intervene to fulfill his purposes; they simply make general statements about the way the world works—God directs man's steps in general, not simply when there is conflict between God and man.

Success and failure come from God, for we read, "For not from the east or from the west and not from the wilderness comes lifting up; but it is God who executes judgment, putting down one and lifting up another" (Ps. 75:6–7). So Mary can say, "He has put down the mighty from their thrones, and exalted those of low degree" (Luke 1:52). The LORD gives children, for children "are a heritage from the LORD, the fruit of the womb a reward" (Ps. 127:3).

All our talents and abilities are from the Lord, for Paul can ask the Corinthians, "What have you that you did not receive? If then you received it, why do you boast as if it were not a gift?" (1 Cor. 4:7). David knew that to be true regarding his military skill, for, though he must have trained many hours in the use of a bow and arrow, he could say of God, "He trains my hands for war, so that my arms can bend a bow of bronze" (Ps. 18:34).

God influences rulers in their decisions, for "the king's heart is a stream of water in the hand of the LORD; he turns it wherever he will" (Prov. 21:1). An illustration of this was when the Lord "turned the heart of the king of Assyria" to his people, "so that he aided them in the work of the house of God, the God of Israel" (Ezr. 6:22), or when "the LORD stirred up the spirit of Cyrus king of Persia" (Ezr. 1:1) to help the people of Israel. But it is not just the heart of the king that God influences, for he looks down "on all the inhabitants of the earth" and "fashions the hearts of them all" (Ps. 33:14–15). When we realize that the heart in Scripture is the location of our inmost thoughts and desires, this is a significant passage. God especially guides the desires and inclinations of believers, working in us "both *to will* and to work for his good pleasure" (Phil. 2:13).

All of these passages, reporting both general statements about God's work in the lives of all people and specific examples of God's work in the lives of individuals, lead us to conclude that God's providential work of concurrence extends to all aspects of our lives. Our words, our steps, our movements, our hearts, and our abilities are all from the Lord.

But we must guard against misunderstanding. Here also, as with the lower creation, God's providential direction as an unseen, behind-the-scenes, "primary cause," should not lead us to deny the reality of our choices and actions. Again and again Scripture affirms that we really do *cause* events to happen. We are significant and we are responsible. We *do have choices,* and these are real choices that bring about real results. Scripture repeatedly affirms these truths as well. Just as a rock is *really hard* because God has made it with the property of hardness, just as water is *really wet* because God has made it with the property of wetness, just as plants are *really alive* because God has made them with the property of life, so our choices are *real choices* and do have significant effects, because God has made us in such a wonderful way that he has endowed us with the property of willing choice.

One approach to these passages about God's concurrence is to say that if our choices are real, they *cannot* be caused by God (see below for further discussion of this viewpoint). But the number of passages that affirm this providential control of God is so considerable, and the difficulties involved in giving them some other interpretation are so formidable, that it does not seem to me that this can be the right approach to them. It seems better to affirm that God causes all things that happen, but that he does so in such a way that he somehow upholds our ability to make *willing, responsible choices,* choices that have *real and eternal results,* and for which we are *held accountable.* Exactly how God combines his providential control with our willing and significant choices, Scripture does not explain to us. But rather than deny one aspect or the other (simply because we cannot explain how both can be true), we should accept both in an attempt to be faithful to the teaching of all of Scripture.

The analogy of an author writing a play may help us to grasp how both aspects can be true. In the Shakespearean play *Macbeth*, the character Macbeth murders King Duncan. Now (if we assume for a moment that this is a fictional account), we may ask, "Who killed King Duncan?" On one level, the correct answer is "Macbeth." Within the play, he carried out the murder and he is rightly to blame for it. But on another level, a correct answer to the question, "Who killed King Duncan?" would be "William Shakespeare caused his death": he wrote the play, he created all the characters in it, and he wrote the part where Macbeth killed King Duncan.

It would not be correct to say that because Macbeth killed King Duncan, William Shakespeare did not (somehow) cause his death. Nor would it be correct to say that because William Shakespeare caused King Duncan's death, Macbeth did not kill him. Both are true. On the level of the characters in the play Macbeth fully (100%) caused King Duncan's death, but on the level of the creator of the play, William Shakespeare fully (100%) caused King Duncan's death. In similar fashion, we can understand that God fully causes things in one way (as Creator), and we fully cause things in another way (as creatures). (One word of caution however: The analogy of an author (= writer, creator) of a play should not lead us to say that God is the "author" (= actor, doer, an older sense of "author") of sin, for he never does sinful actions, nor does he ever delight in them.)[4]

Of course, characters in a play are not real persons — they are fictional characters. But God is infinitely greater and wiser than we are. While we can only create fictional characters in a play, our almighty God has created us as real persons who make willing choices. To say that God could not make a world in which he (somehow) causes us to make willing choices (as some would argue today; see discussion below), is limiting the power of God. It seems also to deny a large number of passages of Scripture.

7. What About Evil? If God does indeed cause, through his providential activity, everything that comes about in the world, then the question arises, "What is the relationship

---

[4]I. Howard Marshall, "Predestination in the New Testament" in *Grace Unlimited*, by Clark H. Pinnock, pp. 132–33, 139, objects to the analogy of an author and a play because the actors "are bound by the characters assigned to them and the lines that they have learned" so that even if the dramatist "makes [the characters] say 'I love my creator' in his drama, this is not mutual love in the real sense."

But Marshall limits his analysis to what is possible with human beings acting on a human level. He does not give consideration to the possibility (in fact, the reality!) that God is able to do far more than human beings are able to do, and that he can wonderfully create genuine human beings rather than mere characters in a play. A better approach to

the analogy of an author and a play would be if Marshall would apply to this question a very helpful statement that he made in another part of the essay: "The basic difficulty is that of attempting to explain the nature of *the relationship between an infinite God and finite creatures*. Our temptation is to think of divine causation in much the same way as human causation, and this produces difficulties as soon as we try to relate divine causation and human freedom. It is beyond our ability to explain how God can cause us to do certain things (or to cause the universe to come into being and to behave as it does)" (pp. 137–38). I can agree fully with everything in Marshall's statement at that point, and find that to be a very helpful way of approaching this problem.

between God and evil in the world?" Does God actually cause the evil actions that people do? If he does, then is God not responsible for sin?

In approaching this question, it is best first to read the passages of Scripture that most directly address it. We can begin by looking at several passages that affirm that God did, indeed, cause evil events to come about and evil deeds to be done. But we must remember that in all these passages it is very clear that Scripture nowhere shows God as *directly doing anything evil,* but rather as bringing about evil deeds through the willing actions of moral creatures. Moreover, *Scripture never blames God for evil or shows God as taking pleasure in evil,* and Scripture never excuses human beings for the wrong they do. However we understand God's relationship to evil, we must *never* come to the point where we think that we are not responsible for the evil that we do, or that God takes pleasure in evil or is to be blamed for it. Such a conclusion is clearly contrary to Scripture.

There are literally dozens of Scripture passages that say that God (indirectly) brought about some kind of evil. I have quoted such an extensive list (in the next few paragraphs) because Christians often are unaware of the extent of this forthright teaching in Scripture. Yet it must be remembered that in all of these examples, the evil is actually done not by God but by people or demons who choose to do it.

A very clear example is found in the story of Joseph. Scripture clearly says that Joseph's brothers were wrongly jealous of him (Gen. 37:11), hated him (Gen. 37:4, 5, 8), wanted to kill him (Gen. 37:20), and did wrong when they cast him into a pit (Gen. 37:24) and then sold him into slavery in Egypt (Gen. 37:28). Yet later Joseph could say to his brothers, "*God sent me before you* to preserve life" (Gen. 45:5), and "You meant evil against me; but *God meant it for good,* to bring it about that many people should be kept alive, as they are today" (Gen. 50:20).[5] Here we have a combination of evil deeds brought about by sinful men who are rightly held accountable for their sin and the overriding providential control of God whereby God's own purposes were accomplished. Both are clearly affirmed.

The story of the exodus from Egypt repeatedly affirms that God hardened the heart of Pharaoh: God says, "I will harden his heart" (Ex. 4:21), "I will harden Pharaoh's heart" (Ex. 7:3), "the LORD hardened the heart of Pharaoh" (Ex. 9:12), "the LORD hardened Pharaoh's heart" (Ex. 10:20, repeated in 10:27 and again in 11:10), "I will harden Pharaoh's heart" (Ex. 14:4), and "the LORD hardened the heart of Pharaoh king of Egypt" (Ex. 14:8). It is sometimes objected that Scripture also says that Pharaoh hardened his own heart (Ex. 8:15, 32; 9:34), and that God's act of hardening Pharaoh's heart was only in response to the initial rebellion and hardness of heart that Pharaoh himself exhibited of his own free will. But it should be noted that God's promises that he would harden Pharaoh's heart (Ex. 4:21; 7:3) are made long before Scripture tells us that Pharaoh hardened his own heart (we read of this for the first time in Ex. 8:15). Moreover, our analysis of concurrence given above, in which both divine and human agents can cause the same event, should show us that both factors can be true at the same time: even when Pharaoh hardens his own heart, that is not inconsistent with saying that God is causing Pharaoh to do this and thereby God is hardening the heart of Pharaoh. Finally, if

---

[5]Ps. 105:17 says that God "had sent a man ahead of them, Joseph, who was sold as a slave."

someone would object that God is just intensifying the evil desires and choices that were already in Pharaoh's heart, then this kind of action could still in theory at least cover all the evil in the world today, since all people have evil desires in their hearts and all people do in fact make evil choices.

What was God's purpose in this? Paul reflects on Exodus 9:16 and says, "For the scripture says to Pharaoh, 'I have raised you up for the very purpose of showing my power in you, so that my name may be proclaimed in all the earth'" (Rom. 9:17). Then Paul infers a general truth from this specific example: "So then he has mercy upon whomever he wills, and he hardens the heart of whomever he wills" (Rom. 9:18). In fact, God also hardened the hearts of the Egyptian people so that they pursued Israel into the Red Sea: "I will harden the hearts of the Egyptians so that they shall go in after them, and I will get glory over Pharaoh and all his host, his chariots, and his horsemen" (Ex. 14:17). This theme is repeated in Psalm 105:25: "He turned their hearts to hate his people."

Later in the Old Testament narrative similar examples are found of the Canaanites who were destroyed in the conquest of Palestine under Joshua. We read, "For it was the LORD's doing to harden their hearts that they should come against Israel in battle, in order that they should be utterly destroyed" (Josh. 11:20; see also Judg. 3:12; 9:23). And Samson's demand to marry an unbelieving Philistine woman "was from the LORD; for he was seeking an occasion against the Philistines. At that time the Philistines had dominion over Israel" (Judg. 14:4). We also read that the sons of Eli, when rebuked for their evil deeds, "would not listen to the voice of their father; for it was the will of the LORD to slay them" (1 Sam. 2:25). Later, "an evil spirit from the LORD" tormented King Saul (1 Sam. 16:14).

When David sinned, the LORD said to him through Nathan the prophet, "I will raise up evil against you out of your own house; and I will take your wives before your eyes, and give them to your neighbor, and he shall lie with your wives in the sight of this sun. For you did it secretly; but I will do this thing before all Israel, and before the sun" (2 Sam. 12:11–12; fulfilled in 16:22). In further punishment for David's sin, "the LORD struck the child that Uriah's wife bore to David, and it became sick" and eventually died (2 Sam. 12:15–18). David remained mindful of the fact that God could bring evil against him, because at a later time, when Shimei cursed David and threw stones at him and his servants (2 Sam. 16:5–8), David refused to take vengeance on Shimei but said to his soldiers, "Let him alone, and let him curse; for the LORD has bidden him" (2 Sam. 16:11).

Still later in David's life, the Lord "incited"[6] David to take a census of the people (2 Sam. 24:1), but afterward David recognized this as sin, saying, "I have sinned greatly in what I have done" (2 Sam. 24:10), and God sent punishment on the land because of this sin (2 Sam. 24:12–17). However, it is also clear that "the anger of the LORD was kindled against Israel" (2 Sam. 24:1), so God's inciting of David to sin was a means by which he brought about punishment on the people of Israel. Moreover, the means by which God incited David is made clear in 1 Chronicles 21:1: "Satan stood up against

---

[6]The Hebrew word used when 2 Sam. 24:1 says that the Lord *incited* David against Israel is *sûth,* "to incite, allure, instigate" (BDB, p. 694). It is the same word used in 2 Chron. 21:1 to say that Satan *incited* David to number Israel, in 1 Kings 21:25 to say that Jezebel *incited* Ahab to do evil, in Deut. 13:6(7) to warn against a loved one *enticing* a family member secretly to serve other gods, and in 2 Chron. 18:31 to say that God *moved* the Syrian army to withdraw from Jehoshaphat.

Israel, and *incited* David to number Israel." In this one incident the Bible gives us a remarkable insight into the three influences that contributed in different ways to one action: God, in order to bring about his purposes, worked through Satan to incite David to sin, but Scripture regards David as being responsible for that sin. Again, after Solomon turned away from the Lord because of his foreign wives, "the LORD raised up an adversary against Solomon, Hadad the Edomite" (1 Kings 11:14), and "God also raised up as an adversary to him, Rezon the son of Eliada" (1 Kings 11:23). These were evil kings raised up by God.

In the story of Job, though the LORD gave Satan permission to bring harm to Job's possessions and children, and though this harm came through the evil actions of the Sabeans and the Chaldeans, as well as a windstorm (Job 1:12, 15, 17, 19), yet Job looks beyond those secondary causes and, with the eyes of faith, sees it all as from the hand of the Lord: "the LORD gave, and the LORD has taken away; *blessed be the name of the LORD*" (Job 1:21). The Old Testament author follows Job's statement immediately with the sentence, "In all this Job did not sin or charge God with wrong" (Job 1:22). Job has just been told that evil marauding bands had destroyed his flocks and herds, yet with great faith and patience in adversity, he says, "*The LORD has taken away.*" Though he says that the LORD had done this, yet he does not blame God for the evil or say that God had done wrong: he says, "Blessed be the name of the LORD." To *blame* God for evil that he had brought about through secondary agents would have been to sin. Job does not do this, Scripture never does this, and neither should we.

Elsewhere in the Old Testament we read that the Lord "put a lying spirit in the mouth" of Ahab's prophets (1 Kings 22:23) and sent the wicked Assyrians as "the rod of my anger" to punish Israel (Isa. 10:5). He also sent the evil Babylonians, including Nebuchadnezzar, against Israel, saying, "I will bring them against this land and its inhabitants" (Jer. 25:9). Then God promised that later he would punish the Babylonians also: "I will punish the king of Babylon and that nation, the land of the Chaldeans, for their iniquity, says the LORD, making the land an everlasting waste" (Jer. 25:12). If there is a deceiving prophet who gives a false message, then the Lord says, "if the prophet be deceived and speak a word, I, the LORD, have deceived that prophet, and I will stretch out my hand against him, and will destroy him from the midst of my people Israel" (Ezek. 14:9, in the context of bringing judgment on Israel for their idolatry). As the culmination of a series of rhetorical questions to which the implied answer is always "no," Amos asks, "Is a trumpet blown in a city, and the people are not afraid? Does evil befall a city, unless the LORD has done it?" (Amos 3:6). There follows a series of natural disasters in Amos 4:6–12, where the LORD reminds the people that he gave them hunger, drought, blight and mildew, locusts, pestilence, and death of men and horses, "yet you did not return to me" (Amos 4:6, 8, 9, 10, 11).

In many of the passages mentioned above, God brings evil and destruction on people in judgment upon their sins: They have been disobedient or have strayed into idolatry, and then the LORD uses evil human beings or demonic forces or "natural" disasters to bring judgment on them. (This is not always said to be the case—Joseph and Job come to mind—but it is often so.) Perhaps this idea of judgment on sin can help us to understand, at least in part, how God can righteously bring about evil events.

All human beings are sinful, for Scripture tells us that "all have sinned and fall short of the glory of God" (Rom. 3:23). None of us deserves God's favor or his mercy, but only eternal condemnation. Therefore, when God brings evil on human beings, whether to discipline his children, or to lead unbelievers to repentance, or to bring a judgment of condemnation and destruction upon hardened sinners, none of us can charge God with doing wrong. Ultimately all will work in God's good purposes to bring glory to him and good to his people. Yet we must realize that in punishing evil in those who are not redeemed (such as Pharaoh, the Canaanites, and the Babylonians), God is also glorified through the demonstration of his justice, holiness, and power (see Ex. 9:16; Rom. 9:14–24).

Through the prophet Isaiah God says, "I form the light, and create darkness: I make peace, and create evil:[7] I the LORD do all these things" (Isa. 45:7 KJV; the Hebrew word for "create" here is *bārā'*, the same word used in Gen. 1:1). In Lamentations 3:38 we read, "Is it not from the mouth of the Most High that good and evil come?"[8] The people of Israel, in a time of heartfelt repentance, cry out to God and say, "O LORD, why do you make us err from your ways and harden our heart, so that we fear you not?" (Isa. 63:17).[9]

The life of Jonah is a remarkable illustration of God's concurrence in human activity. The men on board the ship sailing to Tarshish threw Jonah overboard, for Scripture says, "So *they* took up Jonah and threw him into the sea; and the sea ceased from its raging" (Jonah 1:15). Yet only five verses later Jonah acknowledges God's providential direction in their act, for he says to God, "*You* cast me into the deep, into the heart of the seas" (Jonah 2:3). Scripture simultaneously affirms that the men threw Jonah into the sea and that God threw him into the sea. The providential direction of God did not force the sailors to do something against their will, nor were they conscious of any divine influence on them—indeed, they cried to the Lord for forgiveness as they threw Jonah overboard (Jonah 1:14). What Scripture reveals to us, and what Jonah himself realized, was that God was bringing about his plan through the willing choices of real human beings who were morally accountable for their actions. In a way not understood by us and not revealed to us, God *caused* them to make a *willing choice* to do what they did.

The most evil deed of all history, the crucifixion of Christ, was ordained by God—not just the fact that it would occur, but also all the individual actions connected with it. The church at Jerusalem recognized this, for they prayed:

---

[7]Other translations render the Hebrew word *rā'*, "evil," as "disaster" (NIV) or "woe" (RSV) or "calamity" (NASB), and indeed the word can be used to apply to natural disasters such as these words imply. But it may have broader application than natural disasters, for the word is an extremely common word used of evil generally: It is used of the tree of the knowledge of good and *evil* (Gen. 2:9), of the *evil* among mankind that brought the judgment of the flood (Gen. 6:5), and of the *evil* of the men of Sodom (Gen. 13:13). It is used to say, "Depart from *evil* and do good" (Ps. 34:14), and to speak of the wrong of those who call *evil* good and good *evil* (Isa. 5:20), and of the sin of those whose "feet run to *evil*" (Isa. 59:7; see also 47:10, 11; 56:2; 57:1; 59:15; 65:12; 66:4). Dozens of other times throughout the Old Testament it refers to moral evil or sin. The contrast with "peace" (*shālôm*) in the same phrase in Isa. 45:7 might argue that only "calamity" is in view, but not necessarily so, for moral evil and wickedness is certainly also the opposite of the wholeness of God's "shalom" or peace. (In Amos 3:6, *rā'āh* is a different but related word and has a similar range of meanings.) But Isa. 45:7 does not say that God *does* evil (see discussion below).

[8]The Hebrew for "evil" here is *rā 'āh*, as in Amos 3:6.

[9]Another kind of evil is physical infirmity. With regard to this, the Lord says to Moses, "Who has made man's mouth? Who makes him dumb, or deaf, or seeing, or blind? Is it not I, the LORD?" (Ex. 4:11).

> For truly in this city there were gathered together against your holy servant Jesus, whom you anointed, both Herod and Pontius Pilate, with the Gentiles and the peoples of Israel, *to do whatever your hand and your plan had predestined to take place.* (Acts 4:27)

All the actions of all the participants in the crucifixion of Jesus had been "predestined" by God. Yet the apostles clearly attach no moral blame to God, for the actions resulted from the willing choices of sinful men. Peter makes this clear in his sermon at Pentecost: "this Jesus, delivered up according to the definite plan and foreknowledge of God, *you crucified and killed by the hands of lawless men*" (Acts 2:23). In one sentence he links God's plan and foreknowledge with the moral blame that attaches to the actions of "lawless men." They were not forced by God to act against their wills; rather, God brought about his plan *through their willing choices,* for which they were nevertheless responsible.

In an example similar to the Old Testament account of God sending a lying spirit into the mouth of Ahab's prophets, we read of those who refuse to love the truth, "Therefore God sends upon them a strong delusion, to make them believe what is false, so that all may be condemned who did not believe the truth but had pleasure in unrighteousness" (2 Thess. 2:11–12). And Peter tells his readers that those who oppose them and persecute them, who reject Christ as Messiah, "stumble because they disobey the word, as they were destined to do" (1 Peter 2:8).[10]

8. Analysis of Verses Relating to God and Evil. After looking at so many verses that speak of God's providential use of the evil actions of men and demons, what can we say by way of analysis?

a. God Uses All Things to Fulfill His Purposes and Even Uses Evil for His Glory and for Our Good: Thus, when evil comes into our lives to trouble us, we can have from the doctrine of providence a deeper assurance that "God causes all things to work together for good to those who love God, to those who are called according to his purpose" (Rom. 8:28 NASB). This kind of conviction enabled Joseph to say to his brothers, "You meant evil against me; but *God meant it for good*" (Gen. 50:20).

We can also realize that God is glorified even in the punishment of evil. Scripture tells us that "the LORD has made everything for its purpose, even the wicked for the day of trouble" (Prov. 16:4).[11] Similarly, the psalmist affirms, "Surely the wrath of men shall praise you" (Ps. 76:10). And the example of Pharaoh (Rom. 9:14–24) is a clear example of the way God uses evil for his own glory and for the good of his people.

---

[10]The "destining" in this verse is best taken to refer to both the stumbling and the disobedience. It is incorrect to say that God only destined the fact that those who disobey would stumble, because it is not a fact but persons ("they") who are said to be "destined" in this case. (See discussion in Wayne Grudem, *The First Epistle of Peter,* TNTC [Leicester: Inter-Varsity Press, and Grand Rapids: Eerdmans, 1988], pp. 106–10.)

[11]David J. A. Clines, "Predestination in the Old Testament," p. 116, retranslates this, "The Lord has made everything with its counterpart, so the wicked will have his day of doom." He does this in order to avoid the conclusion that the Lord has made some wicked people for the day of evil. But his translation is not convincing. The Hebrew word translated "purpose" in the RSV (*ma 'aneh*) occurs only eight times in the Old Testament and usually refers to an "answer" to a question or a statement. So it means something like "appropriate response" or "corresponding purpose." But the preposition *le* is much more accurately translated "for" (not "with"), so in either

b. Nevertheless, God Never Does Evil, and Is Never to Be Blamed for Evil: In a statement similar to those cited above from Acts 2:23 and 4:27–28, Jesus also combines God's predestination of the crucifixion with moral blame on those who carry it out: "For the Son of man goes *as it has been determined;* but woe to that man by whom he is betrayed!" (Luke 22:22; cf. Matt. 26:24; Mark 14:21). And in a more general statement about evil in the world, Jesus says, "Woe to the world for temptations to sin! For it is necessary that temptations come, but woe to the man by whom the temptation comes!" (Matt. 18:7).

James speaks similarly in warning us not to blame God for the evil we do when he says, "Let no one say when he is tempted, 'I am tempted by God'; for God cannot be tempted with evil and he himself tempts no one; but each person is tempted when he is lured and enticed by his own desire" (James 1:13–14). The verse does not say that God never causes evil; it affirms that we should never think of him as the personal agent who is tempting us or who is to be held accountable for the temptation. We can never blame God for temptation or think that he will approve of us if we give in to it. We are to resist evil and always blame ourselves or others who tempt us, but we must never blame God. Even a verse such as Isaiah 45:7, which speaks of God "creating evil," does not say that God himself *does* evil, but should be understood to mean that God ordained that evil would come about through the willing choices of his creatures.

These verses all make it clear that "secondary causes" (human beings, and angels and demons) are *real,* and that human beings do cause evil and are responsible for it. Though God ordained that it would come about, both in general terms and in specific details, yet *God is removed from actually doing evil,* and his bringing it about through "secondary causes" does not impugn his holiness or render him blameworthy. John Calvin wisely says:

> Thieves and murderers and other evildoers are the instruments of divine providence, and the Lord himself uses these to carry out the judgments that he has determined with himself. Yet I deny that they can derive from this any excuse for their evil deeds. Why? Will they either involve God in the same iniquity with themselves, or will they cloak their own depravity with his justice? They can do neither.[12]

A little later, Calvin heads a chapter, "God So Uses the Works of the Ungodly, and So Bends Their Minds to Carry Out His Judgments, That He Remains Pure From Every Stain."[13]

We should notice that the alternatives to saying that God *uses evil for his purposes,* but that *he never does evil* and is *not to be blamed* for it, are not desirable ones. If we were to say that God himself does evil, we would have to conclude that he is not a good and righteous God, and therefore that he is not really God at all. On the other hand, if we maintain that God does not use evil to fulfill his purposes, then we would have to admit

---

case the sentence affirms that the Lord has made everything for its appropriate purpose or the response appropriate to it. Therefore, whether we translate "purpose" or "counterpart," the verse affirms that even the wicked have been made by the Lord "for [Heb. *le*] the day of evil."

[12]John Calvin, *Institutes of the Christian Religion,* Library of Christian Classics, ed. by John T. McNeill and trans. by F. L. Battles, 2 vols. (Philadelphia: Westminster, 1960), 1:217 (1.16.5).

[13]John Calvin, *Institutes,* 1:228 (1.18.title).

that there is evil in the universe that God did not intend, is not under his control, and might not fulfill his purposes. This would make it very difficult for us to affirm that "all things" work together for good for those who love God and are called according to his purpose (Rom. 8:28). If evil came into the world in spite of the fact that God did not intend it and did not want it to be there, then what guarantee do we have that there will not be more and more evil that he does not intend and that he does not want? And what guarantee do we have that he will be able to use it for his purposes, or even that he can triumph over it? Surely this is an undesirable alternative position.

c. God Rightfully Blames and Judges Moral Creatures for the Evil They Do: Many passages in Scripture affirm this. One is found in Isaiah: "These have *chosen* their own ways, and their soul *delights in* their abominations; I also will choose affliction for them, and bring their fears upon them; because, when I called, no one answered, when I spoke they did not listen; but they did what was evil in my eyes, and *chose* that in which I did not delight" (Isa. 66:3–4). Similarly, we read, "God made man upright, but they have sought out many devices" (Eccl. 7:29). *The blame for evil is always on the responsible creature,* whether man or demon, who does it, and *the creature who does evil is always worthy of punishment.* Scripture consistently affirms that God is righteous and just to punish us for our sins. And if we object that he should not find fault with us because we cannot resist his will, then we must ponder the apostle Paul's own response to that question: "You will say to me then, 'Why does he still find fault? For who can resist his will?' But who are you, a man, to answer back to God? Will what is molded say to its molder, 'Why have you made me thus?'" (Rom. 9:19–20). In every case where we do evil, we know that we *willingly* choose to do it, and we realize that we are rightly to be blamed for it.

d. Evil Is Real, Not an Illusion, and We Should Never Do Evil, for It Will Always Harm Us and Others: Scripture consistently teaches that we never have a right to do evil, and that we should persistently oppose it in ourselves and in the world. We are to pray, "Deliver us from evil" (Matt. 6:13), and if we see anyone wandering from the truth and doing wrong, we should attempt to bring him back. Scripture says, "If any one among you wanders from the truth and someone brings him back, let him know that whoever brings back a sinner from the error of his way will save his soul from death and will cover a multitude of sins" (James 5:19–20). We should never even *will* evil to be done, for entertaining sinful desires in our minds is to allow them to "wage war" against our souls (1 Peter 2:11) and thereby to do us spiritual harm. If we are ever tempted to say, "Why not do evil that good may come?" as some people were slanderously charging Paul with teaching, we should remember what Paul says about people who teach that false doctrine: "Their condemnation is just" (Rom. 3:8).

In thinking about God using evil to fulfill his purposes, we should remember that there are things that are *right* for God to do but *wrong* for us to do: He requires others to worship him, and he accepts worship from them. He seeks glory for himself. He will execute final judgment on wrongdoers. He also uses evil to bring about good purposes, but he does not allow us to do so. Calvin quotes a statement of Augustine with approval:

"There is a great difference between what is fitting for man to will and what is fitting for God. . . . For through the bad wills of evil men God fulfills what he righteously wills."[14] And Herman Bavinck uses the analogy of a parent who will himself use a very sharp knife but will not allow his child to use it, to show that God himself uses evil to bring about good purposes but never allows his children to do so. Though we are to imitate God's moral character in many ways (cf. Eph. 5:1), this is one of the ways in which we are not to imitate him.

e. In Spite of All of the Foregoing Statements, We Have to Come to the Point Where We Confess That We Do Not Understand How It Is That God Can Ordain That We Carry Out Evil Deeds and Yet Hold Us Accountable for Them and Not be Blamed Himself: We can affirm that all of these things are true, because Scripture teaches them. But Scripture does *not* tell us exactly *how* God brings this situation about or how it can be that God holds us accountable for what he ordains to come to pass. Here Scripture is silent, and we have to agree with Berkhof that ultimately "the problem of God's relation to sin remains a mystery."[15]

9. Are We "Free"? Do We Have "Free Will"? If God exercises providential control over all events are we in any sense free? The answer depends on what is meant by the word *free.* In some senses of the word *free,* everyone agrees that we are free in our will and in our choices. Even prominent theologians in the Reformed or Calvinistic tradition concur. Both Louis Berkhof in his *Systematic Theology* (pp. 103, 173) and John Calvin in his *Institutes of the Christian Religion*[16] are willing to speak *in some sense* of the "free" acts and choices of man. However, Calvin explains that the term is so subject to misunderstanding that he himself tries to avoid using it. This is because "free will is not sufficient to enable man to do good works, unless he be helped by grace."[17] Therefore, Calvin concludes:

> Man will then be spoken of as having this sort of free decision, not because he has free choice equally of good and evil, but because he acts wickedly by will, not by compulsion. Well put, indeed, but what purpose is served by labeling with a proud name such a slight thing?

Calvin continues by explaining how this term is easily misunderstood:

> But how few men are there, I ask, who when they hear free will attributed to man do not immediately conceive him to be master of both his own mind and

---

[14]John Calvin, *Institutes,* 1:234 (1.18.3).

[15]Louis Berkhof, *Systematic Theology,* p. 175.

[16]*Institutes,* 1:296 (2.3.5), quoting St. Bernard with approval: "Among all living beings man alone is free. . . . For what is voluntary is also free." Later in the same passage he quotes St. Bernard with approval again, where he admits that the will is in bondage to sin and therefore sins of necessity, but then says that "this necessity is as it were voluntary. . . . Thus the soul . . . is at the same time enslaved and free: enslaved because of necessity; free because of will." A little later Calvin himself says that "man, while he sins of necessity, yet sins

no less voluntarily" (1:309 [2.4.1]). Calvin clearly says that Adam, before there was sin in the world, "by free will had the power, if he so willed, to attain eternal life. . . . Adam could have stood if he wished, seeing that he fell solely by his own will. . . . His choice of good and evil was free" (1:195 [1.15.8]). So Calvin can use the term *free will* if it means "voluntary, willing," and he can use it of Adam before the fall. Yet he carefully avoids applying the term *free will* to sinful human beings if by it people mean "able to do good in one's own strength" (see text above).

[17]*Institutes,* 1:262 (2.2.6).

will, able of his own power to turn himself toward either good or evil. . . . If anyone, then, can use this word without understanding it in a bad sense, I shall not trouble him on this account . . . I'd prefer not to use it myself, and I should like others, if they seek my advice, to avoid it.[18]

Thus, when we ask whether we have "free will," it is important to be clear as to what is meant by the phrase. Scripture nowhere says that we are "free" in the sense of being outside of God's control[19] or of being able to make decisions that are not caused by anything. (This is the sense in which many people seem to assume we must be free; see discussion below.) Nor does it say we are "free" in the sense of being able to do right on our own apart from God's power. But we are nonetheless free in the greatest sense that any creature of God could be free—we make *willing* choices, choices that have *real effects*.[20] We are aware of no restraints on our will from God when we make decisions.[21] We must insist that we have the power of *willing* choice; otherwise we will fall into the error of fatalism or determinism and thus conclude that our choices do not matter, or that we cannot really make willing choices. On the other hand, the kind of freedom that is demanded by those who deny God's providential control of all things, a freedom to be outside of God's sustaining and controlling activity, would be impossible if Jesus Christ is indeed "continually carrying along things by his word of power" (Heb. 1:3, author's translation). If this is true, then to be outside of that providential control would simply be not to exist! An absolute "freedom," totally free of God's control, is simply not possible in a world providentially sustained and directed by God himself.

C. Government

1. Scriptural Evidence. We have discussed the first two aspects of providence, (1) preservation and (2) concurrence. This third aspect of God's providence indicates that *God has a purpose in all that he does in the world and he providentially governs or directs all things in order that they accomplish his purposes.* We read in the Psalms, "His kingdom rules over all" (Ps. 103:19). Moreover, "he does according to his will in the host of heaven and among the inhabitants of the earth; and none can stay his hand or say to him, 'What are you doing?'" (Dan. 4:35). Paul affirms that "from him and through him and to him are all things" (Rom. 11:36), and that "God has put all things in subjection under his feet" (1 Cor. 15:27). God is the one who "accomplishes *all things* according to the counsel of his will" (Eph. 1:11), so that ultimately "at the name of Jesus" every knee will bow "in heaven and on earth and under the earth, and every tongue confess that Jesus Christ

---

[18]Ibid., 1:264, 266 (2.2.7–8).

[19]In fact, our ability to make willing choices at all is simply a created reflection of God's will and his ability to make willing choices. However, if we were to be *totally* free in our choices, we would be equal to God in our will, and that is something we may never expect either in this life or in the one to come.

[20]Arminian theologians dissent from this understanding of free will and argue for a freedom that means our decisions are not caused by anything outside ourselves (see discussion of

Jack Cottrell's objection that freedom must mean more than willing choices on pp. 227–34, below).

[21]John Feinberg says, "If the act is according to the agent's *desires,* then even though the act is causally determined, it is free and the agent is morally responsible" ("God Ordains All Things," in *Predestination and Free Will: Four Views of Divine Sovereignty and Human Freedom,* ed. by David Basinger and Randall Basinger [Downers Grove, Ill.: InterVarsity Press, 1986], p. 37).

is Lord, to the glory of God the Father" (Phil. 2:10–11). It is because Paul knows that God is sovereign over all and works his purposes in every event that happens that he can declare that "God causes all things to work together for good to those who love God, to those who are called according to his purpose" (Rom. 8:28 NASB).

2. Distinctions Concerning the Will of God. Though *in God* his will is unified, and not divided or contradictory, we cannot begin to understand the depths of God's will, and only in a small part is it revealed to us. For this reason, as we saw in chapter 6,[22] two aspects of God's will appear to us. On the one hand, there is God's *moral will* (sometimes called his "revealed" will). This includes the moral standards of Scripture, such as the Ten Commandments and the moral commands of the New Testament. God's moral commands are given as descriptions of how *we* should conduct ourselves if we would act rightly before him. On the other hand, another aspect of God's will is his *providential government* of all things (sometimes called his "secret will"). This includes all the events of history that God has ordained to come about, for example, the fact that Christ would be crucified by "lawless men" (Acts 2:23). It also includes all the other evil acts that were mentioned in the preceding section.

Some have objected to this distinction between two aspects of the will of God, arguing that it means there is a "self-contradiction" in God.[23] However, even in the realm of human experience, we know that we can will and carry out something that is painful and that we do not desire (such as punishing a disobedient child or getting an inoculation that temporarily makes us ill) in order to bring about a long-term result that we desire more than the avoidance of short-term pain (to bring about the obedience of the child, for example, or to prevent us from getting a more serious illness). And God is infinitely greater and wiser than we are. Certainly it is possible for him to will that his creatures do something that in the short term displeases him in order that in the long term he would receive the greater glory. To say that this is a "self-contradiction" in God is to fail to understand the distinctions that have been made so that this explanation is not contradictory.[24]

D. The Decrees of God

The decrees of God are *the eternal plans of God whereby, before the creation of the world, he determined to bring about everything that happens.* This doctrine is similar to the doctrine of providence, but here we are thinking about God's decisions *before the world was created,* rather than his providential actions in time. His providential actions are the outworking of the eternal decrees that he made long ago.

---

[22]See pp. 103–6 for a further discussion of God's secret and revealed will.

[23]This is the objection of I. Howard Marshall, "Predestination in the New Testament," p. 173.

[24]John Calvin says of those who object to two senses of the will of God, "Let them tell me, I pray, whether he exercises his judgments willingly or unwillingly. . . . When we do not grasp how God wills to take place what he forbids to be done, let us recall our mental incapacity." He also quotes with approval the statement of Augustine: "There is a great difference between what is fitting for man to will and what is fitting for God . . . for through the bad wills of evil men God fulfills what he righteously wills" (*Institutes,* 1:233–34 [1.18.3]).

David confesses, "in your book were written, every one of them, the days that were formed for me, when as yet there was none of them" (Ps. 139:16; cf. Job 14:5: the days, months, and bounds of man are determined by God). There was also a "definite *plan and foreknowledge of God*" (Acts 2:23) by which Jesus was put to death, and the actions of those who condemned and crucified him were "predestined" (Acts 4:28) by God. Our salvation was determined long ago because God "chose us in him (Christ) *before the foundation of the world*, that we should be holy and blameless before him" (Eph. 1:4). Our good works as believers are those "which God *prepared beforehand*, that we should walk in them" (Eph. 2:10; cf. Jude 4).

These examples take in many diverse aspects of human activity. It seems appropriate to conclude from these examples that all that God does he has planned before the creation of the world—in fact, these things have been an *eternal plan* with him. The benefit of an emphasis on God's decrees is that it helps us to realize that God does not make up plans suddenly as he goes along. He knows the end from the beginning, and he will accomplish all his good purposes. This should greatly increase our trust in him, especially in difficult circumstances.

E. The Importance of Our Human Actions

We may sometimes forget that God works *through human actions* in his providential management of the world. If we do, then we begin to think that our actions and our choices do not make much difference or do not have much effect on the course of events. To guard against any misunderstanding of God's providence we make the following points of emphasis.

1. We Are Still Responsible for Our Actions. God has made us *responsible* for our actions, which have *real and eternally significant results.* In all his providential acts God will preserve these characteristics of responsibility and significance.

Some analogies from the natural world might help us understand this. God has created a rock with the characteristic of being *hard,* and so it is. God has created water with the characteristic of being *wet,* and so it is. God has created plants and animals with the characteristic of being *alive,* and so they are. Similarly, God has created us with the characteristic of being *responsible for our actions,* and so we are! If we do right and obey God, he will reward us and things will go well with us both in this age and in eternity. If we do wrong and disobey God, he will discipline and perhaps punish us, and things will go ill with us. The realization of these facts will help us have pastoral wisdom in talking to others and in encouraging them to avoid laziness and disobedience.

The fact that we are responsible for our actions means that we should never begin to think, "God made me do evil, and therefore I am not responsible for it." Significantly, Adam began to make excuses for the very first sin in terms that sounded suspiciously like this: "The woman whom you gave to be with me, she gave me fruit of the tree, and I ate" (Gen. 3:12). Unlike Adam, Scripture *never* blames God for sin. If we ever begin to *think* that God is to blame for sin, we have thought *wrongly* about God's providence, for it is always the creature, not God who is to be blamed. Now we may object that it is not right for God to hold us responsible if he has in fact ordained all things that happen, but Paul corrects us: "You will say to me then, 'Why does he still find fault? For who can resist his will?' But who are you, a man, to answer back to God?" (Rom. 9:19–20). We must realize and settle in our hearts that it is *right* for God to rebuke and discipline and punish evil. And, when we are responsible to do so, it is right for us to rebuke and discipline evil in our families, in the church, and even, in some ways, in the society around us. We should never say about an evil event, "God willed it and therefore it is good," because we must recognize that some things that God's will of decree has planned are not in themselves good, and should not receive our approval, just as they do not receive God's approval.

2. Our Actions Have Real Results and Do Change the Course of Events. In the ordinary working of the world, if I neglect to take care of my health and have poor eating habits, or if I abuse my body through alcohol or tobacco, I am likely to die sooner. God has ordained that our *actions* do have effects. God has ordained that *events* will come about *by our causing them.* Of course, we do not know what God has planned even for the rest of this day, to say nothing of next week or next year. But we *do* know that if we trust God and obey him, we will discover that he has planned *good things* to come about through that obedience! We cannot simply disregard others whom we meet, for God brings many people across our paths and gives *us* the responsibility to act toward them in eternally significant ways—whether for good or ill.

Calvin wisely notes that to encourage us to use ordinary caution in life and to plan ahead, "God is pleased to hide all future events from us, in order that we should resist them as doubtful, and not cease to oppose them with ready remedies, until they are either overcome or pass beyond all care. . . . God's providence does not always meet us in its naked form, but God in a sense clothes it with the means employed."[25]

By contrast, if we anticipate that some dangers or evil events may come in the future, and if we do not use reasonable means to avoid them, then we may in fact discover that our lack of action was the means that God used to allow them to come about!

3. Prayer Is One Specific Kind of Action That Has Definite Results and That Does Change the Course of Events. God has also ordained that prayer is a very significant means of bringing about results in the world.[26] When we earnestly intercede for a specific person or situation, we will often find that God had ordained that our prayer would be a *means* he would use to bring about the changes in the world. Scripture reminds us of this when it tells us, "You do not have, because you do not ask" (James 4:2). Jesus says, "Hitherto you have asked nothing in my name; ask, and you will receive, that your joy may be full" (John 16:24).

4. In Conclusion, We Must Act! The doctrine of providence in no way encourages us to sit back in idleness to await the outcome of certain events. Of course, God may impress on us the need to wait on him before we act and to trust in him rather than in our

---

[25]John Calvin, *Institutes,* 1:216 (1.17.4).   [26]See chapter 11 for a more extensive discussion of prayer.

own abilities—that is certainly not wrong. But simply to say that we are trusting in God *instead of* acting responsibly is sheer laziness and is a distortion of the doctrine of providence.

In practical terms, if one of my sons has school work that must be done the next day, I am right to make him complete that work before he can go out to play. I realize that his grade is in God's hands, and that God has long ago determined what it would be, but I do not know what it will be, and neither does he. What I do know is that if he studies and does his school work faithfully, he will receive a good grade. If he doesn't, he will not. So Calvin can say:

> Now it is very clear what our duty is: Thus, if the Lord has committed to us the protection of our life, our duty is to protect it; if he offers helps to us, to use them; if he forewarns us of dangers, not to plunge headlong; if he makes remedies available, not to neglect them. But no danger will hurt us, say they, unless it is fatal, and in this case it is beyond remedies. But what if the dangers are not fatal, because the Lord has provided you with remedies for repulsing and overcoming them?[27]

One good example of vigorous activity combined with trust in God is found in 2 Samuel 10:12, where Joab says, "*Be strong* and let us show ourselves courageous for the sake of our people and for the cities of our God," but then adds immediately in the same sentence, "*and may the Lord do what is good in His sight*" (NASB). Joab will both fight and trust God to do what he thinks to be good.

Similar examples are found in the New Testament. When Paul was in Corinth, in order to keep him from being discouraged about the opposition he had received from the Jews, the Lord appeared to him one night in a vision and said to him, "Do not be afraid, but speak and do not be silent; for I am with you, and no man shall attack you to harm you; for *I have many people in this city*" (Acts 18:9–10). If Paul had been a fatalist with an improper understanding of God's providence, he would have listened to God's words, "I have many people in this city," and concluded that God had determined to save many of the Corinthians, and that therefore it did not matter whether Paul stayed there or not: God had already chosen many people to be saved! Paul would have thought that he may as well pack his bags and leave! But Paul does not make that mistake. He rather concludes that if God has chosen many people, then it will probably be through the *means* of Paul's preaching the gospel that those many people would be saved. Therefore Paul makes a wise decision: "*And he stayed a year and six months,* teaching the word of God among them" (Acts 18:11).

Paul put this kind of responsible action in the light of God's providence into a single sentence in 2 Timothy 2:10, where he said, "I endure everything *for the sake of the elect,* that they also may obtain salvation in Christ Jesus with its eternal glory." He did not argue from the fact that God had chosen some to be saved that nothing had to be done; rather, he concluded that *much* had to be done in order that God's purposes might come about by the *means* that God had also established. Indeed, Paul was willing to endure

---

[27]John Calvin, *Institutes*, 1:216 (1.17.4).

"everything," including all kinds of hardship and suffering, that God's eternal plans might come about. A hearty belief in God's providence is not a discouragement but a spur to action.

A related example is found in the story of Paul's journey to Rome. God had clearly revealed to Paul that no one on the ship would die from the long storm they had endured. Indeed, Paul stood before the passengers and crew and told them to take heart,

> for there will be no loss of life among you, but only of the ship. For this very night there stood by me an angel of the God to whom I belong and whom I worship, and he said, "Do not be afraid, Paul; you must stand before Caesar; and lo, God has granted you all those who sail with you." So take heart, men, for I have faith in God that it will be exactly as I have been told. But we shall have to run on some island. (Acts 27:22–26)

But shortly after Paul had said this, he noticed that the sailors on board the ship were secretly trying to lower a lifeboat into the sea, "seeking to escape from the ship" (Acts 27:30). They were planning to leave the others helpless with no one who knew how to sail the ship. When Paul saw this, he did not adopt an erroneous, fatalistic attitude, thinking that God would miraculously get the ship to shore. Rather, he immediately went to the centurion who was in charge of the sailors and "Paul said to the centurion and the soldiers, 'Unless these men stay in the ship, you cannot be saved'" (Acts 27:31). Wisely, Paul knew that God's providential oversight and even his clear prediction of what would happen still involved the use of ordinary human *means* to bring it about. He was even so bold to say that those means were *necessary*: "Unless these men stay in the ship, *you cannot be saved*" (Acts 27:31). We would do well to imitate his example, combining complete trust in God's providence with a realization that the use of ordinary means is necessary for things to come out the way God has planned them to come out.

5. What If We Cannot Understand This Doctrine Fully? Every believer who meditates on God's providence will sooner or later come to a point where he or she will have to say, "I cannot understand this doctrine fully." In some ways that must be said about every doctrine, since our understanding is finite, and God is infinite (see chapter 1, pp. 25–27; cf. pp. 41–43). But particularly is this so with the doctrine of providence: we should believe it because Scripture teaches it even when we do not understand fully how it fits in with other teachings of Scripture. Calvin has some wise advice:

> Let those for whom this seems harsh consider for a little while how bearable their squeamishness is in refusing a thing attested by clear Scriptural proofs because it exceeds their mental capacity, and find fault that things are put forth publicly, which if God had not judged useful for men to know, he would never have bidden his prophets and apostles to teach. For our wisdom ought to be nothing else than to embrace with humble teachableness, and at least without finding fault, whatever is taught in sacred Scripture.[28]

---

[28]*Institutes*, 1:237 (1.18.4).

F. Further Practical Application

Although we have already begun to speak of the practical application of this doctrine, three additional points should be made.

1. Do Not Be Afraid, but Trust in God. Jesus emphasizes the fact that our sovereign Lord watches over us and cares for us as his children. He says, "Look at the birds of the air: they neither sow nor reap nor gather into barns, and yet your heavenly Father feeds them. Are you not of more value than they? . . . Therefore do not be anxious, saying, 'What shall we eat?' or 'What shall we drink?' or 'What shall we wear?'" (Matt. 6:26, 31). If God feeds the birds and clothes the grass of the field, he will take care of us. Similarly, Jesus says, "Are not two sparrows sold for a penny? And not one of them will fall to the ground without your Father's will. . . . Fear not, therefore; you are of more value than many sparrows" (Matt. 10:29–31).

David was able to sleep in the midst of his enemies, because he knew that God's providential control made him "dwell in safety," and he could say, "In peace I will both lie down and sleep" (Ps. 4:8). Many of the psalms encourage us to trust God and not to fear, because the LORD keeps and protects his people—for example, Psalm 91 ("He who dwells in the shelter of the Most High . . .") or Psalm 121 ("I lift up my eyes to the hills . . ."). Because of our confidence in God's providential care, we need not fear any evil or harm, even if it does come to us—it can only come by God's will and ultimately for our good. Thus Peter can say that "now for a little while you may have to suffer various trials, so that the genuineness of your faith, more precious than gold . . . may redound to praise and glory and honor at the revelation of Jesus Christ" (1 Peter 1:6–7). In all of this we need not worry about the future but trust in God's omnipotent care.

2. Be Thankful for All Good Things That Happen. If we genuinely believe that all good things are caused by God, then our hearts will indeed be full when we say, "Bless the LORD, O my soul, and forget not all his benefits" (Ps. 103:2). We will thank him for our daily food (cf. Matt. 6:11; 1 Tim. 4:4–5); indeed, we will "give thanks in all circumstances" (1 Thess. 5:18).

3. There Is No Such Thing as "Luck" or "Chance." All things come to pass by God's wise providence. This means that we should adopt a much more "personal" understanding of the universe and the events in it. The universe is not governed by impersonal fate or luck, but by a personal God. Nothing "just happens"—we should see God's hand in events throughout the day, causing all things to work together for good for those who love him.

This confidence in God's wise providence certainly does not equal superstition, for that is a belief in impersonal or demonic control of circumstances, or control by a capricious deity concerned for meaningless ritual rather than obedience and faith. A deepened appreciation for the doctrine of providence will not make us more superstitious; it will make us trust in God more and obey him more fully.

G. Another Evangelical View: the Arminian Position

There is a major alternative position held by many evangelicals, which for convenience we shall call the "Arminian" view.[29] Among denominations in contemporary evangelicalism, Methodists and Nazarenes tend to be thoroughly Arminian, whereas Presbyterians and the Christian Reformed tend to be thoroughly Reformed (at least by denominational statement of faith). Both views are found among Baptists, Episcopalians (though the Thirty-Nine Articles have a clearly Reformed emphasis), Dispensationalists, Evangelical Free Churches, Lutherans (though Martin Luther was in the Reformed camp on this issue), the Churches of Christ, and most charismatic and Pentecostal groups (though Pentecostal denominations such as the Assemblies of God have been predominantly Arminian).

Those who hold an Arminian position maintain that in order to preserve the *real human freedom* and *real human choices* that are necessary for genuine human personhood, God cannot cause or plan our voluntary choices. Therefore they conclude that God's providential involvement in or control of history must *not* include *every specific detail* of every event that happens, but that God instead simply *responds* to human choices and actions as they come about and does so in such a way that his purposes are ultimately accomplished in the world.

Those who hold this position argue that God's purposes in the world are more general and could be accomplished through many different kinds of specific events. So God's purpose or plan for the world "is not a blueprint encompassing all future contingencies" but "a dynamic program for the world, the outworking of which depends in part on man."[30] Cottrell says, "God does not have a specific, unconditional purpose for each discrete particle, object, person, and event within the creation."[31] Arminians believe that God achieves his overall goal by responding to and utilizing the free choices of human beings, whatever they may be.[32] Pinnock says that "predestination does not apply to

---

[29]The term *Arminianism* was recently chosen in the title of a responsible series of essays representing this position: See Clark H. Pinnock, ed., *The Grace of God, The Will of Man: A Case for Arminianism* (Grand Rapids: Zondervan, 1989). In the following section I quote extensively from this book and from an earlier book edited by Pinnock, *Grace Unlimited*. These two books are excellent recent defenses of the Arminian position.

Jacob Arminius (1560–1609) was a Dutch theologian who differed with the predominant Calvinism of his day. Though he is not personally quoted or referred to very often by Arminians today, his name has become attached to a range of positions that have in common the fact that they differ from the Calvinist position on the question of man's free will, both with respect to God's providence in general and with respect to predestination or election in specific.

The term *Arminian* should be distinguished from the term *Armenian*, which refers to people who live in or descend from inhabitants of the ancient country of Armenia in western Asia (now part of Turkey, Iran, and the CIS).

[30]Clark Pinnock, "Responsible Freedom in the Flow of Biblical History," in *Grace Unlimited*, p. 18.

[31]Jack Cottrell, "The Nature of the Divine Sovereignty," in *The Grace of God, the Will of Man*, p. 107. Cottrell's essay is, in my view, the most comprehensive and persuasive of the many excellent Arminian essays in this book—the book as a whole is responsibly done and is probably the best recent representation of Arminian thinking. Cottrell does not deny divine omniscience regarding future events as do the essays by Clark Pinnock and Richard Rice in the same volume, and this places him closer to the intuitive Arminianism that seems right to many evangelical laypersons today.

[32]I. Howard Marshall claims this at several points in "Predestination in the New Testament," *Grace Unlimited*, pp. 127–43. Marshall uses the analogy of a jazz band where individual players can improvise freely but the overall goal and unity of the piece are preserved nonetheless (p. 133). Thus, "the Bible has the picture of a God deciding fresh measures in history and interacting with the wills of men alongside the picture of a God planning things in eternity past, and both pictures are equally valid" (Marshall, p. 141).

every individual activity, but is rather the comprehensive purpose of God which is *the structural context* in which history moves."[33]

Moreover, advocates of the Arminian position maintain that God's will cannot include evil. Pinnock says, "The fall of man is an eloquent refutation to the theory that God's will is always done."[34] He states that it "is not the case" that God's will "is also accomplished in the lostness of the lost."[35] And I. Howard Marshall quite clearly affirms, "It is not true that everything that happens is what God desires."[36] These statements make it clear that the differences between the Reformed and Arminian positions are not merely differences in terminology: there is a real disagreement in substance. Several arguments are advanced in defense of the Arminian position. I have attempted to summarize them in the four major points that follow.

1. The Verses Cited as Examples of God's Providential Control Are Exceptions and Do Not Describe the Way That God Ordinarily Works in Human Activity. In surveying the Old Testament passages referring to God's providential involvement in the world, David J. A. Clines says that God's predictions and statements of his purposes refer to limited or specific events:

> Almost all of the specific references to God's plans have in view a particular event or a limited series of events, for example, "his purposes against the land of the Chaldeans" (Jer. 50:45). Furthermore, it is not a matter of a *single* divine plan; various passages speak of various intentions, and some references are in fact to God's plans in the plural. . . . [The passages are] an assertion that within history God is working his purposes out.[37]

Jack Cottrell agrees that in some cases God intervenes in the world in an uncommon way, using "subtle manipulation of such [natural] laws and of mental states." But he calls these unusual events "special providence," and says, "It is natural that the Old Testament teems with accounts of special providence. But we have no reason to assume that God was working in Australia and South America in such ways at the same time."[38]

2. The Calvinist View Wrongly Makes God Responsible for Sin. Those who hold an Arminian position ask, "How can God be holy if he decrees that we sin?" They affirm that God is not the "author of sin," that "God cannot be tempted with evil and he himself tempts no one" (James 1:13), that "God is light and in him is no darkness at all" (1 John 1:5), and that "the LORD is upright . . . and there is no unrighteousness in him" (Ps. 92:15).

The view of God's providence advocated above, they would say, makes us into puppets or robots who cannot do anything other than what God causes us to do. But this brings moral

---

[33]Pinnock, "Responsible Freedom," p. 102.

[34]Ibid., p. 102.

[35]Ibid., p. 106.

[36]Marshall, "Predestination in the New Testament," p. 139.

[37]David J. A. Clines, "Predestination in the Old Testament," p. 122; see also pp. 116–17. Similarly, James D. Strauss, "God's Promise and Universal History," *Grace Unlimited*, p. 196, says

that the example of Jacob and Esau that Paul mentions in Rom. 9:9–13 refers to God's corporate plans for the descendants of Jacob and Esau and should not be taken as an illustration of how God works in people's lives or hearts generally.

[38]Jack Cottrell, "The Nature of the Divine Sovereignty," pp. 112–13.

reproach on God, for Marshall says, "I am responsible for what my agent does."[39] Pinnock affirms that "it is simply blasphemous to maintain, as this theory does, that man's rebellion against God is *in any sense* the product of God's sovereign will or primary causation."[40]

3. Choices Caused by God Cannot Be Real Choices. When the Calvinist claims that God causes us to choose things voluntarily, those who hold an Arminian position would respond that any choices that are ultimately caused by God cannot be real choices, and that, if God really causes us to make the choices we make, then we are not real persons. Cottrell says that the Calvinist view of God as the primary cause and men as secondary causes really breaks down so there is only one cause, God. If a man uses a lever to move a rock, he argues, "the lever is not a true second cause but is only an instrument of the real cause of the movement. . . . In my judgment the concept of cause has no real significance when used in this sense. In such a system man contributes only what has been predetermined."[41]

Pinnock writes:

Personal fellowship of the kind envisioned in the Gospel only exists where consummated in a free decision. If we wish to understand God's grace as personal address to his creatures, we must comprehend it in dynamic, non-manipulative, non-coercive terms, as the Bible does.[42]

He also says:

If the world were a completely determined structure on which no decision of man's would have any effect, that basic intuition of man's that he is an *actor* and a *free agent* would be nonsensical: There would then be no point to his making plans or exerting efforts intended to transform the world. . . . Human freedom is the precondition of moral and intellectual responsibility.[43]

Why then, in the Arminian view, did the fall and sin come about? Pinnock answers that "they occur because God refuses to mechanize man or to force his will upon him."[44] And Marshall says, with respect to the "possibility of my predetermining a course of action involving myself and another subject," that "on the level of free agents it is impossible."[45] He objects that the analogy of God and world as being like an author and a play is unhelpful because if we ask whether the characters are indeed free, "this is an unreal question."[46]

However, it should be noted that Arminian theologians are certainly willing to allow some kinds of influence by God on human beings. Marshall says, "Prayer also influences men. . . . The wills of men can thus be affected by prayer or else we would not pray for them. *To believe in prayer is thus to believe in some kind of limitation of human freedom, and in some kind of incomprehensible influence upon the wills of men.*"[47]

---

[39]Marshall, "Predestination," p. 136.

[40]Pinnock, "Responsible Freedom," p. 102.

[41]Jack Cottrell, "The Nature of the Divine Sovereignty," pp. 104–5.

[42]Pinnock, *Grace Unlimited*, p. 15.

[43]Pinnock, "Responsible Freedom," p. 95.

[44]Ibid., p. 108.

[45]Marshall, "Predestination," p. 132. Similarly, he says, "When we try to think of a person foreordaining the course of a relationship between himself and another person . . . *this concept is logically self-contradictory*" (p. 135).

[46]Ibid., p. 133.

[47]Ibid., pp. 139–40 (emphasis in original text).

To drive home their point about the essential freedom of the human will, advocates of an Arminian position draw attention to the frequency of the free offer of the gospel in the New Testament. They would say that these invitations to people to repent and come to Christ for salvation, if *bona fide,* must imply the *ability* to respond to them. Thus, all people without exception have the ability to respond, not just those who have been sovereignly given that ability by God in a special way.

In further support of this point, Arminians would see 1 Corinthians 10:13 as clearly affirming our ability not to sin. Paul says to the Corinthians, "No temptation has overtaken you that is not common to man. God is faithful, and he will not let you be tempted beyond your strength, but with the temptation will also provide the way of escape, *that you may be able to endure it.*" But, it is said, this statement would be false if God sometimes ordains that we sin, for then we would not be "able" to escape from temptation without sinning.

4. The Arminian View Encourages Responsible Christian Living, While the Calvinistic View Encourages a Dangerous Fatalism. Christians who hold an Arminian position argue that the Calvinist view, when thoroughly understood, destroys motives for responsible Christian behavior. Randall Basinger says that the Calvinist view "establishes that what is ought to be and rules out the consideration that things could and/or should have been different."[48] Basinger continues by saying that Christians

> who evoke and act on the basis of God's sovereignty are guilty of an arbitrary, unlivable, and dangerous fatalism. . . . In contrast to this, the Arminian believes that what actually occurs in the world is, to an extent, consequent on the human will; God's exhaustive control over the world is denied. This means that things can occur that God does not will or want; things not only *can* be different but often *should* be different. And from all this follows our responsibility to work with God to bring about a better world.[49]

However, Basinger goes on to make a further point: Calvinists, in practice, often avoid such fatalism and "live and talk like Arminians."[50] Thus, on the one hand, Basinger's challenge is a warning against the practical extremes to which he claims Calvinism should logically drive Christians. On the other hand, his objection claims that when Calvinists live the way they know they must live, in responsible obedience to God, they are either inconsistent with their view of divine sovereignty or else not allowing their view of God's sovereign control to affect their daily lives.

H. Response to the Arminian Position

Many within the evangelical world will find these four Arminian arguments convincing. They will feel that these arguments represent what they intuitively know about themselves, their own actions, and the way the world functions, and that these arguments best account

---

[48]Randall G. Basinger, "Exhaustive Divine Sovereignty: A Practical Critique," in *The Grace of God, the Will of Man: A Case for Arminianism,* ed. Clark H. Pinnock, p. 94.

[49]Ibid., p. 196.
[50]Ibid., p. 204.

for the repeated emphasis in Scripture on our responsibility and the real consequences of our choices. However, there are some answers that can be given to the Arminian position.

1. Are These Scripture Passages Unusual Examples, or Do They Describe the Way God Works Ordinarily? In response to the objection that the examples of God's providential control only refer to limited or specific events, it may be said first that the examples are so numerous (see above, pp. 204–14) that they seem to be designed to describe to us the ways in which God works all the time. God does not just cause *some* grass to grow; he causes all grass to grow. He does not just send *some* rain; he sends all the rain. He does not just keep *some* sparrows from falling to the ground without his will; he keeps all sparrows from falling to the ground without his will. He does not just know every word on David's tongue before he speaks it; he knows the words on all our tongues before we speak them. He has not just chosen Paul and the Christians in the Ephesian churches to be holy and blameless before him; he has chosen all Christians to be holy and blameless before him. This is why Cottrell's claim, that God was working differently in Australia and South America than in the Old Testament,[51] is so unconvincing: Scripture is given to tell us the ways of God, and when we have dozens of examples throughout Old and New Testaments where there is such clear teaching on this, it is appropriate for us to conclude that this is the way in which God *always* works with human beings. By contrast, there seems to be nothing in Scripture that would indicate that some things are outside God's providential control, or that these ways of God's acting are unusual or unrepresentative of the ways in which he acts generally.

Moreover, many of the verses that speak of God's providence are very general: Christ "continually carries along *all things* by his word of power" (Heb. 1:3, author's translation), and "in him all things hold together" (Col. 1:17). "In him we live and move and have our being" (Acts 17:28). He "accomplishes *all things* according to the counsel of his will" (Eph. 1:11).[52] He provides our food (Matt. 6:11), supplies all our needs (Phil. 4:19), directs our steps (Prov. 20:24) and works in us to will and to do his good pleasure (Phil. 2:13). Such Scripture passages have in view more than exceptional examples of an unusual intervention by God in the affairs of human beings; they describe the way God always works in the world.

---

[51]Jack Cottrell, "The Nature of the Divine Sovereignty," p. 113.

[52]Jack Cottrell, "The Nature of the Divine Sovereignty," argues that the context of Eph. 1:11 shows that it does not include all things in the universe but is restricted to a specific focus: "This focus is 'the mystery of his will' (1:9), which is the uniting of Jews and Gentiles together into one body, the church (3:6)." Thus, he says, the verse only "refers to 'all things' required for uniting Jews and Gentiles under one Head in one body" (p. 116).

But this argument is not convincing. Cottrell must skip over to Eph. 3:6 to get the contextual restriction he seeks for the "all things" in 1:11. In doing this he ignores the clearly cosmic scope of the context as defined in the immediately preceding verse, a verse that is in the same sentence in the Greek text:

"as a plan for the fulness of time, to unite *all things* [*ta panta*] in him, *things in heaven and things on earth*" (Eph. 1:10). All things in heaven and on earth includes the whole universe. Eph. 1:21–22 further explains that God has exalted Christ "far above all rule and authority and power and dominion . . . and he has put *all things* under his feet and has made him the head over *all things* for the church." Once again the scope is universal. The "mystery" of God's will mentioned in Eph. 1:9 is not limited to the uniting of Jews and Gentiles (as in 3:6) but is defined by 1:10 as a plan to unite all things in Christ. The term *mystery* (Gk. *mystērion*) in Paul means something previously hidden but now made known by revelation, and it can refer to different things in different contexts: in Eph. 5:32 it refers to marriage as a symbol of the union between Christ and the church; in 1 Cor. 15:51 it refers to the resurrection body; etc.

2. Does the Calvinistic Doctrine of God's Providence Make God Responsible for Sin?
Against the Calvinistic view of God's providence (which allows that he decrees to permit sin and evil) Arminians would say that God is not responsible for sin and evil *because he did not ordain them or cause them in any way.* This is indeed *one way* of absolving God from responsibility and blame for sin, but is it the biblical way?

The problem is whether the Arminian position can really account for many texts that clearly say that God ordains that some people sin or do evil (see Section B.7, above, pp. 209–14). The death of Christ is the prime example of this, but there are many others in Scripture (Joseph's brothers, Pharaoh, the Egyptians, the Canaanites, Eli's sons, David's census, and the Babylonians, to mention a few). The response could be made that these were unusual events, exceptions to God's ordinary way of acting. But it does not solve the problem, for, on the Arminian view, how can God be holy if he ordains even one sinful act?

The Calvinist position seems preferable: God himself never sins but always brings about his will *through secondary causes;* that is, through personal moral agents who voluntarily, willingly do what God has ordained. These personal moral agents (both human beings and evil angels) are to blame for the evil they do. While the Arminian position objects that, on a human level, people are also responsible for *what they cause others to do,* we can answer that Scripture is not willing to apply such reasoning to God. Rather, Scripture repeatedly gives examples where God in a mysterious, hidden way somehow ordains that people do wrong, but continually places the blame for that wrong on the individual human who does wrong and never on God himself. The Arminian position seems to have failed to show why God *cannot* work in this way in the world, preserving both his holiness and our individual human responsibility for sin.

3. Can Choices Ordained by God Be Real Choices? In response to the claim that choices ordained by God cannot be real choices, it must be said that this is simply an assumption based once again on human experience and intuition, not on specific texts of Scripture.[53] Yet Scripture does not indicate that we can extrapolate from our human experience when dealing with God's providential control of his creatures, especially human beings. Arminians have simply not answered the question, Where does Scripture say that a choice ordained by God is not a real choice?[54] When we read passages indicating that God works through our will, our power to choose, and our personal volition, on

---

[53]This is the case with Cottrell's analogy of the man who uses a lever to move a rock. He says the lever "is not a true second cause, but only an instrument of the real cause" ("The Nature of the Divine Sovereignty," p. 104). But here Cottrell makes a common mistake, assuming that analogies from human experience, rather than the testimony of Scripture itself, can determine what is a real cause and what is not. The analogy of a man using a lever to move a rock does not fit, because God is far greater than any man, and we as real persons are far greater than any lever.

[54]The lack of scriptural support for this fundamental Arminian idea is evident in Jack Cottrell's discussion of free will. After accurately explaining that Calvinists say we are free only in the sense of making voluntary, willing choices, Cottrell says, "*In my judgment,* however, the mere ability to act in accord with one's desires is not a sufficient criterion of freedom" ("The Nature of the Divine Sovereignty," p. 103, emphasis mine). He then gives no evidence from Scripture to show why this is his judgment (pp. 103–4). I would respond that Cottrell has simply imported into the discussion a non-biblical *assumption* about the nature of human freedom and then has pronounced Calvinism incapable of meeting his (nonbiblical) criterion.

what basis can we say that a choice brought about by God through these means is not a real choice? It seems better to affirm that God *says* that our choices are real and to conclude that therefore they *are real.* Scripture repeatedly affirms that our choices are genuine choices, that they have *real* results, and that those results last for eternity. "Do this, and you will live" (Luke 10:28). "For God so loved the world that he gave his only Son, that *whoever believes in him* should not perish but have eternal life" (John 3:16).

This causes us to conclude that God has made us in such a way that (1) he ordains all that we do, and (2) we exercise our personal will and make real, voluntary choices. Because we cannot understand this should we therefore reject it? We cannot understand (in any final sense) how a plant can live, or how a bumblebee can fly, or how God can be omnipresent or eternal. Should we therefore reject those facts? Should we not rather simply accept them as true either because we see that plants in fact do live and bumblebees in fact do fly, or because Scripture itself teaches that God is omnipresent and eternal?

Calvin several times distinguishes between "necessity" and "compulsion" with regard to our will: unbelievers necessarily sin, but no compulsion forces them to sin against their will.[55] In response to the objection that an act cannot be willing or voluntary if it is a necessary act, Calvin points to both the good deeds of God (who *necessarily* does good) and the evil deeds of the devil (who *necessarily* does evil):

> If the fact that he must do good does not hinder God's free will in doing good; if the Devil, who can only do evil, yet sins with his will—who shall say that man therefore sins less willingly because he is subject to the necessity of sinning?[56]

Who are we to say that choices somehow caused by God *cannot* be real? On what basis can we prove that? God in Scripture tells us that he ordains all that comes to pass. He also tells us that our choices and actions are significant *in his sight,* and that we are responsible *before him* for our actions. We need simply to believe these things and to take comfort in them. After all, *he alone* determines what is significant, what is real, and what is genuine personal responsibility in the universe.

But do our actions have any effect on God? At this point Arminians will object that while Calvinists may *say* that a choice caused by God is a real choice, it is not real in any ultimate sense, because, on a Calvinist view, nothing that God does can ever be a response to what we do. Jack Cottrell says:

> Calvinism is still a theology of determinism as long as it declares that nothing God does can be conditioned by man or can be a reaction to something in the world. The idea that a sovereign God must always *act* and never *react* is a point on which almost all Calvinists seem to agree. . . . Reformed theologians agree that the eternal decree is unconditional or absolute. . . . "Decretal theology" decrees that "God cannot be affected by, nor respond to, anything external to him," says Daane.[57]

---

[55]See *Institutes,* 1:294–96 (2.3.5).
[56]Ibid., p. 295 (2.3.5).
[57]Jack Cottrell, "The Nature of the Divine Sovereignty,"

pp. 102–3. The quotation at the end is from James Daane, *The Freedom of God* (Grand Rapids: Eerdmans, 1973), p. 160.

But here Cottrell has misunderstood Reformed theology for two reasons. First, he has quoted James Daane, who, though he belongs to the Christian Reformed Church, has written as an opponent, not a defender, of classical Reformed theology, and his statement does not represent a position Reformed theologians would endorse. Second, Cottrell has confused God's decrees before creation with God's actions in time. It is true that Calvinists would say that God's eternal decrees were not influenced by any of our actions and cannot be changed by us, since they were made *before creation*.[58] But to conclude from that that Calvinists think God does not react *in time* to anything we do, or is not influenced by anything we do, is simply false. No Calvinist theologian known to me has ever said that God is not influenced by what we do or does not react to what we do. He is grieved at our sin. He delights in our praise. He answers our prayers. To say that God does not react to our actions is to deny the whole history of the Bible from Genesis to Revelation.

Now a Calvinist would add that God has eternally decreed that he would respond to us as he does. In fact, he has decreed that we would act as we do and he would respond to our actions. But his responses are still genuine responses, his answers to prayers are still genuine answers to prayer, and his delight in our praise is still genuine delight. Cottrell may of course object that a response that God has planned long ago is not a real response, but this is far different from saying that Calvinists believe God does not respond to what we do. Moreover, we return to the same unsupported assumption underlying this objection: on what scriptural basis can Cottrell say that a response God has planned long ago is not a real response?[59]

Here it is helpful for us to realize that there is no other reality in the universe except what God himself has made. Is a thunderstorm caused by God a *real* thunderstorm? Is a king that God establishes on a throne a *real* king? Is a word that God causes me to speak (Ps. 139:4; Prov. 16:1) a *real* word? Of course they are real! There *is* no other reality than that which God brings about! Then is a human choice that God somehow causes to happen a *real* choice? Yes, it is, in the same way that a thunderstorm or a king is real according to their own characteristics and properties. The choice that I make is not a "forced" or "involuntary" choice—we make choices all the time, and we have absolutely no sense of being forced or compelled to choose one thing rather than another.

Now some may object that this view makes us mere "puppets" or "robots." But we are not puppets or robots; we are *real persons*. Puppets and robots do not have the power of personal choice or even individual thought. We, by contrast, think, decide, and choose. Again the Arminian wrongly takes information from our situation as human beings and then uses that information to place limitations on what God *can* or *cannot* do. All of these analogies from human experience fail to recognize that God is far greater than

[58]See below, p. 287, on God's decrees.

[59]I am not sure if Cottrell would be able to object that a response planned by God long ago is not a real response, because he himself talks about God foreknowing our actions and then planning how he will respond to them. He says, "Even before the creation God foreknew every free-will act. . . . Nothing takes God by surprise. . . . God knew, even before creation, when and how he would have to intervene in his world to accomplish his purposes. . . . God's foreknowledge also enables him to plan his own responses to and uses of human choices even before they are made" ("The Nature of the Divine Sovereignty," p. 112). But if Cottrell is willing to say that God planned long ago how he would respond to human choices, it is hard to see how he can object to the Calvinist position that God decreed long ago how he would respond when we pray or act.

our limited human abilities. Moreover, we are far more real and complex than any robot or puppet would ever be—we are real persons created by an infinitely powerful and infinitely wise God.

Much of our difficulty in understanding how God can cause us to choose something willingly comes from the finite nature of our creaturely existence. In a hypothetical world where all living things created by God were plants rooted in the ground, we might imagine one plant arguing to another that God *could not* make living creatures who could move about on the earth, for how could they carry their roots with them? And if their roots were not in the ground, how could they receive nourishment? An "Arminian" plant might even argue, "In order for God to create a world with living things, he *had to* create them with roots and with the characteristic of living all their lives in a single place. To say that God *could not* create living things that move about on the earth does not challenge God's omnipotence, for that is simply to say that he cannot do things that logically cannot be done. Therefore it is impossible that God could create a world where living things also have the capacity of moving about on the earth." The problem with this plant is that it has limited God's power by virtue of its own "plant-like" experience.

On a higher level, we could imagine a creation that had both plants and animals but no human beings. In that creation, we can imagine an argument between a "Calvinist" dog and a "Arminian" dog, where the "Calvinist" dog would argue that it *is* possible for God to create creatures that not only can communicate by barking to one another but also can record their barks in marks on paper and can send them silently to be understood by other creatures many days' journey distant, creatures who have never been seen by the sending creature who first marked his barks down on paper. The "Arminian" dog would reply that God *cannot* do such a thing, because *essential* to the idea of creaturely communication is *hearing* and *seeing* (and usually *smelling!*) the creature from whom one receives the communication. To say that there can be communication without ever hearing or seeing or smelling the other creature is an absurd idea! It is beyond the range of possible occurrences and is logically inconceivable. Therefore it is impossible to think that God could create a creature with such communicating abilities.

In both cases the "Arminian" plant and the "Arminian" dog are in the wrong, because they have incorrectly limited the kind of thing God could create by deriving what was possible for God (in their opinion) from their own finite creaturely existence. But this is very similar to the Arminian theologian who simply asserts (on the basis of his own perception of human experience) that God *cannot* create a creature who makes willing, voluntary, meaningful choices, and that those choices are nonetheless ordained by God. Similarly, the Arminian theologian who argues that God *cannot* ordain that evil come about and not yet himself be responsible for evil, is limiting God based merely on observation of finite human experience.

4. Does a Calvinistic View of Providence Encourage Either a Dangerous Fatalism or a Tendency to "Live Like Arminians"? The view of providence presented above emphasizes the need for responsible obedience, so it is not correct to say that it encourages the kind of fatalism that says that whatever is, should be. Those who accuse Reformed writers of believing this have simply not understood the Reformed doctrine of providence.

But do Calvinists "live like Arminians" anyway? Both Calvinists and Arminians believe that our actions have real results and that they are eternally significant. Both agree that we are responsible for our actions and that we make voluntary, willing choices. Both groups will agree that God answers prayer, that proclaiming the gospel results in people being saved, and that obedience to God results in blessing in life, while disobedience results in lack of God's blessing.

But the differences are very significant. Calvinists when true to their doctrine will live with a far more comprehensive trust in God in all circumstances and a far greater freedom from worry about the future, because they are convinced, not just that God will somehow cause his major purposes to work out right in the end, but that *all things* work together for good for those who love God and are called according to his purpose (Rom. 8:28). They will also be thankful to God for *all* the benefits that come to us from whatever quarter, for the one who believes in providence is assured that the ultimate reason for all things that happen is not some chance occurrence in the universe, nor is it the "free will" of another human being, but it is ultimately the goodness of God himself. They will also have great patience in adversity, knowing that it has not come about because God was unable to prevent it, but because it, too, is part of his wise plan. So the differences are immense. Calvin says:

> Gratitude of mind for the favorable outcome of things, patience in adversity, and also incredible freedom from worry about the future all necessarily follow upon this knowledge. . . . Ignorance of providence is the ultimate of all miseries; the highest blessedness lies in the knowledge of it.[60]

5. Additional Objections to the Arminian Position. In addition to responding to the four specific Arminian claims mentioned above some remaining objections to it need to be considered.

a. On an Arminian View, How Can God Know the Future?: According to the Arminian view, our human choices are not caused by God. They are totally free. But Scripture gives many examples of God predicting the future and of prophecies being fulfilled exactly. How can God predict the future in this way if it is not certain what will happen?

In response to this question, Arminians give three different kinds of answer. Some say that God is not able to know details about the future; specifically, they deny that God is able to know what choices individual human beings will make in the future.[61] This seems to me to be the most consistent Arminian position, but the result is that, while God may be able to make some fairly accurate predictions based on complete knowledge

---

[60]Calvin, *Institutes*, 1:219–25 (1.17.7, 11).

[61]Richard Rice, "Divine Foreknowledge and Free-Will Theism," in *The Grace of God, the Will of Man*, pp. 121–39, takes this position (see esp. pp. 129, 134–37). Rice says, "God knows a great deal about what will happen. . . . All that God does not know is the content of future free decisions, and this is because decisions are not there to know until they occur" (p. 134). In order to take this position and maintain God's

omniscience, Rice redefines omniscience: "An omniscient being knows everything logically knowable" (p. 128), and then he defines "logically knowable" to exclude future human choices. On this basis, Rice argues that God does not know the results of future free decisions of human beings, since these are not logically knowable.

Clark Pinnock also explains how he came to this position: "I knew the Calvinist argument that exhaustive foreknowledge of the present, these cannot be certain predictions. Ultimately it also means that God is ignorant of *all future human choices,* which means that he does not even know what the stock market will do tomorrow, or who will be elected as the next president of the United States, or who will be converted. On this view, what event of human history *could* God know with certainty in advance? No event. This is a radical revision of the idea of omniscience and seems to be clearly denied by the dozens of examples of unfailing predictive prophecy in Scripture, the fulfillment of which demonstrates that God is the true God in opposition to false gods.[62]

Other Arminians simply affirm that God *knows* everything that will happen, but this does not mean that he has *planned* or *caused* what will happen—it simply means that he has the ability to see into the future. (The phrase sometimes used to express this view is "Foreknowledge does not imply foreordination.") This is probably the most common Arminian view, and it is ably expressed by Jack Cottrell: "I affirm that God has a true foreknowledge of future free-will choices without himself being the agent that causes them or renders them certain."[63]

The problem with this position is that, even if God did not plan or cause things to happen, the fact that they are foreknown means that they will *certainly come about.* And this means that our decisions are predetermined *by something* (whether fate or the inevitable cause-and-effect mechanism of the universe), and they still are not free in the sense the Arminian wishes them to be free. If our future choices are known, then they are fixed. And if they are fixed, then they are not "free" in the Arminian sense (undetermined or uncaused).

A third Arminian response is called "middle knowledge." Those who take this view would say that the future choices of people are not determined by God, but that God knows them anyway, because he knows *all future possibilities,* and he knows how each free creature will respond in any set of circumstances that might occur.[64] William Craig says:

> God's insight into the will of a free creature is of such a surpassing quality that God knows exactly what the free creature would do were God to place him in a certain set of circumstances. . . . By knowing what every possible free creature would do in any possible situation, God can by bringing about that situation know what the creature will freely do. . . . Thus he foreknows with certainty everything that happens in the world.[65]

---

was tantamount to predestination because it implies the fixity of all things from 'eternity past,' and I could not shake off its logical force" ("From Augustine to Arminius: A Pilgrimage in Theology," in *The Grace of God, the Will of Man,* p. 25). He rejected exhaustive foreknowledge and decided that *"God knows everything that can be known,* but that free choices would not be something that can be known even by God because they are not yet settled in reality. Decisions not yet made do not exist anywhere to be known even by God. . . . God too moves into a future not wholly known because not yet fixed" (ibid., pp. 25–26, emphasis mine).

[62]See chapter 4, pp. 62–63, also p. 80, on God's knowledge of the future.

[63]Jack Cottrell, "The Nature of the Divine Sovereignty," p. 111.

[64]See William L. Craig, "Middle Knowledge, a Calvinist-Arminian Rapprochement?" in *The Grace of God, the Will of Man,* pp. 141–64. See also his book *The Only Wise God: The Compatibility of Divine Foreknowledge and Human Freedom* (Grand Rapids: Baker, 1987).

[65]Craig, "Middle Knowledge," pp. 150–51.

But Craig's view does not sustain a view of freedom in the sense Arminians usually maintain: that no cause or set of causes made a person choose the way he or she did. On Craig's view, the surrounding circumstances and the person's own disposition *guarantee* that a certain choice will be made—otherwise, God could not know what the choice would be from his exhaustive knowledge of the person and the circumstances. But if God knows what the choice will be, and if that choice is guaranteed, then it could not be otherwise. Moreover, if both the person and the circumstances have been created by God, then ultimately the outcome has been determined by God. This sounds very close to freedom in a Calvinist sense, but it is certainly not the kind of freedom that most Arminians would accept.

b. On an Arminian View, How Can Evil Exist If God Did Not Want It?: Arminians quite clearly say that the entrance of evil into the world was not according to the will of God. Pinnock says, "The fall of man is an eloquent refutation to the theory that God's will is always done."[66] But how can evil exist if God did not want it to exist? If evil happens in spite of the fact that God does not want it to happen, this seems to deny God's omnipotence: he wanted to prevent evil, but he was unable to do so. How then can we believe that this God is omnipotent?

The common Arminian response is to say that God was *able* to prevent evil but he chose to *allow for the possibility* of evil in order to guarantee that angels and humans would have the freedom necessary for meaningful choices. In other words, God *had to* allow for the possibility of sinful choices in order to allow genuine human choices. Cottrell says, "This God-given freedom includes human freedom to rebel and to sin against the Creator himself. By creating a world in which sin was possible, God thereby bound himself to *react* in certain specific ways should sin become a reality."[67]

But this is not a satisfactory response either, for it implies that God will have to allow for the possibility of sinful choices in heaven eternally. On the Arminian position, if any of our choices and actions in heaven are to be genuine and real, then they will *have to* include the possibility of sinful choices. But this implies that even in heaven, for all eternity, we will face the real possibility of choosing evil—and therefore the possibility of rebelling against God and losing our salvation and being cast out of heaven! This is a terrifying thought, but it seems a necessary implication of the Arminian view.

Yet there is an implication that is more troubling: If *real* choices have to allow for the possibility of choosing evil, then (1) God's choices are not real, since he cannot choose evil, or (2) God's choices are real, and there is the genuine possibility that God might someday choose to do evil—perhaps a little, and perhaps a great deal. If we ponder the second implication it becomes terrifying. But it is contrary to the abundant testimony of Scripture.[68] On the other hand, the first implication is clearly false: God is the definition of what is real, and it is clearly an error to say that his choices are not real. Both implications therefore provide good reason for rejecting the Arminian position that real choices

---

[66]Pinnock, "Responsible Freedom," p. 102.
[67]Cottrell, "The Nature of Divine Sovereignty," p. 109.
[68]See chapter 5, pp. 87–89, 90–92, 93–95, for scriptural testimony to God's goodness, holiness, and righteousness, and chapter 4, pp. 54–59, on God's unchangeableness.

must allow the possibility of choosing evil. But this puts us back to the earlier question for which there does not seem to be a satisfactory answer from the Arminian position: How can evil exist if God did not want it to exist?

c. On an Arminian View, How Can We Know That God Will Triumph Over Evil?: If we go back to the Arminian assertion that evil is *not* according to the will of God, another problem arises: if all the evil now in the world came into the world even though God did not want it, how can we be sure that God will triumph over it in the end? Of course, God *says* in Scripture that he will triumph over evil. But if he was unable to keep it out of his universe in the first place and it came in against his will, and if he is unable to predict the outcome of any future events that involve free choices by human, angelic, and demonic agents, how then can we be sure that God's declaration that he will triumph over all evil is in itself true? Perhaps this is just a hopeful prediction of something that (on the Arminian viewpoint) God simply cannot know. Far from the "incredible freedom from worry about the future" which the Calvinist has because he knows that an omnipotent God makes "all things work together for good" (Rom. 8:28 KJV), the Arminian position seems logically to drive us to a deep-seated anxiety about the ultimate outcome of history.

Both of these last two objections regarding evil make us realize that, while we may have difficulties in thinking about the Reformed view of evil as ordained by God and completely under the control of God, there are far more serious difficulties with the Arminian view of evil as not ordained or even willed by God, and therefore not assuredly under the control of God.

d. The Difference in the Unanswered Questions: Since we are finite in our understanding, we inevitably will have some unanswered questions about every biblical doctrine. Yet on this issue the questions that Calvinists and Arminians must leave unanswered are quite different. On the one hand, Calvinists must say that they do not know the answer to the following questions:

1. Exactly how God can ordain that we do evil willingly, and yet God not be blamed for evil.
2. Exactly how God can cause us to choose something willingly.

To both, Calvinists would say that the answer is somehow to be found in an awareness of God's infinite greatness, in the knowledge of the fact that he can do far more than we could ever think possible. So the effect of these unanswered questions is to increase our appreciation of the greatness of God.

On the other hand, Arminians must leave unanswered questions regarding God's knowledge of the future, why he would allow evil when it is against his will, and whether he will certainly triumph over evil. Their failure to resolve these questions tends to diminish the greatness of God—his omniscience, his omnipotence, and the absolute reliability of his promises for the future. And these unanswered questions tend to exalt the greatness of man (his freedom to do what God does not want) and the power of evil (it comes and remains in the universe even though God does not want it). Moreover, by denying that God can make creatures who have real choices that are nevertheless caused by him, the Arminian position diminishes the wisdom and skill of God the Creator.

QUESTIONS FOR PERSONAL APPLICATION

1. Has thinking about the doctrine of providence increased your trust in God? How has it changed the way you think about the future? Are there difficulties or hardships in your life at this time? Give an example of a specific difficulty that you are now facing and explain how the doctrine of providence will help you in the way you think about it.

2. Can you name five good things that have happened to you so far today? Were you thankful to God for any of them?

3. Do you sometimes think of luck or chance as causing events that happen in your life? If you ever feel that way, does it increase or decrease your anxiety about the future? Now think for a moment about some events that you might have attributed to luck in the past. Instead, begin to think about those events as under the control of your wise and loving heavenly Father. How does that make you feel differently about them and about the future generally?

4. Do you ever fall into a pattern of little "superstitious" actions or rituals that you think will bring good luck or prevent bad luck (such as not walking under a ladder, being afraid when a black cat walks across your path, not stepping on cracks on a sidewalk, carrying a certain item "just for good luck," etc.)? Do you think those actions tend to increase or decrease your trust in God during the day and your obedience to him?

5. Explain how a proper understanding of the doctrine of providence should lead a Christian to a more active prayer life.

6. What has been the overall effect of this chapter on how you think and feel about God and the events of your life?

SPECIAL TERMS

Arminian
Calvinist
concurrence
decrees of God
free choices
free will
government
middle knowledge

preservation
primary cause
providence
Reformed
secondary cause
voluntary choices
willing choices

BIBLIOGRAPHY

Basinger, David, and Randall Basinger, eds. *Predestination and Free Will: Four Views of Divine Sovereignty and Human Freedom.* Downers Grove, Ill.: InterVarsity Press, 1986.

Berkouwer, G. C. *The Providence of God.* Trans. by Lewis B. Smedes. Grand Rapids: Eerdmans, 1952.

Cameron, N. M. de S. "Providence." In *NDT,* pp. 177–79.

Carson, D. A. *Divine Sovereignty and Human Responsibility: Biblical Perspectives in Tension.* New Foundations Theological Library. Atlanta: John Knox, and London: Marshall, Morgan and Scott, 1981.

_____. *How Long, O Lord? Reflections on Suffering and Evil.* Grand Rapids: Baker, and Leicester: Inter-Varsity Press, 1990.

Craig, William Lane. *The Only Wise God: The Compatibility of Divine Foreknowledge and Human Freedom.* Grand Rapids: Baker, 1987.

Feinberg, John. *The Many Faces of Evil: Theological Systems and the Problem of Evil.* Zondervan, 1994.

Flavel, John. *The Mystery of Providence.* Edinburgh and Carlisle, Pa.: Banner of Truth, 1976. Reprint of 1698 edition.

Helm, Paul. *The Providence of God.* Leicester and Downers Grove, Ill.: InterVarsity Press, 1994.

Parker, T. H. L. "Providence of God." In *EDT,* pp. 890–91.

Pink, Arthur W. *The Sovereignty of God.* Grand Rapids: Baker, 1930.

Warfield, B. B. *Calvin and Calvinism.* London and New York: Oxford University Press, 1931.

SCRIPTURE MEMORY PASSAGE

Romans 8:28: *We know that in everything God works for good with those who love him, who are called according to his purpose.*

HYMN

"God Moves in a Mysterious Way"

> God moves in a mysterious way
>   his wonders to perform;
> He plants his footsteps in the sea,
>   and rides upon the storm.
>
> Deep in unfathomable mines
>   of never-failing skill
> He treasures up his bright designs,
>   and works his sovereign will.

Ye fearful saints, fresh courage take;
    the clouds ye so much dread
Are big with mercy, and shall break
    in blessings on your head.

Judge not the Lord by feeble sense,
    but trust him for his grace;
Behind a frowning providence
    he hides a smiling face.

His purposes will ripen fast,
    unfolding every hour;
The bud may have a bitter taste,
    but sweet will be the flow'r.

Blind unbelief is sure to err,
    and scan his work in vain;
God is his own interpreter,
    and he will make it plain.

AUTHOR: WILLIAM COWPER, 1774

Chapter 10

MIRACLES

What are miracles? Can they happen today?

EXPLANATION AND SCRIPTURAL BASIS

A consideration of the subject of miracles is closely connected with God's providence, which was considered in the previous chapter. There we argued that God exercises an extensive, ongoing, sovereign control over all aspects of his creation. This chapter will assume an understanding of that discussion of providence and will build on it in approaching the question of miracles.

A. Definition

We may define a miracle as follows: *A miracle is a less common kind of God's activity in which he arouses people's awe and wonder and bears witness to himself.*[1] This definition takes into account our previous understanding of God's providence whereby God preserves, controls, and governs all things. If we understand providence in this way, we will naturally avoid some other common explanations or definitions of miracles.

For example, one definition of miracle is "a direct intervention of God in the world." But this definition assumes a deistic view of God's relationship to the world, in which the world continues on its own and God only intervenes in it occasionally. This is certainly not the biblical view, according to which God makes the rain to fall (Matt. 5:45), causes the grass to grow (Ps. 104:14), and continually carries along all things by his word of power (Heb. 1:3). Another definition of miracle is "a more direct activity of God in the world." But to talk about a "more direct" working of God suggests that his *ordinary* providential activity is somehow not "direct" and again hints at a sort of deistic removal of God from the world.

Another definition is "God working in the world without using means to bring about the results he wishes." Yet to speak of God working "without means" leaves us with very

---

[1] I have adapted this definition from unpublished lectures given by John Frame, professor of systematic theology at Westminster Theological Seminary.

few if any miracles in the Bible, for it is hard to think of a miracle that came about with no means at all: in the healing of people, for example, some of the physical properties of the sick person's body were doubtless involved as part of the healing. When Jesus multiplied the loaves and fishes, he at least used the original five loaves and two fishes that were there. When he changed water to wine, he used water and made it become wine. This definition seems to be inadequate.[2]

Yet another definition of miracle is "an exception to a natural law" or "God acting contrary to the laws of nature." But the phrase "laws of nature" in popular understanding implies that there are certain qualities inherent in the things that exist, "laws of nature" that operate independently of God, and that God must intervene or "break" these laws for a miracle to occur.[3] Once again this definition does not adequately account for the biblical teaching on providence.

Another definition of miracle is "an event impossible to explain by natural causes." This definition is inadequate because (1) it does not include God as the one who brings about the miracle; (2) it assumes that God does not use some natural causes when he works in an unusual or amazing way, and thus it assumes again that God only occasionally intervenes in the world; and (3) it will result in a significant minimizing of actual miracles and an increase in skepticism, since many times when God works in answer to prayer the result is amazing to those who prayed but it is not absolutely impossible to explain by natural causes, especially for a skeptic who simply refuses to see God's hand at work.

Therefore, the original definition given above, where a miracle is simply a *less common* way of God's working in the world, seems to be preferable and more consistent with the biblical doctrine of God's providence. This definition does not say that a miracle is a different kind of working by God, but only that it is a less common way of God's working and that it is done so as to arouse people's surprise, awe, or amazement in such a way that God bears witness to himself.

The biblical terminology for miracles frequently points to this idea of God's power at work to arouse people's wonder and amazement. Primarily three sets of terms are employed: (1) "sign" (Heb. *'ôth;* Gk. *sēmeion*), which means something that points to or indicates something else, especially (with reference to miracles) God's activity and power; (2) "wonder" (Heb. *môpēth;* Gk. *teras*), an event that causes people to be amazed or astonished;[4] and (3) "miracle" or "mighty work" (Heb. *gᵉbûrāh;* Gk. *dynamis*), an act displaying great power, especially (with reference to miracles) divine power.[5] Often "signs and wonders" is used as a stock expression to refer to miracles (Ex. 7:3; Deut. 6:22; Ps. 135:9; Acts 4:30; 5:12; Rom. 15:19, et al.), and sometimes all three terms are combined, "mighty works and wonders and signs" (Acts 2:22) or "signs and wonders and mighty works" (2 Cor. 12:12; Heb. 2:4).

---

[2]However, if someone defined a miracle as "a work of God apart from the *ordinary* use of means, to arouse people's awe and wonder," this would be similar in force to the definition I proposed above and would be consistent with the Bible's teaching on God's providence (see L. Berkhof, *Systematic Theology,* pp. 176–77).

[3]If the phrase "natural law" is understood by Christians simply to refer to the predictable patterns of behavior that God gives to and maintains in each created thing, then this defi-

nition is less objectionable because it consciously takes into account God's providence. But the phrase "natural law" is not generally understood that way in English today.

[4]The verb *thaumazō,* "to wonder, be amazed," is frequently used in the Gospels to describe people's reaction to miracles.

[5]See the extensive discussion of New Testament vocabulary for miracles in W. Mundle, O. Hofius, and C. Brown, "Miracle, Wonder, Sign," *NIDNTT* 2:620–35.

In addition to the meanings of the terms used for miracles, another reason supporting our definition is the fact that miracles in Scripture do arouse people's awe and amazement and indicate that God's power is at work. The Bible frequently tells us that God himself is the one who performs "miracles" or "wondrous things." Psalm 136:4 says that God is the one "who alone does great wonders" (cf. Ps. 72:18). The song of Moses declares:

> Who is like you, O Lord, among the gods?
>> Who is like you, majestic in holiness,
>> terrible in glorious deeds, doing *wonders?* (Ex. 15:11)

Thus, the miraculous signs that Moses did when his staff turned into a snake and back again, or when his hand became leprous and then clean again (Ex. 4:2–8), were given that Moses might demonstrate to the people of Israel that God had sent him. Similarly, the miraculous signs God did by the hand of Moses and Aaron through the plagues, far surpassing the false miracles or imitation signs done by the magicians in Pharaoh's court (Ex. 7:12; 8:18–19; 9:11), showed that the people of Israel were those who worshiped the one true God. When Elijah confronted the priests of Baal on Mount Carmel (1 Kings 18:17–40), the fire from heaven demonstrated that the Lord was the one true God.

Now if we accept the definition that a miracle is "a less common kind of God's activity in which he arouses people's awe and wonder and bears witness to himself," then we may ask what kinds of things should be considered miracles. Of course, we are right to consider the incarnation of Jesus as God-man and Jesus' resurrection from the dead as the central and most important miracles in all history. The events of the exodus such as the parting of the Red Sea and the fall of Jericho were remarkable miracles. When Jesus healed people and cleansed lepers and cast out demons, those were certainly miracles as well (see Matt. 11:4–5; Luke 4:36–41; John 2:23; 4:54; 6:2; 20:30–31).

But can we consider unusual answers to prayer to be miracles? Apparently so, if they are remarkable enough to arouse people's awe and wonder and cause them to acknowledge God's power at work: the answer to Elijah's prayer that God would send fire from heaven was a miracle (1 Kings 18:24, 36–38), as were the answers to his prayers that the widow's dead son would come back to life (1 Kings 17:21), or that the rain would stop and later start again (1 Kings 17:1; 18:41–45 with James 5:17–18). In the New Testament, the release of Peter from prison in answer to the prayers of the church was certainly a miracle (Acts 12:5–17; note also Paul's prayer for Publius's father in Acts 28:8). But there must have been many miracles not nearly as dramatic as those, because Jesus healed many hundreds of people, "*any* that were sick with *various diseases*" (Luke 4:40). Paul healed "the rest of the people on the island who had diseases" (Acts 28:9).

On the other hand, Christians see answers to prayer every day, and we should not water down our definition of miracle so much that every answer to prayer is called a miracle. But when an answer to prayer is so remarkable that people involved with it are amazed and acknowledge God's power at work in an unusual way, then it seems appropriate to call it a miracle.[6] This is consistent with our definition and seems supported

---

[6]Others may prefer to be more restrictive in their definition of miracles, reserving the term (for example) for events that absolutely could not have happened by ordinary means and that are thoroughly witnessed and documented by several

by the biblical evidence that works of God that aroused people's awe and wonder were called miracles (Gk. *dynamis*).[7]

But whether we adopt a broad or narrow definition of miracle, all should agree that if God really does work in answer to our prayers, whether in common or uncommon ways, it is important that we recognize this and give thanks to him, and that we not ignore it or go to great lengths to devise possible "natural causes" to explain away what God has in fact done in answer to prayer. While we must be careful not to exaggerate in reporting details of answers to prayer, we must also avoid the opposite error of failing to glorify and thank God for what he has done.

B. Miracles as Characteristic of the New Covenant Age

In the New Testament, Jesus' miraculous signs attested that he had come from God: Nicodemus recognized, "No one can do these signs that you do, unless God is with him" (John 3:2). Jesus' changing of water into wine was a "sign" that "manifested his glory; and his disciples believed in him" (John 2:11). According to Peter, Jesus was "a man attested to you by God with *mighty works and wonders and signs* which God did through him in your midst" (Acts 2:22).

Then in the early church, the apostles and others who preached the gospel performed miracles that amazed people and gave confirmation of the gospel that was being preached (Acts 2:43; 3:6–10; 4:30; 8:6–8, 13; 9:40–42, et al.). Even in churches where no apostles were present miracles occurred. For example, Paul, in writing to several churches in the region of Galatia (see Gal. 1:1), assumes this when he asks, "Does he who supplies the Spirit to you and works miracles among you do so by works of the law, or by hearing with faith?" (Gal. 3:5). Similarly, he mentions in the church at Corinth "workers of miracles" (1 Cor. 12:28) and names "the working of miracles" (1 Cor. 12:10) as a gift distributed by the Holy Spirit. These last two verses are especially significant because 1 Corinthians 12:4–31 is not discussing a specific situation at Corinth but the nature of the church in general as the "body of Christ" with many members yet one body.[8]

---

impartial observers. In that case, they will see far fewer miracles, especially in a skeptical, anti-supernatural society. But such a definition may not encompass all the kinds of things Paul had in mind when he talked about miracles in the churches of Corinth (1 Cor. 12:10, 28–29) and Galatia (Gal. 3:5), and may prevent people from recognizing a gift of miracles when it is given to Christians today. (Of course, Christians who hold such a restrictive definition will still readily thank God for many answers to prayer that they would not call miracles.)

[7]The appropriateness of such a definition is not lost simply because the same event might be called a miracle by some people and an ordinary event by others, for people's evaluation of an event will vary depending on their nearness to the event, the assumptions of their worldview, and whether they are Christians or not.

[8]Note, for example, that Paul says that God has appointed in the church, "first apostles ..." (1 Cor. 12:28). But there

were no apostles given specifically to the church at Corinth. Therefore this passage must be talking about the church in general.

B. B. Warfield, *Counterfeit Miracles* (Edinburgh: Banner of Truth, 1972; first published in 1918), notes that in the church at Corinth those who took part in the ordinary church worship service "might often have a miraculous gift to exercise." He says that "there is no reason to believe that the infant congregation at Corinth was singular in this. The Apostle does not write as if he were describing a marvelous state of affairs peculiar to that church.... The hints in the rest of his letters and in the Book of Acts require us, accordingly, to look upon this beautiful picture of Christian worship as one which would be true to life for any of the numerous congregations planted by the Apostles in the length and breadth of the world visited and preached to by them.... We are justified in considering it characteristic of the Apostolic churches

In fact, it seems to be a characteristic of the New Testament church that miracles occur.[9] In the Old Testament, miracles seemed to occur primarily in connection with one prominent leader at a time, such as Moses or Elijah or Elisha. In the New Testament, there is a sudden and unprecedented increase in the miracles when Jesus begins his ministry (Luke 4:36–37, 40–41). However, contrary to the pattern of the Old Testament, the authority to work miracles and to cast out demons was not confined to Jesus himself, nor did miracles die out when Jesus returned to heaven. Even during his ministry, Jesus gave authority to heal the sick and to cast out demons not only to the Twelve, but also to seventy of his disciples (Luke 10:1, 9, 17–19; cf. Matt. 10:8; Luke 9:49–50). Moreover, the passages noted above from 1 Corinthians and Galatians indicate that performing miracles was not confined to the seventy disciples, but was characteristic of the churches of Galatia and the New Testament churches generally. This suggests that the occurrence of miracles is a characteristic of the New Testament church and may be seen as an indication of the powerful new work of the Holy Spirit that began with Pentecost and may be expected to continue through the church age.[10]

C. The Purposes of Miracles

One purpose of miracles is certainly to authenticate the message of the gospel. This was evident in Jesus' own ministry, as people like Nicodemus acknowledged: "We know that you are a teacher come from God; for no one can do these *signs* that you do, unless God is with him" (John 3:2). It also was evident as the gospel was proclaimed by those who heard Jesus, for as they preached, "God also bore witness by *signs and wonders and various miracles* and by gifts of the Holy Spirit distributed according to his own will" (Heb. 2:4). Whether this purpose was valid only when the gospel was first preached (before the New Testament was written), or whether it holds good throughout the church age, depends on what we think the miracles are confirming: are they confirming only the absolute truthfulness of the words of Scripture (as the very words of God), or are miracles given to confirm the truthfulness of the gospel generally, whenever it is preached? In other words, do miracles confirm Scripture or the gospel? As we shall see below, miracles were not limited to those who wrote Scripture or spoke with absolute apostolic authority.[11] This suggests that miracles given in confirmation of the gospel might be expected to continue throughout the church age.

---

that such miraculous gifts should be displayed in them. The exception would be, not a church with, but a church without, such gifts" (pp. 4–5).

[9]Warfield continues, "Everywhere, the Apostolic Church was marked out as itself a gift from God, by showing forth the possession of the Spirit in appropriate works of the Spirit—miracles of healing and miracles of power, miracles of knowledge whether in the form of prophecy or of the discerning of spirits, miracles of speech, whether of the gift of tongues or of their interpretation. The Apostolic Church was characteristically a miracle-working church" (*Counterfeit Miracles*, p. 5).

While I would agree with Warfield's analysis of the New Testament evidence on this question, there is certainly room to disagree with his subsequent point, and the main contention of his book, that the church after the age of the apostles experienced the cessation of miraculous gifts, and that we should not expect such gifts today because God intended them only to confirm the early apostolic message during the time when the apostles were still alive.

[10]See further discussion of this question in chapter 52 below, on spiritual gifts and the question of the time of cessation of some gifts.

[11]See Section D below.

When miracles occur, they give evidence that God is truly at work and so serve to advance the gospel: the Samaritan woman proclaimed to her village, "Come, see a man who told me all that I ever did" (John 4:29), and many of the Samaritans believed in Christ. This was frequently true in Jesus' ministry, but it was also true in the early church: when Philip went to a city in Samaria,

> the multitudes with one accord *gave heed to what was said by Philip,* when they heard him and saw the *signs* which he did. For unclean spirits came out of many who were possessed, crying with a loud voice; and many who were paralyzed or lame were healed. So there was much joy in that city. (Acts 8:6–8)

When Aeneas the paralytic was healed, "all the residents of Lydda and Sharon saw him, and *they turned to the Lord*" (Acts 9:35). When Tabitha was raised from the dead, "it became known throughout all Joppa, and *many believed in the Lord*" (Acts 9:42).[12]

In the New Testament, a second purpose of miracles is to bear witness to the fact that the kingdom of God has come and has begun to expand its beneficial results into people's lives, for the results of Jesus's miracles show the characteristics of God's kingdom: Jesus said, "If it is by the Spirit of God that I cast out demons, then the kingdom of God has come upon you" (Matt. 12:28). His triumph over the destructive forces of Satan showed what God's kingdom was like. In this way, every miracle of healing or deliverance from demonic oppression advanced the kingdom and helped fulfill Jesus' ministry, for he came with the Spirit of the Lord on him "to preach good news to the poor. . . . to proclaim release to the captives and recovering of sight to the blind, to set at liberty those who are oppressed" (Luke 4:18).

Similarly, Jesus gave his disciples "power and authority over all demons and to cure diseases, and he sent them out to preach the kingdom of God and to heal" (Luke 9:1–2). He commanded them, "Preach as you go, saying, 'The kingdom of heaven is at hand.' Heal the sick, raise the dead, cleanse lepers, cast out demons" (Matt. 10:7–8; cf. Matt. 4:23; 9:35; Acts 8:6–7, 13).

A third purpose of miracles is to help those who are in need. The two blind men near Jericho cried out, "Have mercy on us," and Jesus "in pity" healed them (Matt. 20:30, 34).

---

[12]The verses just quoted show the positive value of miracles in bringing people to faith. Some may object that when we say that miracles have value in bearing witness to the gospel this means that we think the gospel message by itself is weak and unable to bring people to faith (see especially James M. Boice, "A Better Way: The Power of Word and Spirit," in Michael Scott Horton, ed., *Power Religion* [Chicago: Moody, 1992], pp. 119–36). But this is not a valid objection, for Jesus and Paul did not reason that way—both performed miracles in conjunction with their preaching of the gospel, and Jesus commanded his disciples to do this as well (Matt. 10:7–8). We must remember that it is God himself who "bore witness" to the gospel "by signs and wonders and various miracles and by gifts of the Holy Spirit distributed according to his own will" (Heb. 2:4), and we cannot say that he has an inappropriate view of the power of the gospel message.

John's gospel is especially instructive in showing the value of miracles in encouraging people to believe in Christ (see John 2:11, 23; 3:2; 4:53–54; 6:2, 14; 7:31; 9:16; 11:48; 12:11; and, in summary, 20:30–31). This positive emphasis in John stands in contrast to the view of D. A. Carson in "The Purpose of Signs and Wonders in the New Testament," in Horton, *Power Religion,* pp. 100–101, where he admits but minimizes the positive role of miracles in bringing people to faith in John's gospel. Surprisingly, he fails to discuss several of the positive passages mentioned above and sees a depreciation of miracles in passages where no such negative evaluation exists, such as John 2:23–25; 4:48; and 20:29–31. We should not think that when miracles accompany the gospel those who believe will have inferior faith (as Carson suggests, p. 101), for that would lead us to say that those who believed the preaching of Jesus, Peter, and Paul had inferior faith—a conclusion hardly advanced by the New Testament!

When Jesus saw a great crowd of people, "he had compassion on them, and healed their sick" (Matt. 14:14; see also Luke 7:13). Here miracles give evidence of the compassion of Christ toward those in need.

A fourth purpose of miracles, related to the second, is to remove hindrances to people's ministries. As soon as Jesus had healed Peter's mother-in-law, "she rose and served him" (Matt. 8:15). When God had mercy on Epaphroditus and restored his health (whether through miraculous means or not, Paul attributes it to God's mercy in Phil. 2:27), Epaphroditus was then able to minister to Paul and complete his function as a messenger returning to the Philippian church (Phil. 2:25–30). Although the text does not explicitly say that Tabitha (or Dorcas) resumed her "good works and acts of charity" (Acts 9:36) after the Lord through Peter raised her from the dead (Acts 9:40–41), by mentioning her good works and those who bore witness to her selfless care for the needs of others (Acts 9:39), it suggests that she would resume a similar ministry of mercy when she was raised from the dead. Related to this category would be the fact that Paul expects people to be edified when miraculous gifts are used in the church (1 Cor. 12:7; 14:4, 12, 26).

Finally, a fifth purpose for miracles (and one to which all the others contribute) is to bring glory to God. After Jesus healed a paralytic, the crowds "were afraid, and they glorified God, who had given such authority to men" (Matt. 9:8). Similarly, Jesus said that the man who had been blind from birth was blind "that the works of God might be made manifest in him" (John 9:3).

D. Were Miracles Restricted to the Apostles?

1. An Unusual Concentration of Miracles in the Apostles' Ministry. Some have argued that miracles were restricted to the apostles or to the apostles and those closely connected with them. Before considering their arguments, it is important to note that there are some indications that a remarkable concentration of miracles was characteristic of the apostles as special representatives of Christ. For example, God was pleased to allow extraordinary miracles to be done through both Peter and Paul. In the very early days of the church,

> many signs and wonders were done among the people by the hands of the apostles. . . . And more than ever believers were added to the Lord, multitudes both of men and women, so that they even carried out the sick into the streets, and laid them on beds and pallets, that as Peter came by at least his shadow might fall on some of them. The people also gathered from the towns around Jerusalem, bringing the sick and those afflicted with unclean spirits, and they were all healed. (Acts 5:12–16)

Similarly, when Paul was in Ephesus, "God did *extraordinary miracles* by the hands of Paul, so that handkerchiefs or aprons were carried away from his body to the sick, and diseases left them and the evil spirits came out of them" (Acts 19:11–12).[13] Another

---

[13]In neither case should these events be thought of as some kind of "magic" that came automatically through Peter's shadow or handkerchiefs that Paul had touched, but rather as an indication of the fact that the Holy Spirit was pleased to give such a full and remarkable empowering to the ministry of these men that on occasion he extended his work beyond their individual bodily presence even to things that they came near or touched.

example is found in the raising of Tabitha: when she had died, the disciples at Joppa sent for Peter to come and pray for her to be raised from the dead (Acts 9:36–42), apparently because they thought that God had given an unusual concentration of miraculous power to Peter (or to the apostles generally). And Paul's ministry generally was characterized by miraculous events, because he summarizes his ministry by telling the Romans of the things that Christ had worked through him to win obedience from the Gentiles "by the power of *signs and wonders,* by the power of the Holy Spirit" (Rom. 15:19).

Nevertheless, the unusual concentration of miracles in the ministries of the apostles does not prove that *no* miracles were performed by others! As we have clearly seen, the "working of miracles" (1 Cor. 12:10) and other miraculous gifts (1 Cor. 12:4–11 mentions several) were part of the ordinary functioning of the Corinthian church, and Paul knows that God "works miracles" in the churches of Galatia as well (Gal. 3:5).

2. What Are the "Signs of an Apostle" in 2 Corinthians 12:12? Why then have some argued that miracles were uniquely the signs that distinguished an apostle? Their case is largely based on 2 Corinthians 12:12, where Paul says, "The *signs of a true apostle* were performed among you in all patience, with signs and wonders and mighty works" (2 Cor. 12:12).[14] They say that this implies that others who were not the apostles (or their close companions) did not have that authority or could not work these miraculous signs.[15] They further maintain that the working of the miracles ceased when the apostles and their close associates died. Therefore, they conclude, no further miracles are to be expected today. (Those who hold this position are sometimes known as "*cessationists,*" since they hold to the ceasing or "cessation" of miracles early in the history of the church.)

In considering this question, it should be remembered that in the key passage used to establish this point, where Paul talks about "the signs of a true apostle" in 2 Corinthians 12:12, he is *not* attempting to prove that he is an apostle *in distinction from other Christians* who are not apostles. He is rather attempting to prove that he is a true representative of Christ in distinction from others who are "false apostles" (2 Cor. 11:13), false representatives of Christ, servants of Satan who are disguising themselves as "servants of righteousness" (2 Cor. 11:14–15). In short, the contrast is not between apostles who could work miracles and ordinary Christians who could not, but between genuine Christian apostles through whom the Holy Spirit worked and *non-Christian pretenders to the apostolic office,* through whom the Holy Spirit did not work at all. Therefore, even if we understand the "signs of an apostle" to be miracles, we should recognize that those who use this passage to argue that miracles cannot be done through *Christians* today are taking the phrase "signs of an apostle" out of its context and using it in a way that Paul

---

[14]The word "true" is not actually in the Greek text, which simply says, "the signs of an apostle." The RSV (which is quoted here) and NASB have added "true" to give the sense: Paul is contrasting his ministry with that of the false apostles.

[15]See Walter J. Chantry, *Signs of the Apostles,* 2d ed. (Edinburgh: Banner of Truth, 1976), esp. pp. 17–21; B. B. Warfield, *Counterfeit Miracles;* Norman Geisler, *Signs and Wonders* (Wheaton: Tyndale House, 1988).

never intended. Paul is distinguishing himself from non-Christians, whereas they use the passage to distinguish Paul from other Christians.

Moreover, a close examination of 2 Corinthians 12:12 shows it to be very doubtful that the phrase "signs of an apostle" in this passage means miraculous signs. In this very verse, Paul distinguishes the "signs of a true apostle" from miracles, which he calls "signs and wonders and mighty works," noting that the miracles were done along with the signs of an apostle: "The *signs of a true apostle* were performed among you in all patience, *with signs and wonders and mighty works.*"[16] The latter phrase, "with signs and wonders and mighty works," has a piling up of all three terms used for miracles and therefore must refer to miracles (note "signs and wonders" in Acts 4:30; 5:12; 14:3; 15:12; Rom. 15:19; Heb. 2:4, et al.). Therefore the former phrase, "signs of a true apostle," must refer to something different, something that was *accompanied by* (done "with") signs and wonders.

In fact, although the word *sign* in Greek (*sēmeion*) often refers to miracles, it has a much broader range of meaning than just *miracle: sēmeion* simply means "something which indicates or refers to something else."[17] In 2 Corinthians 12:12, the "signs" of an apostle are best understood as everything that characterized Paul's apostolic mission and showed him to be a true apostle.[18] We need not guess at what these signs were, for elsewhere in 2 Corinthians Paul tells what marked him as a true apostle:

1. Spiritual power in conflict with evil (10:3–4, 8–11; 13:2–4, 10)
2. Jealous care for the welfare of the churches (11:1–6)

---

[16]The grammar of the Greek text forces us to this distinction, since "the signs of an apostle" is in the nominative case, while "signs and wonders and mighty works" is in the dative, and cannot therefore be simply a restatement of "signs of an apostle" in apposition to it: nouns in apposition in Greek must be in the same case. (The NIV ignores the grammar here and translates the two phrases as if they were in apposition; the RSV and NASB are more precise.)

[17]Many nonmiraculous things are called "signs." For example, Paul's handwritten signature is his "sign" (2 Thess. 3:17; RSV "mark"); circumcision is a "sign" of Abraham's imputed righteousness (Rom. 4:11); Judas's kiss is a "sign" to the Jewish leaders (Matt. 26:48); the rainbow is a "sign" of the covenant (Gen. 9:12, LXX); eating unleavened bread during Passover every year is a "sign" of the Lord's deliverance (Ex. 13:9, LXX); Rahab's scarlet cord is a "sign" that the spies told her to hang in her window (1 Clem. 12:7).

[18]Among modern commentators on 2 Corinthians, I found only three who understand the "signs of a true apostle" in 2 Cor. 12:12 to be miracles: Colin Kruse, *The Second Epistle of Paul to the Corinthians*, TNTC (Leicester: Inter-Varsity Press, and Grand Rapids: Eerdmans, 1987), p. 209; Jean Héring, *The Second Epistle of Saint Paul to the Corinthians*, trans. A. W. Heathcote and P. J. Allcock (London: Epworth, 1967), pp. 95–96; and Murray Harris, "2 Corinthians," *EBC*, 10:398, take it that way, but none of them gives any argument to

support this view, and Harris notes an alternative view where the "signs" are the changed lives of the Corinthians and the Christlike character of Paul.

The majority of commentators understand "signs of a true apostle" to have a much broader meaning, including the qualities of Paul's life and the character and results of his ministry: see Philip E. Hughes, *Paul's Second Epistle to the Corinthians*, NIC (Grand Rapids: Eerdmans, 1962), pp. 456–58 (following Chrysostom and Calvin); Ralph P. Martin, *II Corinthians*, WBC (Waco, Tex.: Word, 1986), pp. 434–38 (with extensive discussion); Alfred Plummer, *A Critical and Exegetical Commentary on the Second Epistle of St. Paul to the Corinthians*, ICC (Edinburgh: T. & T. Clark, 1915), p. 359; R. V. G. Tasker, *2 Corinthians*, TNTC (London: Tyndale Press, 1958), p. 180; Charles Hodge, *An Exposition of 1 and 2 Corinthians* (Wilmington, Del.: Sovereign Grace, 1972 [reprint]), pp. 359–60; John Calvin, *The Second Epistle of Paul the Apostle to the Corinthians. . .*, trans. T. A. Smail, ed. by D. W. Torrance and T. F. Torrance (Edinburgh: Oliver and Boyd, and Grand Rapids: Eerdmans, 1964), pp. 163–64; see also J. B. Lightfoot, *The Epistle of St. Paul to the Galatians* (Grand Rapids: Zondervan, 1957), p. 99. Some of these commentators understand the "signs of a true apostle" as accompanied by or including miracles, but none understand the phrase to refer primarily or exclusively to miracles.

3. True knowledge of Jesus and his gospel plan (11:6)
4. Self-support (selflessness) (11:7–11)
5. Not taking advantage of churches; not striking people physically (11:20–21)
6. Suffering and hardship endured for Christ (11:23–29)
7. Being caught up into heaven (12:1–6)
8. Contentment and faith to endure a thorn in the flesh (12:7–9)
9. Gaining strength out of weakness (12:10).

The first item may have included miracles, but that is certainly not the primary focus of his reference to the "signs of a true apostle."

Another evidence that the "signs of a true apostle" in 2 Corinthians 12:12 were all these things and not simply miracles is the fact that Paul says, "The signs of a true apostle were performed among you *in all patience.*" Now it would make little sense to say that miracles were performed "in all patience," for many miracles happen quite quickly, but it would make much sense to say that Paul's Christlike endurance of hardship for the sake of the Corinthians was performed "in all patience."

We should note that nowhere in this list does Paul claim miracles to prove his genuine apostleship. In fact, most of the things he mentions would not distinguish him from other true Christians. But these things do distinguish him from servants of Satan, false apostles who are not Christians at all: their lives will not be marked by humility, but pride; not by selflessness, but selfishness; not by generosity, but greed; not by seeking the advantage of others, but by taking advantage of others; not by spiritual power in physical weakness, but by confidence in their natural strength; not by enduring suffering and hardship, but by seeking their own comfort and ease.[19] When Paul acted in a Christlike manner among them, his actions were "signs" that his claim to be an apostle was a true claim: thus, these things were "signs of a true apostle." In this context, the "signs" that mark a true apostle need not be things that showed an absolute difference between him and other Christians, but rather things that showed his ministry to be genuine, in distinction from false ministries. He is not here telling the Corinthians how to tell who an apostle was in distinction from other Christians (he did that in 1 Cor. 9:1–2; 15:7–11; Gal. 1:1, 11–24, mentioning seeing the risen Christ and being commissioned by him as an apostle), but here he is telling how to recognize what a genuine, Christ-approved ministry was.

Why then does he add that all these signs of a true apostle were done among the Corinthians "with signs and wonders and mighty works"? He is simply adding one additional factor to all the previous marks of his genuine apostleship. Miracles of course had a significant function in confirming the truth of Paul's message, and Paul here makes explicit what the Corinthians may or may not have assumed to be included in the phrase "signs of a true apostle": in addition to all these other signs of a true apostle, his ministry showed miraculous demonstrations of God's power as well.[20]

---

[19]Some interpreters assume that the false apostles were working miracles and claiming revelations from God, so that Paul would have to claim greater miracles and revelations. But nothing in 2 Corinthians says that the false apostles claimed miracles or revelations.

[20]The following verse also gives confirmation to this interpretation: Paul says, "For in what were you less favored than the rest of the churches . . . ?" (2 Cor. 12:13). The fact that they were not lacking in any of Paul's care and attention would prove to them that the "signs of a true apostle" were performed

There is yet another very significant reason why miracles did not prove someone to be an apostle. In the larger context of the New Testament it is clear that miracles were worked by others than apostles, such as Stephen (Acts 6:8), Philip (Acts 8:6–7), Christians in the several churches in Galatia (Gal. 3:5), and those with gifts of "miracles" in the body of Christ generally (1 Cor. 12:10, 28). Miracles as such cannot then be regarded as exclusively signs of an apostle. In fact, "workers of miracles" and "healers" are actually distinguished from "apostles" in 1 Corinthians 12:28: "And God has appointed in the church first *apostles,* second prophets, third teachers, then *workers of miracles,* then healers. . . ."

Similar evidence is seen in Mark 16:17–18: Though there are serious questions about the authenticity of this passage as part of Mark's gospel,[21] the text is nonetheless very early[22] and at least bears witness to one strand of tradition within the early church. This text reports Jesus as saying,

> And these signs will accompany those who believe: in my name they will cast out demons; they will speak in new tongues; they will pick up serpents, and if they drink any deadly thing, it will not hurt them; they will lay their hands on the sick, and they will recover.

Here also the power to work miracles is assumed to be the common possession of Christians. Those who wrote and passed on this early tradition, and who thought it represented the genuine teaching of Jesus, were certainly not aware of any idea that miracles were to be limited to the apostles and their close associates.[23]

The argument that many other Christians in the New Testament worked miracles is sometimes answered by the claim that it was only the apostles *and those closely associated with them* or those on whom the apostles laid their hands who could work miracles.[24] However, this really proves very little because the story of the New Testament church is the story of what was done through the apostles and those closely associated with them. A similar argument might be made about evangelism or the founding of churches: "In the New Testament, churches were only founded by the apostles or their close associates; therefore, we should not found churches today." Or, "In the New Testament, missionary work in other countries was only done by the apostles or their close associates; therefore, we should not do missionary work in other countries today." These analogies show the inadequacy of the argument: the New Testament primarily shows how the church *should* seek to act, not how it *should not* seek to act.

But if many other Christians throughout the first-century church were working miracles by the power of the Holy Spirit, then the power to work miracles could not be a sign to distinguish the apostles from other Christians.

---

among them only if these "signs" included all of Paul's ministry to them, but not if the "signs of a true apostle" were just miracles.

[21]The manuscript evidence and considerations of style suggest that these verses were not originally part of the gospel that Mark wrote.

[22]It is included in several manuscripts of Tatian's Diates-

saron (A.D. 170) and is quoted by Irenaeus (d. A.D. 202) and Tertullian (d. A.D. 220).

[23]I am grateful to Professor Harold Hoehner of Dallas Theological Seminary for suggesting to me the arguments given here regarding 1 Cor. 12:28 and Mark 16:17–18 (though he may disagree with my conclusion in this section).

[24]So Chantry, *Signs,* pp. 19–21.

3. Norman Geisler's Restrictive Definition of Miracles. A more recent attempt to deny that miracles occur today has been made by Norman Geisler.[25] Geisler has a much more restrictive definition of *miracle* than that presented in this chapter, and he uses that definition to argue against the possibility of contemporary miracles. Geisler says that "miracles (1) are always successful, (2) are immediate, (3) have no relapses, and (4) give confirmation of God's messenger" (pp. 28–30). He finds support for this thesis largely in the ministry of Jesus, but when he passes beyond the life of Jesus and attempts to show that others who had the power to work miracles were never unsuccessful, his thesis is much less convincing. With regard to the demon-possessed boy whom the disciples could not set free from the demon (Matt. 17:14–21), Geisler says that "the disciples simply forgot for the moment to faithfully exercise the power that Jesus had already given them" (p. 150). But this is an unpersuasive argument: Geisler says that the power to work miracles was always successful, and when the Bible talks about some who were unsuccessful (and who contradict his thesis) he simply says they "forgot." Jesus, however, gives a different reason than Geisler: "Because of your little faith" (Matt. 17:20). Lesser faith resulted in lesser power to work miracles.

With regard to Paul's failure to heal Epaphroditus (Phil. 2:27), Geisler is forced to make the dubious claim that perhaps Paul never attempted to heal Epaphroditus (though he had come to him in prison and was so ill he almost died), or that "Paul no longer possessed the gift of healing at this time" (p. 150). He employs the same claim to explain the fact that Paul left Trophimus ill at Miletus (2 Tim. 4:20). In these instances Geisler goes well beyond the usual cessationist claim that miracles ended with the death of the apostles—he is claiming that miracles ceased in the life of the greatest apostle before his first Roman imprisonment. That is simply an unconvincing argument with respect to the apostle whose ministry was repeatedly characterized "by the power of signs and wonders, by the power of the Holy Spirit" (Rom. 15:19), and who could say with triumph in his last epistle, "I have fought the good fight, I have finished the race, I have kept the faith" (2 Tim. 4:7).

Geisler's description of miracles does not fit the case of the blind man upon whom Jesus laid his hands, for at first the man did not see clearly but said he saw men who "look like trees, walking." After Jesus laid his hands on him a second time, the man "saw everything clearly" (Mark 8:24–25). Geisler responds that it was Jesus' intention to heal in two stages, to teach the disciples by using an object lesson about the gradual growth of their spiritual lives (pp. 153–54). Though the text says nothing to this effect, it may have been true, but even so it disproves Geisler's thesis, for if it was Jesus' intention to heal in two stages then, it may also be his intention to heal people in two stages today—or in three or four or more stages. Once Geisler admits that it may be God's intention to work a miracle in stages, in order to accomplish his own purposes, then his entire claim that miracles must be immediate and complete is lost.[26]

---

[25]Norman Geisler, *Signs and Wonders*. His definition of miracles is found on pp. 28–32 and 149–55.

[26]Geisler also has much difficulty explaining Mark 5:8 (where Jesus more than once commanded some demons to leave) and Mark 6:5 (where the text says that Jesus was not able to do any miracles in Nazareth because of the unbelief of the people there)(see pp. 149, 152).

Instead of accepting Geisler's definition, it seems better to conclude that even those whom God gifts with the ability to perform miracles may not be able to perform them whenever they wish, for the Holy Spirit continually is distributing them to each person "as he wills" (1 Cor. 12:11; the word *distributes* is a present participle in Greek, indicating a continuing activity of the Holy Spirit). Moreover, there seems no reason to exclude (as Geisler apparently wants to do) unusual or remarkable answers to prayer from the category of "miracle," thus making the definition extremely restrictive. If God answers persistent prayer, for instance, for a physical healing for which there is no known medical explanation, and does so only after several months or years of prayer, yet does so in such a way that it seems quite clearly to be in response to prayer so that people are amazed and glorify God, there seems no reason to deny that a miracle has occurred simply because the earlier prayers were not answered immediately. Finally, Geisler fails to recognize that several New Testament texts indicate that spiritual gifts, whether miraculous or nonmiraculous in nature, may vary in strength or degree of intensity.

4. Hebrews 2:3–4. Another passage that is sometimes used to support the idea that miracles were limited to the apostles and their close associates is Hebrews 2:3–4. There the author says that the message of salvation "was declared at first by the Lord, and it was attested to us by those who heard him, while God also bore witness[27] by signs and wonders and various miracles and by gifts of the Holy Spirit distributed according to his own will."

Since the miracles here are said to come through those who heard the Lord firsthand ("those who heard him"), it is argued that we should not expect them to be done through others who were not firsthand witnesses to the Lord's teaching and ministry.[28]

But this argument also attempts to draw more from the passage than is there. First, the phrase "those who heard him" (Heb. 2:3) is certainly not limited to the apostles, for many others heard Jesus as well. But more importantly, this position is claiming something that the text simply does not say: the fact that (1) the gospel message was confirmed by miracles when it was preached by those who heard Jesus says nothing at all about (2) whether it would be confirmed by miracles when preached by others who did not hear Jesus. Finally, this passage says the message was confirmed not only by "signs and wonders and various miracles" but also by *"gifts of the Holy Spirit."* If someone argues that this passage limits miracles to the apostles and their companions, then he or she must also argue that gifts of the Holy Spirit are likewise limited to the first-century church. But few would argue that there are no gifts of the Holy Spirit today.[29]

---

[27]The KJV translates, "God also bearing *them* witness, both with signs and wonders...." This translation suggests that the miracles bore witness to the people who heard Jesus and first preached. But the word "them" is represented by no word in the Greek text, and this translation is not followed by modern versions.

[28]So Chantry, *Signs of the Apostles,* pp. 18–19: "New Testament miracles are viewed in Scripture itself as God's stamp of approval upon the message of the apostles, which was an inspired record of the things they had seen and heard while with Jesus. Recalling these wonders should deepen our respect for the authority of their words and prompt us to give the more careful heed."

[29]Another argument limiting miracles to the first century is based on the claim that some miracles, such as the gift of prophecy, always give new Scripture-quality revelation.

5. Conclusion: Were Miracles Restricted to the Apostles? If ministry in the power and glory of the Holy Spirit is characteristic of the new covenant age (2 Cor. 3:1–4:18), then our expectation would be just the opposite: we would expect that second and third and fourth generation Christians, who also know Christ and the power of his resurrection (Phil. 3:10), who are continually being filled with the Holy Spirit (Eph. 5:17), who are participants in a war that is not a worldly war, but one that is carried on with weapons that have divine power to destroy strongholds (2 Cor. 10:3–4), who have not been given a spirit of timidity but a "spirit of power and love and self-control" (2 Tim. 1:7), who are strong in the Lord and in the strength of his might, and who have put on the whole armor of God in order to be able to stand against principalities and powers and spiritual hosts of wickedness in the heavenly places (Eph. 6:10–12), would *also* have the ability to minister the gospel not only in truth and love but also with accompanying miraculous demonstrations of God's power. It is difficult to see, from the pages of the New Testament, any reason why only the preaching of the apostles should come "not in plausible words of wisdom, but *in demonstration of the Spirit and of power, that your faith might not rest in the wisdom of men but in the power of God" (1 Cor. 2:4–5).

Though there does seem to have been an unusual concentration of miraculous power in the ministry of the apostles, this is not a reason for thinking that there would be few or no miracles following their deaths. Rather, the apostles were the leaders in a new covenant church whose life and message were characterized by the power of the Holy Spirit at work in miraculous ways. Furthermore, they set a pattern that the church throughout its history may well seek to imitate in its own life, insofar as God the Holy Spirit is pleased to work miracles for the edification of the church.[30]

E. False Miracles

Pharaoh's magicians were able to work some false miracles (Ex. 7:11, 22; 8:7), though they soon had to admit that God's power was greater (Ex. 8:19). Simon the sorcerer in the city of Samaria amazed people with his magic (Acts 8:9–11), even though the miracles done through Philip were much greater (Acts 8:13). In Philippi Paul encountered a slave girl "who had a spirit of divination and brought her owners much gain by soothsaying" (Acts 16:16), but Paul rebuked the spirit and it came out of her (Acts 16:18). Moreover, Paul says that when the man of sin comes it "will be with all power and with pretended signs and wonders, and with all wicked deception for those who are to perish" (2 Thess. 2:9–10), but those who follow them and are deceived do so "because they refused to love the truth and so be saved" (2 Thess. 2:10). This indicates that those who work false miracles in the end times by the power of Satan will not speak the truth but will preach a false gospel. Finally, Revelation 13 indicates that a second beast will rise "out of the earth," one that has "all the authority of the first beast" and "works great signs, even making fire

---

[30]However, Christians should be very cautious and take extreme care to be accurate in their reporting of miracles if they do occur. Much harm can be done to the gospel if Christians exaggerate or distort, even in small ways, the facts of a situation where a miracle has occurred. The power of the Holy Spirit is great enough to work however he wills, and we should never "embellish" the actual facts of the situation simply to make it sound even more exciting than it actually was. God does exactly what he is pleased to do in each situation.

come down from heaven to earth in the sight of men; and by the signs which it is allowed to work in the presence of the beast, it deceives those who dwell on earth" (Rev. 13:11–14). But once again a false gospel accompanies these miracles: this power is exercised in connection with the first beast who utters "haughty and blasphemous words . . . it opened its mouth to utter blasphemies against God, blaspheming his name and his dwelling" (Rev. 13:5–6).

Two conclusions become clear from this brief survey of false miracles in Scripture: (1) *The power of God is greater than the power of Satan* to work miraculous signs, and God's people triumph in confrontations of power with those who work evil. In connection with this, John assures believers that "he who is in you is greater than he who is in the world" (1 John 4:4).[31] (2) The identity of these workers of false miracles *is always known through their denial of the gospel. There is no indication anywhere in Scripture that genuine Christians with the Holy Spirit in them will work false miracles.* In fact, in a city filled with idolatry and demon worship (see 1 Cor. 10:20), Paul could say to the Corinthian believers, many of whom had come out of that kind of pagan background, that "no one can say 'Jesus is Lord' except by the Holy Spirit" (1 Cor. 12:3). Here he gives them reassurance that those who make a genuine profession of faith in Jesus as Lord do in fact have the Holy Spirit in them. It is significant that he immediately goes on to a discussion of spiritual gifts possessed by "each" true believer (1 Cor. 12:7).

This should reassure us that if we see miracles being worked by those who make a genuine profession of faith (1 Cor. 12:3), who believe in the incarnation and deity of Christ (1 John 4:2), and who show the fruit of the Holy Spirit in their lives and bear fruit in their ministry (Matt. 7:20; cf. John 15:5; Gal. 5:22–23), we should not be suspicious that they are false miracles but should be thankful to God that the Holy Spirit is working, even in those who may not hold exactly the same convictions that we do on every point of doctrine.[32] Indeed, if God waited to work miracles only through those who were perfect in both doctrine and conduct of life, no miracles would be worked until Christ returns.

F. Should Christians Seek Miracles Today?

It is one thing to say that miracles might occur today. It is quite another thing to ask God for miracles. Is it right then for Christians to ask God to perform miracles?

The answer depends on the purpose for which miracles are sought. Certainly it is

---

[31]Some may object that one exception to this may be the vision of the end times in Rev. 13:7, where the beast "was allowed to make war on the saints and to conquer them" (Rev. 13:7). But even here there is no indication that the miraculous powers of the beast are greater than the power of the Holy Spirit. This seems to be best understood not as a confrontation of miraculous power but simply as a persecution by military force, for we read later of "those who had been beheaded for their testimony to Jesus and for the word of God, and who had not worshiped the beast or its image and had not received its mark on their foreheads or their hands" (Rev. 20:4).

[32]The fact that people who name the name of Christ are able to prophesy and cast out demons and do "many mighty works" in his name (Matt. 7:21–23) does not contradict this, because these are non-Christians: Jesus says to them, "I never knew you; depart from me, you evildoers" (Matt. 7:23). Although it is possible that these are false miracles worked by demonic power, it seems more likely that they are operations of common grace (see chapter 31) that God worked through non-Christians, similar to the effectiveness of the gospel that God sometimes allows when it is preached by those who have impure motives and do not know Christ in their hearts (cf. Phil. 1:15–18).

wrong to seek miraculous power to advance one's own power or fame, as Simon the magician did: Peter said to him, "your heart is not right before God. Repent therefore of this wickedness of yours, and pray to the Lord that, if possible, the intent of your heart may be forgiven you" (Acts 8:21–22).

It is also wrong to seek miracles simply to be entertained, as Herod did: "When Herod saw Jesus, he was very glad, for he had long desired to see him, because he had heard about him, and he was hoping to see some sign done by him" (Luke 23:8). But Jesus would not even answer Herod's questions.

It is also wrong for skeptical unbelievers to seek miracles simply to find ground to criticize those who preach the gospel:

> And the Pharisees and Sadducees came, and *to test him* they asked him to show them a sign from heaven. He answered them, ". . . An evil and adulterous generation seeks for a sign, but no sign shall be given to it except the sign of Jonah." (Matt. 16:1–4)

This rebuke against seeking signs is repeated elsewhere in the Gospels, but it is important to note that rebukes against seeking signs are always directed against hostile unbelievers who are seeking a miracle only as an opportunity to criticize Jesus.[33] Never does Jesus rebuke anyone who comes in faith, or in need, seeking healing or deliverance or any other kind of miracle, whether for himself or herself, or for others.

What shall we say then about 1 Corinthians 1:22–24, where Paul says, "For *Jews demand signs* and Greeks seek wisdom, but we preach Christ crucified, a stumbling block to Jews and folly to Gentiles, but to those who are called, both Jews and Greeks, Christ the power of God and the wisdom of God"? Does Paul mean that he did not work miracles ("signs") at Corinth, or perhaps in his evangelistic work generally?

Here Paul cannot be denying that he performed miracles in connection with the proclamation of the gospel. In fact, in Romans 15:18–19, a passage he wrote while in Corinth, he said,

> For I will not venture to speak of anything except what Christ has wrought through me to win obedience from the Gentiles, by word and deed, *by the power of signs and wonders,* by the power of the Holy Spirit, so that from Jerusalem and as far round as Illyricum I have fully preached the gospel of Christ.

And 2 Corinthians 12:12 affirms clearly that Paul did work "signs and wonders and mighty works" among them.

---

[33]The fact that Jesus only rebukes hostile unbelievers who seek miracles is surprisingly never mentioned by D. A. Carson, "The Purpose of Signs and Wonders in the New Testament," in M. Horton, ed., *Power Religion,* pp. 89–118, or by James M. Boice, "A Better Way: The Power of Word and Spirit," in *Power Religion,* pp. 119–36. Both articles use Jesus' rebukes as a means of discouraging believers from seeking miracles today, but to do this they must apply Jesus' statements in a way not justified by the New Testament contexts. (See esp. Boice, p. 126, who quotes with approval a statement from John Woodhouse, "A desire for further signs and wonders is sinful and unbelieving.")

The explicit statement of intent "to test him" is also found in Mark 8:11 and Luke 11:16, parallel contexts where Jesus rebukes an evil generation for seeking a sign from him. The only other context where this rebuke occurs, Matt. 12:38–42, does not include an explicit statement of the intent to test, but Jesus is clearly responding to the "scribes and Pharisees" (v. 38), and the incident follows just after Matt. 12:14, where the Pharisees "went out and took counsel against him, how to destroy him," and Matt. 12:24, where the Pharisees say, "It is only by Beelzebul, the prince of demons, that this man casts out demons."

So 1 Corinthians 1:22–24 cannot mean that Paul was denying the validity of *wisdom* or the validity of *signs,* for through Christ he worked signs and he taught wisdom. Rather, here he is saying that signs and wisdom do not themselves save people, but the gospel saves people. Signs and the wisdom that Jews and Greeks were seeking were not the signs and wisdom of Christ but simply signs to entertain or to fuel their hostility and skepticism and wisdom that was the wisdom of the world rather than the wisdom of God.

There is nothing inappropriate in seeking miracles for the proper purposes for which they are given by God: to confirm the truthfulness of the gospel message, to bring help to those in need, to remove hindrances to people's ministries, and to bring glory to God (see Section C above). In the Gospels many people came to Jesus seeking miracles, and he healed them for these purposes. Moreover, when he sent his disciples out preaching that the kingdom of heaven was at hand, he told them, "Heal the sick, raise the dead, cleanse lepers, cast out demons" (Matt. 10:7–8). How could they do this without seeking God for miracles everywhere they went? Jesus' command required them to seek for miracles to happen.

After Pentecost, the early church prayed both for boldness to preach the gospel and for God to grant miracles to accompany its preaching. They cried out to God,

> And now, Lord, look upon their threats, and grant to your servants to speak your word with all boldness, *while you stretch out your hand to heal,* and *signs and wonders* are performed through the name of your holy servant Jesus. (Acts 4:29–30)

Far from teaching that we should not ask God for miracles, this example of the early church gives us some encouragement to do so. Similarly, the disciples in Lydda sent for Peter to come and pray for Tabitha after she had died, thereby seeking a miraculous intervention by God (Acts 9:38). And James directs that the elders of the church should pray and seek healing for those who are ill (James 5:14). Of course, we should not assume that an obviously miraculous answer to prayer is somehow better than one that comes through ordinary means (such as medical help for sickness), and we must also realize that asking God for a particular need does not guarantee that the prayer will be answered. On the other hand, our faith that God will work in powerful and even miraculous ways may be far too small. We must beware of being infected by a secular worldview that assumes that God will answer prayer only very seldom, if ever. And we should certainly not be embarrassed to talk about miracles if they occur—or think that a nonmiraculous answer to prayer is better! Miracles are God's work, and he works them to bring glory to himself and to strengthen our faith. When we encounter serious needs in people's lives today, it is right for us to seek God for an answer, and where miraculous intervention seems to be needed, then to ask God if he would be pleased to work in that way.[34] This would seem to be especially appropriate when our motivation is a Christlike compassion for those in need and a burning desire to see Christ's kingdom advance and his name glorified.

---

[34]John Walvoord, the late President of Dallas Theological Seminary, understood the gift of miracles to be "the power to perform miracles at will in the name of Christ." Therefore he held that the gift of miracles has ceased. But he still argued that we can pray for miracles today: "A Christian can still appeal to God to do wonders, and God does answer prayer. God can still heal and even raise the dead if he chooses, but these miracles are sovereign and individual. . . . While therefore the gift of miracles is not part of the present program of God, the power of God to perform miracles must be affirmed" (*The Holy Spirit* [Wheaton, Ill.: Van Kampen, 1954], pp. 179–80).

QUESTIONS FOR PERSONAL APPLICATION

1. When you first came to faith in Christ, did the stories of miracles in the Bible have any influence (negative or positive) on your believing the message of Scripture?

2. Before reading this chapter, have you thought of the church at the time of the New Testament as a church with frequent miracles? Have you thought of the contemporary church as one with frequent miracles? After reading this chapter, how has your position changed, if at all?

3. If you think that miracles should be characteristic of the church until Christ returns, then why have we not seen very many miracles at many points in the history of the church, and why do we not see many miracles in large sections of the Christian church today?

4. If you hold a "cessationist" position, what kinds of unusual answers to prayer might you still think possible today? (For example, prayer for physical healing, for deliverance from danger, victory over demonic attack through prayer and/or verbal rebuke of an evil spirit, or sudden and unusual insight into a passage of Scripture or a situation in someone's life.) How would you distinguish these things that you might think possible today from "miracles" according to the definition given in this chapter? (You may wish to argue for a different definition of "miracle" as well.)

5. Do miracles have to be large and "remarkable" (such as raising the dead or healing a man blind from birth) to accomplish useful purposes in the church today? What kinds of "small-scale" miracles might also accomplish some of the purposes for miracles listed in this chapter? Have you known of any answers to prayer in your own church (or your own life) that you would characterize as "miraculous" according to the definition given at the beginning of the chapter?

6. Would you like to see more miraculous power of the Holy Spirit (or more unusual answers to prayer) at work in your own church today, or not? If more miracles did occur, what might be the dangers? What might be the benefits?

SPECIAL TERMS

cessationist
mighty work
miracle
natural law

sign
"signs of a true apostle"
wonder

BIBLIOGRAPHY

Berkouwer, G. C. "Providence and Miracles." In *The Providence of God*. Trans. by Lewis B. Smedes. Grand Rapids: Eerdmans, 1952, pp. 188–231.

Boice, James Montgomery. "A Better Way: The Power of Word and Spirit." In *Power Religion: The Selling Out of the Evangelical Church?* Michael Scott Horton, ed. Chicago: Moody Press, 1992.

Bridge, Donald. *Signs and Wonders Today.* Leicester: Inter-Varsity Press, 1985.

Brown, Colin. "Miracle." In *NDT,* pp. 433–34.

_____. *That You May Believe: Miracles and Faith — Then and Now.* Grand Rapids: Eerdmans, 1985.

Carson, D. A. "The Purpose of Signs and Wonders in the New Testament," In *Power Religion: The Selling Out of the Evangelical Church?* Michael Scott Horton, ed. Chicago: Moody Press, 1992.

Deere, Jack. *Surprised by the Power of the Spirit: A Former Dallas Seminary Professor Discovers That God Still Speaks and Heals Today.* Grand Rapids: Zondervan, 1993.

Geisler, Norman. *Signs and Wonders.* Wheaton: Tyndale, 1988.

_____. *Miracles and Modern Thought.* With a response by R. C. Sproul. Grand Rapids: Zondervan, and Dallas: Probe Ministries, 1982.

Greig, Gary S., and Kevin N. Springer, eds. *The Kingdom and the Power.* Ventura, Calif.: Regal, 1993.

Gross, Edward N. *Miracles, Demons, and Spiritual Warfare: An Urgent Call for Discernment.* Grand Rapids: Baker, 1990.

Grudem, Wayne. *Power and Truth: A Response to the Critiques of Vineyard Teaching and Practice by D. A. Carson, James Montgomery Boice, and John H. Armstrong in "Power Religion".* Anaheim, Calif.: Association of Vineyard Churches, 1993.

_____. "Should Christians Expect Miracles Today? Objections and Answers From the Bible." In *The Kingdom and the Power.* Gary Greig and Kevin Springer, eds. Ventura, Calif.: Regal, 1993, pp. 55–110.

Horton, Michael S., ed. *Power Religion: The Selling Out of the Evangelical Church?* Chicago: Moody, 1992.

Kirk, J. A. "Power." In *NDT,* pp. 524–25.

Lewis, C. S. *Miracles: A Preliminary Study.* New York: Macmillan, 1947.

Moule, C. F. D., ed. *Miracles.* London: Mowbray, 1965.

Spiceland, J. D. "Miracles." In *EDT,* pp. 723–24.

Wenham, David, and Craig Blomberg, eds. *Miracles of Jesus.* Sheffield, England: JSOT, 1986.

Williams, Don. *Signs, Wonders, and the Kingdom of God: A Biblical Guide for the Skeptic.* Ann Arbor, Mich.: Servant, 1989.

Wimber, John, with Kevin Springer. *Power Evangelism.* Revised edition. San Francisco: Harper and Row, and London: Hodder and Stoughton, 1992.

SCRIPTURE MEMORY PASSAGE

Hebrews 2:3–4: *How shall we escape if we neglect such a great salvation? It was declared at first by the Lord, and it was attested to us by those who heard him, while God also bore witness by signs and wonders and various miracles and by gifts of the Holy Spirit distributed according to his own will.*

HYMN

"A Mighty Fortress Is Our God"

A mighty fortress is our God, a bulwark never failing;
Our helper he amid the flood of mortal ills prevailing.
For still our ancient foe doth seek to work us woe;
His craft and pow'r are great; and, armed with cruel hate,
On earth is not his equal.

Did we in our own strength confide, our striving would be losing;
Were not the right man on our side, the man of God's own choosing.
Dost ask who that may be? Christ Jesus, it is he,
Lord Sabaoth his name, from age to age the same,
And he must win the battle.

And though this world, with devils filled, should threaten to undo us,
We will not fear, for God hath willed his truth to triumph through us.
The prince of darkness grim, we tremble not for him;
His rage we can endure, for lo! his doom is sure;
One little word shall fell him.

That word above all earthly powers, no thanks to them, abideth;
The Spirit and the gifts are ours through him who with us sideth;
Let goods and kindred go, this mortal life also;
The body they may kill: God's truth abideth still;
His kingdom is forever.

AUTHOR: MARTIN LUTHER, 1529

Chapter 11

PRAYER

Why does God want us to pray?
How can we pray effectively?

EXPLANATION AND SCRIPTURAL BASIS

The character of God and his relationship to the world, as discussed in the previous chapters, lead naturally to a consideration of the doctrine of prayer. Prayer may be defined as follows: *Prayer is personal communication with God.*

This definition is very broad. What we call "prayer" includes prayers of request for ourselves or for others (sometimes called prayers of petition or intercession), confession of sin, adoration, praise and thanksgiving, and also God communicating to us indications of his response.

A. Why Does God Want Us to Pray?

Prayer is not made so that God can find out what we need, because Jesus tells us, "Your Father knows what you need before you ask him" (Matt. 6:8). God wants us to pray because prayer expresses our trust in God and is a means whereby our trust in him can increase. In fact, perhaps the primary emphasis of the Bible's teaching on prayer is that we are to pray with faith, which means trust or dependence on God. God as our Creator delights in being trusted by us as his creatures, for an attitude of dependence is most appropriate to the Creator/creature relationship. Praying in humble dependence also indicates that we are genuinely convinced of God's wisdom, love, goodness, and power—indeed of all of the attributes that make up his excellent character. When we truly pray, we as persons, in the wholeness of our character, are relating to God as a person, in the wholeness of his character. Thus, all that we think or feel about God comes to expression in our prayer. It is only natural that God would delight in such activity and place much emphasis on it in his relationship with us.

The first words of the Lord's Prayer, "Our Father who art in heaven" (Matt. 6:9), acknowledge our dependence on God as a loving and wise Father and also recognize that he rules over all from his heavenly throne. Scripture many times emphasizes our need to trust God as we pray. For example, Jesus compares our praying to a son asking his father for a fish or an egg (Luke 11:9–12) and then concludes, "If you then, who are evil, know how to give good gifts to your children, how much more will the heavenly Father give the Holy Spirit to those who ask him!" (Luke 11:13). As children look to their fathers to provide for them, so God expects us to look to him in prayer. Since God is our Father, we should ask in faith. Jesus says, "Whatever you ask in prayer, you will receive, if you have faith" (Matt. 21:22; cf. Mark 11:24; James 1:6–8; 5:14–15).

But God does not only want us to trust him. He also wants us to love him and have fellowship with him. This, then, is a second reason why God wants us to pray: Prayer brings us into deeper fellowship with God, and he loves us and delights in our fellowship with him.

A third reason God wants us to pray is that in prayer God allows us as creatures to be involved in activities that are eternally important. When we pray, the work of the kingdom is advanced. In this way, prayer gives us opportunity to be involved in a significant way in the work of the kingdom and thus gives expression to our greatness as creatures made in God's image.

B. The Effectiveness of Prayer

How exactly does prayer work? Does prayer not only do us good but also affect God and the world?

1. Prayer Changes the Way God Acts. James tells us, "You do not have, because you do not ask" (James 4:2). He implies that failure to ask deprives us of what God would otherwise have given to us. We pray, and God responds. Jesus also says, "Ask, and it will be given you; seek, and you will find; knock, and it will be opened to you. For every one who asks receives, and he who seeks finds, and to him who knocks it will be opened" (Luke 11:9–10). He makes a clear connection between seeking things from God and receiving them. When we ask, God responds.

We see this happening many times in the Old Testament. The Lord declared to Moses that he would destroy the people of Israel for their sin (Ex. 32:9–10): "But Moses besought the LORD his God, and said, 'O Lord. . . . Turn from your fierce wrath, and repent of this evil against your people'" (Ex. 32:11–12). Then we read, "And the LORD repented of the evil which he thought to do to his people" (Ex. 32:14). When God threatens to punish his people for their sins he declares, "If my people who are called by my name humble themselves, *and pray and seek my face,* and turn from their wicked ways, *then I will hear* from heaven, and will forgive their sin and heal their land" (2 Chron. 7:14). If and when God's people pray (with humility and repentance), *then* he will hear and forgive them. The prayers of his people clearly affect how God acts. Similarly, "If we confess our sins, he is faithful and just, and will forgive our sins and cleanse us from all unrighteousness" (1 John 1:9). We confess, and then he forgives.[1]

---

[1]Other examples of God answering prayer in Scripture are too numerous to comment on (Gen. 18:22–33; 32:26; Dan. 10:12; Amos 7:1–6; Acts 4:29–31; 10:31; 12:5–11, et al.).

If we were really convinced that prayer changes the way God acts, and that God does bring about remarkable changes in the world in response to prayer, as Scripture repeatedly teaches that he does, then we would pray much more than we do. If we pray little, it is probably because we do not really believe that prayer accomplishes much at all.

2. Effective Prayer Is Made Possible by Our Mediator, Jesus Christ. Because we are sinful and God is holy, we have no right on our own to enter into his presence. We need a mediator to come between us and God and to bring us into God's presence. Scripture clearly teaches, "There is one God, and there is one mediator between God and men, the man Christ Jesus" (1 Tim. 2:5).

But if Jesus is the only mediator between God and man, will God hear the prayers of those who do not trust in Jesus? The answer depends on what we mean by "hear." Since God is omniscient, he always "hears" in the sense that he is aware of the prayers made by unbelievers who do not come to him through Christ. God may even, from time to time, answer their prayers out of his mercy and in a desire to bring them to salvation through Christ. However, God has nowhere promised to respond to the prayers of unbelievers. The only prayers that he has promised to "hear" in the sense of listening with a sympathetic ear and undertaking to answer when they are made according to his will, are the prayers of Christians offered through the one mediator, Jesus Christ (cf. John 14:6).

Then what about believers in the Old Testament? How could they come to God through Jesus the mediator? The answer is that the work of Jesus as our mediator was foreshadowed by the sacrificial system and the offerings made by the priests in the temple (Heb. 7:23–28; 8:1–6; 9:1–14, et al.). There was no saving merit inherent in that system of sacrifices (Heb. 10:1–4), however. Through the sacrificial system believers were accepted by God only on the basis of the future work of Christ foreshadowed by that system (Rom. 3:23–26).

Jesus' activity as a mediator is especially seen in his work as a priest: he is our "great high priest who has passed through the heavens," one who "in every respect has been tempted as we are, yet without sin" (Heb. 4:14–15).

As recipients of the new covenant, we do not need to stay "outside the temple," as all believers except the priests were required to do under the old covenant. Nor do we need to stay outside of the "Holy of Holies" (Heb. 9:3), the inner room of the temple where God himself was enthroned above the ark of the covenant and where only the high priest could go, and he but once a year. But now, since Christ has died as our mediational High Priest (Heb. 7:26–27), he has gained for us boldness and access to the very presence of God. Therefore "we have confidence to enter *into the holy places* by the blood of Jesus" (Heb. 10:19, author's literal translation), that is, into the holy place and into the holy of holies, the very presence of God himself! We enter "by the new and living way" (Heb. 10:20) that Christ opened for us. The author of Hebrews concludes that since these things are true, "and since we have a great priest over the house of God, let us draw near with a true heart in full assurance of faith" (Heb. 10:22). In this way, Christ's mediational work gives us confidence to approach God in prayer.

We do not just come into God's presence as strangers, or as visitors, or as laypersons, but as priests—as people who belong in the temple and have a right and even a duty to be in the most sacred places in the temple. Using imagery from the ceremony for ordination of priests (see Ex. 29:4, 21), the author of Hebrews pictures all believers as having been ordained as priests to God and thus able to enter into his presence, for he says that we draw near "with our hearts sprinkled clean from an evil conscience and our bodies washed with pure water" (Heb. 10:22; cf. 1 Peter 2:9). Does all this make sense to a modern Christian? No one today goes to Jerusalem to enter the temple and there "draw near" to God. Even if we did go to Jerusalem, we would find no temple standing, since it was destroyed in A.D. 70. What then does the author of Hebrews mean when he says we enter into the "holy places"? He is talking about a reality in the unseen spiritual realm: With Christ as our Mediator we enter not into the earthly temple in Jerusalem, but into the true sanctuary, into "heaven itself," where Christ has gone "to appear in the presence of God on our behalf " (Heb. 9:24).

3. What Is Praying "in Jesus' Name"? Jesus says, "Whatever you ask *in my name,* I will do it, that the Father may be glorified in the Son; if you ask anything in my name, I will do it" (John 14:13–14). He also says that he chose his disciples "so that whatever you ask the Father *in my name,* he may give it to you" (John 15:16). Similarly, he says, "Truly, truly, I say to you, if you ask anything of the Father, he will give it to you in my name. Hitherto you have asked nothing *in my name;* ask, and you will receive, that your joy may be full" (John 16:23–24; cf. Eph. 5:20). But what does this mean?

Clearly it does not simply mean adding the phrase "in Jesus' name" after every prayer, because Jesus did not say, "If you ask anything and add the words 'in Jesus' name' after your prayer, I will do it." Jesus is not merely speaking about adding certain words as if these were a kind of magical formula that would give power to our prayers. In fact, none of the prayers recorded in Scripture have the phrase "in Jesus' name" at the end of them (see Matt. 6:9–13; Acts 1:24–25; 4:24–30;[2] 7:59; 9:13–14; 10:14; Rev. 6:10; 22:20).

To come in the name of someone means that another person has authorized us to come on his authority, not on our own. When Peter commands the lame man, "in the name of Jesus Christ of Nazareth, walk" (Acts 3:6), he is speaking on the authority of Jesus, not on his own authority. When the Sanhedrin asks the disciples, "By what power or *by what name* did you do this?" (Acts 4:7), they are asking, "By whose authority did you do this?" When Paul rebukes an unclean spirit "in the name of Jesus Christ" (Acts 16:18), he makes it clear that he is doing so on Jesus' authority, not his own. When Paul pronounces judgment "in the name of the Lord Jesus" (1 Cor. 5:4) on a church member who is guilty of immorality, he is acting with the authority of the Lord Jesus. *Praying in Jesus' name is therefore prayer made on his authorization.*

In a broader sense the "name" of a person in the ancient world represented the person himself and therefore all of his character. To have a "good name" (Prov. 22:1; Eccl. 7:1) was to have a good reputation. Thus, the name of Jesus represents all that he is, his entire character. This means that praying "in Jesus' name" is not only praying in his authority,

---

[2]In Acts 4:30 the phrase, "through the name of your holy servant Jesus," which appears at the end of a prayer, modifies the main clause immediately preceding it, "and signs and wonders are performed." It is not a general statement about the way in which the whole prayer is made.

but *also praying in a way that is consistent with his character,* that truly represents him and reflects his manner of life and his own holy will.[3] In this sense, to pray in Jesus' name comes close to the idea of praying "according to his will" (1 John 5:14–15).[4]

Does this mean that it is wrong to add "in Jesus' name" to the end of our prayers? It is certainly not wrong, as long as we understand what is meant by it, and that it is not necessary to do so. There may be some danger, however, if we add this phrase to every public or private prayer we make, for very soon it will become to people simply a formula to which they attach very little meaning and say without thinking about it. It may even begin to be viewed, at least by younger believers, as a sort of magic formula that makes prayer more effective. To prevent such misunderstanding, it would probably be wise to decide not to use the formula frequently and to express the same thought in other words, or simply in the overall attitude and approach we take toward prayer. For example, prayers could begin, "Father, we come to you in the authority of our Lord Jesus, your Son . . ." or, "Father, we do not come on our own merits but on the merits of Jesus Christ, who has invited us to come before you . . ." or, "Father, we thank you for forgiving our sins and giving us access to your throne by the work of Jesus your Son. . . ." At other times even these formal acknowledgments should not be thought necessary, so long as our hearts continually realize that it is our Savior who enables us to pray to the Father at all. Genuine prayer is conversation with a Person whom we know well, and who knows us. Such genuine conversation between persons who know each other never depends on the use of certain formulas or required words, but is a matter of sincerity in our speech and in our heart, a matter of right attitudes, and a matter of the condition of our spirit.

4. Should We Pray to Jesus and to the Holy Spirit? A survey of the prayers of the New Testament indicates that they are usually addressed neither to God the Son nor to the Holy Spirit, but to God the Father. Yet a mere count of such prayers may be misleading, for the majority of the prayers we have recorded in the New Testament are those of Jesus himself, who constantly prayed to God the Father, but of course did not pray to himself as God the Son. Moreover, in the Old Testament, the trinitarian nature of God was not so clearly revealed, and it is not surprising that we do not find much evidence of prayer addressed directly to God the Son or God the Holy Spirit before the time of Christ.

Though there is a clear pattern of prayer directly to God the Father through the Son (Matt. 6:9; John 16:23; Eph. 5:20) there are indications that prayer spoken directly to Jesus is also appropriate. The fact that it was Jesus himself who appointed all of the other apostles, suggests that the prayer in Acts 1:24 is addressed to him: "Lord, who knows the hearts of all men, show which one of these two you have chosen. . . ." The dying Stephen prays, "Lord Jesus, receive my spirit" (Acts 7:59). The conversation between Ananias

[3]In fact, Paul says that not just our prayers but everything we do is to be done in Jesus' name: "And whatever you do, in word or deed, *do everything in the name of the Lord Jesus,* giving thanks to God the Father through him" (Col. 3:17).

[4]Leon Morris says of John 14:13, "This does not mean simply using the name as a formula. It means that prayer is to be in accordance with all that the name stands for. It is prayer proceeding from faith in Christ, prayer that gives expression to a unity with all that Christ stands for, prayer which seeks to set forward Christ himself. And the purpose of it all is the glory of God" (*The Gospel According to John* [Grand Rapids: Eerdmans, 1971], p. 646).

and "the Lord" in Acts 9:10–16 is with Jesus, because in verse 17 Ananias tells Saul, "The Lord Jesus . . . has sent me that you may regain your sight." The prayer, "Our Lord, come!" (1 Cor. 16:22) is addressed to Jesus, as is the prayer in Revelation 22:20, "Come, Lord Jesus!" And Paul also prayed to "the Lord" in 2 Corinthians 12:8 concerning his thorn in the flesh.[5]

Moreover, the fact that Jesus is "a merciful and faithful high priest" (Heb. 2:17) who is able to "sympathize with our weaknesses" (Heb. 4:15), is viewed as an encouragement to us to come boldly before the "throne of grace" in prayer "that we may receive mercy and find grace to help in time of need" (Heb. 4:16). These verses must give us encouragement to come directly to Jesus in prayer, expecting that he will sympathize with our weaknesses as we pray.

There is therefore clear enough scriptural warrant to encourage us to pray not only to God the Father (which seems to be the primary pattern, and certainly follows the example that Jesus taught us in the Lord's Prayer), but also to pray directly to God the Son, our Lord Jesus Christ. Both are correct, and we may pray either to the Father or to the Son.

But should we pray to the Holy Spirit? Though no prayers directly addressed to the Holy Spirit are recorded in the New Testament, there is nothing that would forbid such prayer, for the Holy Spirit, like the Father and the Son, is fully God and is worthy of prayer and is powerful to answer our prayers. (Note also Ezekiel's invitation to the "breath" or "spirit" in Ezek. 37:9.) To say that we cannot pray to the Holy Spirit is really saying that we cannot talk to him or relate to him personally, which hardly seems right. He also relates to us in a personal way since he is a "Comforter" or "Counselor" (John 14:16, 26), believers "know him" (John 14:17), and he teaches us (cf. John 14:26), bears witness to us that we are children of God (Rom. 8:16), and can be grieved by our sin (Eph. 4:30). Moreover, the Holy Spirit exercises personal volition in the distribution of spiritual gifts, for he "continually distributes to each one individually as he wills" (1 Cor. 12:11, author's translation). Therefore, it does not seem wrong to pray directly to the Holy Spirit at times, particularly when we are asking him to do something that relates to his special areas of ministry or responsibility.[6] In fact, through the history of the church several well-used hymns have been prayers to the Holy Spirit. But this is not the New Testament pattern, and it should not become the dominant emphasis in our prayer life.

5. The Role of the Holy Spirit in Our Praying. In Romans 8:26–27 Paul says:

> Likewise the Spirit helps us in our weakness; for we do not know how to pray as we ought, but the Spirit himself intercedes for us with sighs too deep for words. And he who searches the hearts of men knows what is the mind of the Spirit, because the Spirit intercedes for the saints according to the will of God.

---

[5]The name Lord (Gk. kyrios) is used in Acts and the Epistles primarily to refer to the Lord Jesus Christ.

[6]J. I. Packer says, "Is it proper to pray to the Spirit? There is no example of doing this anywhere in Scripture, but since the Spirit is God, it cannot be wrong to invoke and address him if there is good reason to do so" (Keep in Step With the Spirit [Old Tappan, N.J.: Revell, 1984], p. 261).

Interpreters differ on whether the "sighs too deep for words" are the sighs the Holy Spirit himself makes or our own sighs and groans in prayer, which the Holy Spirit makes into effective prayer before God. It seems more likely that the "sighs" or "groans" here are our groans. When Paul says, "The Spirit helps us in our weakness" (v. 26), the word translated "helps" (Gk. *sunantilambanomai*) is the same word used in Luke 10:40, where Martha wants Mary to come and *help* her. The word does not indicate that the Holy Spirit prays instead of us, but that the Holy Spirit takes part with us and makes our weak prayers effective.[7] Thus, such sighing or groaning in prayer is best understood to be sighs or groans which we utter, expressing the desires of our heart and spirit, which the Holy Spirit then makes into effective prayer.

Related to this is the question of what it means to pray "in the Spirit." Paul says, "Pray at all times in the Spirit, with all prayer and supplication" (Eph. 6:18), and Jude says, "pray in the Holy Spirit" (Jude 20).[8] In order to understand this phrase, we should realize that the New Testament tells us that many different activities can be done "in the Holy Spirit." It is possible just to be "in the Spirit" as John was on the Lord's day (Rev. 1:10; cf. 4:2). And it is possible to rejoice in the Holy Spirit (Luke 10:21), to resolve or decide something in the Holy Spirit (Acts 19:21), to have one's conscience bear witness in the Holy Spirit (Rom. 9:1), to have access to God in the Holy Spirit (Eph. 2:18), and to love in the Holy Spirit (Col. 1:8). These expressions seem to refer to dwelling consciously in the presence of the Holy Spirit himself, a presence characterized by the Godlike qualities of power, love, joy, truth, holiness, righteousness, and peace. To pray "in the Holy Spirit," then, is to pray with the conscious awareness of God's presence surrounding us and sanctifying both us and our prayers.

C. Some Important Considerations in Effective Prayer

Scripture indicates a number of considerations that need to be taken into account if we would offer the kind of prayer that God desires from us.

1. Praying According to God's Will. John tells us, "This is the confidence which we have in him, that if we ask anything according to his will he hears us. And if we know that he hears us in whatever we ask, we know that we have obtained the requests made of him" (1 John 5:14–15). Jesus teaches us to pray, "Your will be done" (Matt. 6:10), and he himself gives us an example, by praying in the garden of Gethsemane, "Nevertheless, not as I will, but as you will" (Matt. 26:39).

---

[7]Other reasons why these sighs or groans are best understood to be our "groanings" in prayer are (1) v. 23 says that "we ourselves ... groan," using a verb (*stenazō*) that is cognate to the noun translated "sighs" (*stenagmos*) in v. 26; (2) such "groanings," which seem to imply a degree of distress or anguish, are appropriate for creatures (vv. 22, 23) but not for the Creator; and (3) v. 26b, which mentions "sighs too deep for words," explains the first clause in v. 26, which says that the Spirit "helps" us, not that the Spirit replaces our prayers.

The phrase "too deep for words" does not necessarily mean "silent or noiseless," but can rather mean "not able to be put into words."

[8]Some have thought this refers to speaking in tongues, since Paul calls speaking in tongues praying "with the spirit" (1 Cor. 14:15). But that is not a correct understanding, since in 1 Cor. 14:15 "the spirit" refers not to the Holy Spirit but to Paul's own human spirit: note the contrast between "my spirit" and "my mind" in v. 14.

But how do we know what God's will is when we pray? If the matter we are praying about is covered in a passage of Scripture in which God gives us a command or a direct declaration of his will, then the answer to this question is easy: His will is that his Word be obeyed and that his commands be kept. We are to seek for perfect obedience to God's moral will on earth so that God's will may be done "on earth as it is in heaven" (Matt. 6:10). For this reason knowledge of Scripture is a tremendous help in prayer, enabling us to follow the pattern of the first Christians who quoted Scripture when they prayed (see Acts 4:25–26). The regular reading and memorization of Scripture, cultivated over many years of a Christian's life, will increase the depth, power, and wisdom of his or her prayers. Jesus encourages us to have his words within us as we pray, for he says, "If you abide in me, *and my words abide in you,* ask whatever you will, and it shall be done for you" (John 15:7).

This means, for example, that if we are seeking wisdom in the making of an important decision, we do not have to wonder whether it is God's will that we receive wisdom to act rightly. Scripture has already settled that question for us, because there is a promise of Scripture that applies:

> If any of you lacks wisdom, let him ask God, who gives to all men generously and without reproaching, and it will be given him. But let him ask in faith, with no doubting, for he who doubts is like a wave of the sea that is driven and tossed by the wind. For that person must not suppose that a double-minded man, unstable in all his ways, will receive anything from the Lord. (James 1:5–8)

We should have great confidence that God will answer our prayer when we ask him for something that accords with a specific promise or command of Scripture like this. In such cases, we know what God's will is, because he has told us, and we simply need to pray believing that he will answer.

However, there are many other situations in life where we do not know what God's will is. We may not be sure, because no promise or command of Scripture applies, whether it is God's will that we get the job we have applied for, or win an athletic contest in which we are participating (a common prayer among children, especially), or be chosen to hold office in the church, and so on. In all of these cases, we should bring to bear as much of Scripture as we understand, perhaps to give us some general principles within which our prayer can be made. But beyond this, we often must admit that we simply do not know what God's will is. In such cases, we should ask him for deeper understanding and then pray for what seems best to us, giving reasons to the Lord why, in our present understanding of the situation, what we are praying for seems to be best. But it is always right to add, either explicitly or at least in the attitude of our heart, "Nevertheless, if I am wrong in asking this, and if this is not pleasing to you, then do as seems best in your sight," or, more simply, "If it is your will." Sometimes God will grant what we have asked. Sometimes he will give us deeper understanding or change our hearts so that we are led to ask something differently. Sometimes he will not grant our request at all but will simply indicate to us that we must submit to his will (see 2 Cor. 12:9–10).

Some Christians object that to add the phrase "if it is your will" to our prayers "destroys our faith." What it actually does is express uncertainty about whether what we pray for is God's will or not. And it is appropriate when we do not really know what God's will is. But at other times this would not be appropriate: to ask God to give us wisdom to make a decision and then say, "If it is your will to give me wisdom here" would be inappropriate, for it would be saying that we do not believe God meant what he said in James 1:5–8 when he told us to ask in faith and he would grant this request.[9]

Even when a command or promise of Scripture applies, there may be nuances of application that we do not at first fully understand. Therefore it is important in our prayer that we not only talk to God but also listen to him. We should frequently bring a request to God and then wait silently before him. In those times of waiting on the Lord (Pss. 27:14; 38:15; 130:5–6), God may change the desires of our heart, give us additional insight into the situation we are praying about, grant us additional insight into his Word, bring a passage of Scripture to mind that would enable us to pray more effectively, impart a sense of assurance of what his will is, or greatly increase our faith so that we are able to pray with much more confidence.

2. Praying With Faith. Jesus says, "Therefore I tell you, whatever you ask in prayer, believe that you have received it, and it will be yours" (Mark 11:24). Some translations vary, but the Greek text actually says, "believe that you *have received it.*" Later scribes who copied the Greek manuscripts and some later commentators have taken it to mean "believe that you *will* receive it." However, if we accept the text as it is in the earliest and best manuscripts ("believe that you have received it"), Jesus is apparently saying that when we ask for something, the kind of faith that will bring results is a settled assurance that when we prayed for something (or perhaps after we had been praying over a period of time), God agreed to grant our specific request. In the personal communion with God that occurs in genuine prayer, this kind of faith on our part could only come *as God gives us a sense of assurance that he has agreed to grant our request.* Of course, we cannot "work up" this kind of genuine faith by any sort of frenzied prayer or great emotional effort to try to make ourselves believe, nor can we force it upon ourselves by saying words we don't think to be true. This is something that only God can give us, and that he may or may not give us each time we pray. This assured faith will often come when we ask God for something and then quietly wait before him for an answer.

In fact, Hebrews 11:1 tells us that "faith is the *assurance* of things hoped for, the conviction of things not seen." Biblical faith is never a kind of wishful thinking or a vague hope that does not have any secure foundation to rest upon. It is rather trust in a person, God himself, based on the fact that we take him at his word and believe what he has said. This trust or dependence on God, when it has an element of assurance or confidence, is genuine biblical faith.

Several other passages encourage us to exercise faith when we pray. "Whatever you ask in prayer, you will receive, if you have faith," Jesus teaches his disciples (Matt. 21:22). And James tells us we are to "ask in faith, with no doubting" (James 1:6). Prayer is never

[9]To add, "If it is your will" to a prayer is still very different from not asking at all. If my children come and ask if I will take them to get ice cream, but then (feeling in a cooperative mood) add, "but only if you think it's right, Dad," that is still far removed from not asking me at all. If they had not asked, I would not have considered going to get ice cream. Once they ask, even with the qualification, I will often decide to take them.

wishful thinking, for it springs from trust in a personal God who wants us to take him at his word.

3. Obedience. Since prayer is a relationship with God as a person, anything in our lives that displeases him will be a hindrance to prayer. The psalmist says, "If I had cherished iniquity in my heart, the Lord would not have listened" (Ps. 66:18). Though "The sacrifice of the wicked is an abomination to the LORD," by contrast, "the prayer of the upright is his delight" (Prov. 15:8). Again we read that "the LORD . . . hears the prayer of the righteous" (Prov. 15:29). But God is not favorably disposed to those who reject his laws: "If one turns away his ear from hearing the law, even his prayer is an abomination" (Prov. 28:9).

The apostle Peter quotes Psalm 34 to affirm that "the eyes of the Lord are upon the righteous, and his ears are open to their prayer" (1 Peter 3:12). Since the previous verses encourage good conduct in everyday life, in speaking and turning away from evil and doing right, Peter is saying that God readily hears the prayers of those who live lives of obedience to him. Similarly, Peter warns husbands to "live considerately" with their wives, "in order that your prayers may not be hindered" (1 Peter 3:7). Likewise, John reminds us of the need for a clear conscience before God when we pray, for he says, "If our hearts do not condemn us, we have confidence before God; and we receive from him whatever we ask, because we keep his commandments and do what pleases him" (1 John 3:21–22).

Now this teaching must not be misunderstood. We do not need to be freed from sin completely before God can be expected to answer our prayers. If God only answered the prayers of sinless people, then no one in the whole Bible except Jesus would have had his or her prayers answered. When we come before God through his grace, we come cleansed by the blood of Christ (Rom. 3:25; 5:9; Eph. 2:13; Heb. 9:14; 1 Peter 1:2). Yet we must not neglect the biblical emphasis on personal holiness of life. Prayer and holy living go together. There is much grace in the Christian life, but growth in personal holiness is also a route to much greater blessing, and that is true with respect to prayer as well. The passages quoted teach that, all other things being equal, more exact obedience will lead to increased effectiveness in prayer (cf. Heb. 12:14; James 4:3–4).

4. Confession of Sins. Because our obedience to God is never perfect in this life, we continually depend on his forgiveness for our sins. Confession of sins is necessary in order for God to "forgive us" in the sense of restoring his day-by-day relationship with us (see Matt. 6:12; 1 John 1:9). It is good when we pray to confess all known sin to the Lord and to ask for his forgiveness. Sometimes when we wait on him, he will bring other sins to mind that we need to confess. With respect to those sins that we do not remember or are unaware of, it is appropriate to pray the general prayer of David, "Clear me from hidden faults" (Ps. 19:12).

Sometimes confessing our sins to other trusted Christians will bring an assurance of forgiveness and encouragement to overcome sin as well. James relates mutual confession to prayer, for in a passage discussing powerful prayer, James encourages us, "Therefore *confess your sins to one another,* and pray for one another, that you may be healed" (James 5:16).

5. Forgiving Others. Jesus says, "If you forgive men their trespasses, your heavenly Father also will forgive you; but if you do not forgive men their trespasses, neither will your Father forgive your trespasses" (Matt. 6:14–15). Similarly, Jesus says, "Whenever you stand praying, forgive, if you have anything against any one; so that your Father also who is in heaven may forgive you your trespasses" (Mark 11:25). Our Lord does not have in mind the initial experience of forgiveness we know when we are justified by faith, for that would not belong in a prayer that we pray every day (see Matt. 6:12 with vv. 14–15). He refers rather to the *day-by-day relationship with God* that we need to have restored when we have sinned and displeased him. In fact, Jesus commands us to build into our prayers a request that God forgive us in the same way that we have forgiven others who have harmed us (in the same "personal relationship" sense of "forgive"—that is, not holding a grudge or cherishing bitterness against another person or harboring any desire to harm them): "Forgive us our sins, *as we also have forgiven those who sin against us*" (Matt. 6:12, author's translation). If there are those whom we have not forgiven when we pray this prayer, then we are asking God not to restore a right relationship with us after we sin, in just the same way as we have refused to do so with others.

Since prayer presumes a relationship with God as a person, this is not surprising. If we have sinned against him and grieved the Holy Spirit (cf. Eph. 4:30), and the sin has not been forgiven, it interrupts our relationship with God (cf. Isa. 59:1–2). Until sin is forgiven and the relationship is restored prayer will, of course, be difficult. Moreover, if we have unforgiveness in our hearts against someone else, then we are not acting in a way that is pleasing to God or helpful to us. So God declares (Matt. 6:12, 14–15) that he will distance himself from us until we forgive others.

6. Humility. James tells us that "God opposes the proud, but gives grace to the humble" (James 4:6; also 1 Peter 5:5). Therefore he says, "Humble yourselves before the Lord and he will exalt you" (James 4:10). Humility is thus the right attitude to have in praying to God, whereas pride is altogether inappropriate.

Jesus' parable about the Pharisee and the tax collector illustrates this. When the Pharisee stood to pray, he was boastful: "God, I thank you that I am not like other men, extortioners, unjust, adulterers, or even like this tax collector. I fast twice a week, I give tithes of all that I get" (Luke 18:11–12). By contrast, the humble tax collector "would not even lift up his eyes to heaven, but beat his breast, saying, 'God, be merciful to me a sinner!'" (Luke 18:13). Jesus said that he "went down to his house justified," rather than the Pharisee, "for every one who exalts himself will be humbled, but he who humbles himself will be exalted" (Luke 18:14). This is why Jesus condemned those who "for a pretense make long prayers" (Luke 20:47) and those hypocrites who "love to stand and pray in the synagogues and at the street corners, that they may be seen by men" (Matt. 6:5).

God is rightly jealous for his own honor.[10] Therefore he is not pleased to answer the prayers of the proud who take honor to themselves rather than giving it to him. True humility before God, which will also be reflected in genuine humility before others, is necessary for effective prayer.

---

[10]See discussion of God's attribute of jealousy, pp. 95–96 above.

7. Continuing in Prayer Over Time. Just as Moses twice stayed on the mountain forty days before God for the people of Israel (Deut. 9:25–26; 10:10–11), and just as Jacob said to God, "I will not let you go, unless you bless me" (Gen. 32:26), so we see in Jesus' life a pattern of much time given to prayer. When great multitudes were following him, "he himself was often withdrawing into the wilderness regions and praying" (Luke 5:16, author's translation).[11] At another time, "*all night* he continued in prayer to God" (Luke 6:12).

Sometimes, as in the case of Moses and Jacob, prayer over a long period of time may be prayer for one specific item (cf. Luke 18:1–8). When we are earnestly seeking God for an answer to a specific prayer, we may in fact repeat the same request several times. Paul asked the Lord "three times" (2 Cor. 12:8) that his thorn in the flesh would be taken from him. Jesus himself, when he was in the garden of Gethsemane, asked the Father, "Remove this cup from me; yet not what I will, but what you will" (Mark 14:36). Then after he came and found the disciples sleeping, Jesus prayed again, making the same request in the same words: "And again he went away and prayed, *saying the same words*" (Mark 14:39). These are instances of earnest repetition in prayer for a deeply felt need. They are not examples of what Jesus forbids — the heaping up of "empty phrases" in the mistaken belief that "many words" will earn a hearing (Matt. 6:7).

There is also an element of a continual fellowship with God in praying over time. Paul calls on us to "pray constantly" (1 Thess. 5:17), and he encourages the Colossians to "continue steadfastly in prayer, being watchful in it with thanksgiving" (Col. 4:2). Such continual devotion to prayer even while about daily duties should characterize the life of every believer. The apostles are a telling example. They freed themselves from other responsibilities in order to give more time to prayer: "But *we will devote ourselves to prayer* and to the ministry of the word" (Acts 6:4).

8. Praying Earnestly. Jesus himself, who is our model for prayer, prayed earnestly. "In the days of his flesh, Jesus offered up prayers and supplications, with loud cries and tears, to him who was able to save him from death, and he was heard for his godly fear" (Heb. 5:7). In some of the prayers of Scripture, we can almost hear the great intensity with which the saints pour out their hearts before God. Daniel cries out, "O LORD, hear! O LORD, forgive! O LORD, listen and take action! For Thine own sake, O my God, do not delay, because Thy city and Thy people are called by Thy name" (Dan. 9:19 NASB). When God shows Amos the judgment that he is going to bring on his people, Amos pleads, "O Lord GOD, forgive, I beseech you! How can Jacob stand? He is so small!" (Amos 7:2).

In personal relationships, if we attempt to fake emotional intensity and put on an outward show of emotion that is not consistent with the feelings of our hearts, others involved will usually sense our hypocrisy at once and be put off by it. How much more is this true of God, who fully knows our hearts. Therefore, intensity and depth of emotional involvement in prayer should never be faked: we cannot fool God. Yet, if we truly begin to see situations as God sees them, if we begin to see the needs of a hurting

---

[11]The periphrastic imperfect tense here (Gk. *ēn hypochōrōn*) emphasizes, even more than a simple imperfect would, the repeated or habitual nature of the activity of withdrawing into the wilderness (see BDF, 353[1]).

and dying world as they really are, then it will be natural to pray with intense emotional involvement and to expect God, as a merciful Father, to respond to heartfelt prayer. And where such intensely felt prayer finds expression in group prayer meetings, Christians should certainly accept and be thankful for it, for it often indicates a deep work of the Holy Spirit in the heart of the person praying.

9. Waiting on the Lord. After crying out to God for help in distress, David says, "Wait for the LORD; be strong, and let your heart take courage; yea, wait for the LORD!" (Ps. 27:14). Similarly, he says, "But for you, O LORD, do I wait; it is you, O LORD my God, who will answer" (Ps. 38:15). The psalmist likewise says,

> I wait for the LORD, my soul waits,
>   and in his word I hope;
> my soul waits for the LORD
>   more than watchmen for the morning,
>   more than watchmen for the morning. (Ps. 130:5–6)

An analogy from human experience may help us to appreciate the benefit of waiting before the Lord for a response to prayer. If I wish to invite someone home for dinner, there are various ways I can do so. First, I can issue a vague, general invitation: "It would be nice to have you come to dinner sometime." Almost no one will come to dinner based on that kind of invitation alone. This is rather like the vague, general prayer, "God bless all my aunts and uncles and all the missionaries. Amen." Second, I could make a specific but hurried and impersonal kind of invitation: "Fred, can you come to dinner Friday night at 6:00?"—but as soon as the words are out of my mouth, I rush away leaving Fred with a puzzled expression on his face because I didn't allow him time to respond. This is like many of our prayer requests. We simply speak words to God as if the very act of voicing them, without any heart involvement in what we are saying, will itself bring an answer from God. But this kind of request forgets that prayer is a relationship between two persons, myself and God.

There is a third kind of invitation, one that is heartfelt, personal, and specific. After waiting until I'm sure I have Fred's full attention, I can look him directly in the eye and say, "Fred, Margaret and I would really love to have you come to dinner at our home this Friday at 6:00 p.m. Could you come?"—and then, continuing to look him in the eye, I wait silently and patiently while he decides what to answer. He knows from my facial expression, my tone of voice, my timing, and the setting in which I chose to talk to him that I am putting my whole self into this request, and that I am relating to him as a person and as a friend. Waiting patiently for an answer shows my earnestness, my sense of expectancy, and my respect for him as a person. This third kind of request is like that of the earnest Christian who comes before God, gains a sense of being in his presence, earnestly pours out a request to him, and then waits quietly for some sense of assurance of God's answer.

This is not to say that all our requests must be of this nature, or even that the first two kinds of requests are wrong. Indeed, in some situations we pray quickly because we have little time before we need an answer (see Neh. 2:4). And sometimes we do pray generally because we do not have more specific information about a situation, or because it is far removed from us or because of shortness of time. But the material in Scripture on earnest prayer and on waiting for the Lord, and the fact that prayer is personal communication between ourselves and God, do indicate that prayers such as the third kind of request are much deeper and will undoubtedly bring many more answers from God.

10. Praying in Private. Daniel went to his upper chamber and "got down upon his knees three times a day and prayed and gave thanks before his God" (Dan. 6:10).[12] Jesus frequently went out into solitary places to be alone to pray (Luke 5:16 et al.). And he also teaches us, "When you pray, go into your room and shut the door and pray to your Father who is in secret; and your Father who sees in secret will reward you" (Matt. 6:6). This statement is in the context of avoiding the error of the hypocrites who loved to pray at the street corners "that they may be seen by men" (Matt. 6:5). There is wisdom in Jesus' encouragement to pray in secret, not only that we might avoid hypocrisy, but also that we might not be distracted by the presence of other people and therefore modify our prayers to suit what we think they will expect to hear. When we are truly alone with God, in the privacy of a room to which we have "shut the door" (Matt. 6:6), then we can pour out our hearts to him.[13]

The need to pray in private may also have implications for small-group or church prayer meetings: when believers come together to seek the Lord earnestly about a specific matter, it is often helpful if they can be in the privacy of a home where the door is shut and they can collectively cry out to God. Apparently this was the way the early Christians prayed when they were making earnest supplication to God for the release of Peter from prison (see Acts 12:5, 12–16).

11. Praying With Others. Believers find strength in praying together with others. In fact, Jesus teaches us, "Again, I say to you, if two of you agree on earth about anything they ask, it will be done for them by my Father in heaven. For where two or three are gathered in my name, there am I in the midst of them" (Matt. 18:19–20).[14]

There are many other examples in Scripture where groups of believers prayed together or where one person led the entire congregation in prayer (note Solomon's prayer "in the presence of all the assembly of Israel" at the dedication of the temple in 1 Kings 8:22–53 or the prayer of the early church in Jerusalem when "they lifted their voices together to God" in Acts 4:24). Even the Lord's Prayer is put in the plural: It does not say, "Give me this day my daily bread" but "Give *us* this day *our* daily bread" and "Forgive *us our*

---

[12]Though Daniel's enemies saw him praying, it was only because they "came by agreement" and apparently spied on him.

[13]At this point we may also mention that Paul discusses a use of the gift of speaking in tongues during private prayer: "If I pray in a tongue, my spirit prays but my mind is unfruitful. What am I to do? I will pray with the spirit and I will pray with the mind also; I will sing with the spirit and I will sing with the mind also" (1 Cor. 14:14–15). When Paul says "my spirit prays," he is not referring to the Holy Spirit but to his own

human spirit, for the contrast is with "my mind." His own spirit is pouring out requests before God, and those requests are understood by God and result in personal edification: "He who speaks in a tongue edifies himself" (1 Cor. 14:4).

[14]Although the previous four verses (vv. 15–18) have to do with church discipline, the word "again" at the beginning of v. 19 signals a slight change in subject, and it is not inappropriate to take vv. 19–20 as a broader statement about prayer in general in the context of the church.

sins" and "Lead *us* not into temptation but deliver *us* from evil" (Matt. 6:11 – 13, author's translation). Praying with others, then, is also right and often increases our faith and the effectiveness of our prayers.

12. Fasting. Prayer is often connected with fasting in Scripture. Sometimes these are occasions of intense supplication before God, as when Nehemiah, on hearing of the ruin of Jerusalem, "continued *fasting* and praying before the God of Heaven" (Neh. 1:4), or when the Jews learned of the decree of Ahasuerus that they would all be killed, and "there was great mourning among the Jews, with *fasting* and weeping and lamenting" (Esth. 4:3), or when Daniel sought the LORD "by prayer and supplications with *fasting* and sackcloth and ashes" (Dan. 9:3). At other times fasting is connected with repentance, for God says to the people who have sinned against him, " 'Yet even now,' says the LORD, 'return to me with all your heart, with fasting, with weeping, and with mourning' " (Joel 2:12).

In the New Testament, Anna was "worshiping with *fasting* and prayer night and day" (Luke 2:37) in the temple, and the church at Antioch was "worshiping the Lord and *fasting*" when the Holy Spirit said, "Set apart for me Barnabas and Saul for the work to which I have called them" (Acts 13:2). The church responded with further fasting and prayer before sending Barnabas and Saul on their first missionary journey: "Then after fasting and praying they laid their hands on them and sent them off " (Acts 13:3). In fact, fasting was a routine part of seeking the Lord's guidance with regard to church officers, for on Paul's first missionary journey, we read that he and Barnabas, as they traveled back through the churches they had founded, "appointed elders for them in every church, with prayer and fasting" (Acts 14:23).

So fasting appropriately accompanied prayer in many situations: in times of intensive intercession, repentance, worship, and seeking of guidance. In each of these situations, several benefits come from fasting, all of which affect our relationship to God: (1) Fasting increases our sense of humility and dependence on the Lord (for our hunger and physical weakness continually remind us how we are not really strong in ourselves but need the Lord). (2) Fasting allows us to give more attention to prayer (for we are not spending time on eating), and (3) it is a continual reminder that, just as we sacrifice some personal comfort to the Lord by not eating, so we must continually sacrifice all of ourselves to him.[15] Moreover, (4) fasting is a good exercise in self-discipline, for as we refrain from eating food, which we would ordinarily desire, it also strengthens our ability to refrain from sin, to which we might otherwise be tempted to yield. If we train ourselves to accept the small "suffering" of fasting willingly, we will be better able to accept other suffering for the sake of righteousness (cf. Heb. 5:8; 1 Peter 4:1 – 2). (5) Fasting also heightens spiritual and mental alertness and a sense of God's presence as we focus less on the material things of this world (such as food) and as the energies of our body are freed from digesting and processing food. This enables us to focus on

---

[15]Similar reasons (devoting more time to prayer and giving up some personal pleasure) probably explain Paul's permission to married couples to give up sexual relations "by mutual consent and for a time, so that you may devote yourselves to prayer" (1 Cor. 7:5 NIV).

eternal spiritual realities that are much more important.[16] Finally, (6) fasting expresses earnestness and urgency in our prayers: if we continued to fast, eventually we would die. Therefore, in a symbolic way, fasting says to God that we are prepared to lay down our lives that the situation be changed rather than that it continue. In this sense fasting is especially appropriate when the spiritual state of the church is low.

> "Yet even now," says the LORD,
> > "return to me with all your heart,
> > with fasting, with weeping, and with mourning;
> > > and rend your hearts and not your garments." (Joel 2:12–13a)

Though the New Testament does not specifically require that we fast, or set special times when we must fast, Jesus certainly assumes that we will fast, for he says to his disciples, "And *when* you fast" (Matt. 6:16). Moreover, Jesus also says, "The days will come, when the bridegroom is taken away from them, and then they will fast" (Matt. 9:15). He is the Bridegroom, we are his disciples, and during this present church age he has been "taken" away from us until the day he returns. Most western Christians do not fast, but, if we were willing to fast more regularly—even for one or two meals—we might be surprised how much more spiritual power and strength we would have in our lives and in our churches.

13. What About Unanswered Prayer? We must begin by recognizing that as long as God is God and we are his creatures, there must be some unanswered prayers. This is because God keeps hidden his own wise plans for the future, and even though people pray, many events will not come about until the time that God has decreed. The Jews prayed for centuries for the Messiah to come, and rightly so, but it was not until "the time had fully come" that "God sent forth his Son" (Gal. 4:4). The souls of martyrs in heaven, free from sin, cry out for God to judge the earth (Rev. 6:10), but God does not immediately answer; rather he tells them to rest a little longer (Rev. 6:11). It is clear that there can be long periods of delay during which prayers go unanswered, because the people praying do not know God's wise timing.

Prayer will also be unanswered because we do not always know how to pray as we ought (Rom. 8:26), we do not always pray according to God's will (James 4:3), and we do not always ask in faith (James 1:6–8). And sometimes we think that one solution is best, but God has a better plan, even to fulfill his purpose through suffering and hardship. Joseph no doubt prayed earnestly to be rescued from the pit and from being carried off into slavery in Egypt (Gen. 37:23–36), but many years later he found how in all of these events "God meant it for good" (Gen. 50:20).

[16]In Mark 9:29, when the disciples asked why they could not drive out a certain demon, Jesus replied, "This kind cannot be driven out by anything but prayer." Many early and quite reliable Greek manuscripts and several early manuscripts in other languages read "by prayer *and fasting.*" In either case, it cannot mean prayer that is spoken at the time the demon is being cast out, for Jesus simply cast out the demon with a word and did not engage in an extended time of prayer. It must mean rather that the disciples had not previously been spending enough time in prayer and that their spiritual strength was weak. Therefore the "fasting" that is mentioned in many ancient manuscripts fits the pattern of an activity that increases one's spiritual strength and power.

When we face unanswered prayer, we join the company of Jesus, who prayed, "Father, if you are willing, remove this cup from me; nevertheless not my will, but yours, be done" (Luke 22:42). We join also the company of Paul, who asked the Lord "three times" that his thorn in the flesh be removed, but it was not; rather, the Lord told him, "My grace is sufficient for you, for my power is made perfect in weakness" (2 Cor. 12:8–9). We join the company of David, who prayed for his son's life to be saved, but it was not, so he "went into the house of the Lord, and worshiped" and said of his son, "I shall go to him, but he will not return to me" (2 Sam. 12:20, 23). We join the company of the martyrs throughout history who prayed for deliverance that did not come, for they "loved not their lives even unto death" (Rev. 12:11).

When prayer remains unanswered we must continue to trust God, who "causes all things to work together for good" (Rom. 8:28 NASB), and to cast our cares on him, knowing that he continually cares for us (1 Peter 5:7). We must keep remembering that he will give strength sufficient for each day (Deut. 33:25) and that he has promised, "I will never fail you nor forsake you" (Heb. 13:5; cf. Rom. 8:35–39).

We also must continue to pray. Sometimes an answer, long awaited, will suddenly be given, as it was when Hannah after many years bore a child (1 Sam. 1:19–20), or when Simeon saw with his own eyes the long-expected Messiah come to the temple (Luke 2:25–35).

But sometimes prayers will remain unanswered in this life. At times God will answer those prayers after the believer dies. At other times he will not, but even then the faith expressed in those prayers and their heartfelt expressions of love for God and the people he has made will still ascend as a pleasing incense before God's throne (Rev. 5:8; 8:3–4) and will result in "praise and glory and honor at the revelation of Jesus Christ" (1 Peter 1:7).

D. Praise and Thanksgiving

Praise and thanksgiving to God are essential elements of prayer. The model prayer that Jesus left us begins with a word of praise: "Hallowed be your name" (Matt. 6:9). And Paul tells the Philippians, "in everything by prayer and supplication *with thanksgiving* let your requests be made known to God" (Phil. 4:6), and the Colossians, "Continue steadfastly in prayer, being watchful in it *with thanksgiving*" (Col. 4:2). Thanksgiving, like every other aspect of prayer, should not be a mechanical mouthing of a "thank you" to God, but the expression of words that reflect the thankfulness of our hearts. Moreover, we should never think that thanking God for the answer to something we ask for can somehow force God to give it to us, for that changes the prayer from a genuine, sincere request to a demand that assumes we can make God do what we want him to do. Such a spirit in our prayers really denies the essential nature of prayer as dependence on God.

By contrast, the kind of thanksgiving that appropriately accompanies prayer must express thankfulness to God for all circumstances, for every event of life that he allows to come to us. When we join our prayers with humble, childlike thanksgiving to God "in all circumstances" (1 Thess. 5:18), they will be acceptable to God.

QUESTIONS FOR PERSONAL APPLICATION

1. Do you often have difficulty with prayer? What things in this chapter have been helpful to you in this regard?

2. When have you known the most effective times of prayer in your own life? What factors contributed to making those times more effective? Which other factors need most attention in your prayer life? What can you do to strengthen each of these areas?

3. How does it help and encourage you (if it does) when you pray together with other Christians?

4. Have you ever tried waiting quietly before the Lord after making an earnest prayer request? If so, what has been the result?

5. Do you have a regular time each day for private Bible reading and prayer? Are you sometimes easily distracted and turned aside to other activities? If so, how can distractions be overcome?

6. Do you enjoy praying? Why or why not?

SPECIAL TERMS

faith   prayer
"in Jesus' name"   waiting for the Lord

BIBLIOGRAPHY

Bennett, Arthur, ed. *The Valley of Vision: A Collection of Puritan Prayer and Devotions.* Edinburgh and Carlisle, Pa.: Banner of Truth, 1975.

Bounds, E. M. *Power Through Prayer.* Grand Rapids: Baker, 1963.

Brother Lawrence. *The Practice of the Presence of God.* New York: Revell, 1895.

Carson, D. A., ed. *Teach Us To Pray: Prayer in the Bible and the World.* Grand Rapids: Baker, and Exeter: Paternoster, 1990.

Clowney, Edmund. *Christian Meditation.* Philadelphia: Presbyterian and Reformed, 1979.

_____. "Prayer, Theology of." In *NDT,* pp. 526–27.

Forsyth, P. T. *The Soul of Prayer.* Grand Rapids: Eerdmans, 1967 (reprint).

Foster, Richard J. *Celebration of Discipline: The Path to Spiritual Growth.* San Francisco: Harper and Row, 1988.

Hallesby, O. *Prayer.* Trans. by Clarence J. Carlsen. Minneapolis: Augsburg, 1959 (reprint).

Houston, James. *The Transforming Friendship.* Oxford and Batavia, Ill.: Lion, 1989.

Hunter, W. Bingham. *The God Who Hears.* Downers Grove, Ill.: InterVarsity Press, 1986.

Kelly, Thomas R. *A Testament of Devotion.* New York: Harper, 1941.

Law, William. *A Serious Call to a Devout and Holy Life.* Philadelphia: Westminster, 1948 (reprint).

M'Intyre, D. M. *The Hidden Life of Prayer*. Minneapolis: Bethany Fellowship Press, 1962 (reprint). (The author's name is sometimes spelled MacIntyre in other editions of this book.)

Murray, Andrew. *The Ministry of Intercessory Prayer*. Minneapolis: Bethany House, 1981 (reprint; originally published in 1897 as *The Ministry of Intercession*).

Ortlund, Raymond C., Jr. *A Passion for God: Prayers and Meditations on the Book of Romans*. Wheaton, Ill.: Crossway, 1994.

Prince, Derek. *Shaping History Through Prayer and Fasting*. Old Tappan, N.J.: Fleming H. Revell, 1973.

Smith, David R. *Fasting: A Neglected Discipline*. Fort Washington, Pa.: Christian Literature Crusade, 1969.

Spear, Wayne. *The Theology of Prayer*. Grand Rapids: Baker, 1979.

Thomas à Kempis. *The Imitation of Christ*. Grand Rapids: Baker, 1973 (reprint).

Unknown Christian. *The Kneeling Christian*. Grand Rapids: Zondervan, 1945.

Wallis, Arthur. *God's Chosen Fast: A Spiritual and Practical Guide to Fasting*. Fort Washington, Pa.: Christian Literature Crusade, 1987.

White, John. *Daring to Draw Near*. Downers Grove, Ill.: InterVarsity Press, 1977.

Willard, Dallas. *The Spirit of the Disciplines*. San Francisco: Harper and Row, 1988.

SCRIPTURE MEMORY PASSAGE

Hebrews 4:14–16: *Since then we have a great high priest who has passed through the heavens, Jesus, the Son of God, let us hold fast our confession. For we have not a high priest who is unable to sympathize with our weaknesses, but one who in every respect has been tempted as we are, yet without sin. Let us then with confidence draw near to the throne of grace, that we may receive mercy and find grace to help in time of need.*

HYMN

"From Every Stormy Wind"

From ev'ry stormy wind that blows,
from ev'ry swelling tide of woes,
There is a calm, a sure retreat;
'tis found beneath the Mercy Seat.

There is a place where Jesus sheds
the oil of gladness on our heads,
A place than all besides more sweet;
it is the blood-stained Mercy Seat.

There is a spot where spirits blend,
where friend holds fellowship with friend,

Tho' sundered far; by faith they meet
    around the common Mercy Seat.

Ah, whither could we flee for aid,
    when tempted, desolate, dismayed,
Or how the hosts of hell defeat,
    had suff'ring saints no Mercy Seat?

There, there on eagle wings we soar,
    and time and sense seem all no more,
And heav'n comes down our souls to greet,
    and glory crowns the Mercy Seat.

O may my hand forget her skill,
    my tongue be silent, cold, and still,
This bounding heart forget to beat,
    if I forget the Mercy Seat.

AUTHOR: HUGH STOWELL, 1828, 1831

12

ANGELS

What are angels? Why did God create them?

EXPLANATION AND SCRIPTURAL BASIS

A. What Are Angels?

We may define angels as follows: *Angels are created, spiritual beings with moral judgment and high intelligence, but without physical bodies.*

1. Created Spiritual Beings. Angels have not always existed; they are part of the universe that God created. In a passage that refers to angels as the "host" of heaven (or "armies of heaven"), Ezra says, "You are the LORD, you alone; you have made heaven, the heaven of heavens, *with all their host* . . . and the host of heaven worships you" (Neh. 9:6; cf. Ps. 148:2, 5). Paul tells us that God created all things "visible and invisible" through Christ and for him, and then specifically includes the angelic world with the phrase "whether thrones or dominions or principalities or authorities" (Col. 1:16).

That angels exercise moral judgement is seen in the fact that some of them sinned and fell from their positions (2 Peter 2:4; Jude 6; see chapter 13). Their high intelligence is seen throughout Scripture as they speak to people (Matt. 28:5; Acts 12:6–11, et al.) and sing praise to God (Rev. 4:11; 5:11).

Since angels are "spirits" (Heb. 1:14) or spiritual creatures, they do not ordinarily have physical bodies (Luke 24:39). Therefore they cannot usually be seen by us unless God gives us a special ability to see them (Num. 22:31; 2 Kings 6:17; Luke 2:13). In their ordinary activities of guarding and protecting us (Ps. 34:7; 91:11; Heb. 1:14), and joining with us in worship to God (Heb. 12:22), they are invisible. However, from time to time angels took on a bodily form to appear to various people in Scripture (Matt. 28:5; Heb. 13:2).

2. Other Names for Angels. Scripture sometimes uses other terms for angels, such as "sons of God" (Job 1:6; 2:1), "holy ones" (Ps. 89:5, 7), "spirits" (Heb. 1:14), "watchers" (Dan. 4:13, 17, 23), "thrones," "dominions," "principalities," and "authorities" (Col. 1:16).

3. Other Kinds of Heavenly Beings. There are three other specific types of heavenly beings named in Scripture. Whether we think of these as special types of "angels" (in a broad sense of the term), or whether we think of them as heavenly beings distinct from angels, they are nonetheless created spiritual beings who serve and worship God.

a. The "Cherubim":[1] The cherubim were given the task of guarding the entrance to the Garden of Eden (Gen. 3:24), and God himself is frequently said to be enthroned on the cherubim or to travel with the cherubim as his chariot (Ps. 18:10; Ezek. 10:1–22). Over the ark of the covenant in the Old Testament were two golden figures of cherubim with their wings stretched out above the ark, and it was there that God promised to come to dwell among his people: "There I will meet with you, and from above the mercy seat, from between the two cherubim that are upon the ark of testimony, I will speak with you of all that I will give you in commandment for the people of Israel" (Ex. 25:22; cf. vv. 18–21).

b. The "Seraphim":[2] Another group of heavenly beings, the seraphim, are mentioned only in Isaiah 6:2–7, where they continually worship the Lord and call to one another, "Holy, holy, holy is the LORD of hosts; the whole earth is full of his glory" (Isa. 6:3).

c. The Living Creatures: Both Ezekiel and Revelation tell us of yet other kinds of heavenly beings known as "living creatures" around God's throne (Ezek. 1:5–14; Rev. 4:6–8).[3] With their appearances like a lion, an ox, a man, and an eagle, they are the mightiest representatives of various parts of God's entire creation (wild beasts, domesticated animals, human beings, and birds), and they worship God continually: "Day and night they never cease to sing, 'Holy, holy, holy, is the Lord God Almighty, who was and is and is to come!'" (Rev. 4:8)

4. Rank and Order Among the Angels. Scripture indicates that there is rank and order among the angels. One angel, Michael, is called an "archangel" in Jude 9, a title that indicates rule or authority over other angels. He is called "one of the chief princes" in Daniel 10:13. Michael also appears to be a leader in the angelic army: "Now war arose in heaven, Michael and his angels fighting against the dragon; and the dragon and his angels fought, but they were defeated" (Rev. 12:7–8). And Paul tells us that the Lord will return from heaven "with the archangel's call" (1 Thess. 4:16). Whether this refers to Michael as the only archangel, or whether there are other archangels, Scripture does not tell us.

5. Names of Specific Angels. Only two angels are specifically named in Scripture.[4] Michael is mentioned in Jude 9 and Revelation 12:7–8 as well as in Daniel 10:13, 21,

---

[1] In Hebrew, the word *cherub* is singular, while the plural form is *cherubim*.

[2] The Hebrew word *seraph* is singular, while *seraphim* is the plural form.

[3] The descriptions differ somewhat between Ezekiel and Revelation but also have many similarities. It is difficult to tell whether these are different groups of creatures or whether those in Revelation have been transformed from the form they took in Ezekiel's vision.

[4] I have not counted Satan here, who is a fallen angel, and who is sometimes called by other names as well. (See chapter 13, on Satan and demons.)

where he is called "Michael, one of the chief princes" (v. 13). The angel Gabriel is mentioned in Daniel 8:16 and 9:21 as a messenger who comes from God to speak to Daniel. Gabriel is also identified as God's messenger to Zechariah and Mary in Luke 1: the angel answers Zechariah, "I am Gabriel, who stand in the presence of God" (Luke 1:19). Then we read, "In the sixth month the angel Gabriel was sent from God to a city of Galilee named Nazareth, to a virgin . . . and the virgin's name was Mary" (Luke 1:26–27).

6. Only One Place at One Time. Scripture frequently represents angels as traveling from one place to another, as in the verse mentioned above where Gabriel "was sent from God to a city of Galilee named Nazareth" (Luke 1:26). This is made explicit when an angel comes to Daniel and says:

> I have come because of your words. The prince of the kingdom of Persia withstood me twenty-one days; but Michael, one of the chief princes, came to help me, so I left him there with the prince of the kingdom of Persia and came to make you understand what is to befall your people in the latter days. (Dan. 10:12–14)

The idea that an angel can be in only one place at one time is consistent with the fact that angels are created beings. Unlike God, who is omnipresent, they are finite creatures and therefore limited to being in one place at one time, as is everything else that God has created.[5]

7. How Many Angels Are There? Though Scripture does not give us a figure for the number of angels God created, it is apparently a very great number. We read that God on Mount Sinai "came from the *ten thousands of holy ones,* with flaming fire at his right hand" (Deut. 33:2). We also learn that, "the chariots of God are tens of thousands and thousands of thousands" (Ps. 68:17 NIV). When we come to worship we come into the presence of "*innumerable* angels" (Heb. 12:22).[6] Their number is even more strikingly emphasized in Revelation 5:11, where John says, "I heard around the throne and the living creatures and the elders the voice of many angels, numbering *myriads of myriads* and thousands of thousands." This expression indicates an amazingly large number (from a human standpoint)—an innumerable assembly of angelic beings praising God.

8. Do People Have Individual Guardian Angels? Scripture clearly tells us that God sends angels for our protection: "He will give his angels charge of you to guard you in all your ways. On their hands they will bear you up, lest you dash your foot against a stone" (Ps. 91:11–12). But some people have gone beyond this idea of general protection and

---

[5]Nevertheless, it seems that a very large number of angels can be in one place at the same time, at least if the example of evil angels or demons is a good indication of this fact. When Jesus asked the demonic forces in the Gadarene demoniac, "What is your name?" he said, "Legion"; for "many demons had entered him" (Luke 8:30). Even if we do not understand this literally to mean a number equal to a legion of the Roman army (3,000–6,000 men), and even if we allow that since Satan is the father of lies, the demons in the man could be greatly exaggerating, Luke still says that "many demons had entered him."

[6]The Greek term *myrias* ("myriad") is an expression referring to "a very large number, not exactly defined" (BAGD, p. 529). (See also Jer. 33:22.)

wondered if God gives a specific "guardian angel" for each individual in the world, or at least for each Christian. Support for this idea has been found in Jesus' words about little children, "in heaven *their angels* always behold the face of my Father who is in heaven" (Matt. 18:10). However, our Lord may simply be saying that angels who are assigned the task of protecting little children have ready access to God's presence. (To use an athletic analogy, the angels may be playing "zone" rather than "man-on-man" defense.)[7] When the disciples in Acts 12:15 say that Peter's "angel" must be knocking at the door, this does not necessarily imply belief in an individual guardian angel. It could be that an angel was guarding or caring for Peter just at that time. There seems to be, therefore, no convincing support for the idea of individual "guardian angels" in the text of Scripture.

9. Angels Do Not Marry. Jesus taught that in the resurrection people "neither marry nor are given in marriage, but are like angels in heaven" (Matt. 22:30; cf. Luke 20:34–36). This would suggest that angels do not have the kind of family relationships that exist among human beings. Scripture is otherwise silent on this point, so it is wise not to attempt to engage in speculation.[8]

10. The Power of Angels. Angels apparently have very great power. They are called "you mighty ones who do his word" (Ps. 103:20) and "powers" (cf. Eph. 1:21) and "dominions" and "authorities" (Col. 1:16). Angels are seemingly "greater in might and power" than rebellious human beings (2 Peter 2:11; cf. Matt. 28:2). At least for the time of their earthly existence, human beings are made "lower than the angels" (Heb. 2:7). Though the power of angels is great, it is certainly not infinite, but it is used to battle against the

---

[7]Another possibility is that "angel" in Matt. 18:10 and in Acts 12:15 (where the disciples think that Peter's "angel" is knocking at the gate) means not an angelic being but the "spirit" of the person who has died: for a defense of this view see B. B. Warfield, "The Angels of Christ's 'Little Ones,'-" in *Selected Shorter Writings*, ed. John E. Meeter (Nutley, N.J.: Presbyterian and Reformed, 1970), 1:253–66; also D. A. Carson, "Matthew," *EBC*, 8:400–401.

The problem with this interpretation is that not one clear example has been found where the word *angel* (Gk. *angelos*) means "spirit of a person who has died." Warfield (pp. 265–66), followed by Carson, quotes two supposed examples from extrabiblical Jewish literature, 1 Enoch 51:4 and 2 Baruch 51:5, 12. But these texts are not convincing: 1 Enoch 51:4 simply says, "And the faces of [all] the angels in heaven shall be lighted up with joy" (R. H. Charles, *The Apocrypha and Pseudepigrapha of the Old Testament*, 2 vols. [Oxford: Clarendon Press, 1913], 2:219), but does not say that people will become angels. 2 Baruch 51:5 states that the righteous will be transformed "into the splendor of angels" (Charles, 2:508), but this simply means that they will have brightness like the angels, not that they will become angels.

In two related passages, 2 Baruch 51:12 states that the righteous will have excellency "surpassing that in the angels,"

and 2 Baruch 51:10 says that "they shall be made like unto the angels" (Charles, 2:509), but these texts do not say that people will become angels, either. Moreover, since no extant Greek text is available for any of these three passages (1 Enoch is an Ethiopic text with some Greek fragments and 2 Baruch is a Syriac text), they are not useful for determining the meaning of the Greek word *angelos*.

Warfield also cites *Acts of Paul and Thecla*, ed. Tischendorf, p. 42, para. 5, ad finem, as saying, "Blessed are they that fear God, for they shall become angels of God," but the text dates from the late second century A.D. (*ODCC*, p. 1049) and is an unreliable source of information about what the early church believed or what the New Testament teaches.

[8]We should note that this statement of Jesus is given in answer to the Sadducees' question about a woman who had been married seven times, and that Jesus said that their question showed lack of knowledge both of Scripture and of "the power of God" (Matt. 22:29). Jesus' answer, therefore, should comfort us and not trouble us: we should contemplate heaven not with sorrow at the anticipation of diminished interpersonal relationships, but with joy at the prospect of enriched relationships. (See chapter 13, p. 297, for a discussion of the "sons of God" in Gen. 6:2, 4.)

evil demonic powers under the control of Satan (Dan. 10:13; Rev. 12:7–8; 20:1–3).[9] Nonetheless, when the Lord returns, we will be raised to a position higher than that of angels (1 Cor. 6:3; see section C.1, below).

11. Who Is the Angel of the Lord? Several passages of Scripture, especially in the Old Testament, speak of the angel of the Lord in a way that suggests that he is God himself taking on a human form to appear briefly to various people in the Old Testament.

In some passages "*the* angel of the LORD" (not "*an* angel of the LORD") is spoken of as the Lord himself. So "the angel of the LORD" who found Hagar in the wilderness promises her, "I will so greatly multiply your descendants that they cannot be numbered for multitude" (Gen. 16:10), and Hagar responds by calling "the name of *the* LORD *who spoke to her,* 'You are a God of seeing'" (Gen. 16:13). Similarly, when Abraham is about to sacrifice his son Isaac, "the angel of the LORD" calls to him from heaven and says, "Now I know that you fear God, seeing you have not withheld your son, your only son, *from me*" (Gen. 22:12). When "the angel of God" appeared to Jacob in a dream, he said, "I am the God of Bethel, where you anointed a pillar and made a vow to me" (Gen. 31:11, 13). Again, when "the angel of the LORD" appeared to Moses in a flame of fire out of the midst of a bush, he then said, "*I am the God of your father,* the God of Abraham, the God of Isaac, and the God of Jacob" (Ex. 3:2, 6). These are clear instances of the angel of the Lord or the angel of God appearing as God himself, perhaps more specifically as God the Son taking on a human body for a short time in order to appear to human beings.

At other times the angel of the Lord seems to be distinguished from God (see 2 Sam. 24:16; Ps. 34:7; Zech. 1:11–13), and passages that mention "*an* angel of the Lord" (e.g., Luke 1:11) usually indicate an angel sent by God.

B. When Were Angels Created?

All the angels must have been created before the seventh day of creation, for we read, "Thus the heavens and the earth were finished, and all the host of them" (Gen. 2:1, understanding "host" to be the heavenly creatures that inhabit God's universe). Even more explicit than this is the statement, "In six days the LORD made heaven and earth, the sea, *and all that is in them,* and rested the seventh day" (Ex. 20:11). Therefore all the angels were created at least by the sixth day of creation.

But can we be any more specific? There may be a hint at the creation of angelic beings on the first day of creation when we read that "in the beginning God created the heavens and the earth" (Gen. 1:1), and then immediately after we read that "the *earth* was without form and void" (Gen. 1:2), but with no mention of the heavens in this second verse. This may suggest that the uninhabitable state of the earth is contrasted with the heavens where, perhaps, God had already created angelic beings and assigned them various roles and orders. This idea is made more plausible when we read that "the morning stars sang together, and all the sons of God shouted for joy" at the time when God laid

---

[9]Whether the angels who sinned lost some of their power when they rebelled against God and became demons, or whether their power is still the same as it was when they were angels, Scripture does not tell us.

the "cornerstone" of the earth and sunk its "bases" in the process of forming or founding it (Job 38:6–7). If the angels ("the sons of God") shouted for joy when God was making the earth inhabitable, this could imply that God created the angelic beings early on the first day.

However, since we have only hints in Scripture, we must remain content with the fact that God has not given us much information about the time of the creation of the angels. Further speculation, apart from clear scriptural data, would seem to be useless. "The secret things belong to the LORD our God; but the things that are revealed belong to us and to our children for ever, that we may do all the words of this law" (Deut. 29:29).

Some time before Satan tempted Eve in the garden (Gen. 3:1), a number of angels sinned and rebelled against God (2 Peter 2:4; Jude 6). This event occurred apparently after the sixth day of creation when "God saw everything that he had made, and behold, it was very good" (Gen. 1:31), but beyond this, Scripture gives us no further information.

C. The Place of Angels in God's Purpose

1. Angels Show the Greatness of God's Love and Plan for Us. Human beings and angels (using the term broadly) are the only moral, highly intelligent creatures that God has made. Therefore we can understand much about God's plan and love for us when we compare ourselves with angels.

The first distinction to be noted is that angels are never said to be made "in the image of God," while human beings are several times said to be in God's image (Gen. 1:26–27; 9:6). Since being in the image of God means to be like God, it seems fair to conclude that we are more like God even than the angels are.

This is supported by the fact that God will someday give us authority over angels, to judge them: "Do you not know that *we are to judge angels?*" (1 Cor. 6:3). Though we are "for a little while lower than the angels" (Heb. 2:7), when our salvation is complete we will be exalted above angels and rule over them. In fact, even now, angels already serve us: "Are they not all ministering spirits sent forth *to serve,* for the sake of those who are to obtain salvation?" (Heb. 1:14).

The ability of human beings to bear children like themselves (Adam "became the father of a son in his own likeness, after his image," Gen. 5:3) is another element of our superiority to angels, who apparently cannot bear children (cf. Matt. 22:30; Luke 20:34–36).

Angels also demonstrate the greatness of God's love for us in that, though many angels sinned, none were saved. Peter tells us that "*God did not spare the angels when they sinned, but cast them into hell and committed them to pits of nether gloom to be kept until the judgment*" (2 Peter 2:4). Jude says that "the angels that did not keep their own position but left their proper dwelling have been kept by him in eternal chains in the nether gloom until the judgment of the great day" (Jude 6). And we read in Hebrews, "For surely it is not with angels that he is concerned but with the descendants of Abraham" (Heb. 2:16).

We see, therefore, that God created two groups of intelligent, moral creatures. Among the angels, many sinned, but God decided to redeem none of them. This was perfectly just for God to do, and no angel can ever complain that he has been treated unfairly by God.

Now among the other group of moral creatures, human beings, we also find that a large number (indeed, all) have sinned and turned away from God. As with the angels that sinned: God could have let all of us go on our self-chosen path toward eternal condemnation. Had God decided to save no one out of the entire sinful human race, he would be perfectly just to do so, and no one could complain of unfairness on his part.

But God decided to do much more than merely meet the demands of justice. He decided to save some sinful human beings. If he had decided to save only five human beings out of the entire human race, that would have been much more than justice: it would have been a great demonstration of mercy and grace. If he had decided to save only one hundred out of the whole human race, it would have been an amazing demonstration of mercy and love. But God in fact has chosen to do much more than that. He has decided to redeem out of sinful mankind a great multitude, whom no man can number, "from every tribe and tongue and people and nation" (Rev. 5:9). This is incalculable mercy and love, far beyond our comprehension. It is all undeserved favor: it is all of grace. The striking contrast with the fate of angels brings this truth home to us.

The fact that we have been saved from a life of rebellion against God means that we are able to sing songs that angels will never be able to sing for all eternity.

> Redeemed—how I love to proclaim it!
> Redeemed by the blood of the lamb;
> Redeemed through his infinite mercy—
> His child, and forever, I am.

This song, and all the great songs proclaiming our redemption in Christ, are ours alone to sing. Unfallen angels see us sing these songs and they rejoice (Luke 15:10), but they will never be able to make them their own.

2. Angels Remind Us That the Unseen World Is Real. Just as the Sadducees in Jesus' day said that "there is no resurrection, nor angel, nor spirit" (Acts 23:8), so many in our day deny the reality of anything they cannot see. But the biblical teaching on the existence of angels is a constant reminder to us that there is an unseen world that is very real. It was only when the Lord opened the eyes of Elisha's servant to the reality of this invisible world that the servant saw that "the mountain was full of horses and chariots of fire round about Elisha" (2 Kings 6:17; this was a great angelic army sent to Dothan to protect Elisha from the Syrians). The psalmist, too, shows an awareness of the unseen world when he encourages the angels, "Praise him, all his angels, praise him, all his host!" (Ps. 148:2). The author of Hebrews reminds us that when we worship we come into the heavenly Jerusalem to gather with "innumerable angels in festal gathering" (Heb. 12:22), whom we do not see, but whose presence should fill us with both awe and joy. An unbelieving world may dismiss talk of angels as mere superstition, but Scripture offers it as insight into the state of affairs as they really are.

3. Angels Are Examples for Us. In both their obedience and their worship angels provide helpful examples for us to imitate. Jesus teaches us to pray, "Your will be done, on earth as it is in heaven" (Matt. 6:10). In heaven God's will is done by angels, immediately, joyfully, and without question. We are to pray daily that our obedience and the obedience of others would be like that of the angels in heaven. Their delight is to be God's humble servants, each faithfully and joyfully performing their assigned tasks, whether great or small. Our desire and prayer should be that we ourselves and all others on earth would do the same.

Angels also serve as our examples in their worship of God. The seraphim before God's throne see God in his holiness and continue to cry out, "Holy, holy, holy is the LORD of hosts; the whole earth is full of his glory" (Isa. 6:3). And John sees around God's throne a great angelic army, "numbering myriads of myriads and thousands of thousands, saying with a loud voice, 'Worthy is the Lamb who was slain, to receive power and wealth and wisdom and might and honor and glory and blessing!'" (Rev. 5:11–12). As angels find it their highest joy to praise God continuously, should we not also delight each day to sing God's praise, counting this as the highest and most worthy use of our time and our greatest joy?

4. Angels Carry Out Some of God's Plans. Scripture sees angels as God's servants who carry out some of his plans in the earth. They bring God's messages to people (Luke 1:11–19; Acts 8:26; 10:3–8, 22; 27:23–24). They carry out some of God's judgments, bringing a plague upon Israel (2 Sam. 24:16–17), smiting the leaders of the Assyrian army (2 Chron. 32:21), striking King Herod dead because he did not give God glory (Acts 12:23), or pouring out bowls of God's wrath on the earth (Rev. 16:1). When Christ returns, angels will come with him as a great army accompanying their King and Lord (Matt. 16:27; Luke 9:26; 2 Thess. 1:7).

Angels also patrol the earth as God's representatives (Zech. 1:10–11) and carry out war against demonic forces (Dan. 10:13; Rev. 12:7–8). John in his vision saw an angel coming down from heaven, and he records that the angel "seized the dragon, that ancient serpent, who is the Devil and Satan, and bound him for a thousand years, and threw him into the pit . . ." (Rev. 20:1–3). When Christ returns, an archangel will proclaim his coming (1 Thess. 4:16; cf. Rev. 18:1–2, 21; 19:17–18, et al.).

5. Angels Directly Glorify God. Angels also serve another function: they minister directly to God by glorifying him. Thus, in addition to human beings, there are other intelligent, moral creatures who glorify God in the universe.

Angels glorify God for who he is in himself, for his excellence.

> Bless the LORD, O you his angels,
>> you mighty ones who do his word,
>> hearkening to the voice of his word!
>>> (Ps. 103:20; cf. 148:2)

The seraphim continually praise God for his holiness (Isa. 6:2–3), as do the four living creatures (Rev. 4:8).

Angels also glorify God for his great plan of salvation as they see it unfold. When Christ was born in Bethlehem, a multitude of angels praised God and said, "Glory to God in the highest, and on earth peace among men with whom he is pleased!" (Luke 2:14; cf. Heb. 1:6). Jesus tells us, "There is joy before the angels of God over one sinner who repents" (Luke 15:10), indicating that angels rejoice every time someone turns from his or her sins and trusts in Christ as Savior.

When Paul proclaims the gospel so that people from diverse racial backgrounds, both Jews and Greeks, are brought into the church, he sees God's wise plan for the church as being displayed before the angels (and demons), for he says that he was called to preach to the Gentiles "that through the church the manifold wisdom of God might now be *made known to the principalities and powers in the heavenly places*" (Eph. 3:10). And Peter tells us that "angels long to look" (1 Peter 1:12) into the glories of the plan of salvation as it works out in the lives of individual believers each day.[10] Paul also notes that Christ was "seen by angels" (1 Tim. 3:16), suggesting that they glorified God for Christ's life of obedience. Moreover, the fact that women were to have clothing that appropriately signaled that they were women, "because of the angels" (1 Cor. 11:10), when the church assembled for worship, indicates that angels witness the lives of Christians and glorify God for our worship and obedience. Indeed, Paul reminds Timothy, when he wants to emphasize the seriousness of a command, that our actions are carried out in the presence of angelic witnesses: "In the presence of God and of Christ Jesus *and of the elect angels* I charge you to keep these rules without favor, doing nothing from partiality" (1 Tim. 5:21; cf. 1 Cor. 4:9). If Timothy follows Paul's instructions, angels will witness his obedience and glorify God; if he neglects to obey, angels will also see and be grieved.

D. Our Relationship to Angels

1. We Should Be Aware of Angels in Our Daily Lives. Scripture makes it clear that God wants us to be aware of the existence of angels and of the nature of their activity. We should not therefore assume that its teaching about angels has nothing whatsoever to do with our lives today. Rather, there are several ways in which our Christian lives will be enriched by an awareness of the existence and ministry of angels in the world even today.

When we come before God in worship, we are joining not only with the great company of believers who have died and come into God's presence in heaven, "the spirits of just men made perfect," but also with a great throng of angels, "innumerable angels in festal gathering" (Heb. 12:22–23). Though we do not ordinarily see or hear evidence of this heavenly worship, it certainly enriches our sense of reverence and joy in God's presence if we appreciate the fact that angels join us in the worship of God.

Moreover, we should be aware that angels are watching our obedience or disobedience to God through the day. Even if we think our sins are done in secret and bring grief to no one else, we should be sobered by the thought that perhaps even hundreds of angels witness our disobedience and are grieved.[11] On the other hand, when we are

---

[10] The present tense verb *epithymousin*, "long," gives the sense "are continually longing, even at the present time" to look into these things. This longing includes a holy curiosity to watch and delight in the glories of Christ's kingdom as they find ever fuller realization in the lives of individual Christians throughout the history of the church. (See discussion in Wayne Grudem, *1 Peter,* TNTC [Downers Grove, Ill.: InterVarsity Press, 1990], p. 73.)

[11] This is not to deny that the primary deterrent against sinning must be fear of displeasing God himself; it is just to say that as the presence of other human beings serves as an additional deterrent, so the knowledge of the presence of angels should also serve as a deterrent to us.

discouraged and think that our faithful obedience to God is witnessed by no one and is an encouragement to no one, we can be comforted by the realization that perhaps hundreds of angels witness our lonely struggle, daily "longing to look" at the way Christ's great salvation finds expression in our lives.

As if to make the reality of angelic observation of our service to God more vivid, the author of Hebrews suggests that angels can sometimes take human form, apparently to make "inspection visits," something like the newspaper's restaurant critic who disguises himself and visits a new restaurant. We read, "Do not neglect to show hospitality to strangers, for thereby some have entertained angels unawares" (Heb. 13:2; cf. Gen. 18:2–5; 19:1–3). This should make us eager to minister to the needs of others whom we do not know, all the while wondering if someday we will reach heaven and meet the angel whom we helped when he appeared temporarily as a human being in distress here on earth.

When we are suddenly delivered from a danger or distress, we might suspect that angels have been sent by God to help us, and we should be thankful. An angel shut the mouths of the lions so they would not hurt Daniel (Dan. 6:22), delivered the apostles from prison (Acts 5:19–20), later delivered Peter from prison (Acts 12:7–11), and ministered to Jesus in the wilderness at a time of great weakness, immediately after his temptations had ended (Matt. 4:11).[12]

When a car suddenly swerves from hitting us, when we suddenly find footing to keep from being swept along in a raging river, when we walk unscathed in a dangerous neighborhood, should we not suspect that God has sent his angels to protect us? Does not Scripture promise, "For he will give his angels charge of you to guard you in all your ways. On their hands they will bear you up, lest you dash your foot against a stone" (Ps. 91:11–12)? Should we not therefore thank God for sending angels to protect us at such times? It seems right that we should do so.

2. Cautions Regarding Our Relationship to Angels.

a. Beware of Receiving False Doctrine From Angels: The Bible warns against receiving false doctrine from supposed angels: "But even if we, or an angel from heaven, should preach to you a gospel contrary to that which we preached to you, let him be accursed" (Gal. 1:8). Paul makes this warning because he knows that there is a possibility of deception. He says, "Even Satan disguises himself as an angel of light" (2 Cor. 11:14). Similarly, the lying prophet who deceived the man of God in 1 Kings 13 claimed, "*An angel spoke to me* by the word of the LORD, saying, 'Bring him back with you into your house that he may eat bread and drink water'" (1 Kings 13:18). Yet the text of Scripture immediately adds in the same verse, "But he lied to him."

These are all instances of *false* doctrine or guidance being conveyed by angels. It is interesting that these examples show the clear possibility of satanic deception tempting us to disobey the clear teachings of Scripture or the clear commands of God (cf. 1 Kings 13:9). These warnings should keep any Christians from being fooled by the claims of Mor-

---

[12]Note also the report in Luke 22:43 that when Jesus was praying in the Garden of Gethsemane, "there appeared to him an angel from heaven, strengthening him." This text has substantial ancient attestation.

mons, for example, that an angel (Moroni) spoke to Joseph Smith and revealed to him the basis of the Mormon religion. Such "revelation" is contrary to the teachings of Scripture at many points (with respect to such doctrines as the Trinity, the person of Christ, justification by faith alone, and many others), and Christians should be warned against accepting these claims.[13] The closing of the canon of Scripture should also warn us that no further revelation of doctrine is to be given by God today, and any claims to have received additional revelation of doctrine from angels today should be immediately rejected as false.

b. Do Not Worship Angels, Pray to Them, or Seek Them: "Worship of angels" (Col. 2:18) was one of the false doctrines being taught at Colossae. Moreover, an angel speaking to John in the book of Revelation warns John not to worship him: "You must not do that! I am a fellow servant with you and your brethren who hold the testimony of Jesus. Worship God" (Rev. 19:10).

Nor should we pray to angels. We are to pray only to God, who alone is omnipotent and thus able to answer prayer and who alone is omniscient and therefore able to hear the prayers of all his people at once. By virtue of omnipotence and omniscience, God the Son and God the Holy Spirit are also worthy of being prayed to, but this is not true of any other being. Paul warns us against thinking that any other "mediator" can come between us and God, "for there is one God, and there is *one mediator* between God and men, the man Christ Jesus" (1 Tim. 2:5). If we were to pray to angels, it would be implicitly attributing to them a status equal to God, which we must not do. There is no example in Scripture of anyone praying to any specific angel or asking angels for help.

Moreover, Scripture gives us no warrant to seek for appearances of angels to us. They manifest themselves unsought. To seek such appearances would seem to indicate an unhealthy curiosity or a desire for some kind of spectacular event rather than a love for God and devotion to him and his work. Though angels did appear to people at various times in Scripture, the people apparently never sought those appearances. Our role is rather to talk to the Lord, who is himself the commander of all angelic forces. However, it would not seem wrong to ask God to fulfill his promise in Psalm 91:11 to send angels to protect us in times of need.

c. Do Angels Appear to People Today? In the earliest period of the church's history angels were active. An angel told Philip to travel south on a road that goes from Jerusalem to Gaza (Acts 8:26), instructed Cornelius to send a messenger to get Peter to come from Joppa (Acts 10:3–6), urged Peter to get up and walk out of the prison (Acts 12:6–11), and promised Paul that no one on his ship would be lost and that he himself would stand before Caesar (Acts 27:23–24). Moreover, the author of Hebrews encourages his readers, none of whom are apostles or even first-generation believers associated with the apostles (see Heb. 2:3), that *they* should continue to show hospitality to strangers, apparently with the expectation that they too might sometime entertain angels without realizing it (Heb. 13:2).

---

[13]Of course, there were times in Scripture when doctrinal truth came through angels (Luke 1:13–20, 30–37; 2:10–14; Acts 1:11; Heb. 2:2). The warning passages mentioned above forbid receiving doctrine contrary to Scripture from angels.

There seems, therefore, no compelling reason to rule out the possibility of angelic appearances today. Some would dispute this on the grounds that the sufficiency of Scripture and the closing of its canon rule out the possibility of angelic manifestations now. They would say that we are not to expect God to communicate to us through angels. However, this conclusion does not follow. Though angels would not add to the doctrinal and moral content of Scripture, God *could* communicate information to us through angels as he also does through prophecy or through ordinary communication from other persons, or through our observation of the world. If God can send another human being to warn us of danger or encourage us when we are downcast, there seems no inherent reason why he could not occasionally send an angel to do this as well.

However, we should use *extreme caution* in receiving guidance from an angel should such an unusual event happen. (It is perhaps noteworthy that very few instances of such events are recorded today, and many of these involve the communication of antiscriptural doctrine, indicating that they are actually demonic appearances.) The fact that demons can appear as angels of light (see 2 Cor. 11:14) should warn us that the appearance of any angel-like creature does not guarantee that this being speaks truthfully: *Scripture* is our guide, and no angelic creature can give authoritative teaching that is contrary to Scripture (see Gal. 1:8).

An angelic appearance today would be unusual. If one should (apparently) occur, we should evaluate it with caution. But there is no convincing reason for saying that such an event absolutely could not happen, particularly in a time of extreme danger or intense conflict with the forces of evil.

QUESTIONS FOR PERSONAL APPLICATION

1. How might this chapter affect how you think about angels from now on? What difference would it make in your attitude in worship if you consciously thought about being in the presence of angels when you were singing praises to God?

2. Do you think there are angels watching you right now? What attitude or attitudes do you think they have as they watch you? Have you ever experienced a remarkably elevated sense of joy just after praying with someone to receive Christ as personal Savior? Do you think one aspect contributing to that joy might be that angels are also rejoicing with you because a sinner has repented (Luke 15:10)?

3. Have you had a remarkable rescue from physical or other kinds of danger and wondered if angels were involved in helping you at the time?

4. How can the example of angels who joyfully and faithfully perform their assigned tasks, whether great or small, be of help to you in the responsibilities that you face today, whether at work or at home or in the church?

5. How do you think you will feel when God asks you to judge angels (1 Cor. 6:3)? Explain what that fact tells you about the greatness of your humanity as created in the image of God.

SPECIAL TERMS

angel	Michael
angel of the Lord	principalities and powers
archangel	seraphim
cherubim	sons of God
living creature	watchers

BIBLIOGRAPHY

Bromiley, G. W. "Angel." In *EDT*, pp. 46–47.
Dickason, C. Fred. *Angels, Elect and Evil.* Chicago: Moody, 1975.
Graham, Billy. *Angels: God's Secret Agents.* Revised and expanded edition. Waco, Tex.: Word, 1986.
Joppie, A. S. *The Ministry of Angels.* Grand Rapids: Baker, 1953.
McComiskey, T. E. "Angel of the Lord." In *EDT*, pp. 47–48.

SCRIPTURE MEMORY PASSAGE

Revelation 5:11–12: *Then I looked, and I heard around the throne and the living creatures and the elders the voice of many angels, numbering myriads of myriads and thousands of thousands, saying with a loud voice, "Worthy is the Lamb who was slain, to receive power and wealth and wisdom and might and honor and glory and blessing!"*

HYMN

"Angels From the Realms of Glory"

Angels, from the realms of glory,
    wing your flight o'er all the earth
Ye who sang creation's story,
    now proclaim Messiah's birth:
Come and worship, come and worship,
    worship Christ the newborn King.

Shepherds, in the fields abiding,
    watching o'er your flocks by night;
God with man is now residing,
    yonder shines the infant light:
Come and worship, come and worship,
    worship Christ the newborn King.

Sages, leave your contemplations,
    brighter visions beam afar;

Seek the great desire of nations;
 ye have seen his natal star:
Come and worship, come and worship,
 worship Christ the newborn King.

Saints, before the altar bending,
 watching long in hope and fear,
Suddenly the Lord, descending,
 in his temple shall appear:
Come and worship, come and worship,
 worship Christ the newborn King.

All creation, join in praising
 God the Father, Spirit, Son;
Evermore your voices raising
 to th' eternal Three in One:
Come and worship, come and worship,
 worship Christ the newborn King.

AUTHOR: JAMES MONTGOMERY, 1816

Chapter 13

SATAN AND DEMONS

How should Christians think of Satan and demons today? Spiritual warfare.

EXPLANATION AND SCRIPTURAL BASIS

The previous chapter leads naturally to a consideration of Satan and demons, since they are evil angels who once were like the good angels but who sinned and lost their privilege of serving God. Like angels, they are also created, spiritual beings with moral judgment and high intelligence but without physical bodies. We may define demons as follows: *Demons are evil angels who sinned against God and who now continually work evil in the world.*

A. The Origin of Demons

When God created the world, he "saw everything that he had made, and behold, it was very good" (Gen. 1:31). This means that even the angelic world that God had created did not have evil angels or demons in it at that time. But by the time of Genesis 3, we find that Satan, in the form of a serpent, was tempting Eve to sin (Gen. 3:1–5). Therefore, sometime between the events of Genesis 1:31 and Genesis 3:1, there must have been a rebellion in the angelic world with many angels turning against God and becoming evil.

The New Testament speaks of this in two places. Peter tells us, "God did not spare the angels when they sinned, but cast them into hell and committed them to pits of nether gloom to be kept until the judgment" (2 Peter 2:4).[1] Jude also says that "the angels that did not keep their own position but left their proper dwelling have been kept by him in

---

[1]This does not mean that these sinful angels have no current influence on the world, for in v. 9 Peter says that the Lord also knows how "to keep the unrighteous under punishment until the day of judgment," here referring to sinful human beings who were obviously still having influence in the world and even troubling Peter's readers. 2 Peter 2:4 simply means that the wicked angels have been removed from the presence of God and are kept under some kind of restraining influence until the final judgment, but this does not rule out their continued activity in the world meanwhile.

eternal chains in the nether gloom until the judgment of the great day" (Jude 6). Once again the emphasis is on the fact that they are removed from the glory of God's presence and their activity is restricted (metaphorically, they are in "eternal chains"), but the text does not imply either that the influence of demons has been removed from the world or that some demons are kept in a place of punishment apart from the world while others are able to influence it.[2] Rather, both 2 Peter and Jude tell us that some angels rebelled against God and became hostile opponents to his Word. Their sin seems to have been pride, a refusal to accept their assigned place, for they "did not keep their own position but left their proper dwelling" (Jude 6).

It is also possible that there is a reference to the fall of Satan, the prince of demons, in Isaiah 14. As Isaiah is describing the judgment of God on the king of Babylon (an earthly, human king), he then comes to a section where he begins to use language that seems too strong to refer to any merely human king:

> How you are fallen from heaven,
>   O Day Star,[3] son of Dawn!
> How you are cut down to the ground,
>   you who laid the nations low!
> You said in your heart,
>   "*I will ascend to heaven;*
> *above the stars of God*
>   *I will set my throne on high;*
> I will sit on the mount of assembly
>   in the far north;
> I will ascend above the heights of the clouds,
>   *I will make myself like the Most High.*"
> But you are brought down to Sheol,
>   to the depths of the Pit. (Isa. 14:12–15)

This language of ascending to heaven and setting his throne on high and saying, "I will make myself like the Most High" strongly suggests a rebellion by an angelic creature of great power and dignity. It would not be uncommon for Hebrew prophetic speech to pass from descriptions of human events to descriptions of heavenly events that are parallel to them and that the earthly events picture in a limited way.[4] If this is so, then the sin of Satan is described as one of pride and attempting to be equal to God in status and authority. (Also, Ezek. 28:11–19 possibly alludes to Satan's fall.)

---

[2] 2 Peter 2:4 does not say, "God did not spare some of the angels when they sinned," or, "God cast some of the sinning angels into hell," but it speaks generally of "the angels" when they sinned, implying all of them who sinned. Similarly, Jude 6 speaks of "the angels that did not keep their own position," implying all who sinned. Therefore, these verses must say something that is true of all demons. Their current home, their dwelling place, is "hell" and "pits of nether gloom," although they can range from there to influence people in the world.

[3] The KJV translates "Day Star" as "Lucifer," a name meaning "bearer of light." The name Lucifer does not appear elsewhere in the KJV and does not appear at all in more modern translations of the Bible.

[4] See, for example, Ps. 45, which moves from a description of an earthly king to a description of a divine Messiah.

However, it is unlikely that Genesis 6:2–4 refers to the fall of demons. In these verses, we are told that "the sons of God saw that the daughters of men were fair; and they took to wife such of them as they chose. . . . The Nephilim were on the earth in those days, and also afterward, when the sons of God came in to the daughters of men, and they bore children to them." Although some have thought that the "sons of God" in this passage are angels who sinned by marrying human women, this is not a likely interpretation, for the following reasons:[5]

Angels are nonmaterial beings and according to Jesus do not marry (Matt. 22:30), facts that cast doubt on the idea that "the sons of God" are angels who married human wives. Moreover, nothing in the *context* of Genesis 6 itself indicates that the "sons of God" should be understood as angels (this makes this passage unlike Job 1–2, for example, where the context of a heavenly council makes it clear to the reader that angels are being referred to). It is far more likely that the phrase "sons of God" here (as in Deut. 14:1) refers to people belonging to God and, like God, walking in righteousness (note Gen. 4:26 as an introduction to Gen. 5, marking the beginning of Seth's line at the same time as "men began to call upon the name of the LORD"). In fact, there is an emphasis on sonship as including likeness to one's father in Genesis 5:3. Moreover, the text traces the descendants from God through Adam and Seth to many "sons" in all of chapter 5. The larger purpose of the narrative seems to be to trace the parallel development of the godly (ultimately messianic) line of Seth and the ungodly descendants of the rest of mankind. Therefore, the "sons of God" in Genesis 6:2 are men who are righteous in their imitation of the character of their heavenly Father, and the "daughters of men" are the ungodly wives whom they marry.

B. Satan as Head of the Demons

"Satan" is the personal name of the head of the demons. This name is mentioned in Job 1:6, where "the sons of God came to present themselves before the LORD, and *Satan* also came among them" (see also Job 1:7–2:7). Here he appears as the enemy of the Lord who brings severe temptations against Job. Similarly, near the end of David's life, "Satan stood up against Israel, and incited David to number Israel" (1 Chron. 21:1). Moreover, Zechariah saw a vision of "Joshua the high priest standing before the angel of the LORD, and Satan standing at his right hand to accuse him" (Zech. 3:1). The name "Satan" is a Hebrew word (*sātān*) that means "adversary."[6] The New Testament also uses the name "Satan," simply taking it over from the Old Testament. So Jesus, in his temptation in the wilderness, speaks to Satan directly saying, "Begone, Satan!" (Matt. 4:10), or "I saw Satan fall like lightning from heaven" (Luke 10:18).

The Bible uses other names for Satan as well. He is called "the devil"[7] (only in the New Testament: Matt. 4:1; 13:39; 25:41; Rev. 12:9; 20:2, et al.), "the serpent" (Gen. 3:1,

---

[5]For a more detailed argument see W. Grudem, *The First Epistle of Peter*, pp. 211–13, which is summarized in the discussion here. Later Jewish interpreters of these verses were about equally divided between those who thought the "sons of God" were angels and those who thought they were human beings.

[6]BDB, p. 966.

[7]The word *devil* is an English translation of Greek *diabolos*, which means "slanderer" (BAGD, p. 182). In fact, the English word *devil* is ultimately derived from this same Greek word, but the sound of the word changed considerably as the word passed from Greek to Latin to Old English to modern English.

14; 2 Cor. 11:3; Rev. 12:9; 20:2), "Beelzebul" (Matt. 10:25; 12:24, 27; Luke 11:15), "the ruler of this world" (John 12:31; 14:30; 16:11),[8] "the prince of the power of the air" (Eph. 2:2), or "the evil one" (Matt. 13:19; 1 John 2:13). When Jesus says to Peter, "Get behind me, Satan! You are a hindrance to me; for you are not on the side of God, but of men" (Matt. 16:23), he recognizes that Peter's attempt to keep him from suffering and dying on the cross is really an attempt to keep him from obedience to the Father's plan. Jesus realizes that opposition ultimately comes not from Peter, but from Satan himself.

C. The Activity of Satan and Demons

1. Satan Was the Originator of Sin. Satan sinned before any human beings did so, as is evident from the fact that he (in the form of the serpent) tempted Eve (Gen. 3:1–6; 2 Cor. 11:3). The New Testament also informs us that Satan was a "murderer from the beginning" and is "a liar and the father of lies" (John 8:44). It also says that "the devil has sinned *from the beginning*" (1 John 3:8). In both of these texts, the phrase "from the beginning" does not imply that Satan was evil from the time God began to create the world ("from the beginning of the world") or from the beginning of his existence ("from the beginning of his life"), but rather from the "beginning" parts of the history of the world (Genesis 3 and even before). The devil's characteristic has been to originate sin and tempt others to sin.

2. Demons Oppose and Try to Destroy Every Work of God. Just as Satan tempted Eve to sin against God (Gen. 3:1–6), so he tried to get Jesus to sin and thus fail in his mission as Messiah (Matt. 4:1–11). The tactics of Satan and his demons are to use lies (John 8:44), deception (Rev. 12:9), murder (Ps. 106:37; John 8:44), and every other kind of destructive activity to attempt to cause people to turn away from God and destroy themselves.[9] Demons will try every tactic to blind people to the gospel (2 Cor. 4:4) and keep them in bondage to things that hinder them from coming to God (Gal. 4:8). They will also try to use temptation, doubt, guilt, fear, confusion, sickness, envy, pride, slander, or any other means possible to hinder a Christian's witness and usefulness.

3. Yet Demons Are Limited by God's Control and Have Limited Power. The story of Job makes it clear that Satan could only do what God gave him permission to do and nothing more (Job 1:12; 2:6). Demons are kept in "eternal chains" (Jude 6) and can be successfully resisted by Christians through the authority that Christ gives them (James 4:7).

Moreover, the power of demons is limited. After rebelling against God they do not have the power they had when they were angels, for sin is a weakening and destructive influence. The power of demons, though significant, is therefore probably less than the power of angels.

---

[8]John frequently uses "the world" or "this world" to refer to the present evil world system in opposition to God: John 7:7; 8:23; 12:31; 14:17, 30; 15:18, 19; 16:11; 17:14. Scripture does not teach that Satan rules over the entire world, but that he is ruler over the system of sinful opposition to God. Compare Paul's phrase "the god of this world" (2 Cor. 4:4).

[9]Cf. John 10:10: "The thief comes only to steal and kill and destroy."

In the area of knowledge, *we should not think that demons can know the future or that they can read our minds or know our thoughts.* In many places in the Old Testament, the Lord shows himself to be the true God in distinction from the false (demonic) gods of the nations by the fact that *he alone can know the future:* "I am God, and there is none like me, declaring the end from the beginning and from ancient times things not yet done" (Isa. 46:9–10).[10]

Even angels do not know the time of Jesus' return (Mark 13:32), and there is no indication in Scripture that they or demons know anything else about the future either.

With respect to knowing our thoughts, the Bible tells us that Jesus knew people's thoughts (Matt. 9:4; 12:25; Mark 2:8; Luke 6:8; 11:17) and that God knows people's thoughts (Gen. 6:5; Ps. 139:2, 4, 23; Isa. 66:18), but there is no indication that angels or demons can know our thoughts. In fact, Daniel told King Nebuchadnezzar that no one speaking by any other power than the God of heaven could tell the king what he had dreamed:

> Daniel answered the king, "No wise men, enchanters, magicians, or astrologers can show to the king the mystery which the king has asked, but there is a God in heaven who reveals mysteries, and he has made known to King Nebuchadnezzar what will be in the latter days. Your dream and the visions of your head as you lay in bed are these. . . ." (Dan. 2:27–28)[11]

But if demons cannot read people's minds, how shall we understand contemporary reports of witch doctors, fortune-tellers, or other people evidently under demonic influence who are able to tell people accurate details of their lives which they thought no one knew, such as (for example) what food they had for breakfast, where they keep some hidden money in their house, etc.? Most of these things can be explained by realizing that demons can *observe* what goes on in the world and can probably draw some conclusions from those observations. A demon may know what I ate for breakfast simply because it saw me eat breakfast! It may know what I said in a private telephone conversation because it listened to the conversation. Christians should not be led astray if they encounter members of the occult or of other false religions who seem to demonstrate such unusual knowledge from time to time. These results of observation do not prove that demons can read our thoughts, however, and nothing in the Bible would lead us to think they have that power.

4. There Have Been Differing Stages of Demonic Activity in the History of Redemption.

a. In the Old Testament: Because in the Old Testament the word *demon* is not often used, it might at first seem that there is little indication of demonic activity. However,

---

[10]See the discussion of God's knowledge of the future in chapter 4, pp. 62–63, and chapter 5, pp. 80–83.

[11]Paul also says, "For what person knows a man's thoughts except the spirit of the man which is in him?" (1 Cor. 2:11), suggesting that there is no other creature who can know a person's thoughts (although admittedly the inclusion of angelic or demonic creatures in Paul's idea is not made explicit in this context as it is in Dan. 2). See also 1 Cor. 14:24–25, where the disclosure of the "secrets" of a visitor's heart is clear evidence that God himself is present, working through the gift of prophecy. This is significant in Corinth, which was filled with demon worship in idol temples (1 Cor. 10:20)—it indicates that demons could not know the secret thoughts in a person's heart. (On Acts 16:16, see the next paragraph.)

the people of Israel often sinned by serving false gods, and when we realize that these false "gods" were really demonic forces, we see that there is quite a bit of Old Testament material referring to demons. This identification of false gods as demons is made explicit, for example, when Moses says,

> "They stirred him [God] to jealousy with strange gods;
>> with abominable practices they provoked him to anger.
> *They sacrificed to demons which were no gods,*
>> to gods they had never known." (Deut. 32:16–17)

Moreover, in reflecting on the horrible practice of child sacrifice, which the Israelites imitated from the pagan nations, the psalmist says,

> "They mingled with the nations
>> and learned to do as they did.
> They served their idols,
>> which became a snare to them.
> They sacrificed their sons
>> and their daughters *to the demons.*" (Ps. 106:35–37)

These references demonstrate that the worship offered to idols in all the nations surrounding Israel was really worship of Satan and his demons. This is why Paul can say of the false religions of the first-century Mediterranean world, "What pagans sacrifice *they offer to demons* and not to God" (1 Cor. 10:20). It is thus fair to conclude that all the nations around Israel that practiced idol worship were engaging in the worship of demons. The battles the Israelites fought against pagan nations were battles against nations who were controlled by demonic forces and thus "in the power of the evil one" (cf. 1 John 5:19). They were as much spiritual battles as physical battles: the people of Israel needed to depend on God's power to help them in the spiritual realm as much as in the physical.

In light of this, it is significant that there is no clear instance of the casting out of demons in the Old Testament. The nearest analogy is the case of David playing the lyre for King Saul: "And whenever the evil spirit from God was upon Saul, David took the lyre and played it with his hand; so Saul was refreshed, and was well, and the evil spirit departed from him" (1 Sam. 16:23). However, Scripture speaks of this as a recurring event ("whenever"), indicating that the evil spirit returned after David left Saul. This was not the completely effective triumph over evil spirits that we find in the New Testament.

Consistent with the purpose of Satan to destroy all the good works of God, pagan worship of demonic idols was characterized by destructive practices such as the sacrifice of children (Ps. 106:35–37), inflicting bodily harm on oneself (1 Kings 18:28; cf. Deut. 14:1), and cult prostitution as a part of pagan worship (Deut. 23:17; 1 Kings 14:24; Hos. 4:14).[12] Worship of demons will regularly lead to immoral and self-destructive practices.

---

[12]Even today, one distinguishing mark of many non-Christian religions is that their most devoted adherents engage in religious rituals that destroy one or several aspects of humanity, such as their physical health, their mental or emotional stability, or their human sexuality as God intended it to function. Such things clearly fulfill the goals of Satan to destroy everything that God has created good (cf. 1 Tim. 4:1–3). Since Satan is "a liar and the father of lies" (John 8:44), distortion or denial of the truth is always present in false religions as well, particularly when there is strong demonic influence.

b. During the Ministry of Jesus: After hundreds of years of inability to have any effective triumph over demonic forces,[13] it is understandable that when Jesus came casting out demons with absolute authority, the people were amazed: "And they were all amazed, so that they questioned among themselves, saying, 'What is this? A new teaching! With authority he commands even the unclean spirits, and they obey him'" (Mark 1:27). Such power over demonic forces had never before been seen in the history of the world.

Jesus explains that his power over demons is a distinguishing mark on his ministry to inaugurate the reign of the kingdom of God among mankind in a new and powerful way:

> But if it is by the Spirit of God that I cast out demons, *then the kingdom of God has come upon you.* Or how can one enter a strong man's house and plunder his goods, unless he first binds the strong man? Then indeed he may plunder his house. (Matt. 12:28–29)

The "strong man" is Satan, and Jesus had bound him, probably at the time of his triumph over him in the temptation in the wilderness (Matt. 4:1–11). During his earthly ministry, Jesus had entered the strong man's "house" (the world of unbelievers who are under the bondage of Satan), and he was plundering his house, that is, freeing people from satanic bondage and bringing them into the joy of the kingdom of God. It was "by the Spirit of God" that Jesus did this; the new power of the Holy Spirit working to triumph over demons was evidence that in the ministry of Jesus "the kingdom of God has come upon you."

c. During the New Covenant Age: This authority over demonic powers was not limited to Jesus himself, for he gave similar authority first to the Twelve (Matt. 10:8; Mark 3:15), and then to seventy disciples. After a period of ministry, the seventy "returned with joy, saying, 'Lord, even the demons are subject to us in your name!'" (Luke 10:17). Then Jesus

---

[13]There were Jewish exorcists in the period between the Old and the New Testaments who attempted to deal with demonic forces, but it is doubtful whether they were very effective: Acts 19:13 mentions some "itinerant Jewish exorcists" who attempted to use the name of the Lord Jesus as a new magic formula, though they were not Christians and did not have any spiritual authority from Jesus himself. They met with disastrous results (vv. 15–16). Also when confronting the Pharisees, Jesus said, "If I cast out demons by Beelzebul, by whom do your sons cast them out?" (Matt. 12:27). His statement does not mean that their sons were very successful but only that they were casting out demons, or were trying to, with some limited success. In fact, Jesus' argument works very well if they generally failed: "If my great success in casting out demons is due to Satan, then what is your sons' limited success due to? Presumably a power less than Satan; certainly not God!" The suggestion is that the Jewish exorcists' limited power was not from God but was from Satan.

Josephus does record an apparently effective example of exorcism by a Jew named Eleazar who used an incantation said to be derived from Solomon (*Antiquities* 8:45–48; cf. a rabbinic story in Numbers Rabbah 19:8; Tobit 8:2–3; and The Testament of Solomon, throughout). It is difficult to know exactly how widespread and how successful such practices were. On the one hand, God himself could have granted some degree of spiritual power over demons to the faithful remnant of Jewish believers in all ages: he certainly did protect the faithful people of Israel in general from the demonic forces of the nations around them. On the other hand, it is not impossible that Satan would work among unbelieving Jews, as well as among many other unbelieving cultures, to give some appearance of limited power to exorcists, witch doctors, etc., but always with the result of bringing people ultimately into greater spiritual bondage. What is certain is that Jesus came with much more spiritual power over demons than the people had ever seen before, and they were amazed. (An extensive discussion of Jewish exorcism is found in Emil Schürer, *The History of the Jewish People in the Age of Jesus Christ,* rev. English ed., ed. G. Vermes et al. [3 vols. in 4; Edinburgh: T. & T. Clark, 1973–87], vol. 3.1, pp. 342–61, 376, 440.)

responded, "I saw Satan fall like lightning from heaven" (Luke 10:18), indicating again a distinctive triumph over Satan's power (once again, this was probably at the time of Jesus' victory in the temptation in the wilderness, but Scripture does not explicitly specify that time).[14] Authority over unclean spirits later extended beyond the seventy disciples to those in the early church who ministered in Jesus' name (Acts 8:7; 16:18; James 4:7; 1 Peter 5:8–9), a fact consistent with the idea that ministry in Jesus' name in the new covenant age is characterized by triumph over the powers of the devil (1 John 3:8).

d. During the Millennium: During the millennium, the future thousand-year reign of Christ on earth mentioned in Revelation 20, the activity of Satan and demons will be further restricted. Using language that suggests a much greater restriction of Satan's activity than we see today, John describes his vision of the beginning of the millennium as follows:

> Then I saw an angel coming down from heaven, holding in his hand the key of the bottomless pit and a great chain. And he seized the dragon, that ancient serpent, who is the Devil and Satan, and *bound him for a thousand years, and threw him into the pit, and shut it and sealed it over him, that he should deceive the nations no more,* till the thousand years were ended. After that he must be loosed for a little while. (Rev. 20:1–3)

Here Satan is described as completely deprived of any ability to influence the earth. During the millennium, however, there will still be sin in the hearts of the unbelievers, which will grow until the end of the thousand years when there will be a large-scale rebellion against Christ, led by Satan who, having been "loosed from his prison" (Rev. 20:7), will come to lead that rebellion (Rev. 20:8–9). The fact that sin and rebelliousness persist in people's hearts apart from the activity of Satan, even during the thousand-year reign of Christ, shows that we cannot blame all sin in the world on Satan and his demons. Even when Satan is without influence in the world, sin will remain and be a problem in people's hearts.

e. At the Final Judgment: At the end of the millennium, when Satan is loosed and gathers the nations for battle, he will be decisively defeated and "thrown into the lake of fire and sulphur" and "tormented day and night for ever and ever" (Rev. 20:10). Then the judgment of Satan and his demons will be complete.

D. Our Relationship to Demons

1. Are Demons Active in the World Today? Some people, influenced by a naturalistic worldview that only admits the reality of what can be seen or touched or heard, deny that demons exist today and maintain that belief in their reality reflects an obsolete worldview taught in the Bible and other ancient cultures. For example, the German New

[14]Another interpretation says that in the mission of the seventy Jesus saw the fall of Satan.

Testament scholar Rudolf Bultmann emphatically denied the existence of a supernatural world of angels and demons. He argued that these were ancient "myths" and that the New Testament message had to be "demythologized" by removing such mythological elements so that the gospel could be received by modern, scientific people. Others have thought that the contemporary equivalent to the (unacceptable) demonic activity mentioned in Scripture is the powerful and sometimes evil influence of organizations and "structures" in our society today—evil governments and powerful corporations that control thousands of people are sometimes said to be "demonic," especially in the writings of more liberal theologians.

However, if Scripture gives us a true account of the world as it really is, then we must take seriously its portrayal of intense demonic involvement in human society. Our failure to perceive that involvement with our five senses simply tells us that we have some deficiencies in our ability to understand the world, not that demons do not exist. In fact, there is no reason to think that there is any less demonic activity in the world today than there was at the time of the New Testament. We are in the same time period in God's overall plan for history (the church age or the new covenant age), and the millennium has not yet come when Satan's influence will be removed from the earth. Much of our western secularized society is unwilling to admit the existence of demons—except perhaps in "primitive" societies—and relegates all talk of demonic activity to a category of superstition. But the unwillingness of modern society to recognize the presence of demonic activity today is, from a biblical perspective, simply due to people's blindness to the true nature of reality.

But what kind of activity do demons engage in today? Are there some distinguishing characteristics that will enable us to recognize demonic activity when it occurs?

2. Not All Evil and Sin Is From Satan and Demons, but Some Is. If we think of the overall emphasis of the New Testament epistles, we realize that very little space is given to discussing demonic activity in the lives of believers or methods to resist and oppose such activity. The emphasis is on telling believers not to sin but to live lives of righteousness. For example, in 1 Corinthians, when there is a problem of "dissensions," Paul does not tell the church to rebuke a spirit of dissension, but simply urges them to "agree" and "be united in the same mind and the same judgment" (1 Cor. 1:10). When there is a problem of incest, he does not tell the Corinthians to rebuke a spirit of incest, but tells them that they ought to be outraged and that they should exercise church discipline until the offender repents (1 Cor. 5:1–5). When there is a problem of Christians going to court to sue other believers, Paul does not command them to cast out a spirit of litigation (or selfishness, or strife), but simply tells them to settle those cases within the church and to be willing to give up their own self-interest (1 Cor. 6:1–8). When there is disorder at the Lord's Supper, he does not command them to cast out a spirit of disorder or gluttony or selfishness, but simply tells them that they should "wait for one another" and that each person should "examine himself, and so eat of the bread and drink of the cup" (1 Cor. 11:33, 28). These examples could be duplicated many times in the other New Testament epistles.

With regard to preaching the gospel to unbelievers, the New Testament pattern is the same: although occasionally Jesus or Paul would cast out a demonic spirit that was causing significant hindrance to proclaiming the gospel in a certain area (see Mark

5:1–20 [Gerasene demoniac]; Acts 16:16–18 [soothsaying girl at Philippi]), that is not the usual pattern of ministry presented, where the emphasis is simply on preaching the gospel (Matt. 9:35; Rom. 1:18–19; 1 Cor. 1:17–2:5). Even in the examples above, the opposition was encountered in the process of gospel proclamation. In marked contrast to the practice of those who today emphasize "strategic level spiritual warfare," in no instance does anyone in the New Testament (1) *summon a "territorial spirit" upon enter-ing an area to preach the gospel* (in both examples above the demon was in a person and the demon-influenced person initiated the confrontation), or (2) *demand informa-tion from demons about a local demonic hierarchy,* (3) *say that we should believe or teach information derived from demons,* or (4) teach by word or example that certain *"demonic strongholds" over a city have to be broken* before the gospel can be proclaimed with effec-tiveness. Rather, Christians just preach the gospel, and it comes with power to change lives! (Of course, demonic opposition may arise, or God himself may reveal the nature of certain demonic opposition, which Christians would then pray and battle against, according to 1 Cor. 12:10; 2 Cor. 10:3–6; Eph. 6:12.)

Therefore, though the New Testament clearly recognizes the influence of demonic activity in the world, and even, as we shall see, upon the lives of believers, its primary focus regarding evangelism and Christian growth is on the choices and actions taken by people themselves (see also Gal. 5:16–26; Eph. 4:1–6:9; Col. 3:1–4:6, et al.). Similarly, this should be the primary focus of our efforts today when we strive to grow in holiness and faith and to overcome the sinful desires and actions that remain in our lives (cf. Rom. 6:1–23) and to overcome the temptations that come against us from an unbelieving world (1 Cor. 10:13).[15] We need to accept our own responsibility to obey the Lord and not to shift blame for our own misdeeds onto some demonic force.

Nevertheless, a number of passages show that the New Testament authors were defi-nitely aware of the presence of demonic influence in the world and in the lives of Chris-tians themselves. Writing to the church at Corinth, which was filled with temples devoted to worship of idols, Paul said that "what pagans sacrifice they offer to demons and not to God" (1 Cor. 10:20), a situation true not only of Corinth but also of most other cit-ies in the ancient Mediterranean world. Paul also warned that in the latter days some would "depart from the faith by giving heed to deceitful spirits and doctrines of demons" (1 Tim. 4:1), and that this would lead to claims for avoiding marriage and avoiding cer-tain foods (v. 3), both of which God had created as "good" (v. 4). Thus he saw some false doctrine as being demonic in origin. In 2 Timothy, Paul implies that those who oppose sound doctrine have been captured by the devil to do his will: "And the Lord's servant must not be quarrelsome but kindly to every one, an apt teacher, forbearing, correcting his opponents with gentleness. God may perhaps grant that they will repent and come to know the truth, and they may *escape from the snare of the devil, after being captured by him to do his will*" (2 Tim. 2:24–26).

Jesus had similarly asserted that the Jews who obstinately opposed him were following their father the devil: "You are of your father the devil, and your will is to do your father's

---

[15]A common way of summarizing the three sources of evil in our lives today is "the world, the flesh, and the devil" (where "flesh" refers to our own sinful desires).

desires. He was a murderer from the beginning and has nothing to do with the truth, because there is no truth in him. When he lies, he speaks according to his own nature, for he is a liar and the father of lies" (John 8:44).

Emphasis on the hostile deeds of unbelievers as having demonic influence or sometimes demonic origin is made more explicit in John's first epistle. He makes a general statement that "he who commits sin is *of the devil*" (1 John 3:8), and goes on to say, "By this it may be seen who are the children of God, and who are the children of the devil: whoever does not do right is not of God, nor he who does not love his brother" (1 John 3:10). Here John characterizes all those who are not born of God as children of the devil and subject to his influence and desires. So Cain, when he murdered Abel, "was *of the evil one* and murdered his brother" (1 John 3:12), even though there is no mention of influence by Satan in the text of Genesis (Gen. 4:1–16). John also says, "We know that we are of God, and *the whole world is in the power of the evil one*" (1 John 5:19). Then in Revelation Satan is called "the deceiver of the whole world" (Rev. 12:9). As we noted above, Satan is also called "the ruler of this world" (John 14:30), "the god of this world" (2 Cor. 4:4), and "the spirit that is now at work in the sons of disobedience" (Eph. 2:2).

When we combine all of these statements and see that Satan is thought of as the originator of lies, murder, deception, false teaching, and sin generally, then it seems reasonable to conclude that the New Testament wants us to understand that there is some degree of demonic influence in nearly all wrongdoing and sin that occurs today. Not all sin is caused by Satan or demons, nor is the major influence or cause of sin demonic activity, but demonic activity is probably a factor in almost all sin and almost all destructive activity that opposes the work of God in the world today.

In the lives of Christians, as we noted above, the emphasis of the New Testament is not on the influence of demons but on the sin that remains in the believer's life. Nevertheless, we should recognize that sinning (even by Christians) does give a foothold for some kind of demonic influence in our lives. Thus Paul could say, "Be angry but do not sin; do not let the sun go down on your anger, and *give no opportunity to the devil*" (Eph. 4:26). Wrongful anger apparently can give opportunity for the devil (or demons) to exert some kind of negative influence in our lives — perhaps by attacking us through our emotions and perhaps by increasing the wrongful anger that we already feel against others. Similarly, Paul mentions "the breastplate of righteousness" (Eph. 6:14) as part of the armor that we are to use standing against "the wiles of the devil" and in contending "against the principalities, against the powers, against the world rulers of this present darkness, against the spiritual hosts of wickedness in the heavenly places" (Eph. 6:11–12). If we have areas of continuing sin in our lives, then there are weaknesses and holes in our "breastplate of righteousness," and these are areas in which we are vulnerable to demonic attack. By contrast, Jesus, who was perfectly free from sin, could say of Satan, "He has no power over me" (John 14:30). We may also note the connection between not sinning and not being touched by the evil one in 1 John 5:18: "We know that any one born of God does not sin,[16] but He who was born of God keeps him, and the evil one does not touch him."

---

[16]The present tense of the Greek verb here gives the sense "does not continue to sin."

The preceding passages suggest, then, that where there is a pattern of persistent sin in the life of a Christian in one area or another, the primary responsibility for that sin rests with the individual Christian and his or her choices to continue that wrongful pattern (see Rom. 6, esp. vv. 12–16; also Gal. 5:16–26). Nevertheless, there could possibly be some demonic influence contributing to and intensifying that sinful tendency. For a Christian who has prayed and struggled for years to overcome a bad temper, for example, there might be a spirit of anger that is one factor in that continued pattern of sin. A Christian who has struggled for some time to overcome a sense of depression may have been under attack by a spirit of depression or discouragement, and this could be one factor contributing to the overall situation.[17] A believer who has struggled in other areas, such as unwillingness to submit to rightful authority, or lack of self-control in eating, or laziness, or bitterness, or envy, etc., may consider whether a demonic attack or influence could be contributing to this situation and hindering his or her effectiveness for the Lord.

3. Can a Christian Be Demon Possessed? The term *demon possession* is an unfortunate term that has found its way into some English translations of the Bible but is not really reflected in the Greek text. The Greek New Testament can speak of people who "have a demon" (Matt. 11:18; Luke 7:33; 8:27; John 7:20; 8:48, 49, 52; 10:20), or it can speak of people who are suffering from demonic influence (Gk. *daimonizomai*),[18] but it never uses language that suggests that a demon actually "possesses" someone.

The problem with the terms *demon possession* and *demonized* is that they give the nuance of such strong demonic influence that they seem to imply that the person who is under demonic attack has no choice but to succumb to it. They suggest that the person is unable any longer to exercise his or her will and is completely under the domination of the evil spirit. While this may have been true in extreme cases such as that of the Gerasene demoniac (see Mark 5:1–20; note that after Jesus cast the demons out of him, he was then "in his right mind," v. 15), it is certainly not true with many cases of demonic attack or conflict with demons in many people's lives.

So what should we say to the question, "Can a Christian be demon possessed?" The answer depends on what someone means by "possessed." Since the term does not reflect any word found in the Greek New Testament, people can define it to mean various things without having clear warrant to anchor it to any verse of Scripture, and it becomes difficult to say that one person's definition is right and another one's wrong. My own

---

[17]Not all depression is demonic in origin. Some may be caused by chemical factors that will respond to medical treatment. Other depression may be due to a variety of behavioral patterns or interpersonal relationships that are not being conducted according to biblical standards. But we should not rule out demonic influence as a possible factor.

[18]This word *diamonizomai*, which may be translated "under demonic influence" or "to be demonized," occurs thirteen times in the New Testament, all in the Gospels: Matt. 4:24; 8:16, 28, 33; 9:32; 12:22; 15:22 ("badly demonized"); Mark 1:32; 5:15, 16, 18; Luke 8:36; and John 10:21. All of these instances indicate quite severe demonic influence. In light of this, it is perhaps better to reserve the English word *demonized* for more extreme or severe cases such as those represented by the instances that are used in the Gospels. The word *demonized* in English seems to me to suggest very strong demonic influence or control. (Cf. other similar "-ized" words: pasteurized, homogenized, tyrannized, materialized, nationalized, etc. These words all speak of a total transformation of the object being spoken about, not simply of mild or moderate influence.) But it has become common in some Christian literature today to speak of people under any kind of demonic attack as being "demonized." It would be wiser to reserve the term for more severe cases of demonic influence.

preference, for reasons explained above, is not to use the phrase *demon possessed* at all, for any kinds of cases.

But if people explain clearly what they mean by "demon possessed," then an answer can be given depending on the definition they give. If by "demon possessed" they mean that a person's will is completely dominated by a demon, so that a person has no power left to choose to do right and obey God, then the answer to whether a Christian could be demon possessed would certainly be no, for Scripture guarantees that sin shall have no dominion over us since we have been raised with Christ (Rom. 6:14, see also vv. 4, 11).

On the other hand, most Christians would agree that there can be differing degrees of demonic attack or influence in the lives of believers (see Luke 4:2; 2 Cor. 12:7; Eph. 6:12; James 4:7; 1 Peter 5:8). A believer may come under demonic attack from time to time in a mild or more strong sense.[19] (Note the "daughter of Abraham" whom "Satan bound for eighteen years" so that she "had a spirit of infirmity" and "was bent over and could not fully straighten herself " [Luke 13:16, 11].) Though Christians after Pentecost have a fuller power of the Holy Spirit working within them to enable them to triumph over demonic attacks, they do not always call upon or even know about the power that is rightfully theirs. So how severe can demonic influence become in the life of a Christian after Pentecost who is indwelt by the Holy Spirit?

Before answering this question, we should note that it is similar to a question about sin: "How much can a genuine Christian let his or her life be dominated by sin, and still be a born-again Christian?" It is difficult to answer that question in the abstract, because we realize that when Christians are not living as they ought to live, and when they are not benefiting from regular fellowship with other Christians and from regular Bible study and teaching, they can stray into significant degrees of sin and still can be said to be born-again Christians. But the situation is abnormal; it is not what the Christian life should be and can be. Similarly, if we ask how much demonic influence can come into the life of a genuine Christian, it is hard to give an answer in the abstract. We are simply asking how abnormal a Christian's life can become, especially if that person does not know about or make use of the weapons of spiritual warfare that are available to Christians, persists in some kinds of sin that give entrance to demonic activity, and is outside the reach of any ministry that is accustomed to giving spiritual help against demonic attack. It would seem that in such cases the degree of demonic attack or influence in a Christian's life could be quite strong. It would not be correct to say there can be no such influence because the person is a Christian. Therefore when someone asks, "Can a Christian be demon possessed?" but really means, "Can a Christian come under quite strong influence or attack by demons?" then the answer would have to be a positive one but with the caution that the word *possessed* is here being used in a confusing way. Since the term *demon possessed* is a misleading one to use in all cases, especially when referring to Christians, I would prefer to avoid it altogether. It seems better simply to recognize that there can be varying degrees of demonic attack or influence on people, even on

---

[19]It does not seem very helpful to attempt to define categories or degrees of demonic influence, as has sometimes been done, with words such as "depressed," "oppressed," "obsessed," etc., for Scripture does not define a list of categories like this for us to use, and such categories only tend to make complicated what is a simple truth: that there can be varying degrees of demonic attack or influence in a person's life.

Christians, and to leave it at that. In all cases the remedy will be the same anyway: rebuke the demon in the name of Jesus and command it to leave (see discussion below).

4. How Can Demonic Influences Be Recognized? In severe cases of demonic influence, as reported in the Gospels, the affected person would exhibit bizarre and often violent actions, especially opposition to the preaching of the gospel. When Jesus came into the synagogue in Capernaum, "immediately there was in their synagogue a man with an unclean spirit; and he cried out, 'What have you to do with us, Jesus of Nazareth? Have you come to destroy us? I know who you are, the Holy One of God'" (Mark 1:23–24). The man stood up and interrupted the service by shouting these things (or, more precisely, the demon within the man shouted them).

After Jesus came down from the Mount of Transfiguration, a man brought his son to Jesus saying, "He has a dumb spirit; and wherever it seizes him, it dashes him down; and he foams and grinds his teeth and becomes rigid." Then they brought the boy to Jesus, "and when the spirit saw him, immediately it convulsed the boy, and he fell on the ground and rolled about, foaming at the mouth." The father said, "It has often cast him into the fire and into the water, to destroy him" (Mark 9:17–18, 20, 22). Such violent actions, especially those tending toward destruction of the affected person, were clear indications of demonic activity. Similar actions are seen in the case of the Gerasene demoniac,

> a man with an unclean spirit, who lived among the tombs; and no one could bind him any more, even with a chain; for he had often been bound with fetters and chains, but the chains he wrenched apart, and the fetters he broke in pieces; and no one had the strength to subdue him. Night and day among the tombs and on the mountains he was always crying out, and bruising himself with stones. (Mark 5:2–5)

When Jesus cast out the demons so that they could not destroy the man in whom they had lived, they destroyed the herd of swine into which they immediately entered (Mark 5:13). Satanic or demonic activity always tends toward the ultimate destruction of parts of God's creation and especially of human beings who are made in the image of God (cf. Ps. 106:37, on child sacrifice).

In this regard, it is interesting to note that in one case when Jesus healed an epileptic he did it by casting out a demon (Matt. 17:14–18), but elsewhere epileptics are distinguished from those who are under demonic influence: "They brought him all the sick, those afflicted with various diseases and pains, *demoniacs, epileptics,* and paralytics, and he healed them" (Matt. 4:24). So it is with other cases of physical sickness: in some cases, Jesus simply prayed for the person or spoke a word and the person was healed. In other cases there are hints or implicit statements of demonic influence in the affliction: a woman who had had "a spirit of infirmity for eighteen years" (Luke 13:11) was healed by Jesus, and then he explicitly said that she was "a daughter of Abraham *whom Satan bound* for eighteen years" (Luke 13:16). In healing Peter's mother-in-law, Jesus "rebuked the fever, and it left her" (Luke 4:39), suggesting that there was some personal influence (probably therefore demonic) that was capable of receiving a rebuke from Jesus.

In other cases, the Epistles indicate that demonic influence will lead to blatantly false doctrinal statements, such as exclaiming, "Jesus be cursed" (1 Cor. 12:3), or a refusal to confess "that Jesus Christ has come in the flesh" (1 John 4:2–3). In both instances, the context deals with the testing of people who may be "false prophets" and who want to use spiritual gifts to speak in the assembly of the church (1 Cor. 12) or specifically to prophesy (1 John 4:1–6). These passages do not indicate that all false doctrine should be thought to be demonically inspired, but blatantly false doctrinal statements made by those who profess to be speaking by the power of the Holy Spirit would certainly fall into this category. When at Corinth there was active, entrenched opposition to Paul's apostolic authority by those who claimed to be apostles but were not, Paul saw them as servants of Satan disguised as servants of righteousness (2 Cor. 11:13–15).

In addition to these outwardly evident indications, demonic activity was sometimes recognized by a subjective sense of the presence of an evil spiritual influence. In 1 Corinthians 12:10, Paul mentions "the ability to distinguish between spirits" ("discerning of spirits," KJV) as one kind of spiritual gift. This gift would seem to be an ability to sense or discern the difference in the working of the Holy Spirit and the working of evil spirits in a person's life.[20] The gift would apparently include an awareness of demonic influence that would be registered both in terms of objective, observable facts, and also in terms of emotional and/or spiritual uneasiness or perception of the presence of evil.

But does this ability to perceive demonic influence have to be limited to those with this special gift? As with all spiritual gifts, it would seem that there are degrees of intensity or strength in the development of this gift as well. So some may have this gift developed to a very high degree and others may find it functioning only occasionally. Moreover, in the lives of all believers, there may be something analogous to this gift, some kind of ability to sense in their spirits the presence of the Holy Spirit or to sense demonic influence from time to time in other people. In fact, Paul speaks of a *positive* kind of spiritual perception that believers have when they encounter him and his co-workers: "For we are the aroma of Christ to God among those who are being saved and among those who are perishing, to one a fragrance from death to death, to the other a fragrance from life to life" (2 Cor. 2:15–16). In the ordinary course of life today, sometimes Christians will have a subjective sense that someone else is a Christian before they have opportunity to find out that that is in fact the case. And it seems likely that an opposite spiritual perception could also occur from time to time, whereby the believer would sense the presence of demonic influence in a person's life before there were other, more objective indications of that fact.

Moreover, sometimes a person who is under spiritual attack from a demonic power will know it or sense it. A mature pastor or a Christian friend, in counseling someone about a difficult problem, may find it wise to ask, "Do you think that an attack by any evil spiritual force could be a factor in this situation?" The person may simply say, "No," but in many instances the person being counseled will have thought of that possibility or even have been quite clearly aware of it, but afraid to say anything for fear of being thought strange. Such a person will be encouraged that another Christian would consider this as a possible factor.

---

[20]For an extensive analysis of the meaning of the Greek phrase *diakriseis pneumatōn*, "distinguishing between spirits," in 1 Cor. 12:10, see W. Grudem, "A Response to Gerhard Dautzenberg on 1 Corinthians 12:10," in *Biblische Zeitschrift*, NF, 22:2 (1978), pp. 253–70.

In all of these attempts to recognize demonic influence, we must remember that no spiritual gift functions perfectly in this age, nor do we have a full knowledge of people's hearts. "We all make many mistakes," as James recognizes (James 3:2). There are many cases where we are somewhat unsure whether a person is a genuine Christian or not, or where we are somewhat unsure whether a person's motives are sincere. There are also times when we are unclear as to the direction God is leading us in our lives, or we may be uncertain about whether it is appropriate to speak or remain silent about a certain matter. So it should not surprise us that there may be some degree of uncertainty in our perception of the presence of demonic influence as well. This does not mean that we should ignore the possibility of demonic influence, however, and as we grow in spiritual maturity and sensitivity, and as we gain experience in ministering to the needs of others, our ability to recognize demonic influence in various situations will no doubt increase.

5. Jesus Gives All Believers Authority to Rebuke Demons and Command Them to Leave. When Jesus sent the twelve disciples ahead of him to preach the kingdom of God, he "gave them power and authority over all demons" (Luke 9:1). After the seventy had preached the kingdom of God in towns and villages, they returned with joy, saying, "Lord, *even the demons are subject to us in your name!*" (Luke 10:17), and Jesus told them, "I have given you authority . . . over all the power of the enemy" (Luke 10:19). When Philip, the evangelist, went down to Samaria to preach the gospel of Christ, "unclean spirits came out of many who had them" (Acts 8:7, author's translation), and Paul used spiritual authority over demons to say to a spirit of divination in a soothsaying girl, "I charge you in the name of Jesus Christ to come out of her" (Acts 16:18).

Paul was aware of the spiritual authority he had, both in face-to-face encounters such as he had in Acts 16, and in his prayer life as well. He said, "For though we live in the world we are not carrying on a worldly war, for the weapons of our warfare are not worldly but have divine power to destroy strongholds" (2 Cor. 10:3–4). Moreover, he spoke at some length of the struggle Christians have against "the wiles of the devil" in his description of conflict "against the spiritual hosts of wickedness in the heavenly places" (see Eph. 6:10–18). James tells all his readers (in many churches) to "*resist the devil* and he will flee from you" (James 4:7). Similarly, Peter tells his readers in many churches in Asia Minor, "Your adversary the devil prowls around like a roaring lion, seeking some one to devour. *Resist him*, firm in your faith" (1 Peter 5:8–9).[21]

Some may object that Jude 9 teaches that Christians should not command or rebuke evil spirits. It says: "But when the archangel Michael, contending with the devil, disputed about the body of Moses, he did not presume to pronounce a reviling judgment upon him, but said, 'The Lord rebuke you.'"

However, in context Jude is not talking about Christians in their encounters with demonic forces, but is pointing out the error of immoral and rebellious false teachers who "reject authority" in general and "slander celestial beings" (v. 8 NIV): on their own authority they foolishly speak blasphemous words against heavenly beings, whether

---

[21]Of course, our greatest example of dealing with demonic powers by speaking to them directly and commanding them to leave is the example of Jesus himself, who frequently did this in the Gospels, and by example and word he taught the disciples to imitate him.

angelic or demonic. The reference to Michael is simply to show that the greatest angelic creature, no matter how powerful, did not presume to go beyond the limits of the authority that God had given him. The false teachers, however, have far overstepped their bounds, and they show their foolishness when they "revile whatever they do not understand" (v. 10). The lesson of the verse is simply, "Don't try to go beyond the authority God has given you!" When Jude 9 is viewed in this way, the only question that arises for a Christian from this verse is, "What authority has God given us over demonic forces?" And the rest of the New Testament speaks clearly to that in several places. Not only Jesus, and not only his twelve disciples, but also the seventy disciples, and Paul, and Philip (who was not an apostle) are given authority over demons by the Lord Jesus (see verses above). Jude 9 therefore simply cannot mean that it is wrong for human beings to rebuke or command demons, or that it is wrong for any but the apostles to do so. In fact, both Peter and James encourage all Christians to "resist" the devil, and Paul encourages believers in general to put on spiritual armor and prepare for spiritual warfare.

Before we examine in more detail how that authority works out in practice, it is important, first, that we recognize that the work of Christ on the cross is the ultimate basis for our authority over demons.[22] Though Christ won a victory over Satan in the wilderness, the New Testament epistles point to the cross as the moment when Satan was decisively defeated. Jesus took on flesh and blood, "that through death He might render powerless him who had the power of death, that is, the devil" (Heb. 2:14 NASB). At the cross God "disarmed the principalities and powers and made a public example of them, triumphing over them in him" (Col. 2:15). Therefore Satan hates the cross of Christ, because there he was decisively defeated forever. Because the blood of Christ speaks clearly of his death, we read in Revelation of those who overcame Satan by Christ's blood during conflict in this world: "And they have conquered him by the blood of the Lamb and by the word of their testimony" (Rev. 12:11). Because of Christ's death on the cross, our sins are completely forgiven, and Satan has no rightful authority over us.

Second, our membership as children in God's family is the firm spiritual position from which we engage in spiritual warfare. Paul says to every Christian, "For in Christ Jesus you are all sons of God, through faith" (Gal. 3:26). When Satan comes to attack us, he is attacking one of God's own children, a member of God's own family: this truth gives us authority to successfully wage war against him and defeat him.

If we as believers find it appropriate to speak a word of rebuke to a demon, it is important to remember that we need not fear demons. Although Satan and demons have much less power than the power of the Holy Spirit at work within us, one of Satan's tactics is to attempt to cause us to be afraid. Instead of giving in to such fear, Christians should remind themselves of the truths of Scripture, which tell us, "You are of God, and have overcome them; for *he who is in you is greater than he who is in the world*" (1 John 4:4), and "God did not give us a spirit of timidity but a spirit of power and love and self-control" (2 Tim. 1:7). What Paul says about the Philippians in their relationship to human opponents can also be applied when facing demonic opposition to the gospel—Paul tells them

---

[22]In this paragraph and the following one on adoption I am indebted to the fine work of Timothy M. Warner, *Spiritual Warfare* (Wheaton, Ill.: Crossway, 1991), pp. 55–63.

to stand firm and to be *"not frightened in anything by your opponents.* This is a clear omen to them of their destruction, but of your salvation, and that from God" (Phil. 1:28). He also tells the Ephesians that in their spiritual warfare they are to use the "shield of faith" with which they can "quench all the flaming darts of the evil one" (Eph. 6:16). This is very important, since the opposite of fear is faith in God. He also tells them to be bold in their spiritual conflict, so that, having taken the whole armor of God, they "may be able to withstand in the evil day, and having done all, to stand" (Eph. 6:13). In their conflict with hostile spiritual forces, Paul's readers should not run away in retreat or cower in fear, but should stand their ground boldly, knowing that their weapons and their armor "have divine power to destroy strongholds" (2 Cor. 10:4; cf. 1 John 5:18).

We may ask, however, why does God want Christians to speak directly to the demon who is troubling someone rather than just praying and asking God to drive away the demon for them? In a way, this is similar to asking why Christians should share the gospel with another person rather than simply praying and asking God to reveal the gospel to that person directly. Or why should we speak words of encouragement to a Christian who is discouraged rather than just praying and asking God himself to encourage that person directly? Why should we speak a word of rebuke or gentle admonition to a Christian whom we see involved in some kind of sin, rather than just praying and asking God to take care of the sin in that person's life? The answer to all these questions is that in the world that God has created, he has given us a very *active* role in carrying out his plans, especially his plans for the advancement of the kingdom and the building up of the church. In all of these cases, our *direct involvement* and *activity* is important in addition to our prayers. And so it seems to be in our dealing with demonic forces as well. Like a wise father who does not settle all of his children's disputes for them, but sometimes sends them back out to the playground to settle a dispute themselves, so our heavenly Father encourages us to enter directly into conflict with demonic forces in the name of Christ and in the power of the Holy Spirit. Thereby he enables us to gain the joy of participating in eternally significant ministry and the joy of triumphing over the destructive power of Satan and his demons in people's lives. It is not that God could not deal with demonic attacks every time we prayed and asked him to do so, for he certainly could and he no doubt sometimes does. But the New Testament pattern seems to be that God ordinarily expects Christians themselves to speak directly to the unclean spirits.

In actual practice, this authority to rebuke demons may result in briefly speaking a command to an evil spirit to leave when we suspect the presence of demonic influence in our personal lives or the lives of those around us.[23] We are to "resist the devil" (James 4:7), and he will flee from us.[24] Sometimes a very brief command in the name of Jesus will be enough. At other times it will be helpful to quote Scripture in the process of commanding an evil spirit to leave a situation. Paul speaks of "the sword of the Spirit, which is the

---

[23]Because Scripture gives no indication that demons can know our thoughts (see above, pp. 298–99), it would seem that the command should be spoken audibly.

[24]For example, if we or one of our children wakes up with a frightening dream, in addition to praying to Jesus for comfort and protection, we might also say, "In the name of Jesus, I command any evil spirit causing this frightening dream, begone!" Children from a very young age can be taught to say, "In Jesus' name, go away!" to any images of witches, goblins, etc. that may appear in their dreams or in mental images that trouble them at night, and then to pray to Jesus for protection and happy thoughts of him. Such action by those

word of God" (Eph. 6:17).[25] And Jesus, when he was tempted by Satan in the wilderness, repeatedly quoted Scripture in response to Satan's temptations (Matt. 4:1–11). Appropriate Scriptures may include general statements of the triumph of Jesus over Satan (Matt. 12:28–29; Luke 10:17–19; 2 Cor. 10:3–4; Col. 2:15; Heb. 2:14; James 4:7; 1 Peter 5:8–9; 1 John 3:8; 4:4; 5:18),[26] but also verses that speak directly to the particular temptation or difficulty at hand.

In our own personal lives, if we find sinful emotions that are unusually strong welling up in our minds or hearts (whether they be emotions of irrational fear, anger, hatred, bitterness, lust, greed, etc.), in addition to praying and asking Jesus for help in overcoming them, it would also be appropriate for us to say something like, "Spirit of fear, in Jesus' name, I command you, go away from here and don't return!" Even though we may be unsure whether there is a demonic factor in that particular situation, and even though a demon's presence may be only one factor contributing to the situation, nonetheless, such words of rebuke will sometimes be very effective. Though we do not have in the New Testament a complete record of the personal prayer life of the apostle Paul, he talks openly about wrestling "not . . . against flesh and blood, but . . . against the spiritual hosts of wickedness in the heavenly places" (Eph. 6:12) and about "not carrying on a worldly war" (2 Cor. 10:3). It is reasonable to think that his own extensive prayer life included this kind of verbal rebuke of demonic forces as one aspect of his spiritual warfare.

Moreover, such wrestling against "the spiritual hosts of wickedness" may mean that in our private times of intercessory prayer for others we will include an element of verbal rebuke to demonic forces that may be a component in situations for which we are praying. (This kind of spiritual warfare would not be in the presence of the person for whom we are concerned, who in many cases would be confused or frightened unnecessarily.) For example, parents may appropriately include a brief word of rebuke to a spirit of rebelliousness in one child, of laziness in another, or of anger in yet another, in addition to praying that the Lord would give victory in those areas, and in addition to teaching and disciplining their children.[27]

6. Appropriate Use of the Christian's Spiritual Authority in Ministry to Other People.
When we pass from the discussion of private spiritual warfare in our own personal lives and perhaps the lives of close family members, we move to the question of direct personal ministry to others who have come under spiritual attack. For example, we may at times be involved in counseling or prayer with another person when we suspect that demonic activity is a factor in their situation. In these cases, some additional considerations must be kept in mind.

---

little ones who trust in Christ will often be remarkably effective, for their faith in Jesus is very simple and genuine (see Matt. 18:1–4).

[25]The Greek word here translated "word" is *rhēma*, which usually refers to spoken words (whether by God or by others). It is sometimes used to speak of the words of Scripture when they are spoken by God or by people quoting Scripture (Matt. 4:4; John 15:7; 17:8; Rom. 10:17; Heb. 6:5; 1 Peter 1:25 [twice]), and that is the sense in which Paul seems to use it in Eph. 6:17: as we speak the words of Scripture they are accompanied by the work of the Holy Spirit and have the power of a spiritual sword.

[26]It would be good for Christians to memorize the verses in the list just mentioned so as to be able to speak them from memory when involved in any spiritual warfare.

[27]Since Scripture gives no indication that demons can read our minds, such rebukes against demons would probably have to be spoken audibly, even if softly. By contrast, God of course knows our thoughts, and prayer to him can be in our minds only, without being spoken aloud.

First, it is important not to frighten people by talking very glibly about an area that may be familiar to us but quite unfamiliar and somewhat frightening to others. The Holy Spirit is a Spirit of gentleness and peace (see 1 Cor. 14:33). Because of this, it is often considerate simply to ask questions of the person we are helping. We might ask, "Do you think an evil spirit may be attacking you in this situation?" or "Would you mind if I spoke a word of rebuke to any evil spirit that may be a factor in this?" It would also be important to assure the person that if there is a demonic factor involved, it should not be thought of as a negative reflection on the person's spiritual condition but may simply indicate that Satan is trying to attack the person to keep him or her from more effective ministry for the Lord. Each Christian is a soldier in the Lord's spiritual army and therefore subject to attacks from the forces of the enemy.

If the other person gives permission to do so, a brief command should be spoken aloud, telling the evil spirit to leave.[28] Since the person under attack will often have had a sense of a demonic presence, it would be appropriate, after commanding the evil spirit to leave, to ask the person if he or she felt or sensed anything different when those words were spoken. If there really was a demonic influence in the situation, the person may express an immediate feeling of relief or freedom, often with a sense of joy and peace as well.

All of this does not have to be a highly dramatic or emotionally charged procedure. Some contemporary stories tell of long, drawn-out battles in which the Christian counselor argues with the demon and shouts at it repeatedly over a period of several hours. But there is no indication in the New Testament that demons are hard of hearing, nor are there examples of such long periods of conflict in order to get a demon to leave. Jesus simply "cast out the spirits with a word" (Matt. 8:16), even though in one case (with the Gerasene demoniac) the evil spirit showed some initial resistance (see Mark 5:8; Luke 8:29). Jesus then asked its name and then cast out many demons at once (Mark 5:9–13; Luke 8:30–33). The power to cast out demons comes not from our own strength or the power of our own voice, but from the Holy Spirit (Matt. 12:28; Luke 11:20). Thus, a quiet, confident, authoritative tone of voice should be sufficient.

Second, to avoid being drawn into a long conversation or battle with the demon itself the Christian counselor should focus not on the demon but on the person being ministered to and the truths of the Bible that need to be affirmed and believed. The "belt of truth" (Eph. 6:14 NIV) is part of the armor that protects us against Satan, as is the "sword of the Spirit, which is the word of God" (Eph. 6:17). If the person who is receiving ministry will focus on and believe the truth of Scripture and will renounce sin and thereby put on the "breastplate of righteousness" (Eph. 6:14), then the evil spirit will have no foothold in that person's life. If the demon refuses to leave in spite of the command given in the name of Jesus, then it may be best to wait until another time after more prayer and personal spiritual preparation on the part of the person being ministered to and the persons who are engaging in this ministry (Matt. 17:19–20; Mark 9:29; see discussions below).[29]

---

[28]The verb *exorcise* in English means "to drive out (an evil spirit) by a magic formula or a spoken command." An "exorcism" is defined as the action of driving out an evil spirit in this way. These words do not occur in the Bible (although Acts 19:13 mentions Jewish exorcists). Because these terms are used in pagan as well as Christian contexts throughout history, there is room for Christians to differ over whether it is wise to use them to refer to Christian practices today.

[29]It would often be wise, in difficult cases, to have help from someone with more maturity and experience in this area.

Third, it is important for Christians not to become overly curious in this area of demonic conflict. Though it is a ministry that the Lord gives all Christians authority to engage in, Scripture nonetheless tells us that we are to be "babes in evil" (1 Cor. 14:20). That is, we are not to become overly fascinated with matters of evil and attempt to become "experts" in some kinds of evil just to satisfy our curiosity.[30]

Fourth, if the person being ministered to is not a Christian, it is important that he or she be urged to come to Christ as Savior immediately after the demon is cast out so that the Holy Spirit will reside in the person and protect him or her from future attacks. Otherwise there may be a worse result later.

> When the unclean spirit has gone out of a man, he passes through waterless places seeking rest, but he finds none. Then he says, "I will return to my house from which I came." And when he comes he finds it empty, swept, and put in order. Then he goes and brings with him seven other spirits more evil than himself, and they enter and dwell there; and the last state of that man becomes worse than the first. So shall it be also with this evil generation. (Matt. 12:43–45)

Fifth, effectiveness in difficult cases of demonic influence may be related to our own spiritual condition. When Jesus had cast a demon out of an epileptic boy, and "the boy was cured instantly," the disciples privately came to Jesus and asked, "Why could we not cast it out?" (Matt. 17:18–19). Jesus said to them, "Because of your little faith" (Matt. 17:20). Mark's gospel reports that Jesus also said in response to the disciples, "This kind cannot be driven out by anything but prayer" (Mark 9:29). The disciples apparently were at that time weak in faith; they had not spent enough time in prayer recently and they were not walking fully in the power of the Holy Spirit.[31]

Jesus issues a clear warning that we should not rejoice too much or become proud in our power over demons, but that we should rejoice rather in our great salvation. We must keep this in mind lest we become proud and the Holy Spirit withdraw his power from us. When the seventy returned with joy saying, "Lord, even the demons are subject to us in your name!" (Luke 10:17) Jesus told them, "Do not rejoice in this, that the spirits are subject to you; but rejoice that your names are written in heaven" (Luke 10:20).[32]

7. We Should Expect the Gospel to Come in Power to Triumph Over the Works of the Devil. When Jesus came preaching the gospel in Galilee, "demons also came out of many" (Luke 4:41). When Philip went to Samaria to preach the gospel, "unclean

---

[30]Christians should therefore not be preoccupied with matters concerning the occult or the New Age movement. We should think about things that are "honorable" and "pure" and "worthy of praise" (Phil. 4:8).

[31]When Jesus said, "This kind cannot be driven out by anything but prayer" (Mark 9:29), he cannot have meant that it was necessary to pray for a long time about that specific situation before the demon would be cast out, for he did not pray at all but simply spoke a word and cast out the demon at once. He must have meant, rather, that a continual life of

prayer and abiding in God will result in a spiritual preparedness and a possession of a spiritual power through the anointing of the Holy Spirit that will be effective in conflict even over very severe demonic attack or influence.

[32]Jesus cannot mean that it is wrong to rejoice when the enemy is vanquished and people are set free from bondage, for that is certainly a good reason for rejoicing. He must rather be putting a relative contrast in absolute terms in telling the disciples that the greatness of their salvation is the primary thing that they should be rejoicing in.

spirits came out of many . . . crying with a loud voice" (Acts 8:7). Jesus commissioned Paul to preach among the Gentiles "that they may turn from darkness to light and from the power of Satan to God, that they may receive forgiveness of sins and a place among those who are sanctified by faith in me" (Acts 26:18). Paul's proclamation of the gospel, he said, was "not in plausible words of wisdom, but in demonstration of the Spirit and of power, that your faith might not rest in the wisdom of men but in the power of God" (1 Cor. 2:4–5; cf. 2 Cor. 10:3–4). If we really believe the scriptural testimony to the existence and activity of demons, and if we really believe that "the reason the Son of God appeared was *to destroy the works of the devil*" (1 John 3:8), then it would seem appropriate to expect that even today when the gospel is proclaimed to unbelievers, and when prayer is made for believers who have perhaps been unaware of this dimension of spiritual conflict, there will be a genuine and often immediately recognizable triumph over the power of the enemy. We should expect that this would happen, think of it as a normal part of the work of Christ in building up his kingdom, and rejoice in Christ's victory in it.

QUESTIONS FOR PERSONAL APPLICATION

1. Before reading this chapter, did you think that most demonic activity was confined to the time of the New Testament or to other cultures than your own? After reading this chapter, are there areas in your own society where you think there might be some demonic influence today? Do you feel some fear at the prospect of encountering demonic activity in your own life or the lives of others around you? What does the Bible say that will specifically address that feeling of fear? Do you think that the Lord wants you to feel that fear, if you do?

2. Are there any areas of sin in your own life now that might give a foothold to some demonic activity? If so, what would the Lord have you do with respect to that sin?

3. Are there cases where you have had victory over some demonic force by speaking to it in the name of Jesus? How can the material in this chapter help you be more effective in this kind of spiritual conflict? What are the dangers of becoming too interested in or too deeply involved in this kind of ministry? How can you safeguard against that excessive emphasis? What do you think Paul's procedure was when he came to preach the gospel in city after city where it had never been heard before and where there was demon worship? How could the church today profit from Paul's example?

SPECIAL TERMS

demonized	distinguishing between spirits
demon possession	exorcism
demons	Satan

BIBLIOGRAPHY

Anderson, Neil. *The Bondage Breaker.* Eugene, Ore.: Harvest House, 1990.

_____. *Victory Over the Darkness.* Ventura, Calif.: Regal, 1990.

Dickason, C. Fred. *Angels, Elect and Evil.* Chicago: Moody, 1975.

_____. *Demon Possession and the Christian: A New Perspective.* Westchester, Ill.: Crossway, 1991.

Green, Michael. *I Believe in Satan's Downfall.* Grand Rapids: Eerdmans, 1981.

Lewis, C. S. *The Screwtape Letters.* New York: Macmillan, 1961.

MacMillan, John A. *The Authority of the Believer: A Compilation of "The Authority of the Believer" and "The Authority of the Intercessor."* Harrisburg, Pa.: Christian Publications, 1980.

McClelland, S. E. "Demon, Demon Possession." In *EDT,* pp. 306–8.

Mallone, George. *Arming for Spiritual Warfare.* Downers Grove, Ill.: InterVarsity Press, 1991.

Penn-Lewis, Jessie, with Evan Roberts. *War on the Saints.* Unabridged ed. New York: Thomas E. Lowe, 1973.

Pentecost, Dwight. *The Adversary, the Devil.* Grand Rapids: Zondervan, 1969.

Twelftree, G. H. "Devil and Demons." In *NDT,* pp. 196–98.

Unger, M. F. "Satan." In *EDT,* pp. 972–73.

_____. *Demons in the World Today: A Study of Occultism in the Light of God's Word.* Wheaton, Ill.: Tyndale, 1971.

Warner, Timothy M. *Spiritual Warfare: Victory Over the Powers of This Dark World.* Wheaton, Ill.: Crossway, 1991.

Wright, Nigel. *The Satan Syndrome: Putting the Power of Darkness In Its Place.* Grand Rapids: Zondervan, 1990.

SCRIPTURE MEMORY PASSAGE

James 4:7–8: *Submit yourselves therefore to God. Resist the devil and he will flee from you. Draw near to God and he will draw near to you. Cleanse your hands, you sinners, and purify your hearts, you men of double mind.*

HYMN

"Christian, Dost Thou See Them?"

Christian, dost thou see them on the holy ground,
   How the pow'rs of darkness rage thy steps around?
Christian, up and smite them, counting gain but loss,
   In the strength that cometh by the holy Cross.

Christian, dost thou feel them, how they work within,
   Striving, tempting, luring, goading into sin?

Christian, never tremble; never be downcast;
   Gird thee for the battle, watch and pray and fast.

Christian, dost thou hear them, how they speak thee fair?
   "Always fast and vigil? Always watch and prayer?"
Christian, answer boldly, "While I breathe I pray!"
   Peace shall follow battle, night shall end in day.

Hear the words of Jesus: "O my servant true;
   Thou art very weary, I was weary too;
But that toil shall make thee some day all mine own,
   And the end of sorrow shall be near my throne."

AUTHOR: JOHN MASON NEALE, 1862

Alternative hymns: "Soldiers of Christ Arise"; "Lead On, O King Eternal"; or "Onward, Christian Soldiers."

We want to hear from you. Please send your comments about this book to us in care of zreview@zondervan.com. Thank you.

ZONDERVAN.com/
AUTHORTRACKER
follow your favorite authors